Keeping the Faith

Essays in Memory of Roger H. Prentice

MERCER UNIVERSITY PRESS

Endowed by

TOM WATSON BROWN
and
THE WATSON-BROWN FOUNDATION, INC.

Keeping the Faith

Essays in Memory of Roger H. Prentice

Edited by Paul L. Harris and Karen E. Smith
with William H. Brackney†

MERCER UNIVERSITY PRESS
Macon, Georgia

MUP/ P669

© 2023 by Mercer University Press
Published by Mercer University Press
1501 Mercer University Drive
Macon, Georgia 31207
All rights reserved

27 26 25 24 23   5 4 3 2 1

Books published by Mercer University Press are printed on acid-free paper
that meets the requirements of the American National Standard for
Information Sciences—Permanence of Paper for Printed Library Materials.

Printed and bound in the United States.

This book is set in Adobe Caslon Pro.

Cover/jacket design by Burt&Burt.

ISBN   978-0-88146-890-8
Cataloging-in-Publication Data is available from the Library of Congress

Praise to God the Father holy;
　The world He formed;
Praise his Son in manger lowly
　Whom Herod scorned;
Praise the Holy Ghost who shows us
To our God who always loves us,
And in turn, to service moves us:
　Our hearts are warmed. Amen.

Third verse of a "Hymn of Dismissal" written by RHP for use in
the Manning Memorial Chapel at Acadia University.

Contents

Preface   viii

Contributors   x

THE LIFE AND MINISTRY OF ROGER PRENTICE   1

In Memory of My Great and Good Friend Roger H. Prentice, by Kelvin K. Ogilvie   3

In Appreciation of a Friendship, by Paul L. Harris   8

Roger H. Prentice: A Bibliography, 1969 to 2022, by Patricia Townsend   13

BAPTIST IDENTITY, THEOLOGY, AND SPIRITUALITY   19

Voluntarism, Human Rights, and a Global Mission: The Progressive/Liberal Tradition among Canadian Baptists, by William H. Brackney†   21

"Man that is born of a woman is of few days and full of trouble": Morgan Edwards (1722–1795) and the Book of Common Prayer, by Evan Lynwood Colford   43

Keeping Maturin Honest: Edmund Maturin and John Mockett Cramp Debate the Reformation, by Scott Kindred-Barnes   62

Marking Life's Experiences: The Poems of Frances Cramp Muir (1830–1892), by Karen E. Smith   91

ACADIA UNIVERSITY AND MARITIME CONNECTIONS   121

"Education Seasoned with Grace": A Liberal Education at Acadia College, by Barry M. Moody   123

A Nova Scotia Baptist Family: Four Generations of Leadership in
Church and Academy, by Howard John Whidden 143

Shepherding Soldiers: Maritime Baptist Chaplains of the
First World War, by Carol Anne Janzen and
Zachary Cooper 168

WORSHIP, PREACHING, AND MINISTRY 179

Worship as Theatre, by Robert Ellis 181

A Homiletic Hermeneutic for the Rewriting of Hymn Texts,
by J. Daniel Gibson 206

"Someone's in the Kitchen with Martha": Outlines for a
Eucharistic Homiletic, by Barry Morrison 225

Silence and the Cadences of Worship, by Paul L. Harris 237

Four Dimensions of Christian Ministry in the
New Testament, by Allison A. Trites 250

ENGAGING WITH OTHERS IN THE CHURCH AND
IN THE WIDER WORLD 257

Ecumenisms of Tomorrow: Paradoxes for the Future of Faith,
by David M. Csinos and Lydia Hood 259

State Neutrality and Religion in Europe: What's the Prospect?,
by Malcolm D. Evans 276

Religious Freedom in the Post-Nation-State: The Canadian
Experiment, by Mark Parent 303

Index 325

Preface

The plans for this book were hatched in January 2021. At the time, we hoped to produce a celebratory book of essays which could be presented to our friend, Roger Prentice, on what would have been his eightieth birthday in August 2023. Knowing we needed a Canadian conspirator to help us with our plans, we contacted Bill Brackney and asked if he would like to help with the project. He immediately accepted our invitation, whereupon we began to contact some of Roger's many friends in Canada and in the UK. When they heard about the book project, friends responded enthusiastically by promising an essay. Several friends gave a financial contribution to make the volume possible.

Sadly, in April 2022, with the sudden death of Roger, our plans had to change, as there would be no special celebration. Yet while we could no longer present to him a *Festschrift* volume, we decided that we would use the book as a way of honouring and remembering Roger's life and ministry. Again we contacted contributors, most of whom were still able to contribute, and they readily agreed to our plan for a memorial volume.

Unfortunately, on the day of Roger's funeral, Bill Brackney was himself taken ill, hospitalised, and, sadly, died without being able to do any further work on this volume. In fact, while the material that he himself drafted is substantially his own, the chapter he contributed to the book was not complete and needed considerable editing in order to prepare it for publication. We are grateful to Bill's wife, Kitty, for her help in locating the paper and for granting us permission to edit it so that it could be included in this volume as it now stands.

We would like to thank all those who financially helped with the publication of this special memorial tribute to Roger. We are grateful to Marc Jolley and Marsha Luttrell at Mercer University Press for their support and help. We also appreciate the work of the staff in the Office of Advancement at Acadia University who collected the donations for this volume. Finally, we are grateful for all the hard work and efforts of all of the contributors who, in different ways and in various contexts, knew Roger as a friend. While the names of all the contributors are listed elsewhere in this volume, we would like to acknowledge the special help given to us by Patricia Townsend, the archivist at the library at Acadia University, and herself a close friend of Roger. In addition to putting together the bibliography of Roger's works, Pat located and identified photographs, and in many other ways she encouraged the project and offered valuable advice and ongoing support to us.

The essays, as will become apparent, reflect a number of diverse themes which were of interest to Roger. Of course, it was not possible to incorporate essays on every subject about which he was knowledgeable. If we had, we would have included themes such as Canadian maritime history, the life and work of the novelist and former governor general of Canada John Buchan (whose books he collected), philately, trains, and travel guides that noted restaurants with the best desserts! Of course, no volume could ever say all there is to say about Roger. However, we are pleased to offer this collection of essays as a tribute to one whose life and friendship meant so much to us and to so many others as well.

Paul L. Harris
Karen E. Smith

Contributors

William H. Brackney was the Millard R. Cherry Distinguished Professor of Christian Thought Emeritus at Acadia University in Wolfville, Nova Scotia, Canada, where he also directed the Acadia Centre for Baptist and Anabaptist Studies. Previously, he taught at Colgate Rochester Crozer Divinity Schools, McMaster University, Baylor University, and Carey Theological College. He was curator of the Samuel Colgate Baptist Historical Library of the American Baptist Historical Society. A specialist in post-Reformation Protestantism and the Free Churches, he is also remembered for his work in human rights, world religions, and poverty. Dr. Brackney was educated at the University of Maryland (BA), Eastern Baptist Theological Seminary (MAR), and Temple University (MA, PhD), where he graduated with distinction.

Evan Lynwood Colford (MA, Acadia Divinity College, Acadia University) was formerly senior pastor at Berwick Baptist Church. He currently teaches Bible, history, and Christian ethics at Halifax Christian Academy in Halifax, Nova Scotia. With William H. Brackney, he helped with the publication of two edited books, *Maritime Baptist Old First Churches* (Gaspereau Press, 2017) and *Come Out from among Them, and Be Ye Separate, Saith the Lord* (Pickwick Publications, 2019). He is also the coeditor of the forthcoming volume of the historical works of Morgan Edwards in the *Baptists in Early North America* series with Mercer University Press. He is husband to Kayla and father to Elias.

Zachary Cooper has family antecedents reaching deep into Nova Scotia's settler era, including connections with early Baptists. While pursuing a BA in history at Acadia University, he developed a deep friendship with the late Rev. Dr. Roger Prentice, whom he credits as having been a mentor, counselor, and guide. Zachary lives in the Annapolis Valley and is working in small business.

David M. Csinos is associate professor of practical theology at Atlantic School of Theology in Halifax, Nova Scotia. He is also founder and president of Faith Forward, an ecumenical network for innovation in ministry with children, youth, and families. He is the author and editor of many books, including *A Gospel for All Ages* and *Little Theologians*. Dave lives in Halifax, Nova Scotia, with his wife and their two children.

Robert Ellis is a minister of the Baptist Union of Great Britain. He served as pastor to churches in Milton Keynes and Bristol, and taught Christian doctrine at Bristol Baptist College before being appointed fellow in pastoral theology at Regent's Park College, Oxford. He then served as principal at Regent's from 2007 until 2021, and continues there as a senior research fellow. He has published articles on a wide range of theological topics and books on the theology of intercession and the theology of sport: this last area provides his current main research projects. He is married to Sue, and they live in rural Oxfordshire.

Professor Sir Malcolm D. Evans, KCMG, OBE, FLSW, is the principal of Regent's Park College, Oxford. Prior to becoming principal, he was professor of public international law at the University of Bristol. His particular areas of academic focus include torture and torture prevention, the protection of religious liberty under international law, and the law of the sea. From 2009 to 2020, he was a member, and from 2011 to 2020 chair, of the UN Subcommittee for Prevention of Torture (the SPT). From 2015 to 2022, he was a member of the statutory panel of the Independent Inquiry into Child Sexual Abuse in England and Wales (IICSA). From 2002 to 2013, he was a member of the OSCE ODIHR advisory council on the Freedom of Religion or Belief. He is general editor of the *International and Comparative Law Quarterly* and coeditor in chief of the *Oxford Journal of Law and Religion*. He is an editor of the journals *Torture*, *Ocean Development and International Law*, and *Religion and Human Rights*.

J. Daniel Gibson is a retired pastor, with an MDiv from Acadia Divinity College, a DMin from Trinity Evangelical Divinity College, and an MTh from Waterloo Lutheran Seminary. He was ordained in 1971 and served in pastorates in Nova Scotia and Ontario, and was involved in denominational and ecumenical work throughout his career. Music has always been an important part of worship for him, and as a hobby, he built several small pipe organs over the years. He is married to Susan, and they have a daughter, Catherine.

Paul L. Harris is a retired British Baptist minister who studied at Regent's Park College, Oxford, and at the Carver School of Church Social Work in Louisville, Kentucky. He served as pastor of Rehoboth Welsh Baptist Church, Briton Ferry, from 1992 to 2018.

Lydia Hood has served the church through a wide variety of roles: as a project coordinator for the Roman Catholic Archdiocese of Halifax-Yarmouth, as pastoral associate at Our Lady of Guadalupe Parish, and as recruitment coordinator at Atlantic School of Theology, all in Nova Scotia. Originally from Charlottetown, Prince Edward Island, Lydia lives in Halifax, Nova Scotia, with her husband and their two children, but tries to put her feet on the red soil of PEI as often as possible.

Carol Anne Janzen is one of a group of friends who met regularly with Roger. Her friendship with him was grounded in a shared appreciation for Baptist history, choral and organ music, and stimulating conversation. While her career meandered through historical research, arts and crafts, and ministry in Canadian Baptist churches, she eventually earned a PhD in Religious and Moral Education from the University of Alberta. She joined the faculty at Acadia Divinity College in 2003, and over the course of fifteen years, taught in practical theology, including oversight of the chaplaincy program for a time.

Scott Kindred-Barnes (BA, MDiv, MTh, PhD) worked as an adjunct faculty member at Toronto School of Theology from 2007 to 2011, where he taught in the Historical Department. From 2011 to 2018, Scott served as the minister of the congregation at First Baptist Church Ottawa before moving to Wolfville, where he now serves as the senior pastor of Canada's oldest continuing Baptist church. Scott is the current editor of the CABF Bulletin.

Barry M. Moody is professor emeritus in the Department of History and Classics at Acadia University. He holds a BA (Hons.) degree from Acadia University and MA and PhD degrees from Queen's University. He taught history at Acadia from 1970 to 2013. He has written extensively on the history of the New England Planters, eighteenth-century Nova Scotia, and higher education in Canada.

Barry Morrison has served Baptist congregations in four Canadian provinces—Saskatchewan, Quebec, Ontario, and Nova Scotia. His ThD dissertation (Regis College, University of Toronto) was on the theology and spirituality of the Lord's Supper in the context of worship in the Baptist tradition. In 1999, he was appointed to the faculty of Acadia Divinity College, Nova Scotia, where he served as the John N. Gladstone Professor of Preaching and Worship. In 2004, he accepted the call to return to pastoral ministry at Wolfville Baptist Church, Canada's oldest continuing Baptist church, dating to 1763. In retirement, Barry continues to pursue his interest in the liturgy and spirituality of the Eastern Christian churches, including studies in iconography and the ministry of spiritual direction.

Hon. Kelvin Kenneth Ogilvie, CM, PhD, DSc, FCIC, H. Col, Senator(r) is a leading expert on biotechnology, bioorganic chemistry, and genetic engineering. Formerly president and vice chancellor of Acadia University, he was named to the Senate of Canada and served from 2009 to 2017. His scientific accomplishments include the development of the "Gene Machine," an automated process for the manufacture of DNA, and he invented a drug now in worldwide use. Both of these achievements have been recognized by the Canadian Society of Chemistry. Dr. Ogilvie was inducted into the Nova Scotia Discovery Centre Science and Technology Hall of Fame in 2002 and the Canadian Science and Engineering Hall of Fame in Ottawa in 2011.

Mark Parent is the son of missionary parents and grew up in Bolivia, South America. On his return to Canada, he earned a bachelor of arts at York University, a master of divinity at Acadia Divinity College, and a doctor of philosophy at McGill University. Mark has served as pastor of several churches across Canada and has written two books and countless articles for journals and newspapers. Mark has served as an elected member of the Nova Scotia Legislature in the capacity of minister of Environment and Labour and minister of Agriculture. He and his wife, Margie Jenkins, have five children between them and six grandchildren.

Karen E. Smith is an honorary senior research fellow of the School of History, Archaeology, and Religion, Cardiff University, Wales, UK. She has written widely in the area of Baptist history and Christian spirituality and is coeditor of the *Baptist Quarterly*, the journal of the British Baptist Historical Society.

Patricia Townsend has been an archivist at Acadia University for many years. Her research interests centre on the historical development of the Baptist denomination in Atlantic Canada as well as the history of Acadia University. In 1985, she was a member of the committee that selected Roger Prentice as the university chaplain at Acadia.

Allison A. Trites is the Payzant Distinguished Professor Emeritus of New Testament at Acadia Divinity College, Acadia University, Wolfville, Nova Scotia. His publications include *The New Testament Concept of Witness*; *The Gospel of Luke in the Cornerstone Bible Commentary*, vol. 12; and articles in *The New Interpreter's Dictionary of the Bible*, *The Encyclopedia of the Historical Jesus*, and *The New Living Translation Study Bible*.

Howard John Whidden was born in 1943 in Wolfville, Nova Scotia, where his father taught in the Acadia University School of Theology. He was educated in the Wolfville schools, received a BA in history from Acadia, and taught under the auspices of CUSO for two years in West Africa, where he married. After a year at the University of London Institute of Education, he and his wife, Helen, moved to her hometown of Toronto, where he taught for thirty years at a large college of applied arts and technology. On retirement, they moved to Wolfville, where they have occupied their time with gardening, singing in church and university choirs, and with various tasks and committees in the community and in their local Anglican church of St. John's Horton. He has been interested in local history and has written two short books, one on Wolfville's heritage buildings and the other a biography of his father's early years.

Roger Howard Prentice
Halifax, N.S.
Degree: B.Div.

Roger arrived at Willet House and the "Vatican" in 1967. Having already scaled the heights of academic and ecclesiastical excellence, he set his face steadfastly to the task of teaching up Philistines all things needful — academic tradition, worship, and pre-eminently, propriety. He has contributed much as Secretary, then President of the Theology Club. Few are deceived by his seeming formality for we know his warmth and understanding. We wish him fulfilment in his vocation. Dominus vobiscum!

Bachelor of Divinity degree entry for Roger Howard Prentice in *The Axe*, the Acadia University yearbook, 1969.

The Life and Ministry of
Roger Prentice

In Memory of My Great and Good Friend
Roger H. Prentice

Kelvin K. Ogilvie

Roger Prentice was a remarkable person for whom I have always had the greatest respect, and I valued him as a friend. My first contact with Roger occurred when I was appointed the vice president of academics at Acadia University in 1987 following a research career largely spent at McGill University. Roger was the chaplain of Acadia and presided over his domain from the Manning Memorial Chapel on the campus. This lovely chapel was already a place of special significance to me. It had been constructed during the last years that my future wife, Roleen, and I were undergraduates at Acadia, and we were the second couple to be married there in May 1964.

My association with Roger developed rapidly. He was dedicated to the students of Acadia. He had been appointed chaplain in 1985 and saw his role primarily to minister to students, faculty, and staff on campus as well as to the larger community. Being chaplain on a secular university campus requires a genuine character and a broad sense of ministry. It also helps to have a solid historical and scholarly background in Christian ministry. Roger had those qualities and background and more besides.

Roger took seriously his role as chaplain and felt deeply that chaplaincy belonged in the university. However, early on, he had clearly identified that the chaplaincy was not secure in a university always strapped for funds and a faculty not likely to place chapel funding equal with their academic needs. He initiated a chaplaincy endowment fund intended to protect the role. I became president of Acadia for two terms, from 1993 to 2003, and I would come to say that Roger was so valuable to us at Acadia that had he not existed, it would have been critical to "invent" him. Through his natural and genuine instincts, he demonstrated that the role of chaplain was essential to the whole community.

It is difficult to summarize the many and varied ways Roger influenced generations of students as well as faculty, staff, and the greater community. He quickly developed a role in guiding students needing advice in a secure environment. He provided a solid, safe, and learning environment for students of faith, or seeking faith, through his chaplaincy programs.

These students came from many disciplines and included campus athletics. He conducted eleven chapel services a week, and participation in his Passion plays became one of the most sought-after roles on campus and included memorable performances from athletes, especially from the hockey team. As a result, Roger became a counselor for all students needing guidance regardless of their religious connections. The chapel has a fine organ and always an exceptional organist, too, and, as such, it was often a much appreciated location for quiet reflection on campus. I must also note that regardless of the time of day or night that an "incident" involving students on campus occurred, it was a race between our director of security and Roger as to which would arrive first, and they worked together in the best interests of the student(s) involved.

Roger's ministry to students evolved from his own early years. His life from age five on would be centered in the south end of Halifax. His parents were devoted "churchgoers," attending both morning and evening services at First Baptist Church in Halifax. Roger also attended morning Sunday school, where many of the teachers were Halifax's leading citizens. Daily, in his early school years, he went to religious services and gained further knowledge of the Christian faith. He was also part of the Wolf Cubs and Boy Scouts, both sponsored by churches.

As the 1960s arrived, Roger reached the teenage years and was caught up in the challenge to authority and the role of religion. His deep respect for his parents, and the introduction to intellectual argument from authors such as J. A. T. Robinson, K. Barth, P. Tillich, D. Bonhoeffer, R. Bultmann, and others, helped him to reflect and resolve his views on religion and its role in society. He came to a profound understanding of the Bible and its basis in oral traditions and stories, its reflection on "truths" of human nature and relationships, and the appearance of human life on our planet.

Roger attended Dalhousie University with the intention of teaching history in high school upon graduation. He was particularly influenced by Rev. Dr. John Corston, a respected biblical scholar, and Dr. George Wilson, an eminent historian. Roger continued his close association with First Baptist in Halifax and established and served as chair of a young adult fellowship program. The program was open to all students and, on Sunday afternoons, would discuss "perplexing problems (social, theological, ethical, etc.)" with an invited speaker. Following supper, most would attend the evening service.

In Memory of My Great and Good Friend

During his undergraduate years, Roger volunteered to be part of a project for youth through the Seaview United Baptist Church in Africville. This experience was a great opportunity for personal development and helped solidify his growing feeling that he was being called to be a Christian minister. He was accepted by the Maritime Baptist Home Mission Board as a student summer "minister" and spent two summers in Advocate Harbour, Nova Scotia. He also expanded his courses in subjects such as "The English Bible," "The Psychology of Religion," and "Classical Literature in Translation."

Roger entered the bachelor of divinity program at Acadia in 1966, and the following summer he was a youth minister in Sable River, which he recalled as a wonderful learning experience, especially getting to know the scientist Harrison Lewis. There he also met a young woman, Leanne Oickle, who would have a profound impact on his life. (She was enrolled in a women's leadership course while acquiring her degree at Acadia.)

During his studies, Roger came in contact with Dr. Evan Whidden, Dr. Charles Taylor, Dr. Earl Merrick, and Dr. Allison Trites—all of whom he later felt had been particularly important to his formation. His thesis, "The Spiritual Effect of Fasting," under the supervision of Dr. Merrick, won the "best theological studies thesis" award. Roger was involved in numerous activities during his studies and was president of the Theological Club and a member of the college's "Gospel Team."

Following his ordination in 1969, at which time he established his ability to stand solidly with his position on important religious matters, Roger was called to be the assistant minister and minister of Christian education at First Baptist Church, Amherst, Nova Scotia. He was heavily involved in youth programs and community outreach and also directed plays that were so popular they went "on the road" in the Maritimes.

After six years in Amherst, Roger was called to the pastorate at St. Stephen, New Brunswick. He and Leanne were by this time engaged to be married, with the wedding planned for July 1975. Tragedy struck in May 1975 when Leanne was killed in a car accident. Thereafter, Roger never married, but his personal-loss experience enabled him to become a much respected and valued counselor and guide to others suffering great loss or facing personal turmoil in life.

As he continued his ministry in the church, Roger became deeply interested in the tradition and practice of Baptist worship. While exploring this issue and seeking to understand the experience of churches around the world, he was invited by the Rev. Dr. B. R. White, principal of Regent's

Park College, Oxford University, to begin a doctor of philosophy program. He found Oxford both "exhilarating and exhausting." Roger's studies were intense, and he also was sent out regularly to preach in Baptist churches in the region. After four years, he had run out of funding to continue his studies and returned to Nova Scotia after being called to the First United Baptist Church in Annapolis Royal (and four other churches in the area). Two years later, and after numerous efforts on the part of the university, Roger agreed to become the chaplain at Acadia University in 1985.

Roger always believed that a university offered a great opportunity for young adults to discover their "spiritual being," and through his chaplaincy he attempted to provide the best environment for such exploration. Roger used every opportunity to provide a context whereby students could reflect on faith. Worship services, Passion plays that provided opportunity for students to understand through telling the story themselves, and one-to-one conversation were viewed as moments for a person to explore faith. He spoke in classes and invited faculty and others to "preach" in the chapel services. He officiated at the weddings of a countless number of students. He also held funeral services for faculty, staff, and students. He was invited to say grace at all university functions. He even wrote the university prayer, which is still in use, as well as a university hymn.

Roger believed in the inclusiveness of the university and the surrounding community and sought to bring them together for their mutual benefit. As such, he participated in Advent services, baccalaureate, the Inter-Church Council and Remembrance Day services on campus, and attended services in the wider community on special occasions. Roger was chaplain of the Royal Canadian Legion, and the organ recitals that he planned for the chapel played to full houses from the community.

Roger's theology seems to have been based on the idea that the individual spirit is vitally linked to a larger spirit that may be interpreted as the "Holy Spirit." The activity of the Spirit is discovered in our connection through friends, community, family relationships, and, indeed, in all relationships of life. Roger's theological beliefs were not simply expressed in words, they were all-embracing and meant to be practised in all of life, as well as in specific acts of worship, music, and prayer.

Roger was a dynamic individual with numerous interests, especially in philately, railroads, the Senate of Canada, and literature. He and I even toured Wales together with Dr. Rodger Forsman, all being avid *Cadfael* followers.

In Memory of My Great and Good Friend

Through his life's work, Roger had a profound effect on countless individuals and his community, and he was recognized for his efforts in many ways. While I'm certain he was most truly rewarded by realizing the help he provided individuals, I must note that he was awarded a doctor of humanities degree from Acadia University in 2008 and received the Queen's Diamond Jubilee Medal in 2012, the Senate of Canada Sesquicentennial Medal in 2017, and honorary life membership in the Canadian Association for Baptist Freedoms in 2019. All of these awards indicate the high esteem in which Roger's life and work was held by so many. He was to me a great and good friend.

In Appreciation of a Friendship

Paul L. Harris

It is my privilege, as one who knew Roger for more than forty years, since meeting him first at Regent's Park College, Oxford, in 1979, to write this short appreciation of a dear friend. What I originally planned to write in this book—when it was intended as a *Festschrift* for Roger's eightieth birthday—was a tribute to the ongoing companionship of a great friend, colleague, and "mentor cum confidante." Now, sadly, I am writing of a wonderful legacy of friendship and support offered by Roger to so many friends in different parts of Canada and, indeed, the world. Yet it is with great thanksgiving that I speak of his gift of friendship.

Today, the word friendship is at times used rather loosely to indicate someone who is recognized and accepted on a social media account. However, friendship with Roger could never be reduced to mere contact over the internet or even the occasional phone call. While for many a year Roger and I kept in touch across the miles on a daily basis via email, he always preferred letter writing, and in his view, personal contact was even better. Hence, yearly my family and I would look forward to his arrival to stay with us in Britain. Usually travelling to us by way of a luxury ocean liner, and then in a first-class BritRail seat on a train, when he finally arrived at our home, we would laugh together as he relayed tales from his journey across the Atlantic.

Roger's kindly but always quite humble and very honest friendship to so many was legendary. Whether it was spending time with a friend as they travelled together to a meeting (usually with the gift of a chocolate bar in his pocket aptly named "my buddy") or his regular mealtime gathering with a group of women (jokingly referred to as "the Harem"), he enjoyed being with people. By his own admission, he would meet and greet people all over the province and beyond (indeed, even abroad, too). He did not always remember names or situations—how could he possibly do so with so many contacts that he had worldwide? However, all would be met with wide open arms and a cheery smile—and with an unmistakable grin of sheer delight at recognition. Such encounters, sometimes entirely serendipitous—even at international airports and London underground

In Appreciation of a Friendship

stations—tell the tale of a Christian gentleman who never took himself too seriously and yet was ready to be a friend and support to any who crossed his path, even years after the initial point of contact.

Without in any way betraying a confidence, seemingly it is officially recognized that one of the illnesses which led to his final and sadly very sudden demise in his own home in early April 2022 was an enlarged heart. This seems to be a striking metaphor for his life as a whole. Both as an individual and as an ordained minister, Roger always had a rare degree of openness to others. Roger's nonjudgmental, amicable, fun-loving personality, combined with a personal integrity and deep Christian commitment, led people to trust and respect him. Hence, his friendships extended to all ages and to those of very differing political opinions or theological persuasions as well.

When he was ordained in 1969, Roger's more liberal theological views and contemporary approaches to Scripture and doctrine were challenged by some of the ministerial colleagues then commissioning him. Latterly, some continued to find his insistence on liturgical correctness, including wearing formal attire (a cassock and gown) when presiding at the ministry of Word and Sacrament and the occasional offices of weddings and funerals (of which he officiated at hundreds over the years), out of keeping with the Baptist way. Yet for those who knew Roger, his sense of calling was never in doubt. His warmth of personality was appreciated, his integrity of scholarly understanding was respected, and his pastoral heart was recognized by all who knew him.

While in his early ministry, Roger was an able pastor in several local churches. He was well suited not only by nurture (including extensive training and careful preparation) but also by nature to become the university chaplain and dean of the Manning Memorial Chapel at Acadia. The son of devout parents, his childhood experience and then his own youth and young-adult faith development at the Baptist church in Halifax well prepared him for what would become his paramount role in ministry. The challenge of following Christ's call to discipleship and serving in Christian ministry to those of all faiths or none, with a winsome humour, but also a razor-sharp radical openness and a suitably penetrating, even probing, honesty, was not one which came easily to him. However, he gave himself to the calling which from his youth he knew as his own vocation in life. This was a calling no doubt shaped in large part by his upbringing, his experience of church life, and his own personal path of suffering in the

KEEPING THE FAITH

tragic loss of his fiancée, Leanne Oickle, just before their planned marriage, and then later his own long, arduous struggle with cancer.

By virtue of his role as the official chaplain to students and staff at Acadia from 1985 to 2007, and then again briefly, but wholly comprehensively, in an interim role some years later, he met with countless people in his office. However, he also met frequently with staff and students in various places on and off campus. Such was Roger's generous and hospitable spirit that much of his counseling, and, to a degree, his spiritual direction, was undertaken in an anonymous context at a cafe, restaurant, or other establishment. He was also ready to welcome those who turned up at his door at all hours of the day or night, willing to make himself available to help whenever necessary, even if it meant a short night's sleep. Roger even gave lodging to students who were in need of a place to stay while doing studies at Acadia. On at least one occasion, he hosted an international student for a year, knowing the student would not have been able to continue studying at the university without this assistance.

Roger enjoyed theatre, and his thespian gifts were displayed in various contexts over the years, including at youth camps, an Oxford College dining hall, church buildings, Manning Memorial Chapel in Acadia, and, of course, the local theatre in Wolfville, where for several years at Christmas, Roger acted as Mr. Fezziwig in *A Christmas Carol*. He believed that the theatre could be an important means for exploring faith, which is why he wrote Passion plays during his time as chaplain, and even drew the members of the university hockey team to take part. His mischievous sense of humour drew people in, and his wicked delight in gently teasing others was used not to ridicule but to foster understanding—all with the aim of building up a person or tearing down needless barriers.

Roger's laughter, like his enthusiasm, was infectious. He had a particular gift with young people and could come meaningfully alongside those with little or no interest in the church. Much of his ministry was geared to reaching out to those who were younger in years or, as in his later years as chaplain, to those somewhat estranged from the ambience of traditional Christian faith and institutional religion. He himself was devout without being overly pious, and he was able to draw others who were just seekers, or who even had no inclination to faith, to think about the spiritual dimension of life. He befriended so many in this way, and the testimony of them without exception is that he gave them the opportunity to be truly themselves. In Roger's company, they were able to explore the deeper things of life in a new way without being trapped in what might be

In Appreciation of a Friendship

perceived by them to be a narrow or stuffy, antiquated religious orthodoxy. So, at Acadia, students and staff (including personnel at all levels), as well as chapel assistants and hockey players alike, were able to trust him, and to confide in him, and to find in him a role model of true faith and devotion without the off-putting judgementalism or rigidity so often found in church life.

In his personal life and ministerial formation, Roger had developed the art of speaking the honest word in a way that drew attention to what really mattered. Thus, he could be relied upon for a sincere expression of his opinion on a moot topic whether in the context of the local church, the regional association of Baptist churches, the ecumenical scene in town, or even in the university Senate on which he served for his last few years. Through the years, pastors, tutors, fellow ministers, and even university presidents would seek his personal views on a subject of concern or confide in him when facing difficult personal or relational issues. Roger was a friend who could be relied upon absolutely, and one to whom so many turned for moral support or simply wise counsel.

Roger travelled widely and, unsurprizingly, had many diverse interests, including a particular penchant for philately and literature, with one special other interest, namely rail transportation and trains. Roger built up an amazing stamp collection as well as a vast collection of many and varied editions of the writings of the historian, novelist, and former governor general of Canada John Buchan. He had a huge library of all kinds of books on these topics and others. His many interests meant that he could converse comfortably in all kinds of situations and with all manner of people. However, Roger was especially at home when it came to things of a spiritual nature, where, in discussion on subjects of faith and belief, he showed clearly, but humbly, an understanding of the issues raised by contemporary theology.

Roger had a broad openness when reflecting on issues of faith, spirituality, and ethics which he happily maintained, along with a very traditional sense of the liturgy and an admittedly High Church appreciation for leadership of worship, preaching, and the administration of the sacraments. This passionate inclination and his warm ecumenical spirit meant he was more at home in an Anglican evensong than in many evangelical traditions, which were often less formal liturgically. Naturally, it was this openness which lay behind his willingness to join with others to form the Canadian Association for Baptist Freedoms (CABF). Likewise, his genuine ecumenical spirit led him to give support to the local inter-Church

Council and to forge faithful and lasting relationships with both clergy and members of various denominations.

Roger was, of course, an avowed Baptist by persuasion, but one always willing to listen and to see the strengths in the viewpoint of others on matters of faith and practice. However, his ultimate loyalty was never to a church body or a denomination, nor to a set interpretation of the Christian creed, or even to a given theological school as such, but to the Lord. In his devout life, this allegiance was expressed always to Christ, who had called and equipped him specifically for his distinct vocation, which he worked out in his own quite unique circumstances.

When he celebrated the fiftieth anniversary of his ordination in 2019, it is not surprizing that in addition to attending a celebration with some of those who had been his "young people" in his first church, he also had a special service at Acadia, where he was then serving as interim chaplain. At that service, he knelt down and publicly renewed his ministerial vows to serve the Lord. One of the hymns Roger included in the service was "To Be a Pilgrim," a hymn commonly attributed to the seventeenth-century English Baptist John Bunyan. Truly it can be said of Roger: "His first avowed intent, to be a Pilgrim."

Reflecting upon Roger's life and witness, it is undeniably the case that he lived by his own motto to "keep the faith." I am glad I knew him, and, with so many others who knew him, I give thanks to God for his friendship over so many years. I will always treasure the memories of time spent with him in Nova Scotia and the many visits he made to Wales to stay with my family. Remarkably, when he heard that we were looking for a house in retirement, his advice was always to go to the Cotswolds (which he loved). Knowing the economic constraints of finding a place in such a desirable location, my wife and I laughed at his suggestion. When, strangely, we in fact found ourselves settling a few miles from the Cotswold region, Roger was satisfied. Once more, his sound advice had been heard and in an uncanny way heeded. Of more lasting significance, his encouragement and inspiration in matters of faith will long be remembered and appreciated not only by myself but by countless others.

Roger H. Prentice: A Bibliography, 1969 to 2022

Compiled by Patricia Townsend

BOOKS AND BOOKLETS

Wolfville, Nova Scotia: Baptists in Early North America series. Macon, GA: Mercer University Press, forthcoming.

Hymns at Heaven's Gate: The Use and Abuse of Hymns. Kentville, NS: Gaspereau Press, 2008.

A Quick and Easy History of a Child of Providence: The Story of Acadia University. Wolfville, NS: Acadia University, 2005.

Vespers Little Talks. Wolfville, NS: Acadia University, 1998.

NOVELLAS

Roger wrote these novellas in order to convey the Christmas story in a unique way. He sent them to several hundred friends during the respective Christmas seasons from 2015 to 2021. All were published by Gaspereau Press in Kentville, Nova Scotia.

2015: *Mildred*
2016: *A Letter from Charles*
2017: *Benedictus: A Christmas Story*
2018: *Hear the Angels Sing: A Christmas Story*
2019: *Jesse's Secret*
2020: *Angel Voices*
2021: *Morningstar*

CONTRIBUTIONS TO BOOKS AND BOOKLETS

"'The Cardinal': A Chronicle of the Rev'd (Lieutenant Colonel) John Howard MacDonald FRGS, CBE, D.D." In the *Acadia Centre for Baptist and Anabaptist Studies Booklet Series*, No. 3, 2016, and revised edition, 2018.

"The Impact of Walter Rauschenbusch in Canada." In *In the Shadow of the Prophet: The Legacy of Walter Rauschenbusch.* Edited by William H. Brackney and David P. Gushee. Macon, GA: Mercer University Press and the Acadia Centre for Baptist and Anabaptist Studies, 2020: 93–124.

"Letters of Enquiry: The Correspondence File of the Maritime Baptist Convention Chaplain Service Committee 1939–1941." In *Crossing Baptist Boundaries: A Festschrift in Honor of William Brackney*. Edited by Erich Geldbach. Macon, GA: Mercer University Press 2019: 151–79.

"Two Commemorative Services." In *Maritme Baptist Old First Churches Narratives and Perspectives*, edited by William H. Brackney with Evan L. Colford. Wolfville, NS: ACBAS Publications and the Editorial Committee of the Canadian Baptists of Atlantic Canada Historical Committee, 2017: 225–46. Roger also prepared the index for this volume.

THESIS

"The Spiritual Effect of Fasting." A thesis presented for the bachelor of divinity degree, School of Theology, Acadia University, 1969. https://scholar.acadiau.ca/islandora/object/theses:3672

BOOK REVIEWS

Prentice, Roger H. Review of *The Champions of the Truth: Fundamentalism, Modernism, and the Maritime Baptists*, by George Rawlyk. *Bulletin of the Atlantic Baptist Fellowship* (September 1990): 10.

Prentice, Roger H. Review of *Finding My Way*, by Bert Radford. *Bulletin of the Canadian Association for Baptist Freedoms* (Winter 2022): 14–15.

Prentice, Roger H. Review of *A Life of Bishop John A. T. Robinson: Scholar, Pastor, Prophet*, by Eric James. *Bulletin of the Atlantic Baptist Fellowship* (December 1992): 10.

Prentice, Roger H. Review of *The Spirit among the Dissenters: Other Voices in Understanding the Spirit of God*, by William Brackney. *Bulletin of the Canadian Association for Baptist Freedoms* (Fall 2019): 9.

Prentice, Roger H. Review of *To Be a Pilgrim: A Biography of Silas Tertius Rand, 1810–1889*, by Dorothy May Lovesey. *Bulletin of the Atlantic Baptist Fellowship* (December 1992): 9.

Articles Written by Roger Prentice for Atlantic Baptist

"A Convention Issue: The Evangelical Fellowship of Canada." 24/8 (August 1988): 18–19.

"Regarding renewal of subscription to the newspaper." 8/7 (May 15, 1972): 9.

"University Chaplaincy." 23/8 (August 1987): 35–36.

Articles written by Roger Prentice for The Bulletin of the Atlantic Baptist Fellowship.
"ABF Friends Luncheon Speaker." (Spring 2002): 14.
"ABF Mourns Founding Members." (Summer 2005): 13–15.
"The ABF and University Chaplaincy." (December 1993): 5–6.
"Atlantic United Baptist Convention, 1988: A Personal Report." (December 1988): 4.
"Baptism and the Baptism, Eucharist, and Ministry Document." (October–November 1984): 9–12.
"Booklet Is Ready." (Spring 1997): 12.
"Can This Not Be a Better World?" (Summer 2000): 10–11.
"A Christian Man of Principle." (Winter 1997): 4.
"The Christmas Cycle Gift." (Winter 2002): 11–12.
"Dr. Ferne G. Levy." (Summer 2004): 15.
"God and Government." (Fall 2002): 5.
"The Infection of Lies." (Winter 1996): 3.
"Invitation for a Christian Community." (Spring 1996): 3.
"Looking to the Future." (June 1994): 3.
"Morris Roland Bezantine Lovesey BA, MA, BSC, BD, MTH, D.D." (Fall 2009): 12–16.
"Places We Worship...Manning Memorial Chapel." (Winter 1997): 14.
"Rescuing the Leadership." (June 1995): 3–4.
"Resurrection: A Sign for the Future." (Fall 2001): 5–6.
"Singing from the Same Hymnbook." (Fall 2002): 8–9.
"Some Uncertain Signs: Convention." (December 1985): 8–9.
"Springtime Changes." Editorial comment. (Spring 2003): 9.
"Thanks!" Editorial comment. (Winter 2002): 5.
"...that they may be one." (Summer 1997): 3.
"That They May Be One." (Winter 2001): 3.
"Unexpected Encounters." (Summer 1998): 3.
"University Chaplaincy: The Outside from the INSIDE." (March 1994): 5.
"What Is Missing?" (December 1995): 6.
"A Word for the 21st Century." (Fall 1999): 3.
"The Word in Song." (Autumn 2004): 13–16.
"Working on Credentials." (Summer 2012): 5.

Articles written by Roger Prentice for The Bulletin of the Canadian Association for Baptist Freedoms

"Any Anniversary Ideas?" (Fall 2019): 6.

"Archival Treasures." (Fall 2018): 4.

"Autumn Stampede." Editorial. (Fall 2019): 2.

"Belonging to a New Spirit." Editorial. (Spring 2014): 2.

"Chaplain Extraordinary: The Rev'd Dr. I. Judson Levy." (Winter 2020): 14–15.

"Church Images." (Fall 2018): 4–15.

"Church and State." Editorial. (Spring 2015): 2.

"The Colonel Who Disappeared." (Fall 2018): 11–12.

"Five Delightful Years: A Minister with a View." (Spring 2018): 14–15.

"42 Years Advancing Freedoms." Editorial. (Winter 2014): 2.

"From the Editor...Handling the Tiller." (Fall 2013): 2–3.

"'The Full-Orbed Gospel' The Ministry of Henry Fish Waring." (Winter 2019): 12–15.

"The Golden Calf." Editorial. (Winter 2019): 2.

"The Leadership Challenge." Editorial. (Fall 2016): 2.

"Little Church at the Crossroads: A New Book of Baptist History." (Winter 2019): 8–9.

"Looking to the Future." Editorial. (Fall 2018): 2.

"A Lost Treasure." (Fall 2019): 5–6.

"A Man of Faith: Dr. Rodger Forsman." Editorial. (Fall 2017): 2.

"The Man from Margaree." (Spring 2014): 10–11.

"A New Emmaus Road." Editorial. (Winter 2015): 2.

"Pioneer Baptists of Halifax: The Rev'd John Burton." (Fall 2019): 10–12.

"Pressing Work." (Fall 2019): 13–14.

"Probing the Future." Editorial. (Spring 2019): 2.

"Recognizing the Saints." Editorial. (Spring 2016): 2.

"Reflections of a Former Editor." (Spring 2020): 5–7.

"The Reflector and Its Story." (Spring 2016): 10–12.

"Religion and Sport." Editorial. (Spring 2018): 2.

"A Scholar and a Gentleman." Editorial. (Winter 2018): 2.

"Sesquicentennial." Editorial. (Winter 2017): 2.

"Spring Cleaning." Editorial. (Spring 2017): 2.

"Terry." Editorial. (Fall 2015): 2.

"Thoughts for the Journey." (Winter 2018): 13–14.

"Waving Good-Bye." Editorial. (Winter 2020): 2.

ACBAS Times. (November 2015) 1:1.

PLAYS

But It's History, Mom, a playlet for the 165th anniversary of First Baptist Church Halifax, September 30, 1992.

My Name Is Gabriel: The Story from One Who Was There: A Christmas Pageant. Kentville, NS: Gaspereau Press, 2010.

Manning Memorial Chapel Passion Plays: 1997–2005

A Cry in the Dark: A Passion Play. March 27–30, 2001.

It Happened on Friday, The Passion of Our Lord: A Passion Play. March 2000.

On the Road to Freedom: A Passion Play. March 26–29, 2002.

The Quest of Doubting Thomas: A Passion Play. March 30–April 2, 2004.

Sent to Coventry: A Passion Play. March 29–April 1, 2005.

Through New Eyes: A Passion Play. March 1999.

Uninvited Guests: A Passion Play for a Chancel. March 24–26, 1997.

The Valour of a King: A Passion Play. March 25–28, 2003.

EDITED SERIALS

Acadia Centre for Baptist and Anabaptist Studies Booklet Series. 2014–2018.

Acadia University Chaplaincy Chapel Booklet Series. 1996–1997; 2002.

Acadia Vesper Hymns. Wolfville: Manning Memorial Chapel. 1993.

Atlantic Baptist Fellowship Newsletter. Editor. May 1972–1975.

The Chapel Times. Acadia University. Author and editor. 1994–1999.

Three-year-old Roger with his wheelbarrow, October 1946.

Cast of *On The Road To Freedom* presented
at Manning Memorial Chapel,
Acadia University, March 26-29, 2002.

Roger preaching in Manning Memorial Chapel.

Roger seated in the Andrew H. McCain Arena, Acadia University, most likely while attending a hockey game.

Roger with one of his many favourite desserts.

Roger with Marjorie (Manning) Fountain at Roger's retirement dinner. Fountain Commons, Acadia University, July 28, 2007.

Baptist Identity, Theology, and Spirituality

Adoring Thee, we humbly pray
In all which we can give,
That everything we've done today
May make Thy glory live.

Confessing all the sins we have:
Confessing every one,
That we may know Thy power to save:
The Name of Thine own Son.

Absolving all who come to Thee,
Which none of us can claim
Our lives are made completely free
By praying in Thy name.

Discipleship is how we love
Thy place within our lives;
Our faith in Christ will be enough
Enlightening our minds.

In intercession we implore.
For all the world we know,
And in this place may we learn more
That faith in life will grow.

Atonement is the goal we want:
With Thee we will be one;
Our worship flows in fulfillment
And may Thy will be done.

Thy praise we sing, an earthly host
Joins all who love our Lord:
Praise Father, Son and Holy Ghost,
We sing with one accord. Amen.

Acadia Vesper Hymns
(Wolfville: Manning Memorial Chapel, 1993, No.1, RHP)

Voluntarism, Human Rights, and a Global Mission: The Progressive/Liberal Tradition among Canadian Baptists

William H. Brackney

Through the years, it has been assumed, at times, that when rightly expressed, Baptist theology can be stated in a uniform way. Yet those who are familiar with Baptist life realise that even in the local church there are theological differences among Baptists. It has always been so. In fact, from the very beginning of their history, Baptists have not always agreed with one another on every point of doctrine or practice. Sometimes, particularly on a local level, when differences have emerged, members have simply agreed to disagree on certain matters, but have continued to work together in service for Christ. At other times, especially on a denominational level, the differences, regrettably, have led to division.

For many years, a main theological divide among Baptists has been between those who have what might be considered more conservative theological views and those who might be defined as being liberal in their understanding of Christian faith. Unfortunately, the terms "fundamentalist" and "liberal" are often used in a pejorative way and with the assumption that by describing opposing views along a two-party system, it is possible to clearly identify those who are part of each group. Yet even within such groups, always there have been differences of opinion.

While recognizing a broad theological spectrum of views among Baptists, it is sometimes claimed that most Baptists identify with a conservative theological view. Such an assumption, however, overlooks the fact that there has always been a strong, more liberal tradition among Baptists. In Canada, as this study will show, the Baptist liberal/progressive wing has been characterized by an appreciation of education for ministry, theological relevancy, affirmation of both sexes in ministry, ecumenical and interfaith engagement, social concern, human rights, separation of church and state, and an historical/critical understanding of the interpretation of the

Scriptures. Understandably, the tradition is grounded in Western European Christian intellectual thought.[1]

In some ways, a liberal tradition has characterized Baptist life in Canada from the beginning. It is first reflected in diverse origins. Baptists who came to Canada originated not from one stock or confession, but from several, including American Baptists from the northern US colonies, African American Baptists, English Baptists from London and the counties, Scotch Baptists, and Swiss Francophones.[2] Later immigrant groups of Baptists included Germans, Swedes, Russians, Aboriginals, and various Asian groups, producing quite a variety. It is reflected in an urge to be part of the larger Protestant tradition in Canada. Finally, it is also manifest in the character of the global outreach of Canadian Baptists in Asia, South America, the Caribbean, and Africa.

Some recent interpretations of such a Baptist liberal tradition in Canada have not appreciated this rich heritage. Yet Canadian Baptist history adequately demonstrates a liberal/progressive character from its foundations. In fact, the progressive/liberal tradition is inextricably tied to Baptist efforts in higher education. Two institutions and their leadership display a liberal character: the Baptist College in Montreal and Acadia University in Wolfville, Nova Scotia.[3]

---

[1] It was influenced by John Locke, Thomas Jefferson, Benjamin Franklin, Jean Jacques Rousseau, the philosophes, F. D. E. Schleiermacher at Berlin, Johann G. Oncken, William Vidler, Julius Köbner, and the Baptist revolutionaries of 1848, James Shakespeare, John Clifford, and John R. Mott. In the United States, the liberal tradition among Baptists was carried forth by Roger Williams, Elias Smith, Elhanan Winchester, Jonathan Maxcy, Asa Messer, Francis Wayland, Barnas Sears, Crawford H. Toy, and William H. P. Faunce. Twentieth-century American Baptist liberals included Walter Rauschenbusch, Shailer Mathews, William R. Harper, George B. Foster, Nathaniel Schmidt, William Newton Clarke, Milton G. Evans, Morton Scott Enslin, Harry Emerson Fosdick, William L. Poteat, Edwin E. Aubrey, Jitsuo Morikawa, Harvey Cox, William Hamilton, Robert T. Handy, W. Kenneth Cauthen, Ralph H. Elliott, Martin Luther King, Jr., Carlisle Marney, Howard Thurman, and S. Mark Heim.

[2] Theo T. Gibson, *Robert Alexander Fyfe: His Contemporaries and His Influence* (Burlington, ON: Welsh Publishing Co., 1988), 24–31.

[3] On the Baptist College in Montreal, see Thomas A. Higgins, *The Life of John Mockett Cramp, D.D. 1796–1881* (Quebec: Drysdale, 1887), 83–111; Karen E. Smith, "The Baptist College in Montreal, 1836–1849: The British Connexion,

Voluntarism, Human Rights, and a Global Mission

Benjamin Davies and Canada Baptist College

Benjamin Davies (1814–1876) was a key transatlantic influence toward the liberal tradition in both England and Canada. Educated at Bristol Baptist College and the University of Glasgow, he earned a PhD from the University of Leipzig in Oriental studies. He embodied the high-toned scholar among Baptists, distinguishing himself as a Bible scholar and theological educator.

In 1838, Davies was invited to Lower Canada (Quebec) to organize a new theological institution, Canada Baptist College, in Montreal. Initially, he created a university-style, rigorous program of studies that emphasized biblical languages, but his efforts lacked local support, and few students were qualified to study at the school. One of his lasting contributions, however, was the creation of an extensive theological library, the first among Baptists in Canada. He returned to London for three years, where he was principal at Stepney College followed by a return to Montreal for a decade, where he served as professor and chair of the Classical Studies Department at McGill University. Joseph Angus invited Davies to return to London, where he was given the chair in Old Testament and Classical Studies at Stepney. During this period, Davies was one of the principal revisers of the English Bible, and through his scholarship he brought the fruits of German higher criticism to English Nonconformity. In Canada, he was the first recognized scholar among the Baptists and a pioneering educator in what evolved as the McMaster Tradition.[4] Canada Baptist College, while it did not survive as such in Montreal, was the root of a scholastic tradition in training Canadian Baptist ministers.

---

with Special Reference to the Contribution of the Baptist Missionary Society" *Baptist Quarterly* 41/8 (2006), 455–480; William H. Brackney, *Congregation and Campus: North American Baptists in Higher Education* (Macon, GA: Mercer University Press, 2008), 135. On the establishment of Acadia, see *Jubilee of Acadia College and Memorial Exercises, 1888* (Halifax, NS: Holloway Brothers, 1889); Ronald Stewart Longley, *Acadia University 1838–1939* (Wolfville, NS: Acadia University, 1939); and Barry M. Moody, *"Give Us an A": An Acadia Album 1838–1988* (Wolfville, NS: Acadia University, 1988).

[4] When the college closed in Montreal, it relocated under Robert A. Fyfe to Woodstock, Upper Canada, and then to Toronto where it affiliated with the University of Toronto. In 1930, the university moved to Hamilton, Ontario.

Robert A. Fyfe and Religious Voluntarism

One of the differentiating characteristics of Baptists in Canada from their American counterparts has been religious voluntarism. Robert A. Fyfe stepped forward to advance the vision of Benjamin Davies. Fyfe (1816–1878) was the link between the Montreal experiment and the evolution to Toronto Baptist College and McMaster University. Educated at the Baptist College in Montreal, Hamilton Literary and Theological Institution, and Newton Theological Institution, he was one of the best trained Baptist ministers in North America. His orientation was shaped by a liberal, progressive tradition.

Fyfe provided Baptists with two legacies. First was his relentless pursuit of a permanent institution of higher education, primarily for Baptists, but also for others as well. He believed sincerely in general education in a Christian environment. In the school at Woodstock, he boldly opened the school to girls.[5] He lectured across theological disciplines, recognizing the rising importance of the sciences. He wrote, "With almost incredible rapidity old ideas are being exploded and new facts presented for enrolment in every department of science."[6] A biographer has observed that Fyfe's teaching was balanced by a generous toleration toward others and a vigorous participation on the side of justice and truth in matters social, moral, and governmental.[7] Fyfe's extraordinary efforts on Woodstock were rewarded with course transfer recognition at the University of Toronto and an invitation from the governor general to be a member of the senate of the provincial university.[8]

Second was his advocacy of religious voluntarism. With the disposition of the Upper Canada clergy reserves funds, a debate arose over the role of religious denominations in controlling and funding universities and theological programs. Some favoured the establishment churches like the Anglicans, others favoured modified support for denominational schools, and Fyfe wrote strenuously in favour of "undenominational" or "unsectarian" universities and a system of denominational colleges voluntarily supported by those sects which wanted or needed them. His position was

---

[5] Gibson, *Robert Alexander Fyfe*, 268.
[6] Fyfe, quoted in Gibson, *Robert Alexander Fyfe*, 272.
[7] Ibid., 274.
[8] Ibid., 275.

based squarely upon his experience in the United States, where the principle of the separation of church and state was embedded in the Constitution. In 1847, a compromise was reached whereby a compact of existing denominations would share in government funds for ministerial education. The compact included Anglicans, Methodists, Presbyterians, and eventually Baptists. Fyfe's dream of a completely voluntary system was lost, but the universities were set free from denominational ties, and a uniquely Canadian Baptist principle had been articulated.[9]

Acadia and the Maritime Liberal Achievement

Horton Academy, later to evolve as Acadia University, grew up amidst strong university-level institutions in Nova Scotia and New Brunswick: University of King's College in Windsor, Dalhousie University in Halifax, and the University of New Brunswick in Fredericton. Acadia soon earned a regional reputation as a liberal arts school and developed a strong undergraduate feeder program to sister schools in the US: Brown University, Newton Theological Institution, and Colgate University.[10] It had at least one professor in theology from its beginning.

Crawley and Cramp

The cofounders of the Acadia tradition represented different scholarly traditions and were often seen in juxtaposition to each other.[11] Edmund A. Crawley (1799–1888) emigrated to Cape Breton, Nova Scotia, and graduated from King's College in Windsor (BA, MA) as a top scholar who was admitted to the bar in two provinces. He also studied theology at Andover Theological Seminary and Brown University. Crawley was converted to Baptist principles and was baptized at Granville Street Baptist Church in Halifax. He served as pastor at Granville Street for nine years, from 1830

---

[9] The history of the voluntary crusade is covered in Gibson, *Robert Alexander Fyfe*, 147–65.

[10] See William H. Brackney, *Acadia and the Sisterhood* (Wolfville, NS: Acadia Centre for Baptist and Anabaptist Studies, 2014).

[11] The assessment of Crawley and Cramp as the "two founders" in A. C. Chute's *The Religious Life of Acadia* (Wolfville, NS: Kentville Publishing Co., 1933) is more balanced than recent assessments of the founders.

to 1839.[12] He became a leader in the Nova Scotia Baptist community and was a founder of the Education Society, Horton Academy, and later Acadia University. A product of Nova Scotia, he was one of the best educated clergy of his region.[13]

Crawley was influential in the making of Acadia in two respects. First, his own formation as an Anglican undergraduate at King's was definitive.[14] He was also appreciative and thus imitative of Dalhousie University, begun in 1817, where he originally had hoped for a teaching position and had designed a possible curriculum. His denial of a chair at Dalhousie in 1838 led to the plans for a Baptist institution at Horton. He served at Horton from 1839 to 1847. In 1865, Crawley returned to Acadia to assist in reorganizing the theological program, including a chair in Rhetoric in the college, and a second chair in Exegesis and Greek, for which he was awarded honorary doctorates at Brown University and King's College, Windsor.[15] As a biographer declared, "He urged his students to grasp the great principles on which truth rests...and make

---

[12] Crawley was ordained an "evangelist" at First Baptist, Providence, RI, on May 16, 1830. While studying at Brown University, he had attended this church (with its historic connection with Roger Williams). He returned to Halifax the next year to be pastor of Granville Street Baptist Church. Alexis Caswell of Brown University, who had served briefly in Halifax, was one of the examiners at his ordination, as was university president Francis Wayland. See Judge J. W. Johnston, D.C.L., "On the Personal History and Character of the Late Rev. E. A. Crawley, D.D., D.C.L.," 153–71 (esp. 159); and Rev. T. A. Higgins, "On the Public and Professional Work of Rev. E. A. Crawley, D.D., D.C.L.," *Jubilee of Acadia College*, 172–81.

[13] Barry M. Moody, "Crawley, Edmund Albern," in *Dictionary of Canadian Biography*, vol. 11, University of Toronto/Université Laval, 2003–, accessed August 31, 2022, http://www.biographi.ca/en/bio/crawley_edmund_albern_11E.html and "Address by the Rev. E. A. Crawley D.D.: The Rise and Progress of Higher Education in Connection with the Baptist Denomination in the Maritime Provinces," in *Memorials of Acadia College and Horton Academy for the Half Century 1828–1878* (Montreal, QC: Dawson Brothers, 1881), 5–42.

[14] According to a biographer, Crawley was formed in the Episcopalian tradition, much influenced by Rev. Hibbert Binney, the father of the bishop of Nova Scotia. Doubtless this gave attention to the Thirty-Nine Articles of Religion. His education reflected emphases in the classics and French. See also Chute, *Religious Life of Acadia*, 110–11.

[15] "Judge Johnston's Address," in the *Jubilee of Acadia College*, 166.

Voluntarism, Human Rights, and a Global Mission

yourselves men by knowing what can be known and by loving what is noble and true."[16]

John Mockett Cramp (1796–1881), a "second founder" of Acadia,[17] began his career in England, graduating from Canterbury School and the Baptist Academical Institution at Stepney. He was a pastor of several congregations in England and edited the *Baptist Magazine* from 1825 to 1828. He was invited in 1844 to assume the presidency of Canada Baptist College in Montreal, where he remained until its demise in 1849. While in Montreal, Cramp edited a newspaper and two journals. In 1850, he was invited to become the president of Acadia College, then near bankruptcy. He gave himself thoroughly to the school, teaching eight subject-area courses, offering public lectures, and serving as pastor of the Wolfville Baptist Church.[18] In 1853, Cramp became the principal of the theological institute, the origins of the Acadia faculty of Theology.[19] He found time to write, particularly on matters of church polity, biblical themes, and Baptist history. Among his outstanding works are *A Textbook on Popery* (1831), *Baptist History* (1858), and *A Memoir of Madame Feller* (1876) plus a running series of articles in the *Christian Messenger*. Just prior to his death, he reported reading the entire New Testament in Greek sixty-eight times.[20] Numerous prominent graduates of Acadia across the Maritimes were proteges of J. M. Cramp. His biographer wrote of his desire "to free men's minds so that higher goals could be obtained."[21]

Two additional Maritime scholars deserve attention following the Crawley-Cramp era at Acadia: Daniel M. Welton and Calvin Goodspeed. A Nova Scotian, Welton (1931–1904) graduated from Acadia with two

---

[16] Higgins, "Public and Professional Work," 177.

[17] A useful biography of Dr. Cramp is found in Chute, *Religious Life of Acadia*, 112–13.

[18] Cramp's first term as Acadia president was 1851–53, followed by a second term, 1860–69.

[19] Crawley and Cramp disagreed about the nature of Acadia's programs, with Crawley favouring a broader emphasis upon lay education. Both agreed in the "no religious tests" clause in the admission of students and faculty. See Moody, *An Acadia Album*, 22.

[20] Chute, *Religious Life of Acadia*, 113.

[21] Barry M. Moody, "Cramp, John Mockett," in *Dictionary of Canadian Biography*, vol. 11, University of Toronto/Université Laval, 2003–, accessed August 31, 2022, http://www.biographi.ca/en/bio/cramp_john_mockett_11E.html.

degrees[22] and then earned a doctorate at the University of Leipzig in biblical studies and Hebrew. Following Crawley, Weldon redefined the theological program, holding that the Scriptures must be interpreted in light of modern scholarship. He was the first of the Acadia faculty members appointed with an earned academic doctorate. Lured away by Toronto interests, Weldon specialised in higher critical methods and joined the faculty at Toronto Baptist College, later McMaster University, as professor of Hebrew and cognate languages.[23] He is credited with emphasizing a scholarly approach to ministry, much in the tradition of Benjamin Davies at Montreal.[24]

A New Brunswicker, Calvin Goodspeed (1842–1912) was educated at the University of New Brunswick and Newton Theological Institution, with further European studies at Spurgeon's College, the Baptist Academical Institution at Stepney, and the University of Leipzig, where he studied higher criticism in depth. His academic work dovetailed with that of D. M. Welton. Goodspeed's teaching career included the Canadian Literary Institute, McMaster University, Baylor University, and Acadia University. His field was systematic theology, wherein he aligned himself closely to the articles of the New Hampshire Confession of Faith. He often took positions contrary to prevailing evangelical trends, for instance, opposing John Calvin's interpretation of Scripture, declining the tendency toward dispensationalism (he was a post-millennialist), opposing Sabbatarianism and perfectionism, and defining the Kingdom of God in relational terms (here, he reflected the thought of his contemporary Walter Rauschenbusch). His book *The Peculiar Principles of the Baptists* (1878) was long an authority among Canadians with respect to Baptist identity. As a biblical scholar, he completed the work begun by D. M. Welton, "The Book of Genesis," in *An American Commentary on the Old Testament* (1909). A

---

[22] As an undergraduate, he studied under John M. Cramp. On Weldon, see Barry M. Moody, "Welton, Daniel Morse," in *Dictionary of Canadian Biography*, vol. 13, University of Toronto/Université Laval, 2003–, accessed August 31, 2022, http://www.biographi.ca/en/bio/welton_daniel_morse_13E.html.

[23] He was the lynchpin in a plan to consolidate all Baptist theological instruction in Canada at McMaster.

[24] Brackney, *Genetic History of Baptist Thought*, 476. Welton's PhD dissertation was "John Lightfoot, the English Hebraist."

biographer has characterized Goodspeed as "severe and unsparing toward his opponents, with a strong concern for doctrinal truth."[25]

Acadia's Nineteenth-Century Alumni

Among Acadia's early graduates were several exemplary scholar teachers: Stephen W. DeBlois, Jacob G. Schurman, Shirley Jackson Case, Frank A. Starratt, Perry J. Stackhouse, and George B. Cutten. A native of Halifax, Nova Scotia, Stephen W. DeBlois (1827–1884) was one of the most celebrated scholar-pastors of the Maritime Baptist Convention, serving as president in 1878.[26] Awarded three degrees by Acadia (BA, MA, DD), DeBlois was also a graduate of Newton Theological Institution, then the leading Baptist graduate theological program. At Acadia, he studied under the eminent University of Leipzig alumnus Daniel M. Weldon. Among DeBlois's role were teaching at Horton Academy and Acadia College, service on the university's board of governors, and serving as pastor at Chester and Wolfville, Nova Scotia (the latter for thirty-nine years). He was the author of *Historical Sketch of the First Horton Baptist Church* (1879).[27]

Jacob Gould Schurman (1854–1942) was born in Freetown, Prince Edward Island. He was educated at Prince of Wales College, Acadia University, and the University of London. He also studied at Heidelberg, Berlin, and Göttingen Universities. He taught English at Acadia and Dalhousie, ending up in 1886 at Cornell University, where he was professor of Christian ethics and moral philosophy and the founding dean of the university's Sage School of Philosophy. He served as president of Cornell from 1892 to 1920, after which he held US diplomatic posts in the Philippines, Greece, China, and Germany. His published works include *Kantian Ethics and the Ethics of Evolution* (1881) and *Agnosticism and Religion* (1896). At Cornell, Schurman was known for his advocacy of women faculty appointments and racial equality in student life.

---

[25] Allison A. Trites, "A Forgotten Scholar: Professor Calvin Goodspeed," in *An Abiding Conviction: Maritime Baptists and Their World,* ed. Robert S. Wilson (Hantsport, NS: Lancelot Press, 1988), 198–207, esp. 207.

[26] Chute, *Religious Life of Acadia,* 43–45, esp. on the local revival of 1848.

[27] Stephen's son was Austen Kennedy DeBlois, PhD (1866–1945), pastor at First Baptist Elgin, and Chicago, and Boston. He studied at Leipzig and Berlin Universities. He was president at Shurtleff College and the Eastern Baptist Theological Seminary, Philadelphia.

KEEPING THE FAITH

Another Canadian Baptist scholar of international repute was Shirley Jackson Case (1872–1947). Case was born in Hatfield Point, New Brunswick, to a Freewill Baptist family. He was educated at Acadia University and taught at Horton Academy[28] and New Hampton Institute, where he taught Greek. He earned a bachelor of divinity and PhD at Yale University in biblical studies and the history of early Christianity. He began a stellar teaching career at Freewill Baptist-related Bates College in Maine, and in 1908 moved to the University of Chicago at the invitation of William Rainey Harper. He taught New Testament and was chair of the Church History Department, with Shailer Mathews largely defining the famous "Chicago School" by his sociohistorical method. Case's title, "professor of the history of Christianity," was trendsetting, imitated by William Warren Sweet and Winthrop S. Hudson. His literary achievement was astonishing: *The Evolution of Christianity* (1914), *Jesus through the Centuries* (1932) and *The Origins of Christian Supernaturalism* (1946). He was president of the Society of Church History and edited the influential *Journal of Religion*.

One academic theologian from the Acadia tradition who has often been overlooked in Canadian annals is Frank Aubrey Starratt (1865–1943). A contemporary of Howard Primrose Whidden, Starratt graduated (BA) from Acadia and went on to study theology at the newly organized University of Chicago. He served pastorates in North Dakota, Texas, and Massachusetts before being appointed professor of theology at Colgate Theological Seminary. At Colgate, he succeeded the distinguished William Newton Clarke as J. J. Joslin Professor of Theology. Starratt published articles on ethics and theology, the relationship of dogma to theology, and the nature of personality, in which he engaged the Personalist School at Boston University. In holding the Joslin Chair, Starratt occupied ostensibly the most distinguished theology position among Baptists in America, and he was honoured in 1912 by Acadia with the award of a doctor of divinity.

Also associated with the emerging Chicago School was Perry J. Stackhouse (1875–1944). Born in Saint John, West, New Brunswick, and educated at Acadia (BA), the University of Chicago (BD), and recognized by Colgate University (DD), Stackhouse was pastor at St. John and Campbellton, New Brunswick; Amherst, Nova Scotia; Utica, New York; and

---

[28] Case studied under John Mockett Cramp.

30

First Baptist, Chicago. A leading advocate of the Social Gospel and critic of urban housing conditions, alcoholism, child labour, and low wages,[29] he authored *The Baptist Position* (1909), *The Social Ideals of the Lord's Prayer* (1916), *The Sword of Christ and the World War* (1917), and *Chicago and the Baptists: A Century of Progress* (1933).

Another originally liberal thinker who identified with Acadia was George B. Cutten (1874–1962). Reared in Amherst, Nova Scotia, he graduated from Acadia University and was ordained a Baptist minister. He graduated with a BD from Yale and completed his PhD in psychology at Yale. His dissertation, *The Psychology of Alcoholism* (1907), broke new ground, and his subsequent book, *The Psychological Phenomena of Christianity* (1908), integrated the disciplines of theology and psychology.[30] Cutten was president at Acadia from 1910 to 1922, after which he served two decades as president of Colgate University, developing a progressive curriculum plan, though upholding controversial views of race and democracy.[31]

The Progressive Tradition Forges Ahead at Acadia

In the second half of the twentieth century, Acadia's theology faculty tilted toward the liberal perspective. Queen's University historian George Rawlyk observed, "Acadia University and Acadia Divinity College reflected a movement over a period of less than one hundred years from an evangelical

---

[29] Roger H. Prentice, "The Impact of Walter Rauschenbusch in Canada," in *In the Shadow of a Prophet: The Legacy of Walter Rauschenbusch*, eds. William H. Brackney and David P. Gushee (Macon, GA: Mercer University Press, 2020), 105.

[30] Cutten also completed a study of spiritual gifts that combined theology and psychology: *Speaking in Tongues Historically and Psychologically Considered* (New Haven, CT: Yale University Press, 1927).

[31] In later years at Colgate, Cutten declared public prohibitions against the admissions of Blacks and Jews, overtly promoting white supremacist policies, and moving the school away from its Baptist roots. Howard Williams, professor of history at Colgate, argued that Cutten had long maintained a limited view of the potentials of democracy, preferring instead an "intellectual democracy" that should rule society. See Williams, *A History of Colgate University 1819–1969* (New York: Van Nostrand Reinhold, 1969), 285, 290.

position to a liberal evangelical and then a largely liberal one."[32] Among those appointed after the Second World War were Evan M. Whidden, MacGregor Fraser, Morris Lovesey, Charles Taylor, C. B. Lumsden, and Millard R. Cherry. Whidden, a Brandon alumnus, held a BD from Yale Divinity School, studied at Colgate Rochester Divinity School, and did doctoral work at the University of Edinburgh on the Hutterites.[33] A church historian, he had also taught previously at Brandon. Fraser, a close friend and office colleague of Whidden who taught philosophy of religion and systematic theology, was a McMaster University alumnus who also had previously taught at Brandon University. British-born Lovesey (1917–2005) was trained as an engineer at the University of Birmingham and studied theology at Spurgeon's College. Lovesey and Fraser were influenced by German theologians, with Lovesey fully embracing the Graf-Wellhausen Hypothesis in his lectures. Lovesey was also an energetic ecumenist.[34] Lumsden, a well-known Maritime Convention pastor who held a doctorate from Yale, taught Greek at Acadia. Cherry, the lone American of the lot, was invited for a term to come to Acadia by university president Watson Kirkconnell. He was a Kentucky Southern Baptist who had studied under Wayne Ward and Dale Moody at Southern Baptist Seminary. Cherry was an unapologetic neoorthodox thinker who delighted in introducing to his students the works of Paul Tillich, Emil Brunner, Reinhold Niebuhr, Dale Moody, and Karl Barth. In his four decades of teaching at Acadia, he was the leader in establishing a separate divinity college and helping to foster the Atlantic Baptist Fellowship.[35]

The appointment of Jarold K. Zeman (1926–2000) to Acadia in 1968 was of great significance to the Acadia divinity program. Succeeding Prof. Evan Whidden, Zeman was the third faculty member with a European

---

[32] George A Rawlyk, *Is Jesus Your Personal Saviour?: In Search of Canadian Evangelicalism in the 1990s* (Montreal, QC: McGill-Queens University Press, 1996), 44.

[33] Howard John Whidden, *Evan MacDonald Whidden: A Life of Service: The First Half, 1898–1938* (Wolfville, NS: self-pub., Gaspereau Press, 2021), 94–95.

[34] Author's conversation with Dr. Allison Trites, August 25, 2021.

[35] To his dismay, his theological views cost him the college principalship to conservatives in the Maritime Convention. Cherry responded by remaining as systematic theologian and leaving an endowment to establish the Millard R. Cherry Chair in Christian Thought and Ethics.

doctorate,[36] with a reputation as a highly regarded convert from the Reformed Church. A graduate of Knox College, Toronto, he was employed by the Baptist Home Mission Board of Ontario and Quebec to work among European immigrants. During his twenty-three years on the Acadia faculty, he gained a reputation as a scholar-teacher and an informant/apologist in Canadian Baptist identity. His perspective was generated from his Anabaptist scholarship on the Czech brethren. His views on Baptist historiography placed him as a counterpoint to the English Separatist advocates, though his personal library was replete with sources relating to that perspective. One of his chief accomplishments was to establish in 1992 the Acadia Centre for Baptist and Anabaptist Studies (ACBAS) which was nurtured by the gift of his extensive library to establish the Zeman Special Collection in Vaughan Memorial Library.

In his church history classes, Zeman required research papers from his students that were to be based on primary sources in the archives. He also edited *Baptists in Canada: A Search for Identity Amidst Diversity* (1980) and published a bibliography, *Baptists in Canada 1760–1990* (1989). *The Baptist Heritage in Atlantic Canada* series was largely his initiative. His time at Acadia was characterized by independent spirit. He was well respected in the university and an ordained Baptist minister. His legacy in developing ACBAS, however, was realized in the decades to follow by H. Miriam Ross, whose interest in the contribution of Baptist women was well-regarded, and Robert S. Wilson, who edited *An Abiding Conviction: Maritime Baptists and Their World* (1988). William H. Brackney expanded the focus of ACBAS beyond the Maritime Baptist community.

A Broadening Tradition: George B. Foster and Douglas Clyde Macintosh

Two outstanding turn-of-the-century Baptist theologians advanced the liberal tradition in Canada: George Burman Foster and Douglas Clyde

---

[36] Allison A. Trites (1936–), appointed in New Testament in 1965, was the second full-time faculty member appointed with an overseas doctorate (D.Phil., Regent's Park College, Oxford). Trites worked with George B. Caird at Mansfield College and G. Henton Davies at Regent's Park College. He did his initial theological work at the Eastern Baptist Theological Seminary and Princeton Theological Seminary, and is also a student of Canadian Maritime Baptist history, emphasizing Baptists in New Brunswick.

MacIntosh. Foster (1857–1918) was an American-born theologian from West Virginia. He graduated from West Virginia University and studied theology at the Universities of Berlin and Göttingen. Following pastoral ministries in Morgantown, West Virginia, and Saratoga Springs, New York, he took up an academic career with a teaching post in philosophy at McMaster University in Toronto from 1892 to 1896. At the invitation of William R. Harper, he moved to the Divinity School of the University of Chicago, where he taught systematic theology. A member of the "Chicago School," he developed his theology from human experience and the contemporary school of pragmatism. During his time in the divinity school, he shaped a whole generation of liberal thinkers. In 1906/1907, Foster was expelled from the Baptist Ministers' Conference of Chicago and transferred to a new department of philosophy of religion at the university, where he worked mainly with graduate students. The dramatic new departure in Foster's work was revealed in his 1906 book, *The Finality of the Christian Religion*, where he found in other religions moral and theological equivalences to Christianity. His 1909 work, *The Function of Religion in Man's Struggle for Existence*, was semiautobiographical and pioneering in its assessment of religion. He was described as the most intellectual of all American Baptist theologians and had a significant impact upon Canadian Baptist theology and the emerging fundamentalist movement.[37]

Arguably, George B. Foster's most outstanding student at the University of Chicago was Douglas Clyde MacIntosh (1877–1948). MacIntosh was born in Breadalbane, Ontario, and served congregations in the Baptist Convention of Ontario and Quebec. He was educated at McMaster University in Toronto and the University of Chicago under G. B. Foster. Macintosh taught at Baptist-related Brandon University in Manitoba and then took the position in theology at Yale Divinity School. Ordained at historic Hyde Park Baptist Church in Chicago, at Yale he advanced to become the Timothy Dwight Chair in Theology, arguably one of the most prestigious in the US. He developed his own approach to theology, which he called "Empirical Theology," by which he meant that theology could be studied as an empirical science. He was fascinated with measuring the data of religious experience, which he thought could define Christian doctrines, including the doctrine of God. He rejected all forms of dogmatics,

---

[37] Yet he was vilified by Canadian traditionalists, particularly with the publication of his book *The Finality of the Christian Religion*.

other systematic theologies, and the historic doctrine of the inspiration of Scripture. His important works included *Theology as an Empirical Science* (1919), *The Reasonableness of Christianity* (1925), and *The Problem of Religious Knowledge* (1940). Denied US citizenship in 1925 over his refusal to take an oath to bear arms in defence of the United States, he was honoured by a significant portrait in the divinity school's commons room at Yale.

Walter Rauschenbusch and the Social Gospel in Canada

Walter Rauschenbusch (1861–1918) was a contemporary of Foster and Macintosh. Rauschenbusch was an American-born theologian of German extraction, being the son of August Rauschenbusch, a founder of the German Baptist Conference in North America. Walter was educated at the Gütersloh Gymnasium in Germany, the University of Rochester, and Rochester Theological Seminary. He served a German congregation in New York's Lower East Side, "Hell's Kitchen." In 1907, Rauschenbusch published his signature work, *The Social Gospel*, in which he stressed the historic social implications of the message of Jesus.[38] Much of his writing was done at his forest retreat in Ontario, and he had a number of connections with Canadian Baptists. For instance, his student (and biographer) Dores R. Sharpe was from New Brunswick, and the theology of a Social Gospel made an impression on faculty and students at McMaster and Brandon Universities. Above all, Rauschenbusch's ideas were a direct influence on Tommy Douglas in the making of social welfare programs and a national health care policy.[39]

---

[38] His other related works include *Christianizing the Social Order* (1912) and *A Theology for the Social Gospel* (1917), both of which are reproduced with commentaries in William H. Brackney, editor, *Walter Rauschenbusch, Selected Writings*, 3 vols. (Macon, GA: Mercer University Press, 2018).

[39] Among the treatments of Rauschenbusch from a Canadian perspective are: Dores R. Sharpe, *Walter Rauschenbusch* (New York: Macmillan, 1942); Donovan E. Smucker, "Walter Rauschenbusch: Anabaptist, Pietist, and Social Prophet" *Mennonite Life* 36/2 (June 1981): 21–23; Anna Robbins, *Methods in the Madness: Diversity in Twentieth Century Christian Social Ethics* (Carlisle: Paternoster Press, 2004); and Roger H. Prentice, "Impact of Walter Rauschenbusch in Canada," 116–20.

KEEPING THE FAITH

McMaster's Contribution

As we have seen, McMaster University was the fulfilment of Canada Baptist College in Montreal and the Canadian Literary Institute in Woodstock. Among the important contributors to the early McMaster liberal tradition was Howard Primrose Whidden (1871–1952). Whidden was a graduate of Acadia University (Class of 1891), who then went on to the Newton Theological Institution for basic theological studies, and then to McMaster University, where he earned an MA as a student of the eminent Hebrew scholar Daniel M. Welton. Whidden had a distinguished pastoral career at Morden, Manitoba, after which he moved to a pastorate at Galt, Ontario, where he was invited to lecture part-time in public reading and speaking at McMaster in Toronto. After a brief term of studies at the University of Chicago, in 1900, he returned to the West, where he became professor of English and biblical literature at Brandon College, then an affiliate school of McMaster University.[40] Following a pastorate at First Baptist, Dayton, Ohio (home of Denison University), Whidden became president at Brandon College for more than a decade, after which he served for almost two decades as chancellor of McMaster University.[41] Whidden's own widening vision for a Baptist-related university involved scientific research[42] in conjunction with the local industrial establishment, combined with an emphasis upon social questions and world order, with social service projects managed by the theology students. Whidden's "New McMaster" was to be "always Christian,"[43] but progressive and culturally diverse, engaging all manner of classes and creeds in its student body.[44]

---

[40] Whidden, *Evan MacDonald Whidden*, 23–25.

[41] Dr. Whidden was the guiding force in the transition of McMaster University to separate status and a new campus in Hamilton, Ontario. He also served as MP from Brandon, Manitoba, in the Robert Borden Unionist government and as editor of *The Canadian Baptist*. Whidden was a supporter of the right to vote for women. *The Acadia Record 1838–1953*, rev. and enlarged by Watson Kirkonnell (Wolfville, NS: Acadia University, 1953), 43.

[42] A euphemism for industrial chemistry.

[43] This was realized in the Greek university motto "In Christ all things hold together" (Col. 1:16).

[44] Charles M. Johnston, *McMaster University, Vol. 2: The Early Years in Hamilton* (Toronto: University of Toronto Press, 1981), 18, 31, 32, 56.

George P. Gilmour followed Howard Whidden as chancellor of McMaster. Gilmour (1900–1963) was heir to one of the pioneering Baptist families of Upper Canada. The influence of the Gilmours in Canada commenced with John Gilmour (1792–1869), an immigrant from Scotland who established the First Baptist Church, Montreal, and advocated for the establishment of Canada Baptist College in that city.[45] His grandson, George P. Gilmour, was trained as a church historian at McMaster, Oxford, and Yale, teaching at McMaster for twenty-seven years and becoming its youngest chancellor at forty-one years of age. His great contribution was steering the university from being a denominational school to a public institution. His conception of a separate but affiliated McMaster Divinity College became a model for other evolving church-related universities. A university foundation for Baptist theological education gave the instruction of classical religious disciplines to a new Department of Religious Studies while emphasizing pastoral courses in the divinity college. Those appointed to the faculty of theology by Gilmour were no less well qualified academically, and included James R. C. Perkin, Harold Lang, Russell Aldwinckle, Gaylord Albaugh, G. Gerald Harrop, Nathaniel H. Parker, Melvyn R. Hillmer, T. Raymond Hobbs, and Murray J. S. Ford in the first generation. Theological degrees were granted by the university, and symbolically, Gilmour became the embodiment of the "McMaster Tradition." In his 1957 convocation address, in the context of an expanding public university, he stressed his commitment to the important principles of academic and religious freedom.[46]

A neglected figure in Canadian Baptist annals and the McMaster tradition is Cyrus S. Eaton. Eaton (1883–1979) was born on a farm near

---

[45] See "The Rev. John Gilmour," in William H. Brackney, *[The 150th Anniversary] John Gilmour Lectures October 20, 1996, at Murray Street Baptist Church, Peterborough, Ontario* (Peterborough, ON: Murray Street Baptist Church, 1996).

[46] Quoted in Charles M. Johnston, *McMaster University 2/The Early Years in Hamilton, 1930–1957* (Toronto, ON: University of Toronto Press for McMaster University, 1981), 263. Another example of the extended McMaster tradition was Rodger E. W. Forsman (1934–2017), educated at McMaster University (BD, MA) and the University of Toronto (MA, PhD). Forsman taught at York and Brock Universities before teaching in philosophy, religious studies, and business at Acadia University for forty years. He was a published specialist in the thought of Austin Farrer, the nature of the contemporary church, the nature of revelation, and the literary criticism of the Bible.

Pugwash Junction in Cumberland County, Nova Scotia. His father was a Baptist layman and storekeeper, and his uncle was Charles Eaton, the Euclid Ave Baptist Church pastor of John D. Rockefeller in Cleveland, Ohio. Cyrus attended Baptist-related Woodstock (Ontario) College and graduated from McMaster University in Toronto. He intended to prepare for the Baptist ministry and majored in philosophy and finance. Mentored by John D. Rockefeller, he was drawn into Rockefeller's business orbit and built what became the Continental Gas & Electric Corporation, and separately Republic Steel Corporation. He lost an estimated $100 million in the 1929 stock market crash, but recovered his fortunes in the 1940s and 1950s as board chairman of the Chesapeake and Ohio Railroad and the West Kentucky Coal Company. Eaton's philanthropy was directed toward McMaster and its move to Hamilton, Ontario. He also used his wealth to strive for nuclear disarmament, which he sought to achieve through international travel and the creation of Pugwash Conferences on Science and World Affairs. His funding themes included sustainable environments, social justice, cultural enrichment, and peaceful coexistence.[47] His home at Pugwash, "Thinkers Lodge," continues to be a national monument to his legacy and the larger liberal tradition among Baptists in Canada.

Archibald Reekie and the Bolivian Liberal Tradition

One of McMaster University's early outstanding alumni was Archibald B. Reekie (1862–1942). He was born to a farm family in Armow, Ontario, and later in life declared his intention to become a Baptist minister. He studied at McMaster University in Toronto (graduated Class of 1897) and was deputed to begin a new mission field in Bolivia under the auspices of the Ontario and Quebec Foreign Mission Board.[48] Reekie became the pioneer Protestant missionary in Bolivia, planting churches, starting schools, and advocating social reforms. He used an educational approach to

---

[47] He was nominated for the Nobel Peace Prize in 1962, ultimately awarded jointly to the Pugwash Conferences on Science and World Affairs and Joseph Rotblat in 1995. See Marcus Gleiser, *The World of Cyrus Eaton* (Kent, OH: Kent State University Press, 2010) and M. Allen Gibson, *Beautiful upon the Mountains: A Portrait of Cyrus Eaton* (Windsor, NS: Lancelot Press, 1977).

[48] *Bridging Cultures and Hemispheres: The Legacy of Archibald Reekie and Canadian Baptists in Bolivia*, ed. William H. Brackney (Macon, GA: Smyth and Helwys Publishers, 1997), 1–35.

missions that has been embodied in the school that bears his name in Oruro. He supported the liberal political movement in Bolivia (1900–1920) and laid the foundation for Earl Merrick for a later agricultural experiment at Huatajata called "Peniel Farm." This venture brought about land reform and the liberation of serfs and the peasant classes in 1942.[49] Before returning to Canada, Reekie served as a missionary for American Baptists in Cuba.

Mainstream Canadian Baptists and the Ecumenical and Interfaith Movements

The interfaith engagement of Baptists in Canada was driven by Muslim-Christian theological conversations held in the late 1990s. William Brackney participated in American Baptist/Muslim conversations at Andover Newton Theological School and brought the interest with him to Acadia. He became a participant in the Halifax Interfaith Council and was a pioneer organizer and president of the Interfaith Spirituality Network (ISN). He was a plenary presenter in two Halifax-region public events, Spiritual Diversity Conferences I and II, as he published his five-volume series *Human Rights and the World's Religions* (2005; rev. 2013). Prof. Brackney also supervised two interfaith-related MA theses at Acadia, one by Dennis Nickerson, and the second by Nael Abd El-Rahaman, the first Muslim thesis presented at Acadia Divinity College.

Come-outers: The ABF and "The Gathering"

The Atlantic Baptist Fellowship (ABF) was founded among Maritime Baptist ministers in 1971 to offer an alternative to polity decisions in the Maritime Baptist Convention. Of major concern was the tightened qualifications for church representation at the annual convention meetings. This caused some pastors to advocate for "Baptist freedom" at the congregational level.[50] Instead of mandating that only those who were baptized

---

[49] Arturo Nacho L. "Agrarian Reform in Huatajata," in Brackney, *Bridging Cultures and Hemispheres*, 55–65; and also the assessment of J. Samuel Escobar, 115–17. The Baptist experiment was a model in 1953 for the Decree of Agrarian Reform in Bolivia (62).

[50] Among the external influences on the ABF were the formation of the Cooperative Baptist Fellowship and the Alliance of Baptists in the United States.

believers by immersion could be delegates to the convention, those within the ABF wanted to leave the decision to the local congregations to decide who their representatives should be. The intention was not originally to form a new denomination, but to advocate its emphases within the convention family of churches. Among the founders of the ABF were Charles Taylor, I. Judson Levy, J. Daniel Gibson, Marion Grant, Austin MacPherson, Reginald Dunn, John Boyd, Ed Colquhoun, Vincent Rushdon, and John Churchill. Later, Roger Prentice and Jeffrey White became leaders in the ABF.

In the 1990s, debates over social issues began to emerge within the Maritime Baptist family. The first was recognition of women as candidates for ordination. Another was recognition of same-sex marriages in convention churches. ABF ministers supported full recognition of women ministers and the right of a local congregation to decide for itself the validation of same-sex marriages. Ultimately, the need to ensure that its authority to ordain and recognize ministers led to the establishment of a separately chartered organization, the Canadian Association of Baptist Freedoms (CABF), in 2012. The CABF is now a parallel organization to the Convention of Atlantic Baptist Churches and holds recognition in the Canadian Council of Churches. CABF is a Maritime-centered association with several congregations aligning with it from Ontario and inquiries from churches in Western Canada. Among its major public events is the Vincent Rushdon Lectures, featuring ecumenical speakers.

Another association, *sui generis*, was "The Gathering." This was an association of Baptist ministers primarily from Ontario. Initially, this group arose in opposition to what they perceived to be attempts to force McMaster Divinity College into a more conservative mindset. At the time, the college was under the leadership of the chair of the board, John W. Irwin, and Principal William H. Brackney.[51] The Gathering was triggered when the Divinity College Board of Trustees terminated the employment of Prof. P. Kenneth Jackson.[52] Participants in the Gathering

---

Walter B. Shurden's book *Five Fragile Freedoms* became a seminal text among the ABF.

[51] See C. Douglas Koop, "The Unlikely Transformation of McMaster Divinity College," *Christian Week* (December 17, 1991): 8–9.

[52] BCOQ evangelical interest in changing the theological direction of McMaster—and more broadly the convention itself—began with the

from 1995 included a wide variety of people, both ordained and non-ordained.[53] The goal of the group was to defend select Baptist principles, especially congregational freedom and what was loosely defined as the "McMaster Tradition."[54] The Gathering met annually for themed discussions at churches such as First Baptist, Ottawa; Dundas Baptist Church; Burlington Baptist Church; McNeil Baptist Church, Hamilton; Lorne Park Baptist Church, Mississauga; and Highland Baptist Church, Kitchener. From time to time, speakers were invited from the Atlantic region, including Roger Prentice, chaplain at Acadia; G. Gerald Harrop, retired professor of Old Testament at McMaster in Halifax; John Boyd, minister, First Baptist, Halifax; Roger Cann, retired Canadian Baptist Overseas Mission Board (CBOMB) missionary in Wolfville; and Andrew Crowell, pastor at Port Williams Baptist Church. In the Maritime context, John Boyd at First Baptist, Halifax, was a spokesman. McMaster Divinity College professor T. R. Hobbs was considered a prominent biblical studies authority, and Paul Dekar, also of McMaster, was a social activist/historian and leader in the Baptist Peacemakers Fellowship. They were self-declared theological liberals.

Conclusion

While there has always been a strong liberal tradition in Canada, it is notable that over the years there has often been an attempt to downplay its

---

appointment of Clark H. Pinnock in Theology at MDC and the subsequent election of John W. Irwin, a book publisher, to the board of trustees. A small group of ministers founded the Baptist Renewal Fellowship to advocate evangelical concerns in the BCOQ.

[53] Franklin Morgan, Wilf Baxter, Bert Radford, T. Raymond Hobbs, Gary Purdy, Ruby Purdy, John Rook, Gary Caldwell, William Sturgis, Stuart Frayne, Paul Dekar, Fred Demaray, John Furry, David Ogilvie, Cam Watts, John Torrance, Kenneth Jackson, Muriel Aldwinckle, Richard Maxwell, John Dickinson, Joseph Ban, Blake Eady, Elmer Anderson, Prof. John Thomas, Scott Kindred-Barnes, Heather Gilmore, and Barbara Bishop.

[54] The "McMaster tradition" was defined from the time of university president George Peel Gilmour (1900–1963), who lectured in the faculty of Theology and was a role model for ministerial practice. Perceived elements included solid historical biblical interpretation, ecumenism, liturgical formality, practised public speaking and diction, proper pulpit attire and deportment, formal hymnology, and earned academic degrees for ordained ministers.

influence. Yet, perhaps as a counter to perceived liberalism in the 1980s and 1990s, a wide-ranging interdenominational conservative group, the Evangelical Fellowship of Canada, emerged. Historically, the development of the Evangelical Fellowship of Canada in 1964 signalled a coalescing of conservative evangelicals from across the country in witness and policy debates. Brian Stiller (1942–), a Pentecostal minister, became EFC director in 1983 and sought to include as many faith groups under the umbrella as possible. In the Baptist community, as the conservative voice grew louder, debates ensued over membership in the EFC or the Canadian Council of Churches, with only the convention in Ontario and Quebec affiliating with both. Membership in the EFC became a hallmark of Canadian conservative evangelicalism, leaving others to be characterized by the ecumenical (and more liberal) CCC.[55]

The formation of the Atlantic Baptist Fellowship in 1971 and the continued presence of the Canadian Association for Baptist Freedoms, as it became known in 2012, serves as a reminder of the strong liberal tradition among Baptists in Canada. Seeking to bear witness to the key Baptist principle of freedom, members of CABF continue to support joint worship, social action, and ecumenical discussion with non-Baptist communions. CABF represents a long tradition of openness which has been upheld by numerous Baptist churches, leaders, and institutions. Their contribution has not always been fully appreciated, and this paper has sought to highlight the legacy of many key individuals. Roger Prentice played his part in upholding this more open, liberal Baptist tradition, and it is to his memory that this paper is presented.

---

[55] Among Maritime Baptists, Andrew D. MacRae (1933–2014), a transplant from the Baptist Union in Scotland to Acadia Divinity College, became an ardent crusader for the convention and Acadia Divinity College to affiliate with the EFC. In the West, a similar leadership toward the EFC was provided by Roy Bell (1925–2017).

"Man that is born of a woman is of few days and full of trouble": Morgan Edwards (1722–1795) and the Book of Common Prayer

Evan Lynwood Colford

Introduction

Morgan Edwards (1722–1795) is a name little known today, except for by scholars of Baptist history and thought.[1] Even the mention of his name among theology students is bound to be met with confusion and perhaps with the question, "Do you mean Jonathan Edwards?" However, this pastor, theologian, and historian was once described by the nineteenth-century American Baptist historian William Cathcart in the following way: "In his day no Baptist minister equalled him, and none since has surpassed him." In a similar vein, Henry C. Vedder, at Crozer Seminary, evaluated Edwards in the following manner: "His very faults had a leaning toward virtue's side, and in good works he was exceeded by none of his day, if indeed by any of any day."[2] This is high praise for a writer whom few today know anything about. This essay will demonstrate that Morgan Edwards made use of the Book of Common Prayer (1662) in his work on Baptist polity and practice. It will begin by briefly sketching his life, followed by a presentation of Edwards as a theologian and his theological works. It will then focus on his manual of Baptist polity and practice and indicate where he makes use of the Book of Common Prayer (1662).

---

[1] It is my privilege to present this essay in memory of my friend Roger H. Prentice. I always thought of Roger as a "high Baptist," so I believe he would be happy to learn more about one Baptist from the eighteenth century who made use of the *Book of Common Prayer* (1662).

[2] Quoted in Howard R. Stewart, *A Dazzling Enigma: The Story of Morgan Edwards* (Lanham, MD: University Press of America, 1995), 379. See *The Baptist Encyclopedia*, ed. William Cathcart (Philadelphia: Lewis H. Everts, 1881), 362, and Henry C. Vedder, *A Short History of the Baptists* (Philadelphia: American Baptist Publication Society, 1907), 314.

KEEPING THE FAITH

Biographical Sketch of Morgan Edwards (1722–1795)

Welsh historian Jan Morris described David Lloyd George (1863–1945), the former prime minister of Great Britain and a Welsh Baptist, as a "dazzling sort of enigma."[3] Howard R. Stewart, Edwards's most recent biographer, applied this same description to Morgan Edwards, which is most apropos, as a look at his life will bear out.

"This peculiar, but worthy man"[4] was born in Trevethin Parish, Monmouthshire, Wales, on May 9, 1722, and he ended his days thousands of miles away on his farm in the United States of America, in Newark, Delaware, on January 28, 1795.[5] During the more than seventy years between these two dates, Edwards lived a fascinating life which has had a deep impact that continues down to the present day.

Edwards was baptized and raised in the Church of England, but in 1738 he became a Baptist and joined the Penygarn Baptist church, part of the Welsh Baptist Association.[6] Sensing a call into ministry, Edwards began his ministerial training in some of the best schools of the day, the Dissenting academies.[7] Edwards first studied at Tronsant Academy in

---

[3] Jan Morris, *The Matter of Wales* (Oxford: Oxford University Press), 167. Quoted in Stewart, *A Dazzling Enigma*, 3.

[4] This is how John Rippon, editor of the *Baptist Annual Register*, referred to Edwards shortly after Edwards's death. Quoted in Thomas R. McKibbens Jr. and Kenneth L. Smith, *The Life and Works of Morgan Edwards* (New York: Arno Press, 1980), 1.

[5] McKibbens and Smith, *Morgan Edwards*, 2 and 53.

[6] The Penygarn Baptist Church, in Pontypool in the southeast of Wales, was established in 1727. The congregation was a mixture of English-speaking and Welsh-speaking adherents.

[7] See Irene Parker, *Dissenting Academies in England: Their Rise and Progress and Their Place among the Educational Systems of the Country* (Cambridge: University Press, 1914; repr., New York: Octagon Books, 1969); see also the Dissenting Academies Project at https://www.qmul.ac.uk/sed/religionandlite-rature/dissenting-academies/dissenting-academies-online/ On the Baptist contribution to higher education in North America, particularly the link between the congregation and the campus, see William H. Brackney, *Congregation and Campus: North American Baptists in Higher Education* (Macon, GA: Mercer University Press, 2008). For the link between the Old World and the New World, see ch. 2. Of particular import, Brackney notes the following in relation to Morgan Edwards's contribution in this regard: "The link between the accomplishments in Bristol

Morgan Edwards (1722–1795) and the Book of Common Prayer

Wales under John Matthews, starting either in 1738 or 1740[8] and leaving in 1742. He then studied at Bristol Academy from 1742 to 1743 under Bernard Foskett.[9] By the standards of the day, Morgan Edwards was very well educated. As Brown University librarian and historian Reuben A. Guild expressed, Edwards was a "Baptist minister possessed of superior learning."[10] After his formal education, Edwards went on to serve several churches in the British Isles. He first served at Boston, Lincolnshire, England, until 1751; he then spent nine years as an assistant pastor in Cork, Ireland, where he was married to Mary Nun, and where he was also ordained (June 1, 1757); Edwards then ministered for about one year as pastor in Rye, back in England (March 1760–February 1761).[11] Following this short pastorate, Edwards sailed for the American colonies, where he would spend the rest of his days.

From 1760 to 1761, after the death of Jenkin Jones,[12] the First Baptist Church in Philadelphia was in search of a pastor; unable to find a suitable

---

[Bristol Baptist Academy] and North America was Morgan Edwards, a Welshman from Caermarthenshire [*sic*] who studied under Foskett.... Edwards brought many of the traits of his mentor [Foskett] to the Colonies: a rigorous study habit, use of the scriptures in the original languages, and a penchant for correct polity and associational life" (49).

[8] Trosnant Academy, begun by John Griffiths, an ironmonger, in 1732, was associated with Penygarn Chapel. It was the first school of its kind to win the denominational blessing. Cf. Selwyn Gummer, "Trosnant Academy" *Baptist Quarterly* 9/7 (July 1939): 417–23.

[9] McKibbens and Smith, in *The Life and Works of Morgan Edwards,* say that Edwards was at Bristol from 1742–1744 (9). On Bernard Foskett, see Norman Moon, *Education for Ministry: Bristol Baptist College 1679–1979* (Bristol: Bristol Baptist College, 1979), 3–6. See also Ruth Gouldbourne and Anthony R. Cross, *The Story of Bristol Baptist College: Three Hundred Years of Ministerial Formation* (Eugene, OR: Pickwick Publications, 2022), 12–14.

[10] Reuben A. Guild, *Early History of Brown University, Including the Life, Times and Correspondence of President Manning, 1756–1791* (Providence, RI: Snow and Farnham, 1896), 12. Guild was a long-time librarian at Brown University. As quoted in Stewart, *A Dazzling Enigma,* 59.

[11] For an account of Edwards's first pastorates, see Stewart, *A Dazzling Enigma,* ch. 4.

[12] Jenkin Jones (1686–1760), a native of Llandysul, Wales, served Lower Dublin Church 1725–1746. He led in the outgrowth from Lower Dublin of the First Baptist Church Philadelphia in 1746. According to McKibbens and Smith,

candidate in the colonies, they sent a letter to the Particular Baptists in England. The Rev. Dr. John Gill (1697–1771) suggested Morgan Edwards for the job, and Edwards accepted. In what would be his last pastorate, Edwards spent ten years as pastor of the First Baptist Church in Philadelphia (1761–1771), which was by all accounts a very successful ministry.[13] While in the colonies, Edwards became quite well known. He was heavily involved in the Philadelphia Baptist Association (PBA) and authored a manual on Baptist polity. In addition, he was a "prime mover"[14] toward the founding of the Rhode Island College, which became Brown University,[15] and he gathered and wrote historical works on the Baptists in almost all of the original thirteen colonies.[16]

John Gano "supplied the pulpit during the winter of 1760–61, while also serving as the pastor of the Baptist Church in New York" (12).

[13] McKibbens and Smith, in *The Life and Works of Morgan Edwards* (19), report that by 1770, the membership of the Philadelphia First Baptist Church was 150, with hundreds of "hearers" besides, making it "the second largest in the Philadelphia Baptist Association." For more on Edwards's time at First Baptist Church, Philadelphia, see *Baptists in Early North America Vol. VII: First Baptist Church, Philadelphia, Pennsylvania*, ed. Deborah Bingham Van Broekhoven (Macon, GA: Mercer University Press, 2021).

[14] Stewart, *A Dazzling Enigma*, 231. The title of Stewart's chapter on Edwards and Baptist higher education is "A Prime Mover in Education."

[15] On Edwards's contribution in the areas of ministerial training and the founding of Rhode Island College, see Brackney, *Congregation and Campus*, ch. 2, specifically 49, 51, 54, and 62. Brackney notes that when Edwards, a Bristol Baptist Academy-trained minister, came to the American Colonies, he noticed three problems among the Baptists: lack of training, the location of institutions of higher education already in place and their denominational affiliations, and lack of overarching organizational principle among the Baptists. Edwards contributed to rectifying each of these problems by suggesting a union of all Baptists in America, a model ordination certificate for ministers, and Rhode Island as the location for a Baptist college.

[16] Morgan Edwards sought to write a twelve-volume history of the American Baptists; however, he only published two of the volumes in his lifetime, one on Pennsylvania (1770) and the other in New Jersey (1792). He did, however, leave several historical manuscripts and notebooks on the Baptists in other parts of the country. Edwards carried out this historical project so he himself could "know the american Baptists" and "to make them known to one another" in order to bring about the national union of those who practice believers' baptism, which he

Morgan Edwards (1722–1795) and the Book of Common Prayer

However, Edwards's time in the colonies was not without difficulties. He preached a sermon on January 1, 1770, called "A New Year's Gift," which referenced a premonition he had about his own death;[17] he maintained his loyalty to the Crown as the colonies were moving toward independence, only to switch to the patriot cause in 1775; he was eventually excommunicated from the church he once served, only to be restored;[18] he was charged with being both an Arminian and a Universalist;[19] and he also suffered deep personal loss, losing six children either during childbirth or in infancy,[20] and losing his home in Delaware and many possessions therein when it was torched by the British. Edwards is a fascinating character to study for many reasons. He was clearly gifted, yet his flaws were

---

believed was the Baptists' "denominating article." For these quotations, see Morgan Edwards, *Materials towards a History of the Baptists in Pennsylvania* (Philadelphia: Joseph Crukshank and Isaac Collins, 1770), i and iii. For more on Edwards's historical project, including transcriptions with notes of his historical works, see the forthcoming *Baptists in Early North America Vol. XII: The Historical Works of Morgan Edwards*, eds. Evan L. Colford and William H. Brackney (Macon, GA: Mercer University Press).

[17] According to Howard R. Stewart, "Morgan Edwards, 1722–1795," in *A Noble Company: Biographical Essays on Notable Particular-Regular Baptists in America*, vol. 3, ed. Terry Wolever (Springfield, MO: Particular Baptist Press, 2013), Edwards and his wife, Mary, both had premonitions regarding their own deaths: Mary that "she would die in her eighth pregnancy" and Edwards "that he would die on March 1, 1770." Mary's premonition came true, which served only to "reinforce Morgan's own premonition." Apparently, Edwards shared his premonition with Ebenezer Gibbons, who freely shared the information, which led to issues for both Edwards and his sermon, "A New Year's Gift." Some have "accused Edwards of preaching his own funeral sermon"; however, Stewart believed that "a reading of the sermon belies that assertion"; for the information and quotations in this footnote, see pages 127–28.

[18] According to Stewart, "Morgan Edwards, 1722–1795," the reason for his excommunication was his being seen to have "over-imbibed" alcoholic beverages in a pub; however, Stewart points out that Edwards "completely renounced all drinking following that experience" (129). For the minutes that record the report about Edwards's immoral conduct, excommunication, and restoration, see *First Baptist Church, Philadelphia*, ed. Van Broekhoven, 163, 164, 167–169, 184, 189, 194–96, 225–26, 227–28, 234, 236, 243.

[19] Stewart, "Morgan Edwards (1722–1795)," 129–130. See also below.

[20] Stewart, *A Dazzling Enigma*, ch. 6.

equally obvious. As Howard Stewart put it, Edwards was "gifted for greatness, hobbled by his eccentricities."[21] He was a man who failed, as all do; he was also a man who achieved great things. He truly was a dazzling enigma.

Edwards as a Theologian and His Theological Works

Edwards's key spheres of influence on American Baptist life include the following areas: ecclesiology, specifically in his contribution to Baptist polity, his plan for a national Baptist union, and his work as a churchman (as the pastor of the First Baptist Church of Philadelphia, a church of the Philadelphia Baptist Association); historical research methodology,[22] which itself was a work undertaken to bring about the national union of Baptists that he so desired; and, finally, his contributions to American Baptist higher education in his work for Rhode Island College, which, as noted above, would become the prestigious Brown University. For the purposes of this essay, the focus is on the theological work and works of Morgan Edwards, specifically his manual of Baptist church polity and practice.

Morgan Edwards was a pastor-theologian.[23] In the midst of a busy schedule of pastoral responsibilities and associational duties, he carved out time to produce and publish works of a theological nature. Edwards was a prolific author, although only some of his works were published. He is known mainly for his historical writings, namely, his planned twelve-volume history of the American Baptists. However, Edwards also produced and published several theological works in his lifetime, and these works are worthy of study today.

---

[21] Ibid., 1.

[22] Edwin S. Gaustad said of Edwards that "like Backus, Edwards has double significance in his contribution to history and the writing of history." See his "Themes for Research in American Baptist History," *Foundations* 6 (April 1963): 151.

[23] See the typologies of Baptist theologians in William H. Brackney, *A Genetic History of Baptist Thought, With Special Reference to Baptists in Britain and North America* (Macon, GA: Mercer University Press, 2004), 104–164; also Gerald Hiestand and Todd Wilson, *The Pastor Theologian: Resurrecting an Ancient Vision* (Grand Rapids, MI: Zondervan, 2015).

Morgan Edwards (1722–1795) and the Book of Common Prayer

The theological works of Morgan Edwards include the following materials: his church manual, entitled *The Customs of the Primitive Churches* (1768); three theological writings; and his sermons.[24] The first work mentioned is Edwards's manual on Baptist polity and practice—his most significant theological work—a portion of which is analysed below. According to McKibbens and Smith, "It was probably the first book written in America on the polity and practices of Baptist churches."[25] Edwards's intention was that this manual be read, critiqued, and refined by his PBA brethren and that it then be officially adopted by the PBA as their manual of polity and practice. Formal adoption of the manual, however, never came to fruition. A work of more than one hundred pages, the manual covers all manner of ecclesiological matters, from the role and responsibilities of pastors to services for weddings and funerals. It is a valuable work for understanding Edwards's ecclesiology.

Although Edwards never wrote a "systematic" theology, his theological works and sermons touch on most points of doctrine. His three theological treatises are *Res Sacrae* (1788), *Two Academical Exercises on Subjects Bearing the Following Titles: Millennium, and Last-Novelties* (1788), and an unpublished work entitled "Academical Exercises on Subjects Bearing the Following Titles: Prescience, God's Purpose, Predestination, Election, Reprobation, Regeneration, Conversion, and Holy Lump" (1742 and 1743). Finally, his sermons are an important source for understanding his theology; he also touched on some theological points in his historical writings, such as an extended discussion of the Philadelphia Baptist Association in his historical volume on Pennsylvania. All of these works are key for understanding his theology. As McKibbens and Smith point out, he was vitally concerned about theology and "from these [his church manual, theological writings, and sermons] it is possible to construct an outline of his interpretation of the major doctrines usually included in 'systematic theology.'"[26] Notably, Edwards was schooled in and adhered to the 1689 Second London Confession of Faith (1689 Confession) and the American version of this, the 1742 Philadelphia Confession of Faith (1742 Confession). His confession of faith is important for understanding his theology.

---

[24] Edwards's sermons are difficult to access, so the place to begin is the work of McKibbens and Smith, *The Life and Works of Morgan Edwards*.

[25] McKibbens and Smith, *Morgan Edwards*, 126.

[26] Ibid., 113.

After surveying Edwards's theological works, McKibbens and Smith conclude that he "was a Calvinist with many strong theological beliefs" who "no doubt accepted the Philadelphia Confession of Faith."[27] This places Edwards squarely in the mainstream Baptist confessional tradition, which is confirmed by statements made at his funeral. Although Edwards was dogged by controversy in his life (loyalty to the Crown, alcoholism, and charges of doctrinal unorthodoxy), William Rogers, who preached his funeral sermon, confirms that he remained a Calvinist, as evidenced in the following portion of the funeral sermon:

> *A good report* our departed brother also had: the numerous letters brought with him across the Atlantic from the Rev. Dr. John Gill, and others, *reported*, handsome things of him; and so did, in return, the letters that went from America to the then Parent Country. *Evil reports* also fell to his share; but most of these were false reports, and therefore he gave credit to them as a species of persecution: and even the title of *Deceiver* did not escape him. Often has he been told that he was an Arminian, though he professed to be a Calvinist; that he was an Universalist in disguise, &c. yet, he was *true* to his principles. These may be seen in our confession of faith, agreeing with that republished by the Baptist churches assembled at London, in the year 1689. He seldom meddled with the five polemical points; but when he did, he always avoided abusive language. The charge of universalism brought against him was not altogether groundless; for though he was not an universalist himself, he professed a great regard for many who were, and he would sometimes take their part against violent opposers, in order to inculcate moderation.[28]

One work on Edwards's eschatology argues that he was an advocate of a pretribulation version of chiliasm.[29] Finally, the most recent theological analysis of Edwards concerns his ecclesiology. A close examination of

---

[27] Ibid., 133.

[28] Stewart, "Morgan Edwards, 1722–1795," 130.

[29] See Frank Marotta, *Morgan Edwards: An Eighteenth Century Pretribulationist.* Including "A Survey of Early Baptist Prophetical Views and a Brief Answer to Dave MacPherson's The Rapture Plot" (Morganville, NJ: Present Truth Publishers, 1995).

his ecclesiological works, particularly his manual on Baptist church polity, and a comparison of this work with other similar works of his day, places him within the Calvinistic Baptist tradition in his understanding of the church and Baptist church polity, while at the same time differing in some significant issues. The areas in which he differs include the number of officers in a local church and the number of church rites, which will be discussed in greater detail below. Edwards's ecclesiological works show him to be an advocate of several elders within congregationalism and a strong proponent of the Baptist Association. In working out his ecclesiology, he drew from Congregationalist authors such as Thomas Hooker (1586–1647), John Owen (1616–1683), and even the General Baptist Thomas Grantham (1633–1692). In his worship practice, he even cited the Book of Common Prayer (1662).[30]

The Customs of the Primitive Churches (1768) and the Book of Common Prayer (1662)

One of Morgan Edwards's key areas of influence was in the area of ecclesiology. His most extended and thorough work on this topic is *The Customs of the Primitive Churches* (1768). As the extended title of the work makes clear, in this work, Edwards sought to identify "a set of propositions relative to the name, matterials, constitution, power, officers, ordinances, rites, business, worship, discipline, government, &c. of a church; to which are added their proofs from scripture; and historical narratives of the manner in which most of them have been reduced to practice."[31] In 110 pages, he covers fifty-three propositions on all manner of topics relating to Baptist church doctrine, polity, and practice. To each proposition, he added notes in smaller print in which he further explained the proposition, providing Scripture references and quoting other authors in support of his proposition. He also added historical narratives of the positions in the propositions as they were carried out in real life.

---

[30] For more on the ecclesiology of Edwards, see Evan Lynwood Colford, "The Ecclesiology of Morgan Edwards (1722–1795), with Particular Reference to His Understanding of Baptist Church Polity," (Unpublished MA Thesis, Acadia University, 2020).

[31] Morgan Edwards, *The Customs of Primitive Churches, Or a Set of Propositions Relative to the Name, Materials, Constitution, Power, Officers...of a Church* (Philadelphia: Andrew Steuart, 1768), front page.

KEEPING THE FAITH

Overall, this work shows Edwards to be in step with his confessional tradition except for the issues of the church officers and the number of rites and ordinances of the church. His confessional tradition spoke of two officers—those being the office of pastor/elder and the office of deacon—whereas Edwards presents seven in total.[32] On the matter of rites and ordinances of the church, his confessional tradition spoke of two—baptism and the Lord's Supper (1689 Confession)—or three—baptism, the Lord's Supper, and the laying on of hands (1742 Confession)—whereas Edwards discusses fourteen in his manual.[33] Toward the end of his work on polity and practice, Edwards discusses the rites and ordinances in general (Proposition XXVII) and then proceeds to discuss each of the fourteen ordinances and rites in turn, devoting a separate proposition to each (Propositions XXVIII–XL). The last two ordinances are the Christian funeral and the Christian marriage, which will be the focus of the remainder of this essay.

What is most interesting about these two rites or ordinances is not so much Edwards's understanding of them but the evident influence of the Book of Common Prayer on the examples/liturgies that he presents under each proposition. On the matter of the funeral, Edwards believes that "there is foundation in the newtestatment [*sic*] for the following rites of a funeral": inviting the minister to preside over the service, having the deceased's neighbours and relations present, making "lamentation at the internment in an audible voice," and visiting with the family following the service in order to bring them comfort.[34]

---

[32] The seven are as follows: minister, ruling elder, deacon, eldress, deaconess, clerk, and the extra-congregational office of missionary/evangelist.

[33] The fourteen rites and ordinances are as follows: baptism, the Lord's Supper, the laying on of hands, the right hand of fellowship, the love feast, the washing of feet, the kiss of charity, the anointing of the sick with oil, the collection for the saints, the church fast, feast, devoting of children, the Christian funeral, and the Christian marriage.

[34] Edwards, *Customs*, 97. In the small print to this proposition, he adds: "He that appointed death for the living appointed the grave for the dead, Job xxx. 23. Wherefore burying the dead is an institution of God." Edwards also took quite serious the lamentation at the graveside: He grounds the requirement in Acts 8:2, where great lamentation was made at the burial of Stephen, and then says: "This means more than tears or doleful countenances; for *lamentation* implies some audible sound or voice; and in our opinion, justifies funeral orations and singing

52

After discussing his understanding of the funeral, he presents an example of liturgy for a funeral service. Edwards's example of a funeral service (really a graveside service) is as follows:

Here follows an example of the manner in which one funeral hath been conducted. The corps being put on the bier, the minister walked before, and the relations and the neighbours after it to the grave. When the corps was put in the grave, the minister spoke and prayed as follow [*sic*]

"Man that is born of a woman is of few days and full of trouble. He cometh forth as a flower and is cut down, he fleeth also as a shadow and continueth not. The Lord slayeth. The Lord maketh alive. The Lord bringeth down to the grave. The Lord bringeth up again. Blessed be the name of the Lord. I heard a voice from heaven saying: Blessed are the dead which die in the Lord; for they cease from their labours and their works do follow them.

And for as much as it hath pleased the Lord, the father of spirits, to command away the soul of this our departed friend, we, like the disciples of old, carry the body to the burial; commit it to the grave, earth to earth; and bid it our last farewell. And may the Lord of the dead and living take care of this dead body, and quicken it to eternal life at the resurrection of the just! O Lord comfort them that mourn the loss of a near relative! Help them to bear their affliction without a murmuring word or a repining thought, because thou hast done this thing; and takest from them only that which thou gavest! O Lord let us the living, who know that we must die, be savingly affected herewith. Fit us for death, and then let thy servants depart in peace, even so Lord Jesus, *Amen*."[35]

Following these words, a hymn was sung, and the service was to be closed with a benediction.

---

elegies at interments; especially the last, which is the most common sense of lamenting the dead. 2 Sam. I. Music was used at funerals, Matth. ix. 23. So also was showing forth the virtues of the deceased, Act. ix. 39."

[35] Edwards, *Customs*, 98. Before these words, Edwards includes the following: "Here follows an example of the manner in which one funeral hath been conducted. The corps being put on the bier, the minister walked before, and the relations and neighbours after it to the grave. When the corps was put in the grave, the minister spoke and prayed as follows."

Compare the words from Edwards's example with the words from the burial service in the Book of Common Prayer (1662) printed by John Baskerville in 1760, a version from the time of Edwards:

When they come to the Grave, while the Corps is made ready to be laid into the earth, the Priest shall say, or the Priest and Clerks shall sing:

MAN that is born of a woman, hath but a short time to live, and is full of misery. He cometh up, and is cut down like a flower; he fleeth as it were a shadow, and never continueth in one stay.

In the midst of life we are in death: of whom may we seek for succour, but of thee, O Lord, who for our sins art justly displeased?

Yet, O Lord God most holy, O Lord most mighty, O holy and most merciful Saviour, deliver us not into the bitter pains of eternal death.

Thou knowest, Lord, the secrets of our hearts: shut not they merciful ears to our prayers; but spare us, Lord most holy, O God most mighty, O holy and merciful Saviour, thou most worthy Judge eternal, suffer us not at our last hour for any pains of death to fall from thee.

Then while the earth shall be cast upon the Body by some standing by, the Priest shall say,

FORASMUCH as it hath pleased Almighty God of his great mercy to take unto himself the soul of our dear *brother* here departed, we therefore commit *his* body to the ground; earth to earth, ashes to ashes, dust to dust; in sure and certain hope of the resurrection to eternal life, though our Lord Jesus Christ; who shall change our vile body, that it may be like unto his glorious body, according to the mighty working, whereby he is able to subdue all things to himself

Then shall be said, or sung

I Heard a voice from heaven, saying unto me, Write, From henceforth blessed are the dead which die in the Lord: even so faith the Spirit; for they rest from their labours. *Rev.* xiv. 13.[36]

It would appear that either Edwards or some other minister made use of the Book of Common Prayer. It would make sense if this represented a funeral service conducted by Edwards himself, since he had been raised in the Church of England and thus had exposure to the Book of Common Prayer. It is conceivable that this was Edwards's order of service for the burial of the dead, and that he made use of the Book of Common Prayer in writing it. Even if Edwards used material from another minister for his historical example, he surely knew it was from the Book of Common Prayer (1662) from his time in the Church of England. The same can be said for his liturgy for a wedding.

On the topic of marriage, Edwards considers it "an ordinance of God; and therefore it is proper that a divine should be the administrator."[37] The ends of marriage are "mutual help; the preventing of unchastity; and the legitimate procreation of children."[38] Finally, marriage is only to take place

---

[36] *The Book of Common Prayer, and Administration of the Sacraments, and Other Rites and Ceremonies of the Church, According to the Use of the Church of England, Together with the Psalter or Psalms of David, Pointed as They Are to be Sung and Said in Churches* (Cambridge, UK: John Baskerville, 1760). This work can be found at the following link: http://archive.org/details/bookofcommonpray00chur_4 This would be the 1662 version of the *Book of Common Prayer.*

[37] Edwards, *Customs,* 98–99. In the small print to the proposition, verse/note 1, Edwards grounds the "institution" of marriage in three scripture passages: Genesis 2:18–24, Matthew 19:3–9, and Mark 10:2–9. In verse/note 2, he states that a minister should perform weddings because it was God who first "united in the bands of matrimony the first couple" and ministers are God's " ambassadors or proxies." He adds: "It is not incredible that either Christ or one of his apostles performed the rites of marriage at Cana in Galilee. Joh. 1" (99).

[38] Edwards, *Customs,* 99. In the small print to this proposition, verse/note 3, he gives these scripture references: Genesis 2:20–22; 1 Corinthians 7:2, 9; and 1 Corinthians 7:14, respectively. It is interesting to note that the *Book of Common Prayer,* in its order for the solemnization of matrimony, mentions the same three "causes for which Matrimony was ordained."

between one man and one woman and can only be dissolved by adultery or death.[39]

As with his discussion of funerals, after his discussion of the meaning and ends of marriage, Edwards presents an example of a marriage ceremony. We will again compare Edwards's example alongside the order for the solemnization of marriage in the Book of Common Prayer. Edwards's service is as follows:

> Here follows an account of the manner in which we have seen marriage performed. The parties concerned present; and having given satisfaction that there was no let or impediment by reason of precontract, consanguinity, affinity &c. the minister bid the man and the woman stand before him, (he on her right hand) and proceeded thus,
>
> "Dearly beloved! we are come together in the presence of God and this company to join together this man and this woman in marriage. Which is an honourable estate; instituted by God in the time of mans innocence; commended by the gospel as honourable in all; graced by our Saviour himself with his divine presence and miracle; and made an emblem of the sacred union there is between him and his church. Wherefore it is not to be enterprised unadvisedly, but soberly and in the fear of God. Duly considering the ends of it. It is instituted for the mutual help the one ought to have of the other in temporal and spiritual affairs. It was instituted for the preventing of unchastity, that they who have not the gift of continence might marry, and keep themselves undefiled. And it was instituted for the legitimate procreation of children to be brought up in the nurture and admonition of the Lord; for which ends ye are now to enter into that estate. And as ye have satisfied us that there is no impediment in the way, I ask you Sir;
>
> Wilt thou have this woman to be thy wedded wife, to live together, after God's ordinance in the honourable estate of matrimony; wilt thou love her, comfort her, honour her, and keep her

---

[39] Edwards, *Customs*, 99. In the small print to the proposition, verse 5, he gives these scripture references: on adultery, Matthew 19:9; on death, he lists Romans 8:1–4, which surely should read Romans 7:1–4.

in sickness and health, and, forsaking all others, keep thee only unto her, so long as ye both shall live? *Yeas.*

I ask you Madam! wilt thou have this man to be thy wedded husband, to live together after God's ordinance in the honourable estate of matrimony? Wilt thou serve, love, honour and obey him, and keep him in sickness and in health, and, forsaking all others, keep thee only unto him so long as ye both shall live? *Yeas*

Then the minister joining their right hands together, added

In the name of the Lord, and by the authority of law and office we join you together in marriage; pronounce you man and wife; and whom the Lord hath thus joined together let no man put asunder.

And may the God that made you one for another, and hath now brought you together, make you happy one with the other! May he bless (Gen. 1:28) you with all temporal and spiritual blessings. With mutual love! With dear and obedient Children! With health, wealth, and honour! With many and happy days; and with all other family blessings! May he bless you, and yours with grace that you and they may be fitted for heaven, where they neither marry nor are given in marriage, but are as the angels of God. Even so Lord Jesus. *Amen.* The grace of whom be with you; the love of God the father and the communion of the holy Ghost, now, henceforth, *Amen.*"[40]

Compare Edwards's proposed liturgy with the wedding ceremony from the 1760 version of the Book of Common Prayer (1662):

At the day and time appointed for Solemnization of Matrimony, the Persons to be married shall come into the body of the Church with their Friends and Neighbours: and there standing together, the Man on the right Hand, and the Woman on the left, the Priest shall say,

DEARLY beloved, we are gathered together here in the sight of God, and in the face of this congregation, to join together this Man and this Woman in holy Matrimony; which is an honourable estate, instituted of God in the time of man's

---

[40] Edwards, *Customs*, 99–100.

innocency, signifying unto us the mystical union that is betwixt Christ and his Church: which holy estate Christ adorned and beautified with his presence, and first miracle that he wrought in Cana of Galilee; and is commended of Saint Paul to be honourable among all men: and therefore is not by any to be enterprised, nor taken in hand unadvisedly, lightly, or wantonly, to satisfy men's carnal lusts and appetites, like brute beasts that have no understanding; but reverently, discreetly, and advisedly, soberly, and in the fear of God; duly considering the causes for which Matrimony was ordained.

First, it was ordained for the procreation of children, to be brought up in the fear and nurture of the Lord, and to the praise of his holy Name.

Secondly, it was ordained for a remedy against sin, and to avoid fornication; that such persons as have not the gift of continency, might marry, and keep themselves undefiled members of Christ's body.

Thirdly, it was ordained for the mutual society, help, and comfort that the one ought to have of the other, both in prosperity and adversity.

Into which holy estate these two persons present come now to be joined. Therefore if any man can shew any just cause, why they may not lawfully be joined together, let him now speak, or else hereafter for ever hold his peace....

M. WILT thou have this women to thy wedded wife, to live together after God's ordinance in the holy estate of Matrimony? Wilt thou love her, comfort her, honour, and keep her in sickness and in health; and forsaking all other, keep thee only unto her, so long as ye both shall live?

The Man shall answer, I will....

N. WILT thou have this man to thy wedded husband, to live together after God's ordinance in the holy estate of Matrimony? Wilt thou obey him, serve him, love, honour, and keep him in sickness and in health; and forsaking all other, keep thee only unto him, so long as ye both shall live?

The Woman shall answer, I will....

FORASMUCH as *M.* and *N.* have consented together in holy wedlock, and have witnessed the same before God and this company, and thereto have given and pledged their troth either to other, and have declared the same by giving and receiving of a Ring, and by joining of hands; I pronounce that they be Man and Wife together, In the Name of the Father, and of the Son, and of the Holy Ghost. Amen.[41]

As is evident from the preceding comparison, as too with the order presented for burying the dead, some lines in Edwards's wedding ceremony were taken directly from the Book of Common Prayer (1662). Apparently, Edwards was not averse to using sources from those with whom he did not agree; his use of quotations from several Independents/Congregationalist authors throughout his manual corroborates his tendency to draw from diverse sources. These two examples also, perhaps, demonstrate some lasting influence upon him from his time in the Church of England.[42] Furthermore, the manual illustrates Edwards's attempt to provide a resource with ready-made services for ministers of the PBA. As Stewart notes, "Morgan Edwards's background in the Anglican Church spilled over into his life as a Baptist. It was his conviction that Baptists would benefit from having an ordered set of principles by which to conduct church life and which would be compatible with their confessions."[43]

The Customs of the Primitive Churches (1768) can be rightly understood as a work of polity and practice, a discipline and a liturgical guide. Thus, Edwards gives more attention to the form of public worship. In this vein, we see that Edwards borrowed from the Book of Common Prayer (1662) in his services for both a Christian funeral and a Christian wedding. These examples support the contention of Robert T. Handy that Edwards was raised an Anglican and that he never really lost interest in that

---

[41] *The Book of Common Prayer.*

[42] It is my contention that some of the examples Edwards presents in his work are his own services or at least liturgies that he himself designed and wrote, evidently using resources. It would also seem that Edwards's *Customs* could be understood as a minister's manual on both polity and practice (ready-made liturgies for various ceremonies), a "Baptist Book of Common Prayer," or book of church order.

[43] Stewart, *A Dazzling Enigma*, 214. As far as I can tell, Stewart was not aware that Edwards appears to actually quote from the Anglican *Book of Common Prayer* in his *Customs of the Primitive Churches.*

communion.[44] In the words of Norman Maring, Edwards's book of church polity can be understood as "the first manual on Baptist polity produced in America."[45] Certainly this was not the only work in America to touch on Baptist polity, but as a manual it is probably the first on polity *and* practice. It appears to me that Edwards wanted to give to his denomination, the PBA, a book that outlined both polity and practice. Such a work would be similar to a book of church order, similar to modern works such as the *Book of Church Order* of the Orthodox Presbyterian Church or the Presbyterian Church in America.[46] Had Edwards's plan for his book— being critiqued by his PBA brethren and officially adopted by the PBA— come to fruition, the denomination would have had an official confession, a catechism, and a book of church order. Morgan Edwards was in the business of denomination building. He was an eighteenth-century Baptist who took the long view and worked diligently to further the Baptist cause in America. His efforts should not be forgotten.[47]

---

[44] Robert T. Handy, "The Philadelphia Tradition," in *Baptist Concepts of the Church: A Survey of the Historical and Theological Issues Which Have Produced Changes in Church Order*, ed. Winthrop Still Hudson, 30–52 (Philadelphia: Judson Press, 1959), 38–39.

[45] Stewart, *Dazzling Enigma*, 218.

[46] For example, see the Committee on Christian Education of the Orthodox Presbyterian Church, *The Book of Church Order of the Orthodox Presbyterian Church: Containing the Standards of Government, Discipline, and Worship* (Willow Grove, PA: The Committee on Christian Education of the Orthodox Presbyterian Church, 2020).

[47] This essay includes slightly edited material from two of my previous works. The first is from the historical introduction in the forthcoming volume, already cited above: *The Historical Works of Morgan Edwards*, eds. Colford and Brackney, used with permission of the publisher. The second is my MA (Theology) thesis on the ecclesiology of Edwards, also cited above: Colford, "The Ecclesiology of Morgan Edwards (1722–1795)." I would also like to thank Dr. William H. Brackney and Dr. Carol Anne Janzen. Dr. Brackney, as my MA Thesis supervisor and coeditor, made this work what it is by his guidance, suggestions, and additions on the earlier iterations that now make up the contents of this essay. I would like to express my thanks for the help I received from Dr. William H. Brackney and Dr. Carol Anne Janzen: Dr. Brackney's fingerprints can be found throughout this essay thanks to his mentorship, editorship, and guidance; however, he specifically wrote or added to footnotes 6, 8, 12, and 23. Dr. Janzen read through a draft of this essay and provided helpful editorial suggestions.

Conclusion

Morgan Edwards is a name that deserves to be better known by modern Christians, especially modern-day Baptists. Edwards's influence runs deep and touches several areas of Baptist life and thought. He lived during a fascinating and complex time in American history, as the new Republic was emerging into a national entity. He had ambitious plans for the Baptists in America and worked for the advancement of the Baptist cause. He wrote histories of the Baptists in various parts of the country, he was involved in the birth of the first Baptist institution of higher education in the American colonies, he sought the national union of all American Baptists, and he endeavoured to give to his fellow Baptists a manual on Baptist church polity and practice. Although many of his efforts did not come to fruition in his lifetime, his work should be remembered. An examination of Edwards's manual shows that he was not averse to borrowing from other authors, be they Congregationalists, General Baptists, or Anglicans. The main thrust of this essay shows that Edward's *The Customs of the Primitive Churches* (1768) uses examples or liturgies that borrow freely from the Book of Common Prayer (1662). Any modern-day Baptist who appreciates the beauty of this historic Anglican text, and who perhaps even makes use of it in their own life and work, stands on the shoulders of this eighteenth-century Baptist pastor-theologian.

Keeping Maturin Honest:
Edmund Maturin and John Mockett Cramp Debate the Reformation

Scott Kindred-Barnes

On September 30, 2018, I was inducted as the senior minister of Wolfville Baptist Church in Nova Scotia, Canada's oldest continuing Baptist church. On that occasion, my friend and mentor and member of the congregation, the Rev. Dr. Roger H. Prentice, presented me with a copy of John Mockett Cramp's *Scripture and Tradition: A Reply to Mr. Maturin's Letter "The Claims of the Catholic Church."* This gift proved to be the first of several books written by Cramp that were given to me by Roger over the next three years. Along with Cramp's *Scripture and Tradition*, Roger presented a card with the following inscription: "This little gift should not cramp your style in any way but open up the thoughts of one who was here before us. Enjoy the light it shines and pursue the continuing light that is shed along The Way we all tread towards the New Jerusalem." The book has indeed proved rewarding in several ways.[1] First, it introduced me to one of the great Baptist historians of the past, John Mockett Cramp, the so-called "second-founder of Acadia." Second, the book has pulled me out of the Reformation period, where I normally focus most of my intellectual energy, to the nineteenth century.

One may legitimately ask why, in our ecumenical age, anyone would want to reintroduce long-forgotten arguments and debates about church polity, especially when such debates often took on the nature of polemical bickering. It all depends on what we do with this history. Though I am an ordained Baptist minister, I have spent considerable scholarly energy writing about Christians from other traditions, namely Richard Hooker and

---

[1] I am grateful to Patricia Townsend and Wendy Robicheau at the Acadia University Archives for helping me locate some of the primary resources for this paper. I also want to thank Lorraine Slopek, the diocesan archivist for Nova Scotia and Prince Edward Island, for the primary sources she made available to me.

Keeping Maturin Honest

his late Elizabethan world.[2] Why? Because I believe we can celebrate our denominational distinctives without practicing ecclesial tribalism. To study the wider catholic tradition, even the messy parts where one group of Christians unashamedly persecutes another group for ecclesial or doctrinal reasons, is an exercise in receptive ecumenism.[3] This is a lesson I learned in part from my friend Roger Prentice.

Edmund Maturin's Resignation as Curate of St. Paul's Halifax

Sometime between February 3 and 10, 1859,[4] the former curate of the Anglican church of St. Paul's, Halifax, Edmund Maturin, published his controversial pamphlet titled *The Claims of the Catholic Church: A Letter to the Parishioners of Saint Paul's, Halifax, Nova Scotia* (hereafter *Claims of the Catholic Church*). "My Dear Friends," Maturin begins his pamphlet, "You are all aware of the circumstances of my recent conversion to the faith of the Catholic Church, received with much surprise among you, from your knowledge of my former views and principles as a Minister of the Gospel

---

[2] Richard Hooker (1554–1600) died before the Baptist movement in England emerged. But he did write against their genetic theological ancestors of the English Separatist Tradition, namely Henry Barrow. Moreover, Hooker was highly critical of sixteenth-century Christians who rejected infant baptism, labeling them, as did other magisterial reformers, pejoratively as "Anabaptists."

[3] In sum, receptive ecumenism can be described as growing in our faith tradition by entering into the faith tradition of others. We learn about ourselves by learning more about others. We learn about our own tradition by having someone outside share what they see, both good and bad. See *Receptive Ecumenism and the Call to Catholic Learning: Exploring a Way for Contemporary Ecumenism*, ed. Paul Murray (Oxford: Oxford University Press, 2008).

[4] One known simply as "A LOVER OF TRUTH" wrote letters to the editor of *The Church Record* on February 3 and February 10. In the earlier letter, the author addresses the forthcoming publication by Maturin. In the latter letter, he affirms that Maturin has indeed published his short book: "SIR: I enclose a few more extracts, as promised in my last week's letter. Since it was written, Mr. Maturin's pamphlet has made its appearance, and all Protestants will be shocked at reading the confirmation of what was previously suspected, that he has long been illustrating in practice the theories of St. Alfonso."

of Christ."[5] A close examination of Maturin's writings suggests that he was led to this action in stages. Writing from London on October 22, 1858, Maturin made the following announcement about leaving his duties at Saint Paul's, Halifax, where he had served as curate since November 1850:

> My dear Archdeacon,
> I have only just time to write a few lines—as the American mail will shortly be closed—but I am anxious to inform you by the earliest opportunity—that I do not expect to return to my former position in the Parish of St. Paul's—as I can no longer continue to officiate in the Church of England.
> It would be tedious to enter into an explanation of the motives which have led me to this conclusion—but it is sufficient to state that it is the result of full and mature deliberation by which I have been brought to the conclusion that it is my solemn duty to return to the communion of the Holy Catholic Church from which the Protestant Reformers of the 16th Century have separated themselves and us—and therefore I have come to the final resolution of acting to this conviction—
> And believe me dear Sir,
> Yours very sincerely,
> Edmund Maturin[6]

Even though the letter was sent in haste, the decision behind Maturin's move toward the Roman Catholic Church was not yet completed. What is more, his reference above to the Reformation is an important clue as to why he made this move, since it was the study of church history, and particularly the history and theology of the Reformation, that influenced Maturin's conversions, first to Rome and then back to the Church of England again. As we will demonstrate below, the ideas of and charges by John Mockett Cramp played an important part in Maturin's reexamination of the history of the Roman Catholic Church.

---

[5] Edmund Maturin, *The Claims of the Catholic Church: A Letter to the Parishioners of Saint Paul's, Halifax, Nova Scotia* (Halifax, NS: Compton & Bowden, Printers, 1859), 4.

[6] St. Paul's Church archives, vestry minute book. Maturin to the Archdeacon, October 22, 1858. The full letter is recorded in the minutes of St. Paul's vestry meeting held on December 18, 1858.

Keeping Maturin Honest

Neil MacKinnon has suggested that Maturin's interest in Catholicism was further fanned by such Tractarian writers as Henry Edward Manning and John Henry Newman, both Church of England clergymen who by the 1850s had abandoned their church for Catholicism.[7] In a later work, Maturin would suggest that it was on August 14, 1858, at the funeral of the late Catholic archbishop of Halifax, "which I can distinctly trace those deep impressions which finally led me to the conviction of the divine origin of the Catholic Church."[8] The archbishop, whom Maturin does not name, was William Walsh who died August 11, in Halifax. Like Maturin, he was born and educated in the Republic of Ireland. After Walsh's funeral, several weeks elapsed as Maturin wrestled with a course of action. In hindsight, Maturin looked back on this period and described it: "I had made arrangements to proceed to England, partly for the benefit of my health, but chiefly with the view of joining the Catholic Church, and without any fixed intention of returning to this Province. And yet I did not fully announce this plan, because I thought it quite possible that something might yet occur, which would enable me to defer, if not altogether to relinquish, this purpose. "[9] On board a steamer bound for England, October 10, 1858, Maturin officiated at morning and evening services, according to the Liturgy of the Church of England. The following Sunday morning they were in Liverpool, England, where he heard two sermons by the "violent controversialist," the Rev. Dr. Hugh Boyd McNiele, before going to Oxford the next day.[10] According to Maturin's

---

[7] Neil MacKinnon, "Maturin, Edmund," in *Dictionary of Canadian Biography*, vol. 12, University of Toronto/Université Laval, 2003–, accessed April 24, 2022, http://www.biographi.ca/en/bio/maturin_edmund_12E.html.

[8] Edmund Maturin, *A Defence of the Claims of the Catholic Church in Reply to Several Publications* (Halifax, NS: Compton & Bowden, Printers, 1859), 13.

[9] Ibid., 15.

[10] Given McNiele's ardent evangelical opposition to the Oxford (Tractarian) movement, one wonders if these sermons further augmented Maturin's already Anglo-Catholic leanings, since he had already begun to admire the Tractarians before leaving Halifax through the influence Bishop Hibbert Binney. Even before the Maturin controversy unfolded, Cramp himself had no love for the Oxford movement. J. M. Cramp, *A Text-Book of Popery: A Brief History of the Council of Trent and a Complete View of Roman Catholic Theology*, 3rd ed. (London: Houston and Stoneman, 1851), 445, writes: 'The Oxford tractarians have done more injury to Protestantism, than all the Romish vicars apostolic, and all the priests under

own testimony it was at Oxford, in the Cathedral of Christ Church, "that my former plans were fully matured, and on the following Sunday, the 24th of October, I attended the Services of the Catholic Church in London."[11] Maturin was received into the Catholic Church in early November 1858 for All Saints Sunday.[12]

Maturin's conversion to Roman Catholicism caused a considerable stir among Nova Scotian Catholics and Protestants of the late 1850s, but for different reasons. Neil MacKinnon has rightly summarized the political and polemical stir generated by Maturin's conversion to Rome, suggesting Joseph Howe's dispute with Irish Roman Catholics in Nova Scotia over Irish recruits to the Crimean War formed the more immediate backdrop to the controversy.[13] But there was also the pastoral side to Maturin's actions. Maturin's resignation forced St. Paul's Halifax to find a new minister to take on the duties of their former curate. Thus, the main purpose

---

their command. Under pretence of reverent regard for the authority of the wise and good, they have introduced among the people a mean, crouching superstition—substituted the trash of the middle ages for the truths of the gospel—repudiated the great principles of the Reformation—and sought to reduce their adherents to a state of slavish subjection to the priesthood, and dependence on the 'church,' to the neglect (one might almost say, the disavowal) of personal responsibility."

[11] Maturin, *Defence of the Claims*, 16.

[12] Ibid., 16–17, where he writes: "The month of November came, and at that holy season at which the Church celebrates the memory of 'All Saints' who have gone before us, I had the inestimable privilege of being admitted into the 'Communion of Saints' in the 'Holy Catholic Church.'" Maturin, *Thoughts on the Infallibility of the Church* (Halifax, NS: J. B. Strong, Bookseller ETC. 1861), 6, also confirms this by stating: "It was in the month of November, 1858, that I joined the Roman Catholic Church in London, though it was only a few weeks previously that I had seriously commenced to devote my earnest attention to this study, and only a few days before that I finally decided on this step."

[13] "His [Maturin's] conversion and pamphlet fell upon a province caught up in religious dissension. A quarrel had erupted between Joseph Howe and the Irish Roman Catholics in Nova Scotia over Howe's efforts in the United States in 1855 to secure Irish recruits for the British army in the Crimea. The ensuing conflict degenerated into an ugly little religious war between Howe's Protestant supporters and the Irish Catholic population. Maturin's publicized conversion prompted a vigorous campaign—in newspapers and pamphlets and on platforms—against his actions and his defence of Catholicism." (MacKinnen, "Maturin, Edmund")

of holding a meeting at the St. Paul's vestry on December 18, 1858, was to allow the churchwarden to announce that the archdeacon had nominated the Rev. Mr. George Hill to resume his duties at St. Paul's.[14] Not mentioned in the paper, but still looming large among the people of the parish, was the question as to why Maturin was no longer serving as the curate, as the details concerning his resignation were not yet widely known. In addition to the typical tasks expected of clergy then, Hill was given the difficult, if not "arduous," duty of having to minister to a parish church that would soon be reeling from the shock of the publication of *The Claims of the Catholic Church: A Letter to the Parishioners of Saint Paul's, Halifax, Nova Scotia*, where they would learn that their former minister had left them because, as he put it, *"my heart was essentially Catholic, while my mind was accidentally Protestant."*[15]

Once published, Maturin's *Claims of the Catholic Church* caused a stir on several levels. According to one newspaper account, Maturin's *Claims* were "industriously circulated."[16] Another reports, "Mr. Maturin's

---

[14] *The Church Record* 1/3 (January 20, 1859). At the time, Hill was serving as the professor of pastoral theology at King's College, Windsor. By January 20, 1859, *The Church Record* announced that the Rev. George Hill, MA, had taken leave of Windsor to return to St. Paul's parish duties: "We heartily welcome him on his return to the city, and wish him God's speed in the arduous and important work committed to him."

[15] Maturin, *Claims of the Catholic Church*, 11.

[16] *The Church Record* 1/6 (February 10, 1859). Moreover, the fact remains that *The Evening Express and Commercial Record* ran the following advertisement for more than a month, between April 29 to June 1, 1859:

Scripture and Tradition.

Reply to Mr. Maturin's Letter on "The Claims of the Catholic Church," BY J. M. CRAMP, D.D.

Review of E. Maturin's Letter, BY REV. JOHN HUNTER.

For sale at the LONDON BOOK STORE

A few copies left of "The Claims of the Catholic Church"—by Edmund Maturin, MA

April 4. J. ANDREW GRAHAM

With the exception to one edition, this advertisement appeared on the front page. On April 8, it was advertised on the back page. Whatever else may be deduced from this advert, we know it was deemed relevant enough to warrant the attention of interested Protestants and Catholics alike.

Pamphlet is still the subject for a host of writers and speakers."[17] Yet, more than just a controversy in provincial and international politics, Maturin's publicized conversion, and the subsequent campaigns for and against his actions and defence of Catholicism, became largely a public debate in theology and church history. To ignore or even downplay this fact is to miss the important role that theology played in nineteenth-century Nova Scotian public life in general.

There were four Protestant replies to Maturin's *Claims of the Catholic Church* published in book form, to say nothing of the many letters written to the editors of several Halifax newspapers. The four authors who published books in reply to Maturin came from across the denominational spectrum, were the Rev. Dr. L. W. D. Gray (Church of England), the Rev. John Hunter (Free Church of Scotland), Judge John G. Marshall (Wesleyan Methodists), and the Rev. Dr. John Mockett Cramp, the Baptist church historian. Maturin's response to these four Protestant critics was titled *A Defence of the Claims of the Catholic Church in Reply to Several Publications*. The four book responses to Maturin's conversion to Rome affirm that his ecclesial shift was perceived by many Protestants as a betrayal. After all, Maturin, prior to his conversion, had been more than vocal in his critique of the Roman Catholic Church. Even before Maturin's *Claims of the Catholic Church* went to press, opinion was expressed about how best to respond to it. In a letter to the editor of *The Church Record*, February 3, 1859, one known by the pseudonym "A LOVER OF TRUTH" suggested Maturin's actions were hypocritical, if not dishonest: "I, myself, have listened to him, when he has gone far out of his way to affix a stigma upon the character of that communion, which he has now so suddenly discovered to be the only true Holy Catholic and Apostolic Church."[18] Hence, this unknown reviewer encouraged his "Protestant brethren" to abstain from purchasing the book:

> I understand that a large impression is to be printed, and no doubt it is expected that curiosity, or the remembrance of former acquaintance, will induce many persons to wish to see it. And we cannot more effectually prove that his influence is completely annihilated, than by treating this statement of his "reason" with merited

---

[17] *The Evening Express and Commercial Record*, 2 (Friday, March 4, 1859).

[18] The Rev. Edmund Maturin's letter, *The Church Record*, 1/6 (February 10, 1859).

contempt. If any of his former friends wish to know what induced him to renounce the faith which once he preached, they cannot expect any satisfaction from this pamphlet, for he is understood to have declared, that he cannot be moved by any arguments, and that nothing less than a Divine revelation can shake his resolution; which proves that his reason has not been convinced, that he believes in the Romish system, because he wishes to believe it, whether it will bear investigation or not.[19]

With this quotation, we see curiosity treated as a vice, rather than a virtue, as the word is more typically defined in our own time. In fact, long before the nineteenth century, "curiosity" was considered a dangerous vice. Samuel Johnson's eighteenth-century *Dictionary*, for instance, defines "curious" in a number of negative ways, such as "inquisitive," "accurate," "difficult to please," "subtle," and "rigid."[20] All these definitions imply that some things are better left unexplored rather than tampered with. How many Protestants may have taken the advice of "A LOVER OF TRUTH" and avoided Maturin's *Claims of the Catholic Church* is impossible to know. Yet we know for certain that John Mockett Cramp did not hold to such a strategy. Instead, Cramp, as a church historian, sought to review Maturin's arguments critically. Hence, he published *Scripture and Tradition: A Reply to Mr. Maturin's Letter "The Claims of the Catholic Church."* Its arguments, while not without polemic, deserve closer consideration for what they reveal about the role of church history and the Reformation in Maturin's conversions.

Maturin on Church History and the Reformation

With the publication of *A Letter to the Parishioners of Saint Paul's, Halifax* in early February 1859, Maturin was determined to provide some account of why he resigned from St. Paul's, and "of my own mental trials, and of the long and painful course of discipline by which I have been led to embrace the communion of the Holy Catholic Church of Christ."[21] Maturin

---

[19] Letter to the Editor, *The Church Record* 1/5 (February 3, 1859), second page, A LOVER OF TRUTH.

[20] Samuel Johnson, "Curious, adj." *A Dictionary of the English Language: A Digital Edition of the 1755 Classic by Samuel Johnson*, ed. Brandi Besalke. https://johnsondictionaryonline.com/curious/_ (accessed April 19, 2022).

[21] Maturin, *Claims of the Catholic Church*, 3.

was indeed conflicted about Protestantism even before taking Holy Orders in the Church of England in 1843. In 1840, he received the highest theological honour in the University of Dublin as the Regius Professor's First Premium in Divinity. This course of studies, he would later claim, "gradually prepared my mind for the more full and impartial investigation of the claims of the Catholic Church."[22] Spiritually unsettled, Maturin had attended services of the Catholic Church until the end of July 1842, even devoting the season of Lent 1842 to prayer and fasting as a way of resolving this existential conflict. Further, Maturin began to question the interpretation of the Reformation he had been taught as a Protestant:

> My chief difficulty was the history of the Protestant Reformation of the 16th Century. It is obvious that the great objection was this, that the very idea of a Reformation, of doctrine was founded upon the supposition of a general corruption of Christianity throughout the whole Church of Christ in every country in Europe, during the long succession of ages, while the Reformers themselves were only fallible men, acting in opposition to the highest ecclesiastical authorities, and unable to agree among themselves on many important points of doctrine.[23]

In the early pages of *Claims of the Catholic Church*, Maturin elaborates on why he had come to leave the Church of England: "I believe it was the study of Ecclesiastical History which first contributed to give a new direction to my thoughts, and materially tended to modify my former views on the subject of religion."[24] Until then, he claimed, his acquaintance with the general facts of church history had been "very slight and superficial, and I was particularly careful to derive all my information on the subject from the statements of Protestant Divines, as I had no confidence in the representations of Catholic historians."[25] By 1859, Maturin could look back and explain that a deeper study of church history had been the most important factor in leading him toward Roman Catholicism. While it had been a gradual process, Maturin grew in his desire to "know what the Catholic

---

[22] Ibid., 4–5.
[23] Maturin, *Infallibility of the Church*, 10.
[24] Maturin, *Claims of the Catholic Church*, 5.
[25] Ibid.

Church really was, not from the accounts of her enemies, but according to her own representation of it."[26]

In addition to careful study of the Decrees of the Council of Trent and the Reformation as a whole, Maturin also credited the influence of the Church Fathers and Cardinal Nicolas Wiseman's lectures as contributing to his conversion. Nicolas Wiseman was the first cardinal resident in England since the Reformation, and the first archbishop of Westminster.[27] Early in 1835, Wiseman began a course of seven lectures in the Royal Sardinian Chapel, Lincoln's-Inn-Fields. As Lent 1835 drew near, he was approached by a "venerable prelate" to undertake the same lectures at St. Mary's, Moorfields, upon the same subjects. It was proposed to confine this series to a few lectures upon one subject, the Rule of Faith, or the authority of the church, the same theme that Maturin would later incorporate into *Claims of the Catholic Church* and other publications related to the controversy.[28] Wiseman's lectures peak through Maturin's lengthy

---

[26] Ibid., 5–6.

[27] Cramp, *A Text-Book of Popery*, 447–50, contextualized with indignation, Pope Pius IX's papal bull titled *Universalis Ecclesiae*. This bull, issued in late September 1850, essentially reestablished a Roman Catholic diocesan hierarchy in England, independent of the Church of England. The bull not only made Wiseman's appointment possible, but it also worked independently of the Protestant establishment by renaming the dioceses where Roman Catholic churches and chapels were organized. Cramp spoke for many Protestants when he wrote that the bull essentially "re-established a Romish hierarchy in England." Further, "While the newly created bishops assert that the act of the pope is entirely spiritual, and relates only to members of the Roman Catholic church, the *Tablet* and the *Universe* boldly declare that the bull is in fact a proclamation issued by the head of the church, demanding the submission of all baptized persons, to whatever denomination belonging, to his authority." Cardinal Wiseman is named by Cramp in a section where he names the Catholic dioceses and breaks down which counties fall under their charge.

[28] "Preface to the First Edition," *Lectures on the Principal Doctrines and Practices of the Catholic Church Delivered at St. Mary's, Moorfields, During the Lent of 1836 by Cardinal Wiseman*, vol I, 6th American ed. (Baltimore, MD: Kelly, Piet and Company, 1870), 7. Later, when these lectures were published, the topic addressed in 1853 filled one volume. The success of the 1835 lectures allowed Wiseman to expand his series for the following Lent, thus producing a second volume. Maturin follows Wiseman so closely at some points that one wonders if the former would have made the move to Rome without the latter.

treatment of both the Catholic Rule of Faith and his critique of the Protestant doctrine of *sola scriptura*. While Wiseman claimed a "rich variety of motives have brought learned men to the Catholic Church," there is a sad meagreness of reasoning behind Catholics who become Protestants. They are, says Wiseman, "possessed of the word of God, of the Bible." So strong is the affinity between Maturin's ideas and those articulated earlier by Wiseman that the *Presbyterian Witness* suggested *Claims of the Catholic Church* is "too clever to be Mr. Maturin's work," it must be "the production of the cunning, meaning or smooth tongued Wiseman."[29]

Echoing the earlier arguments of Wiseman, Maturin claimed that Protestant interpreters had soured his interpretation of the Roman Catholic Church and its history. In fact, Maturin, as a Catholic, looking back at himself as an ordained Anglican, agreed with Cardinal Wiseman's critique of the "naive assumptions" of Protestants. Maturin's critique of Protestantism was largely, but not exclusively, focused on the Reformation period. Most of the topics he addressed had been debated ad infinitum by Catholics and Protestants of the sixteenth and seventeenth centuries. Maturin built upon well-established Roman Catholic critiques of the English Reformation:

> But why talk of the Protestant Divines *of* this period [the sixteenth century], and the effect of their works on public opinion, when it is notorious that such a cause had so little to do with the progress of the English Reformation, which was accomplished, not by the spiritual weapons of theological discussion, but by the strong arm of the civil power? There is no doubt, indeed, that a great improvement took place in the general tone of Protestant controversy in the following age, as exhibited in the works of Ussher, Laud,

---

[29] I am quoting from *The Evening Express and Commercial Record*, Halifax, NS, Friday, March 4, 1859, vol. II. This quotation comes from a summary piece on how Maturin's pamphlet was received by the *Presbyterian Witness* and other papers. This accusation was denied by Maturin, *A Defence of the Claims of the Catholic Church in Reply to Several Publications*, 17. Additionally, Dr. Gray suggested that Maturin's *Claims of the Catholic Church* had most likely passed under the revisions of Wiseman and Bishop Connolly, but Maturin maintained the only one to read the manuscript "was the *Protestant* Bishop of Nova Scotia, though I cannot say that it met with his Lordship's cordial approbation."

Chillingworth, Taylor, Barrow, Stillingfleet, and others, who certainly endeavored to meet the Catholic arguments in a more fair and candid spirit of discussion.[30]

In reaction to statements like these, several Nova Scotian Protestants sought to vindicate their theology from Maturin's accusations that there was neither historical evidence for Roman corruption nor theological grounds for the *sola scriptura* doctrine that so comprehensively shaped Protestant thought since the sixteenth century.

John Mockett Cramp's Reply to Maturin

One Protestant especially weary of Maturin's motives was John Mockett Cramp. Cramp was a prolific Baptist scholar and pastor, who, since September 1856, had served as the "chairman of faculty" until his reappointment as president of Acadia College on January 18, 1860.[31] As a church historian, Cramp was qualified to review critically Maturin's interpretation of the history of the Roman Catholic Church and the Reformation. Cramp was a Protestant authority on the Council of Trent and an historian well acquainted with the Reformation period, which made him a worthy reviewer of Maturin's *Claims of the Catholic Church*. As will be seen below, Cramp's *Scripture and Tradition* sought to encourage Maturin to reassess his assumptions yet again, and to question if he was conducting an honest interpretation of the Roman Catholic past. He pointed out the

---

[30] Maturin, *Claims of the Catholic Church*, 22–23.

[31] In addition to his voluminous publications and work as the editor of several magazines, Cramp also had extensive leadership experience, having already served as the president of Acadia College from June 1851 to September 1853. Prior to his work at Acadia College, Cramp served as principal of the Canada Baptist College in Montreal from 1844 to 1849. Cramp's pastoral work and experience in both England and Canada also shaped his impact on Baptist life on both sides of the Atlantic. For more on his leadership as principal in Montreal, see Karen E. Smith, "The Baptist College in Montreal, 1836–1849. The British Connexion, with special reference to contribution of the Baptist Missionary Society," *Baptist Quarterly* 41/8 (October 2006): 465–80. For more on Cramp's leadership at Acadia College, see Barry M. Moody, "Cramp, John Mockett," in *Dictionary of Canadian Biography*, vol. 11, University of Toronto/Université Laval, 2003–, accessed September 11, 2021, http://www.biographi.ca/en/bio/cramp_john_mockett_11E.html.

KEEPING THE FAITH

weaknesses of Maturin's interpretation of both the council and the larger Reformation itself. Cramp was particularly critical of Maturin's assertion that the doctrines of Roman Catholicism had not changed since the days of the apostles. Maturin defended the Roman Catholic system with "direct testimony to it in the primitive writers," even suggesting that "the modern system of Protestantism stands directly opposed to historical Christianity in every age of the Church."[32]

Cramp was particularly critical of Maturin's Roman Catholic theory of faith and obedience since he saw it as theological sophistry intent on ignoring the Protestant critique of tradition.[33] For Maturin, it was Scripture and tradition together that formed the true rule of faith. While he conceded that some Anglicans had acknowledged a kind of double rule, he argued that the church of his ordination was nonetheless confused on how to *apply* it. Protestants, Maturin claimed, simply confused the period between the first introduction of any doctrine and the date of its formal definition by the church. What is more, history supported the Catholic position:

> Thus, it is found that certain articles of faith were defined by the Pope, or by a General Council approved by the Pope, at some particular period of history, and it is argued from thence that such articles of faith were never held in the Church before that time. *Now every one, who has the slightest knowledge of Church history*, is fully aware of the fallacy of such a theory. It is well known, that no doctrine was ever publicly defined by the Church, until it had been first publicly denied by heretics—as it was quite unnecessary to

---

[32] Maturin, *Claims of the Catholic Church*, 21.

[33] Contrary to popular misunderstandings, the Protestant doctrine of *sola scriptura* did not mean that Protestants were anti-tradition. The best minds of the Reformation were far more nuanced. The Reformers did reject arguments that elevated the authority of tradition as equal to or above the authority of scripture, or taught things contrary to it. The Protestant argument defended the sufficiency of scripture for its intended purpose of saving souls. They rejected arguments that essentially rendered a formula "the bible plus tradition" as necessary for salvation. Hence, the word *sola*, alone, whether applied to *scriptura, gratia, fide, Christo*, or even *soli deo gloria*, sought to challenge the Catholic idea that it was scripture plus something else determined by the church that was necessary for salvation.

promulge a formal explanation of a doctrine which was firmly believed by all Christians.[34]

Maturin makes an important point here, even if he stretches the history to unlikely conclusions. Historically, "heretics" have played an important role in forcing the church to declare her official "orthodox" doctrines. In other words, without both Arius and Athanasius, the Nicene Creed, at least as we know it today, might not have been compiled. Yet, as Cramp demonstrates repeatedly with evidence from church history, Maturin assumes too much when he asserts that such later doctrines, like transubstantiation, were necessarily held by the primitive church but just not stated. Hence, Cramp used church history to challenge Maturin's unprovable assertions: "And so we are actually told, in defence of all history, that the seven sacraments, purgatory, the adoration of images, to which may be added communion in one kind, as finally enacted by the Council of Trent, have been 'held by the Church from the beginning!' These things must be extremely puzzling to the honest searcher after truth."[35]

Cramp's knowledge of the Reformation period acquainted him with sixteenth-century Roman Catholic critiques of Protestantism and vice versa. Charges of innovation were very much part of the ecclesial debates of the sixteenth century. In fact, both Catholic and Protestant polemicists of the period charged one another with doctrinal innovation. During the Reformation debates, Catholics asked Protestants where their religion had been before Martin Luther, while Protestants asked Catholics where such doctrines as transubstantiation, purgatory, and auricular confession could be found in the Scriptures. If Maturin learned how to defend his newly found Catholic faith by reading Roman Catholic writers such as Wiseman, then Cramp himself stood on the shoulders of Protestant giants of the Reformation in offering his own counterarguments. "I observe," writes Cramp, "that Mr. Maturin's rule is to be rejected for its novelty. Lacking the authority of the Scripture, it must of necessity be novel. That fact being established, I care not at how early a period opinions, and practices not found in Scripture were introduced."[36]

---

[34] Maturin, *Claims of the Catholic Church*, 17. Italics mine.
[35] Cramp, *Scripture and Tradition*, 35.
[36] Ibid., 28.

KEEPING THE FAITH

Thus, for Cramp, Maturin's presentation was made "in defiance of all history."[37] Maturin, according to Cramp, had simply surmised that later doctrines existed in the apostolic era even if they could not be found in Scripture. History could say nothing of Peter as the first pope, for instance, and it was intellectually irresponsible to surmise something so important without solid proof. On the contrary, history taught that the primacy of Peter was a later innovation by the church of Rome. "*But history, should he venture to look into its pages, tells a different tale. It shows him the Bishop of Rome, meek as a lamb in the first ages, changed into a roaring lion.*"[38] Cramp then offers quotations from Archbishop Richard Whately: "*There is not a minister in all Christendom who is able to trace up with any approach to certainty his own spiritual pedigree.*"[39] Further, Cramp stands on the shoulders of Whately, "no mean authority," offering a counter to Maturin's claims:

> It is inconceivable that any one even moderately acquainted with history, can feel a certainty, that, amidst all this confusion and corruption, every requisite form was in every instance, strictly adhered to, by men, many of them openly profane and secular, unrestrained by public opinion, through the gross ignorance of the population among which they lived; and that no one, not duly consecrated or ordained, was admitted to sacred offices.[40]

Following the logic of Whately, then, Cramp turned to Maturin's reading of the Council of Trent, describing it as "such a scene of base

---

[37] Ibid., 35.

[38] John Mockett Cramp, *Scripture and Tradition: A Reply to Mr. Maturin's Letter,* "The Claims of the Catholic Church," 2nd ed., rev., with an appendix (Halifax, NS: Printed at the *Christian Messenger* office, 1859), 32.

[39] This italicized line is quoted both on page 32 and 89. The latter is part of appendix 4 on the Apostolic Succession. In 1841 and 1842, Richard Whately, the archbishop of Dublin, published *The Kingdom of Christ Delineated, in Two Essays on Our Lord's Account of His Person and of the Nature of His Kingdom, and on the Constitution, Powers, and Ministry of a Christian Church as Appointed by Himself.* Whately is famous for a number of reasons, including his eccentricities, his association with the so-called "Noetics" (what became known a generation later as the "Broad Churchmen"), and his influence on John Henry Newman, even though with time the latter eventually came to distance himself from Whately intellectually. Cramps quotes from Whately, *The Kingdom of Christ*, pages 217–19.

[40] Cramp, *Scripture and Tradition*, 32–33.

76

Keeping Maturin Honest

intrigue and trickery" before asking, "Can this be the fountain of truth? Is it possible that the decisions of such an assembly can rightfully claim the sanction of heaven?"[41] In a word, Cramp answered no. Much of Cramp's *Reply*, then, sought to demonstrate from church history why Maturin's assertions were without provable foundations.

More than just a personal pilgrimage toward Roman Catholicism, Maturin's conversion was punctuated with a sense of apologetic mission. Thus, Maturin, as a new Catholic convert with a knowledge of Protestant arguments, was elected president of the newly founded Halifax Catholic Institute in early 1859, an association dedicated to "the religious, moral and intellectual advancement of Catholic young men in Halifax."[42] After a successful introductory lecture delivered at the Masonic hall in Halifax by the Rev. Mr. Roles on Christian architecture, a week later, on Wednesday, February 16, 1859, Maturin delivered the second lecture, titled "The Origin and Early History of Christianity in England."[43] The Halifax Catholic Institute published Maturin's talk later that year. Moreover, the public lecture occurred just as the controversy was ramping up, as Maturin's *Claims of the Catholic Church* had been published less than two weeks earlier.

While Maturin asserted that it was not his intention "to enter into any Theological discussion on the present occasion," his claim to objectivity was treated with suspicion by a number of his Protestant contemporaries. Maturin was, after all, a new convert to Rome and one who was under pressure to defend his actions. Nonetheless, he claimed: "My object, then, is rather of an *historical* than a *controversial* nature—it is to deal with *facts*, rather than with *principles*, and I wish to lay before you, with all due impartiality, and plain and unvarnished statement of the principal evidence that relates to the subject before us, with the view of assisting you in arriving at a right conclusion."[44] One sympathetic reviewer described Maturin's talk as a great triumph for the Catholic cause:

---

[41] Ibid., 33.

[42] *Evening Express and Commercial Record* 2/18 (February 11, 1859).

[43] Ibid., 2/21 (February 18, 1859).

[44] Edmund Maturin, *The Origin of Christianity in England: A Lecture Delivered before the Halifax Catholic Institute on Wednesday Evening, February 16th, 1859* (Halifax, NS: Compton & Bowdon, 1859), 3. Further, Maturin, *Origin of Christianity*, 48, concluded his talk with a call to prayer: "Meanwhile the eyes of all

A moment's consideration of the nature and magnitude of this subject, is sufficient to prove, that in order to deal with it as its merits and importance demands, a thorough knowledge of the early history of England—both ecclesiastical and civil—coupled with great logical abilities, are indispensable requisites in enabling a Lecturer to unfold and develop a theme so intricate. That these requisites are possessed by Mr. Maturin in a pre-eminent degree, few who listened to his able elucidation of the subject in hand on Wednesday evening, will be inclined to gainsay. The scholar particularly, and student of history, could not withhold admiration for the glowing and powerful manner in which argumentative reasoning and logical deductions were combined, and the truths of history touching the period treated of, triumphantly vindicated—while the Christian and gentlemanly tone that pervaded the whole discourse, was beyond all praise and well worthy of imitation.[45]

We know that Cramp received a copy of the presentation from Maturin himself, as Cramp included an appendix that dealt directly with the lecture in the second edition of his *Reply*.[46] Though evidence is lacking here, it is likely that Maturin, having read Cramp's first edition, then supplied him with his lecture. The lecture was clearly written and well researched, showing an awareness of the scholarship of the times, yet with an independence of thought. The lecture offered a critical assessment of the various legends of how Christianity came to England and rightly dismissed conjectures and special pleadings that speculated on the Pauline origin of the British church. Loose references to the British Isles, or what were surmised to be so, were gleaned from Clement, Irenaeus, Jerome, and others out of context and were used to support the notion that Christianity

---

Christendom are directed toward Protestant England, and the prayers of thousands are continually ascending to heaven night and day for the conversion of that great country to her ancient faith, and we are all earnestly invited to unite our fervent prayers with theirs, that it may please God to enlighten the minds of the English people by the gracious influence of His Holy Spirit, and to grant that England may be speedily restored to the unity of the Catholic Church, and take her place once more among the nations of Catholic Europe."

[45] *Evening Express and Commercial Record* 2/21 (February 18, 1859).

[46] Cramp, *Scripture and Tradition*, 73, writes: "Since the publication of the first edition, I have received from Mr. Maturin a copy of his Lecture on 'the origin of Christianity in England,' delivered before the 'Halifax Catholic Institute.'"

had come to Britain through one of the earliest Christians such as Paul or Joseph of Arimathea. In contrast to the speculations of such legends, Maturin used more established sources, such as the Venerable Bede's *Ecclesiastical History of the English Nation*, to argue that the conversion of King Lucius in the second century AD, and his alleged commission from Pope Eleutherius, confirmed that the church in England had acknowledged the supremacy of Rome from this early date.

Evidence presented in the lecture sought to answer an important question: "Did the ancient British Church acknowledge the Supremacy of the Pope, or was it independent of the authority of Rome?"[47] Again, this question, too, had implications for the Reformation debate. If the ancient British church acknowledged Roman supremacy, then the Reformation was a schism, at least as far as Maturin was concerned. Yet if the British Church had been planted without Roman supremacy, then the Reformation was a return to such independency.

Cramp, having read Maturin's public lecture "with attention and interest," conceded that Maturin "states the evidence very fairly," though not convincingly. Cramp indicates why he was not persuaded by Maturin's conclusions in the closing comments of his appendix on Maturin's lecture. The missionary labours among the Anglo-Saxons of Augustine in 597 introduced him to the bishops already in England. Augustine found that they had no knowledge of the church in Rome or of spiritual allegiance due to Peter's successor. Moreover, insulated from the rest of Christendom, and unacquainted with changes happening elsewhere, they worshipped and served God as they had been taught by their founders. "Augustine was bent on procuring uniformity and submission. His successors, after a long struggle, accomplished the design. But originally, Britain was independent, in things ecclesiastical, and owned no subjection to the Italian prelate."[48]

---

[47] Maturin, *Origin of Christianity*, 32–33.
[48] Cramp, *Scripture and Tradition*, 78.

KEEPING THE FAITH

Cramp's Critique of Maturin's Submission to Rome

Space will not permit us to explore in detail Cramp's meticulous critique of Maturin, or the latter's counterresponse to Cramp's *Reply*.[49] This all played out rapidly in the press over a period of several months. However, to further demonstrate how Cramp's use of church history played out in the polemical debate, let us look more closely at one of Cramp's points of critique. In *Claims of the Catholic Church*, Maturin highlighted how he was received into the Catholic Church, not according to the usual profession of faith, but according to the pontifical form used by Pope Gregory the Great to receive the Donatists back into the Catholic Church. "My own profession" writes Maturin,

> is therefore more than 1000 years older than the Creed of Pope Pius IV., which is generally adopted on such occasions, but both are essentially the same, as the latter contains only a more complete explanation of Catholic principles and doctrines, which are virtually included, by anticipation in the former. The truth is, that the Supremacy of the Pope as well as all other Roman doctrines, stand before us in a prominent view, as striking facts in the theological system of the ancient Church—and it is impossible to account for this general adoption of such a system on any other principle than that of its Divine and Apostolical origin.[50]

Maturin followed this assertion with the celebrated rule of St. Vincentius and applied it to Roman Catholicism. For Maturin, this rule defended Catholic doctrine: held "in all places, at all times, and by all persons."[51] In many ways, the rule of St. Vincentius was an assertion that Maturin, as a Roman Catholic, seemed unwilling to test. The Roman Catholic Church, he claimed, had remained doctrinally consistent since the days of the apostles, even if these teachings were not as fully stated in the early centuries of the faith.

In opposition to Maturin, Cramp thoroughly rejected what he saw as Maturin's special pleading here, stating his own conviction that the

---

[49] The debate is further complicated by Maturin's counterresponse to Cramp and other critics in his *A Defence of the Claims of the Catholic Church in Reply to Several Publications*.

[50] Maturin, *Claims of the Catholic Church*, 20.

[51] Ibid.

80

Scriptures bear witness to the apostolic doctrines and that nonbiblical teachings were, in fact, innovations of a corrupted Church. Later, in the same work, Cramp criticized Pope Pius's creed itself for both subjecting the Scriptures to the authority of the holy mother church, and for requiring interpretations to be in accord with "the unanimous consent of the Fathers."[52] For Cramp, the Scriptures were the highest authority, and the help of the Church Fathers was not necessary, unless one sought to demonstrate historically how the church had departed over time from the teachings of the apostles. Repeatedly, Cramp's critique pointed out how church history proves that certain doctrines of the Roman Catholic Church were not held by the apostles but were best explained as later innovations. Not only did Cramp doubt the historicity of the Donatists' submission to the Roman apostolic see, but he also recapped what the *ordo ad reconciliandum Apostaltam val Haereticum* meant to anyone brought back into union with the Roman Catholic Church. "The reconciled person promises the Bishop, and, through him, 'holy Peter, Prince of the Apostles, and the most holy Father in Christ, and our Lord, Pope—, and his successors,' that he will never return to schism."

Maturin's claim that he was received into the Roman Catholic Church through a subscription a thousand years older than the creeds embraced at Trent was, in Cramp's view, "a cunning contrivance" since the earlier *ordo* assumed his submission to all subsequent doctrines of the Roman Catholic Church. Had Maturin subscribed to the Roman Church through Pope Pius IV's creed, at least it would not have included the dogma of the "Immaculate Conception," which was still an open question in the 1560s, when the creed was enacted by the Council of Trent and by papal bull of confirmation.[53] However, Maturin's submission to Rome through the *ordo ad reconciliandum*, instead of Pope Pius IV's creed, required him to pledge himself "to the acceptance of all doctrines which had

---

[52] Cramp, *Scripture and Tradition*, 39.

[53] Elsewhere, in Cramp, *A Text-Book of Popery*, 436, he states: "On January 26, 1564, Pius IV published the bull of confirmation, commanding all the faithful to receive and inviolably observe the decrees of the council.... If any doubt or difficulty existed, recourse was to be had to the 'place which the Lord had chosen,'— the apostolic see. A congregation of cardinals was appointed to regulate and announce the legitimate meaning of the decrees. It still continues, and meets usually twice in every month."

been or should be, declared divine by the Roman Pontiffs, comprising Pope Pius's Creed, and something more." For Cramp, the rule of Vincentius to maintain "*what has been believed everywhere, always. And by all*" was completely useless as presented by Maturin. Without the discernment of church history, later pontiffs, no matter how corrupted and misinformed historically, could declare certain doctrines to be apostolic without any foundation whatsoever in primitive Christianity.[54]

For whatever reason, Maturin did not respond directly to Cramp's charge of "cunning contrivance." Maturin's *A Defence of the Claims of the Catholic Church* simply does not address Cramp's charge that the older *ordo ad reconciliandum* was more restricting than the creeds issued at the Council of Trent. Yet later, in 1861, when he had again returned to the Church of England, Maturin makes a passing reference to his earlier reception into the Roman Catholic Church. It comes when Maturin considers the Creed of Pope Pius IV: "This Creed was published by the highest Ecclesiastical authority as the profession of faith of the Roman Catholic Church at the period of the Reformation, *and though it was not proposed to myself at the time of my admission into that communion*, yet it is universally received as containing the most authentic summary of the distinguishing doctrines of Romanism."[55] By 1861, then, Maturin had come himself to see the folly of applying the rule of St. Vincentius to any church without the honest application of church history. By this point, Maturin reinterpreted

---

[54] Cramp elaborated further on the problem of declaring apostolic doctrines not found in the Bible in "Christianity and Popery: Letter III," *Christian Messenger* 5/6 (February 8, 1860): 41. "The faithful might hold different views on the subject, without incurring censure. But the case is now altered. The present pontiff has placed an additional article in the Creed. Ever since the 8th of December 1857, it has been the duty of every Roman Catholic to profess his belief in the 'Immaculate Conception.' Here is a further development. Who can tell how many are yet to come? When will Christianity be perfect? How is it that the Apostles were so ignorant on this subject, and that even the much-vaunted Tradition failed to give clear utterances till the nineteenth century?"

[55] Maturin, *Infallibility of the Church*, 41. Cramp is not cited by Maturin in this latter work, but it seems hardly coincidental that Pope Pius's creed was part of Cramp's critique of Maturin's *Claims of the Catholic Church*. Cramp not only referenced Pope Pius's creed when critiquing Maturin's reception into the Roman Catholic Church, but also for subjecting the Scriptures to the authority of the Church rather than vice versa. Italics mine.

Vincentius's rule according to the logic of the Reformation and the communion of his ordination. When novel contagions attempt to infect the church, the saints are called to keep close to *antiquity*: "This was the remedy proposed by St. Vincentius—not an adherence to the Pope or the existing church of Rome, but an appeal from the present Church to primitive antiquity, and on this principle that Church of England has acted in her own Reformation."[56] Insofar as the church universal was called to reform herself by scrutinizing doctrine and practice according to the authority of the primitive church as found in Scripture, Cramp would agree.

Maturin's Double Conversion and the Reformation Precedent

By the fall of 1861,[57] through "experience, study, reflection, and prayer; and after a long and painful mental conflict," Maturin abandoned his Catholicism, made a public recantation at St. Paul's, and was received back into the Anglican Church, though not exercising his office as prior to leaving.[58] Maturin's double conversion was hardly unique even during the Reformation period. In fact, flip-flopping between Rome and Protestantism and vice versa is part of the historiography of the Reformation itself. Jerome Bolsec, to highlight but one better known case from sixteenth-century Europe, was one such double convert. Bolsec began as a Carmelite friar, then joined the Reformation in Geneva, only to recant again and reestablish his reputation as a solid Catholic intellectual by publishing

---

[56] Maturin, *Infallibility of the Church*, 43.

[57] Once restored to the Anglican Church, he was able to look back as a double convert and lay out the circumstances that led to the publication of the controversial work that caused all the stir: Edmund Maturin, *Infallibility of the Church*, 9, writes, "I was received into the communion of the Church of Rome. At the same time I wrote a Pamphlet, stating the reasons which induced me to take this step, in the form of a Letter to the Parishioners of St. Paul's, under the title of 'The Claims of the Catholic Church.' This was chiefly written in London, before I had actually joined the Church of Rome, and after having laid it aside for a time, I was persuaded to publish it shortly after my return to Halifax, under the impression that the reasons which had convinced my own mind would prove convincing to the minds of others. This pamphlet produced several replies from members of different Protestant denominations, in answer to which I published another and more extended work, in defence of the principles contained in the former essay."

[58] Maturin, *Infallibility of the Church*, 5.

Lives of John Calvin in 1577 and Theodore Beza in 1582.[59] More familiar in an English Protestant context was the example of William Chillingworth (1602–1644), William Laud's godson, who converted to Rome in 1628 largely because of his attraction to the idea of an infallible church. In 1630, he went to the college of Douay, where he was encouraged by Jesuits to put into writing the reasons for his conversion. Whether it was his "brief experience of Continental Catholic authoritarianism" or the rigors of deeper study of the issues, he left Douay in 1631 and returned to Oxford, and, with time, to the Church of England.[60] Chillingworth's most famous book, *The Religion of Protestants*, published at Oxford in 1638, had the added bonus of authorship by one who "having with greatest equality and indifferency, made enquiry and search into the grounds of both sides."[61]

Chillingworth became a champion for the Protestant doctrine of *sola scriptura* over and against Roman Catholic arguments for papal and ecclesial infallibility with his famous dictum "THE BIBLE, THE BIBLE ONLY, IS THE RELIGION OF PROTESTANTS." While Cramp saw Chillingworth's famous epigram as a rallying point, unfortunately many Protestants and their evangelical descendants have often quoted it without understanding that Chillingworth himself believed reason had an important role in interpreting Scripture.[62]

---

[59] "Introduction: Remembering the Reformation," in *Remembering the Reformation*, eds. Brain Cummings, Ceri Law, Karis Riley, and Alexandra Walsham (London and New York: Routledge Taylor & Francis Group, 2020), 3.

[60] The quotation comes from Michael Brydon, *The Evolving Reputation of Richard Hooker: An Examination of Responses 1600–1714* (Oxford: Oxford University Press, 2006), 53–54, who shows Chillingworth was influenced by Richard Hooker's teaching on reason.

[61] William Chillingworth, "The Epistle Dedicatory," in *The Religion of Protestants: A Safe Way to Salvation or an Answer to a Booke Entitled Mercy and Truth or Charity maintained by Catholiques*, 2nd ed. (London: Printed for John Clarke, 1638).

[62] Despite this fact, J. S. Whale (*The Protestant Tradition: An Essay in Interpretation* [Cambridge: Cambridge University Press, 1955], 129), aware of the biblical fundamentalism of his own day, rightly asserted: "Certainly neither Luther nor Calvin would have endorsed this easy generalization just as it stands. Too far from the truth to be a good epigram, and too near it to be a clever caricature, it is a misstatement as crude as it is dull." More recently, Nicholas Tyacke, *Aspects of English Protestantism c. 1530–1700* (Manchester: Manchester University Press,

The memory of conversion stories and their polemical use between Protestants and Catholics alike is relevant to the Maturin conversion controversy since both Maturin and Cramp were aware of such historiography and made use of it in their arguments against one another. Moreover, both Chillingworth's conversions and dictum are relevant to our discussion since both men quote from him in their literary discourse with one another. Long before Cramp took up his pen against Maturin, the preface to his second edition to *A Textbook of Popery* (1839) ended with the following assertion:

> All men ought to know what Popery is, and how it became what it is, and to be put on their guard against its mischievous tendencies. More especially is it needful to explain and enforce Chillingworth's celebrated saying—(now, alas! Forgotten by some, and impugned by others)—THE BIBLE, THE BIBLE ONLY, IS THE RELIGION OF PROTESTANTS. This is the rallying point—may it never be forsaken![63]

Not surprisingly, as a Catholic, Maturin's perspective on the English Reformation challenged the central Protestant assumptions concerning the authority of Scripture. He also rejected any interpretations of church history that assumed the gradual corruption of apostolic teachings over

---

2001), 280–81, has rightly emphasized that *The Religion of Protestants*, as part of a drawn-out Protestant-Catholic exchange, gives reason an important role in interpreting scripture. Hence, the importance of Richard Hooker as an influence on Chillingworth has not been widely appreciated.

[63] John Mockett Cramp, "Preface to the Second Edition," in *A Text-Book of Popery: Comprising a Brief History of the Council of Trent, and a Complete View of Roman Catholic Theology*, 3rd ed. (London: Houlston and Stoneman, Paternoster Row, 1851), viii. Cramp's use of the term "popery" is deeply offensive to our modern ecumenical sensibilities. Yet his use of the word was much more than simply anti-papal, or even anti-Roman Catholic per se; he clearly thought the Church of Rome had been corrupted by medieval innovations. "Popery," for Cramp, was a perversion of biblical doctrine that was by no means limited to the Church of Rome; rather, it was a more pervasive concept that referred to any kind of theological, liturgical, or pastoral "enemies to scriptural truths and godliness." While Cramp clearly had a polemical side to his theology that was characterized by a nineteenth-century Protestant self-understanding and the lens through which he perceived the arguments, his writings also reveal some deeply pastoral components.

time. Maturin challenged the typical Protestant interpretation of church history which assumed a gradual departure from the apostolic faith through

> the accumulation of errors and corruptions which were gradually introduced into the Church, in addition to the Primitive Faith, sanctioned by the authority of Popes and Councils and received by professing Christians during the "dark ages," when all the world was in a state of universal ignorance. I need not stop to show that all this is a *mere fiction*, invented to account for a supposed difficulty, and that it derives no support whatever from historical evidence. But it may be replied, that we have nothing to do with history—our business is with the Bible—and the strongest proofs of the corruptions of the Catholic Church consist in the manifest *opposition* between *its doctrines* and *those of the Bible*. In the language of Chillingworth, which is re-echoed from every Protestant pulpit and platform, "The Bible, and the Bible only, is the religion of Protestants," and by this test alone every point in religious controversy is to be tried and determined. Now, it is evident that there are two important principles involved in this appeal—the one, that the Bible is the *only rule of faith*; and the other, that every one has a right to interpret the Bible *according to his own sense*. [64]

Clearly, Maturin rejects the Protestant rallying point so ardently celebrated and defended by Cramp and others likeminded. Hence, in his critique of Maturin's theory of faith and obedience as presented in *Claims of the Catholic Church*, Cramp quotes Chillingworth's dictum to assert that the Bible has authority over all other authorities, including church tradition. Cramp follows the Chillingworth dictum with a quotation from the sixth article of the Church of England's Thirty-Nine Articles on the sufficiency of Scripture: "Holy Scripture containeth all things necessary to salvation; so that whatever is not read therein, nor may be proved thereby, is not to be required of any man, that it should be believed as an article of Faith, or be thought requisite or necessary to salvation."[65]

As a prolific Baptist scholar and leader, it is not surprising that Cramp drew also upon his own denominational heritage when countering Maturin's view of tradition. As a British-born, -raised, and -trained

---

[64] Maturin, *Claims of the Catholic Church*, 43–44.
[65] Cramp, *Scripture and Tradition*, 13.

Baptist scholar and pastor, Cramp brought this vantage point into the Canadian, and then, more specifically, the Nova Scotian nineteenth-century context. With a quotation from the Thirty-nine Articles in support of the authority of Scripture, Cramp showed his support for the Church of England insofar as it was part of the larger Protestant movement, at least according to some.[66] Cramp also offers a lengthy quotation from chapter one of the English Baptist Confession of Faith of 1689 in support of Scripture as the supreme, infallible rule of interpretation and authority for the church.[67] Further, Cramp, held to the Protestant principle of holy Scripture in the vernacular. It was a crime against God and the people to keep Scripture guarded among the ecclesiastical elite. "Every one who searches the Scriptures with prayer," writes Cramp, "may expect the blessing, and feel assured that in the promises are not to be set aside by the establishment of an earthly tribunal, which indeed would practically render them useless; for why need I search and pray, if there is a judge at hand from whom I am to receive the law, and to whose dictates I must bow? Of such an appointment, and such a judge, I find no mention in Holy Writ."[68] With time, Maturin would himself come to agree with Cramp's approach, though not before leaving the Roman Catholic Church. After his second conversion, Maturin, like Chillingworth before him, saw himself in a better position to defend the church of his ordination, and Protestantism, in general, from Catholic arguments.

Conclusion

By 1861, Maturin dismantled his earlier views and explained his conversions. With "deep contrition and humiliation," he confessed "that he was

---

[66] It might be noted here that Anglicans associated with the Oxford movement tended to downplay the Church of England's affinity with Reformation orthodoxy.

[67] The 1689 Confession is more commonly known today as "the Second London Baptist Confession." For more on the influence and reception of the Second London Confession, see William H. Brackney, *A Genetic History of Baptist Thought: With Special Reference to Baptists in Britain and North America* (Macon, GA: Mercer University Press, 2004), 32–36. Brackney also reminds us that the first edition of the Second London Confession came in 1677 and was modified slightly eleven years later at the First General Assembly (1688/1689).

[68] Cramp, *Scripture and Tradition*, 17.

once deceived by the seductive claims" of the church of Rome.[69] This "confession" is presented by Maturin in the third person, where out of a sense of "duty" he explained the reason for his deception:

> He joined the communion of the Church of Rome, which he believed to be the "One, Holy, Catholic, and Apostolic Church" of Christ; and in consequence of this act, he felt himself under the necessity of separating from the communion with the Church of England, to which he had been strongly attached by early education and religious association, and especially by the sacred office of the Ministry, in which he had been happily engaged for many years. Since that time, he has had ample opportunities for further experience, study, reflection, and prayer; and after a long and painful mental conflict, he is compelled to acknowledge that the whole theory of Church infallibility, as it is now held by the Church of Rome, is a mere delusion of human invention, and especially so, as it is made the foundation of the most dangerous corruptions of the Gospel of Christ in doctrine and in practice.[70]

In part, both the "study" and "reflection" to which Maturin refer were pushed on him by the publicized nature of his conversion to Rome and the vigorous campaign in newspapers and pamphlets as well as on platforms against his actions and his defence of Catholicism.[71] The aforementioned conflict between Howe and the Irish Roman Catholics in Nova Scotia undoubtedly formed the backdrop for political tensions. as MacKinnon highlights,[72] however, so did theological and historical debates. The public response to Maturin's conversion demonstrates that theology and church history were every bit as important as politics, as each area of study was a factor in winning souls to what was perceived as good and sound doctrine. As we have shown above, Cramp used his knowledge of the Council of Trent and the Reformation to challenge Maturin's assertions in favour of

---

[69] Maturin, *Infallibility of the Church*, 5.

[70] Ibid.

[71] Neil MacKinnon, "Maturin, Edmund," in *Dictionary of Canadian Biography*, vol. 12, University of Toronto/Université Laval, 2003–, accessed September 13, 2021, http://www.biographi.ca/en/bio/maturin_edmund_12E.html.

[72] MacKinnon, in "Maturin, Edmund," writes: "The ensuing conflict degenerated into an ugly little religious war between Howe's Protestant supporters and the Irish Catholic population."

Keeping Maturin Honest

the infallibility of the Catholic Church. In so far as these arguments may have had an impact on Maturin's return to the Church of England and were relevant to the ecclesial debates between Catholic and Protestants of the nineteenth century, Cramp's role in the controversy is important and hithertofore underappreciated.

As the editor of the *Christian Messenger*, Cramp often wrote historical pieces for the magazine along with letters to the editor under a variety of pseudonyms. Cramp's letters for January 11 and 25, 1860, each appeared under the title "Christianity and Popery." Cramp used the alias "Tyndale" for both letters and again assumed Chillingworth's celebrated maxim as his foundational starting point. A meeting was held on January 8, 1860, at St. Mary's Chapel, Halifax, "to give expressions of sympathy with the Pope in his present troubles."[73] Maturin is listed as one of five people to deliver speeches. A postscript appearing at the end of a letter to the editor dated January 25, 1860, makes it crystal clear that Cramp, even after his published *Reply* to Maturin's *Claims of the Catholic Church*, saw it as his duty to keep Maturin honest when presenting arguments from church history:

> P.S.—Jan 13.—I have just read an account of the meeting in the Roman Catholic Cathedral, Halifax, speech which is characterized as "one of his most eloquence and happiest efforts." I do not doubt the eloquence, but I demur greatly to the historical accuracy. The most laughable part of the speech is the statement that the sovereignty of the Pope has been held "in rectilinear and unbroken succession for eleven hundred years." It's all moonshine, my dear Sir, as every one who is tolerably acquainted with history knows.
>
> Mr. Maturin, I see, endeavoured at the same meeting to whitewash the Papacy by disclaiming the Pope's right to interfere in the political affairs of the nation, which view of Papal power he says, "was never laid down as an article in the Catholic Church."[74]
>
> The advocates of Roman Catholicism are on an entire equality with ourselves, as they ought to be, and may speak or write as they please. I would advise them to be particularly careful about facts, for "there's a chiel amang them taking notes."[75]

---

[73] *Christian Messenger* (January 18, 1860): 18.

[74] "Christianity and Popery: Letter II," *Christian Messenger*, 5/4 (January 25, 1860): 25.

[75] Ibid.

This latter quotation, itself a loose paraphrase from Robert Burns's famous poem from 1789, "On the Late Captain Grose's Peregrinations thro' Scotland," serves idiomatically to sum up how Cramp understood the church historian's role. In the case of Cramp's *Reply*, the unscriptural and unhistorical claims of Maturin must be scrutinized by the church historian if such claims are to be proved both apostolic and honest.

Marking Life's Experiences:
The Poems of Frances Cramp Muir (1830–1892)

Karen E. Smith

For many years, the stories of women did not figure prominently in the annals of Baptist history. Though women have, for the most part, outnumbered men within local congregations, from their seventeenth-century beginnings and for many years thereafter, men, rather than women, occupied roles of leadership. Given the fact that Baptist history has been presented mainly as institutional history or the development of denominational and congregational life and the respective leaders, the stories of men have primarily been those which have been chronicled.

Over the past thirty years, there has been a growing emphasis on discovering alternative sources and uncovering the stories of Baptist women. In a search for sources, there has been a renewed interest in exploring devotional texts, hymns, poems, prayers, sermon diaries, deathbed testimonies, obituaries, and memoirs which offer insight into what has been described as "lived religion." These sources are particularly important since, until the twentieth century, many Baptist women were not given the opportunity to participate in the "public sphere" of religious life, though their faith and witness was dynamic and influential.

The subject of this essay, Frances Cramp Muir—a daughter of Anne (Burls) Cramp and the well-known Baptist leader and author John Mockett Cramp—is a case in point. While much attention has been given to the life and work of her father as an author, preacher, and past president of Acadia University, her life story and faith—like that of so many women—has not been told. Yet an examination of a memoir of her life and a collection of her poetry reveals that she was, in fact, a person who reflected deeply on matters of faith and should be remembered for her own contribution to her family as well as to the church and its mission.

In many ways, Frances's life was no different from many others living in the late nineteenth century. She was not a great theologian or even a profound poet. Hence, the choice to write on her life as a way of honouring the memory of Roger Prentice may seem a strange one. Yet I think Roger would have approved. As someone who loved the Church and was always supportive and encouraging of women serving within it, I think he would have admired her abiding love for the Church and its work. Likewise, as one who was keenly interested in finding ways of creatively expressing the truths of Christian faith and who even wrote hymns for special occasions, I think he would have appreciated the hymns Frances penned for her church.

More than twenty years ago, I was invited to give a lecture at Acadia Divinity School. On that occasion, my chosen subject was the Baptist College at Montreal, 1836–1849, which, of course, was the college where John Mockett Cramp was president from 1844 until it closed in 1849.[1] The occasion of giving the lecture was a happy one for me and my husband, as it was the first time we had been able to see Roger since we had all been students together at Regent's Park College, Oxford. After we returned home, I received from Roger a photocopy of a transcript of the diary of John Mockett Cramp. In writing this essay, I am pleased that after all these years, I have had the opportunity to turn to that diary material, albeit to reflect on it from the perspective of the early life of his daughter, Frances. I have also looked at a collection of her poetry which was put together by her son, John, after her death. While most of these poems were not written for publication, it is evident that poetry was one medium through which she expressed her faith. More broadly, an exploration of her life provides insight into the life and faith of a nineteenth-century Canadian Baptist woman.

Early Years and the Influence of Parents

Frances Cramp was born in England at St. Peter's, Isle of Thanet, on January 12, 1830. Her birth was noted in her father's diary with these words: "My dear wife was safely delivered of a daughter since named, Fanny."[2] Frances, or Fanny, as she was called by friends and family, was the second child born to Anne and John. Eventually, the family would include ten

---

[1] The lecture was published as "The Baptist College at Montreal, 1836–1849: The British Baptist Connexion, with special reference to the contribution of the Baptist Missionary Society," *The Baptist Quarterly* 4 (October 2006): 455–80.

[2] Photocopy of the journal of John Mockett Cramp (1819–1876), with a note added in 1867 by J. M. C. indicating that he had "revised and some portions expunged or cut out," 40.

children, though one child, Maria (1823–1890), was the daughter of Cramp and his first wife, Maria (Agate), who died in childbirth in 1823.[3]

Frances's upbringing was very much within a Baptist context. Not only were her grandfather and father Baptist ministers, but her maternal grandparents, William (d. 1837) and Mary Burls (d. 1849), were members of the Carter Lane Church in Southwark, where John Rippon served as pastor for many years. William Burls served as a deacon in the church and he was also for many years the London treasurer for the Baptist Missionary Society.[4]

Until 1840 when they moved to Hastings, Frances lived with her family at St Peter's, Isle of Thanet, where her grandfather served as pastor of a Baptist church and her father, John, assisted him. After four years in Hastings, the family left England to go to Montreal when John Mockett Cramp was invited to be the president of the Montreal Baptist College.[5] From there he would move to Wolfville in 1851 in order to become the president of Acadia University.

Growing up in this Baptist home, Frances and her siblings were taught that daily prayer and the reading of Scripture, concern for missions and evangelism, and fellowship within a local church were important. Frances's mother, Anne, was described as a quiet Christian with a faithful

---

[3] Anne Burls (1794–1862) was the second wife of J. M. Cramp. They married in 1826. His first wife, Maria (Agate), died in 1822. See T. A. Higgins, *The Life of John Mockett Cramp, D.D., 1796–1881* (Montreal, QC: W. Drysdale, 1887), 24 and 42. In 1862, when Anne (Burls) died, only five children and her stepdaughter, Maria, had survived to adulthood. These were reported as Thomas, a merchant in Montreal; George, a lawyer in Montreal; Frances, married to G. B. Muir; Eliza, married to T. A. Higgins, Baptist minister; and Mary Ann, who lived with her father. His daughter Maria, by his first wife, married Stephen Seldon, the editor of *Christian Messenger*. See "John M. Cramp," *The Canadian Biographical Dictionary and Portrait Gallery of Eminent and Self-made Men, Quebec and Maritime Provinces* (Chicago, New York, and Toronto: American Biographical Publishing Company, 1881), 496–97. For a more recent biography, see Barry M. Moody, "Cramp, John Mockett," in *Dictionary of Canadian Biography*, vol. 11, University of Toronto/Université Laval, 2003–, accessed August 16, 2022, http://www.biographi.ca/en/bio/cramp_john_mockett_11E.html.

[4] See J. M. Cramp, *A Portraiture from Life by a Bereaved Husband* (Halifax, NS: Christian Messenger Office, 1862), 3.

[5] Higgins, *The Life of John Mockett Cramp*, 83.

witness and a love for the Word. Although she had attended church with her parents, Frances later claimed that she had come to a new consideration of personal faith after hearing Andrew Fuller preach in his church in Kettering. On returning home, in 1812, she was baptized and became a member of the Carter Lane Church.[6]

Describing his wife's personal faith, Cramp claimed that Anne always kept a regular time of devotion, and she kept the Bible "near her at all times," studied it daily, and had committed so many passage to memory that "apt quotations were always at command for direction, consolation or warning."[7] Cramp himself, of course, had a lasting influence on his family. Hence, as it was put later, Frances was brought up in "an atmosphere of Christian culture, and her earliest associations were with the church of Jesus Christ."[8]

Frances recalled and appreciatively described her schooling in such a "Christian culture" in a poem which she wrote on her father's death in 1882. Here she vividly remembers a childhood scene of her father leading the family in singing a hymn, and then on his deathbed leading the family in song.

> Our distant birth-place far across the main,
> The house all ivy-crowned is seen again;
> Within 'tis evening, and the hour of prayer,
> The day of rest is near; a gentle air
> Comes through the open casement soft and sweet.
> As all sing, " Safely through another week";
> Our Father's clear, strong voice uplifts the song,
> A gentle treble leads the children on;
> Ah well remembered hour, and dear old tune,
> Ah happy band to be far scattered soon!
> Father above! when Time's long week is o'er.
> And, one by one, we near the unknown shore,
> May *that* day be, of all the week the best,
> Its dawn the emblem of eternal rest.

---

[6] For an account of Anne's conversion, see J. M. Cramp, *A Portraiture from Life*, 4.

[7] Ibid., 7.

[8] A. G. Upham, "Funeral Address," in John M. C. Muir, *In Affectionate Remembrance of Frances Cramp* (Montreal, QC: Morton Philips & Co., 1892), 5.

Marking Life's Experiences

The years sped on, and in their varied round.
How much of earnest faithful work was found,
In College hall, or from the preacher's desk,
Serving the master with unwearied zest;
His voice and pen maintained the truth and right,
Denouncing error with unsparing might.
Still pressing forward on life's busy way—
As one whose purpose brooked with no delay.

Dear Father! all too soon. Time's silver thread,
With unseen fingers, wove upon his head
A snowy crown! and yet, those precious years,
That tranquil resting place; through misty tears,
We see the children climb their grandsire's knee,
He, giving welcome to their noisy glee.
We look again, the little ones are gone,
And youth is by his side so fair and strong.
Ah loving group! you join with us to-day
A tender tribute to his name to pay;
So, when in coming years, you take our place,
Be yours his heritage of faith and grace.

When the last summons came, all undismayed
He met the thrilling dash of Jordan's wave;
And, as in life, to sing and pray was sweet—
So, at its close one theme would oft repeat,
And said, though full of weariness and pain,
We'll sing, "All hail the power of Jesus' name."
The loving watcher by his dying bed
Essayed the words, repeating them instead,
But he, with feeble voice, took up the strain,
And in clear accents sang the last refrain:

"Oh that with yonder sacred throng
We at his feet may fall.
Join in the everlasting song.
And crown him Lord of all."

When passing through the valley's gloomy shade
In feebleness extreme, he longed for aid.

KEEPING THE FAITH

How precious were his words, "'Tis time for prayer,"
Faith clasped his hands that last request to share;
Then for himself and those he held so dear,
The church of Christ, its laborers far and near.
All were commended to that Heavenly Friend
Whose changeless love supported to the end.

Beloved Father, laid in dreamless sleep,
How beautiful his look of perfect peace!
The weight of years seemed lifted from the brow.
As though Heaven's rapture soothed his spirit now.
And though with aching hearts we know the door
Closed softly, whence he can return no more—
Let us remember, he is laid to rest
Beside the grave of her who loved him best;
There, hushed and still, only the passing breeze
Whispers melodious through the willow trees;
But all beyond there lies a glorious scene,
The distant water, with sweet fields between,
While far above, the cloud-wreaths come and go.
Resting in shadow on the vale below.

God of all comfort! take us by the hand.
Life wearies us, nor do we understand
Earth's sad farewells, its restlessness and pain,
Hopes fondly cherished, then deferred again.
A little while, and near the shining strand,
Our tired feet perchance may faltering stand;
Then, may the hallowed memories of to-day,
The joy of meeting, cheer the gloomy way—
And the same precious faith to us be given,
Leaning on which our Parents entered Heaven.[9]

---

[9] Frances C. Muir, "In Memorium. J. M. Cramp D.D.," written on May 31st, 1882, in John M. C. Muir, *Frances Cramp*, 39–42.

Marking Life's Experiences

Church and Family Life

Since church life had always been at the heart of Frances's family life as she was growing up, not surprizingly, this pattern continued after her marriage to George B. Muir in 1850. George Muir was the son of Ebenezer and Jean Muir, who had come to Montreal from Scotland in 1820. In Scotland, the Muirs had been in membership of the Kilwinnings Baptist Church. Forced to leave Scotland for Montreal in an effort to find work, once there, the family rose to prominence and eventually used their wealth to support Baptist as well as other religious and philanthropic causes.[10]

George and Frances—like their parents before them—were staunch Baptists and became founding members of the Olivet Baptist Church in Montreal. For the opening service, on March 25th, 1879, Frances wrote a hymn of dedication which ended with a prayer that their children would one day sing praise to God in this place of prayer.

God of our fathers! grateful hearts
Are met within these courts to-day,
Now, may Thy glory fill the house,
Make this Thy dwelling-place alway.

Here may the Gospel, full and free.
Proclaimed and taught, the people bless ;
The theme unchanged, yet ever new,
Jesus, "The Lord our Righteousness."

Here, may the Spirit's mighty power,
Descending as in days of old,
Arouse the lost in sin and death.
Bring back the wanderer to the fold.

"The Olivet," a name endeared.
Enshrined in hope, baptized in love.
Hallowed by precious seasons spent
In converse sweet, with Christ above.

---

[10] Patricia Roome, "Henrietta Muir Edwards: The Journey of a Canadian Feminist" (MA dissertation, University of Calgary, 1975, and PhD, Simon Fraser University, 1996), 30.

KEEPING THE FAITH

God of our fathers! when these lips,
Filling Thy courts with praise to-day.
Are hushed and still and others meet
In worship here, to sing and pray:

Then may our children rise and clasp
The sundered links Thy hand has riven,
And join with us to name this place
The house of prayer, the gate of Heaven.[11]

The name given to the church was also the focus of another poem, entitled "The Mount of Olivet." Reflecting on the scriptural scene of Jesus at the place called Olivet, Frances expresses in a simple way the idea that the church should be evangelistic and, as she put it, stand both as a "memorial" to Christ and as a witness to the message of the cross.

A hallowed spot this mount of old,
  When, after breaking bread,
"They sang an hymn," and going forth,
  To "Olivet" were led;
A weary band and full of grief,
  The parting hour so near;
But Christ the Comforter, e'en then.
  Spoke words of hope and cheer.

Gethsemane was just below,
  Near Kedron's gentle brook.
Where those disciples in great fear,
  Their Master all forsook:
Yet resting on the mount awhile,
  And passing o'er the plain.
He gives them promise of a time.
  When He shall come again.

Another scene has Olivet,

---

[11] France C. Muir, "Dedication Hymn," March 25, 1879, in John M. C. Muir, *Frances Cramp*, 21.

Marking Life's Experiences

When Christ the ascending King,
Stands on its summit, leaving earth
 On glad triumphant wing;
And His own followers looking up.
 Where the bright clouds were riven,
Beheld their Master, entering thus,
 As He shall come from Heaven.

And so the name of Olivet,
 Christ's people now may take.
Memorial of His earthly life,
 Precious, for Jesus sake;
Take it, and rear a house of God,
 Where, listening as of old,
The same sweet story of the cross,
 To numbers shall be told.[12]

John Mockett Cramp's continuing guidance and influence on Frances in matters regarding the Christian faith may be seen in letters that he wrote to her. Often including theological reflections on Scripture—even offering outlines of his sermons—Cramp gave his advice and counsel to her.[13] Interestingly, in 1879, when the Olivet church was seeking a new minister, he wrote to his daughter offering strongly worded advice about seeking a new pastor:

> The stealing of ministers from churches is a common offence; but it *is* an offence, and sometimes is followed by punishment. So do not steal. Do not tempt a man to come to Olivet, who is not otherwise known to be desiring a change. If *sheep*-stealers are condemned, surely shepherd-stealers cannot be innocent. Therefore let the Olivet Church be careful. Do not seek the *great*, the *flashy* or the *odd*; be content with the *good*, the *sound* and the *active*—more especially if the man of your choice not only works for the church

---

[12] Frances C. Muir, "The Mount Called Olivet," n.d., in John M. C. Muir, *Frances Cramp*, 24–25.

[13] Higgins, *John Mockett Cramp*, 348–55.

KEEPING THE FAITH

but keeps the church in action. For the great fault of many of our churches is that the members are not personally active.[14]

It is not known to whom Cramp might have been referring when he spoke of taking care to avoid the "great," the "flashy," or the "odd." However, the next year at a welcome service for their new pastor, William Newton Clarke (1841–1912), Frances wrote a poem which seemed to place emphasis on pastor and people working together and actively seeking to reach out to others with the Gospel message.

> Our pastor, welcome! you have left
>   Friends by long years endeared,
> Welcome again and let us prove
>   Our trust as true as theirs.
> If 'neath these skies a stranger flag
>   Seems emblem of your loss,
> Above us all floats braver yet
>   The banner of the Cross!
>
> Our Olivet, in earnest prayer,
>   Has waited for this hour;
> God bless our union, make it strong.
>   With His own mighty power.
> Pastor and people now go forth
>   To sow the precious grain.
> So coming years, in waving corn,
>   Shall welcome you again.
>
> In ages past a voice was heard
>   Which cried "Prepare the way,"
> The heavenly kingdom is at hand,
>   The true light dawns to-day,
> Thus when you preach "Behold the Lamb!"
>   May every heart be stirred.
> And close behind his servant's feet
>   The Master's step be heard.

---

[14] "Letter from John Mockett Cramp to Frances Muir," December 1879, in Higgins, *John Mockett Cramp*, 354.

Marking Life's Experiences

We bid you welcome to our land—
  This young Dominion—where
Strong men and true must strive and delve,
  The nation to uprear.
May numbers who now bear the yoke
  Of priestly power and sway,
Break their hard fetters and unite
  Our Saviour to obey.

And welcome, Pastor, to our homes,
  Always an honored guest,
To share the joys which heaven bestows,
  Welcome when life is blest;
And then when clouds in darkening gloom
  Obscure the toilsome way.
When death draws near, ah! welcome then
  With us to watch and pray.

The wintry months have come and gone,
  Our Church, in joy and pain.
Together, as true brethren should.
  Have mingled both again;
The shock of corn so full and ripe.
  We've laid to quiet rest.
And wept above the tender lamb
  Folded to Jesus' breast.

But spring returns, these ice-bound shores
  Break from their frosty chain.
The great St. Lawrence dashes on
  Unfettered to the main;
With it a brother well beloved
  We welcome back to-night,
And grateful for God's guardian care
  In hearty thanks unite.

No record long has Olivet
  Of the time-honored past,
But earnest, generous men have reared
  A monument to last
For future years; they well have borne

KEEPING THE FAITH

The burden of the day,
Now all will gladly follow where
Their leader marks the way.

Yet closer to our glorious Head
Onward, my brethren, press.
Buried with Him in Jordan's wave,
"The Lord our righteousness";
Till with the Saviour, from the Mount
Of Olivet we rise,
A ransomed throng, redeemed, prepared
For mansions in the skies,

God of our fathers! low we bend
In humble, grateful prayer.
Our Pastor and his loved ones leave
To Thy unchanging care;
Abide with us, control, illume
Thy Church with life and light,
Deign Lord, to consecrate and bless
The Union formed this night.[15]

Clarke only remained in Montreal for three years before moving to Hamilton, New York. He then became professor of theology at Colgate University (later known as Colgate-Rochester Theological Seminary). Later, Clarke became well known for his theological views, which were aligned with a movement that became known as "evangelical liberalism."[16] Refusing to accept the inerrancy of Scripture, he and other so-called "Andover liberals" stood opposed to the fundamentalist movement.[17] Even

---

[15] Frances C. Cramp, "Welcome," April 30, 1880, in John M. C. Muir, *Frances Cramp*, 29–31.

[16] Bernard H. Cochran, "Clarke, William Newton (1841–1912)," in *Encyclopedia of Religious Controversies in the United States*, eds. Bill J. Leonard and Jill Y. Crainshaw (Santa Barbara, CA: ABC-CLIO, 2013), 194.

[17] Harry Emerson Fosdick, who took courses with Clarke, claimed that he was "one of the most inspiring teachers I ever sat under" and said that had it not been for Clarke's influence, he would not have become a Christian minister. Cochran, "Fosdick, Harry Emerson," in *Encyclopedia of Religious Controversies*, 313.

Marking Life's Experiences

during his short time in Montreal, however, he and his wife forged a close relationship with Frances. Hearing of her death, he wrote to her son to express his sympathy to the family, saying,

> I wish I could fitly express, for Mrs. Clarke and myself, our sense of her great beauty of mind and character. Her wonderful delicacy of thought and feeling, her natural gracefulness of mind, her warm affectionateness of spirit, her fidelity to her friends, her patience and cheerfulness, her inward spirituality made their impression upon us long ago, and its impression has only been strengthened by acquaintance. As I think of her now, she seems to me one of the most beautiful human beings that I have ever known. You are happy in having had her so many years for the main element in your life, and you may have the satisfaction, now that she is parted from you, of knowing that you have always profoundly appreciated her.... It is a great loss to us to have so beautiful a spirit go out of the circle of friends whom we can reach. But she remains the same to us all, even while we cannot reach her.[18]

Significantly, in his autobiographical work *Sixty Years with the Bible, A Record of Experience*, Clarke claimed that his move to Montreal marked a period of change for him. He stated that he stopped preaching from a manuscript and found new freedom and "fresh enjoyment in the wealth of the Scriptures."[19] His theology began to change as well, and he claimed that if he were to "give it a name," he would call it "passing over from traditionalism to reality."[20]

When he first came to Olivet, Clarke admitted that he still struggled with the Pauline injunction that "women must keep silent in the church." However, he said that the women at the Olivet church convinced him that they were not governed by Paul, but were followers of Jesus. He wrote:

---

[18] An extract from a letter to Mr. George B. Muir from the Rev. W. N. Clarke, D.D., February 13, 1892, in Muir, *Frances Cramp*, 7.

[19] William Newton Clarke, *Sixty Years with the Bible: A Record of Experience* (New York: Scribner's and Sons, 1909), 126.

[20] Ibid., 129. For a wider discussion of his movement toward evangelical liberalism, see Gary Dorrien, *The Making of American Liberal Theology: Idealism, Realism and Modernity, 1900–1950* (Louisville, KY: Westminster John Knox Press), 2003.

The women were taking part in the meetings of the church, as many of them as wished to do so, with perfect freedom. They knew all the arguments for reading Paul's prohibition as local and temporary, at least the Corinthian one, and so had no fear that they were sinning against the Scriptures. But the real reason of their freedom was that in this matter they were not governed by Paul any more. Some had fine gifts for speaking and something to say, and would have found some way to speak their minds if Paul himself had been there with all the weapons that he was supposed to carry. A few years of such freedom lifted it from me. They were acting out their real life from the heart, and the ancient hand was off from them.[21]

While Clarke does not mention her by name in his autobiography, it is notable that Frances was part of the group of active women at Olivet at the time, and she obviously thought deeply about matters of faith. Several of the poems in the memorial volume were prompted by reflections on sermons and reveal her active and theologically enquiring mind. An example of her poetic reflection may be found, for instance, in a poem which was written after hearing a sermon based on the text "Where Is God My Maker Who Giveth Songs in the Night" (Job 10:10).

> Life hath its rough and lonely ways,
>   When, in the deepening gloom,
> The sunny earth is darkened o'er
>   With shadows from the tomb:
> Then through the ages soft and clear,
>   With solemn sweet refrain,
> These "songs of night" in tender tones,
>   Refresh our hearts again.
>
> "Deep calleth unto deep," says one,
>   "Thy waves and billows all"
> Go over my defenceless head.
>   While angry waters call;
> Yet, in the day time God will still
>   His loving kindness show,
> And in the night His song shall cheer

---

[21] Clarke, *Sixty Years with the Bible*, 153.

Marking Life's Experiences

When hope and trust are low.

Behold! a dark and gloomy cell,
  Within whose inner wall.
Two of God's heroes wait and watch
  The twilight shadows fall:
  'Tis midnight now, they join in prayer.
  Then praise the God of light,
And through the prison, all may hear
  Their glorious "song of night."

Listen again, for later years
  Have heard another strain,
God's martyred saints, on distant hills
  Have sung midst smoke and flame,
Oh precious hope whose mighty power
  Puts doubt and fear to flight.
Death's darkest valley is illumed
  With these sweet songs of night.

But days of suffering come, and then,
  We dread the gloomy way,
And watch the Jordan from afar
  With shudder and dismay:
The waves seem high, they dash and break
  With never-ceasing roar,
While stormy surf with heavy mist.
  Hides Canaan's better shore.

Yet often as the waters rise,
  A heavenly form appears,
The billows firm beneath His tread,
  Awake no anxious fears;
Then "Death where is thy victory?"
  Triumphant song of night!
Beloved lips have caught the strain
  Departing from our sight.

In that fair land, the glorious home
  Where "many mansions" wait
The coming of God's hidden ones,

> Beyond the pearly gate—
> Where tears and weariness are changed,
>   To joy and perfect peace,
> There night is ended, but the songs
>   Of Heaven shall never cease.[22]

While this poem does not reveal original theological reflection, it does point to the fact that Frances was among the women in the church who felt free to reflect on biblical insights. Certainly, there can be no better description of her than one who was "acting out their real life from the heart."

Clarke was not the only minister to note Frances's support. In his address at her funeral, John Upham emphasized his own debt to her, saying that as a "pastor's daughter" she had been sensitive to the problems and difficulties that he sometimes faced. He had also valued her counsel, claiming,

> It was always a refreshment and an inspiration to visit her and to listen to her questions and suggestions concerning the Lord's work committed to our hands. I shall always count it as one of the greatest blessings of my life to have known Mrs. Muir.[23]

Frances and her husband, George, were active in the church. While he served as a deacon, Frances took part in the Women's Foreign Mission Circle and she was a strong supporter of the Grande Ligne Association, which had been founded by Henriette Odin Feller. Madame Feller, as she was known, came to Canada from Switzerland in 1835 after the death of her three-year-old child, followed, a few months later, by the death of her husband. She was a strong, independent, and evangelistic woman who felt called to establish work in Canada, and she came to be revered in many evangelistic circles for her sacrificial service. Frances's father, J. M. Cramp, had written a laudatory biography of Feller's life.[24] Hence, when the mission celebrated the jubilee of their founding in 1885, it is perhaps not

---

[22] Frances C. Muir, "Poem written after hearing a sermon by Professor Richards," February 15, 1880, in Muir, *Frances Cramp*, 22–23.

[23] A. G. Upham, "Funeral Address," in Muir, *Frances Cramp*, 6.

[24] J. M. Cramp, *Memoir of Madame Feller, with an account of the origin of the Grande Ligne Mission* (Montreal, QC: F. E. Grafton and W. Drysdale, 1876).

Marking Life's Experiences

surprizing that Frances wrote a poem in which she praised the evangelistic work that had been done.

> The years speed on, marked in their rapid flight
> By golden sunshine and the hush of night;
> But there are way-marks where the traveller rests,
> The air inspires, the retrospect is blest.
> 'Tis thus to-day, with tender, grateful hearts,
> We lift the curtain of the chequered past,
> And overlook, 'mid smiles and gentle tears,
> The lights and shadows of full fifty years.
>
> Through the long vista, a fair form is seen,
> A noble woman, of sweet, gracious mien.
> Who left her home, her lovely Switzerland,
> For the rough verdure of this northern strand;
> And with one friend, who like herself had given
> His life, his all, to Canada and heaven.
> Came to these shores, a thorny path to take.
> Bearing love's message for the Master's sake.
> Ah! we do well to honor those to-day
> Who toiled and labored on that troubled way.
> Man threatened oft, but God, Himself, drew near;
> The patient workers, strong in faith and cheer,
> Sowed the good seed, and day by day with prayer
> Watered and watched it with such tender care,
> That it took root and blossomed, till they told
> Of thirty, sixty, and a hundred fold.
>
> The little hut, our missionary's home.
> Has given place to stronger walls of stone.
> Rooms where the colporteur with quiet tread.
> Entered alone, and Holy Scriptures read,
> Are empty now, instead, the Churches stand
> Like hallowed sentinels about the land;
> Thousands of souls, some scattered far and wide,
> Have here confessed for them the Saviour died,
> While numbers stand around the great white throne,
> Washed and redeemed by precious blood alone;
> Let all rejoice, and a fresh altar raise,
> Brought "hitherto," to God be all the praise.

KEEPING THE FAITH

Dear, honoured labourers, gathered here to-day,
Bearing the burden of life's busy way,
You, who with loyal, faithful hearts have stood
And toiled so bravely for your country's good;
(Sometimes discouraged, for the foe is strong.
And superstition holds her captives long),
Yet, when with weariness and labour spent,
Has not a day of Pentecost been sent?
When faithful lips have owned Christ's power to save,
And you have seen the early, tender blade
Uprising here and there, take deeper root,
Giving fair promise of abundant fruit.
God spare the labourers long to speak His name.
And garner in rich sheaves of golden grain;
Some time the toil will end, the Master come.
And angels greet them with the glad "well done."

Yet once again, above our sainted dead.
Fresh wreaths of immortelles we fondly spread.
Let coming years to children's children tell
Of "Feller," "Roussy," names remembered well;
And we who meet, and meeting part to-day.
What hallowed memories may we take away!
Zion's sweet strains of gratitude and love
Have blended with the heavenly host above,
Afresh upon these consecrated walls,
Faith, hope, and love in benediction falls,
And all go forth, breathing one earnest prayer,
God bless the mission and His labourers here;
Showers of revival and rich increase
Crown this glad year of unity and peace,
May we all keep, through Jesus' mercy given.
The everlasting Jubilee of Heaven.[25]

---

[25] Frances C. Muir, "Grande Ligne Jubilee, 1885," in Muir, *Frances Cramp*, 43–45.

Marking Life's Experiences

Frances and the women in the Olivet church strongly supported Madame Feller's evangelistic work. No doubt Feller's independent spirit and determination to use her gifts for the cause of Christ set an example that many aspired to emulate in their own context.

Reflecting on the role of women at Olivet, it should be noted that in addition to Frances, other younger women members of the Muir family were evangelistic in spirit and very active in the Olivet church. Henrietta Muir—one of the women who later was part of "famous five" who legally challenged women's rights of eligibility for senate appointment in Canada—was the niece of George and Frances. She married Oliver Edwards (son of William and Anne Edwards, who were also wealthy Baptists) at Olivet Baptist Church in 1876.[26] Both Henrietta and her sister Amelia were active in the Olivet church, and they combined an aggressive feminism with a strong evangelical fervour for missions in order to open the Montreal Women's Printing Office in 1878, from which they began to print a monthly paper called *Women's Work in Canada*.[27]

While no copies of *Women's Work in Canada* appear to have survived, it is not known whether Amelia and Henrietta asked their aunt Frances to contribute to their paper. However, from the small surviving collection of her poems published by her son, it appears that she wrote for other evangelical publications, including *The Link* and *The Sower*. Moreover, since her half sister, Maria, was married to Stephen Seldon, the editor of the *Christian Messenger*, she may have published some of her poetry there, too. Of course, Frances's younger sister, Mary (1843?–1913), who lived with their father and cared for him until his death, was also a writer and supportive of Baptist mission work. In 1892, she published, *Retrospects: A History of the Formation and Progress of the Women's Missionary aid Societies of the Maritime Provinces*. Cramp's son-in-law T. A. Higgins, who compiled the biography of Cramp, noted Mary's assistance in deciphering her father's shorthand notes and also credits her with writing two of the chapters of that biography. Higgins was also responsible for encouraging the admission of women to Horton Academy. [28]

---

[26] Roome, "Henrietta Muir Edwards," 75.

[27] Ibid., 81. Also see Carole Gerson, *Canadian Women in Print, 1750–1918* (Waterloo, ON: Wilfrid Laurier University Press, 2010).

[28] Higgins, *John Mockett Cramp*, iv. See also Barry M. Moody, "Higgins, Thomas Alfred," in *Dictionary of Canadian Biography*, vol. 13, University of

KEEPING THE FAITH

Faith through All the Ups and Downs of Life

At her funeral, it was said that "next to her home, the church had the warmest place" in Frances's heart. Indeed, her church, it was claimed, was her "spiritual home" and she loved it with a "deep and an abiding love."[29] Of course, apart from her involvement in the church and support for related evangelical organisations, Frances did focus much of her attention on her home and family. For women in the Victorian era in general, and in evangelical circles in particular, a woman's place in the family was seen as a sacred obligation and duty. Childbearing and childrearing were viewed, of course, as part of that duty, though given the mortality rate of women and young children in the nineteenth century, these were perilous duties indeed.

Frances took her role as a wife and mother seriously and worried for the well-being of her family. In 1853, for instance, while staying in Wolfville, she wrote a poem to her husband, who had reason to be away from her and their child for a period.

> 'Tis morning, and the song of birds
> Steals on the summer air,
> Gay fields and flowers are gemmed with dew,
> And decked in beauty rare.
> A scattered band, long parted now,
> Together, bend the knee.
> Oh it is sweet, yet dearest then
> My heart thoughts are with thee
>
> 'Tis noon, and in the pleasant shade
> With perfumed breezes nigh.
> We sit together and talk o'er
> The happy days gone by;
> We dearly prize this quiet hour,
> Yet thus can fancy flee
> Far across the bounding wave.
> Back to its home and thee.

Toronto/Université Laval, 2003–, accessed August 16, 2022, http://www.biographi.ca/en/bio/higgins_thomas_alfred_13E.html.

[29] Upham, "Funeral Address," in Muir, *Frances Cramp*, 6.

Marking Life's Experiences

Evening comes on, and golden rays
  On vale and hill-top lie,
Calm twilight falls, hushing each sound,
  To breeze like harmony.
Then little feet of play time tired
  Rest in the mother's knee,
And as I sing my boy to rest
  Remembrance turns on thee.

Still later, and that rosy cheek
  Is softly pressed to mine,
The little arms in love and trust
  Closely my neck entwine;
Thus resting, quiet slumbers fall.
  While thought, unstayed and free.
Oft wanders to thy lonely home
  Dreaming, I'm still with thee.

Dearest, I often muse upon
  The pathway we have trod,
And bless thee for thy patient faith.
  Thy true unchanging love.
Too fearful when dark clouds have lowered
  And shrinking from the blast,
Safe shelter, have I ever found
  In thy kind faithful heart.

This aching heart and feeble frame
  With weariness oppressed.
If severed from love's sympathy
  Would early sink to rest.
Oh dearest, even now I long
  Thy pleasant voice to hear,
God grant through all life's journey,
  Its hopeful power to cheer.

Forgive me all the waywardness
  And folly of the past,
Thy summer of forgetfulness
  Has made the tear drop start;

KEEPING THE FAITH

My daily prayer when e'er I kneel
  Our little one beside,
Is for heaven's blessing on thy path
God's favour for thy guide.

Thy parting gift, so valued then,
  Oh now 'tis very dear,
Earth's best beloved friend it brings
  In pictured semblance near;
Our boy is looking on it now,
  Calling thy cherished name,
God spare thee and protect us all
  In joy to meet again.[30]

The family were eventually united, though Frances and George were not spared the agony of the death of a child. In 1859, Frances wrote a poem lamenting the loss of a son, Henry Havelock Muir, and in the poem mentions that he was the second of their three children to die. This poem is not a theological reflection on death, but it does reflect a parent's struggle to come to terms with the loss. Step by step, Frances remembers the last hours of the child's life and laments the loss even as the child is given over to the arms of Jesus.

Little baby, precious baby,
Longed and hoped for, come and gone,
Mother's arms are sadly folded.
Mother's care for thee is done:
Loving hands about thee ever,
Fain had stayed thy upward flight,
Happy smiles thy morning greeting,
Gushing tears thy last good-night.

Little baby, precious baby,
Must I put his frocks away;
Can the little cot be empty
Gay with ribbons yesterday;

---

[30] Frances C. Muir, "To My Husband," Wolfville, July 9, 1853, in John M. C. Muir, *Frances Cramp*, 14–16.

Marking Life's Experiences

All his pretty things I've gathered.
Weeping o'er them one by one,
Love and hope prepared their tokens
Of our darling come and gone.

Little baby, precious baby.
How we praised his star-bright eyes.
Tearful oft, yet ever wandering
To their home beyond the skies;
Early wearied of life's journey,
Liking not to see us weep,
In his mother's arms our baby
Hushed him for his last long sleep.

Little baby, precious baby,
'Twas so hard to let thee go.
Forth from mother's arms and kisses.
All alone and laid so low;
Not alone, ah, gently take him
Where tall trees in beauty wave,
Where our first born hope lies buried,
Make the little baby's grave.

Little baby, precious baby.
Turn we back to life again.
Solemn life, where bitter partings
Fill with memories of pain;
Two above in Jesus' bosom,
Safely housed from earthly woe.
One is left our hearts to comfort,
One to cherish here below.

When life's path grows dark and dreary,
Heaven sheds down a brighter ray,
Children's voices homeward calling,
Can we miss the upward way?
To the Saviour's tender keeping
We entrust thee, treasured one,
Little baby, precious baby.

Longed and hoped for, come and gone.[31]

Frances and George would go on to have other children, though the pain of loss never left Frances. In 1890, she wrote a poem for her youngest son, Herbert, on his twenty-first birthday, and here she mentioned "fair firstborn," who had died so many years before.

> The years pass on, touched here and there
> By love's sweet golden ray,
> And thus, my boy, our youngest born.
> We give you joy this day;
> With wistful glance we count them o'er.
> The birthdays come and gone,
> And can but marvel that so soon
> They number twenty-one.
>
> God bless thee, dear one; tender love
> Has brightened all the past.
> The future is aglow with light
> From Hope's own radiance cast;
> And near her, watching silently.
> See Faith with outstretched hand,
> Ready to guide, waiting to lead
> Through Time's uncertain land.
>
> Faith, Hope and Love, angelic three.
> Watch o'er my precious boy;
> Whisper with mother's voice sometimes,
> Hallow his days of joy;
> And when life's mountain passes steep
> Unwilling footsteps climb.
> Be swift of wing, and hovering near
> Uphold with strength divine.
>
> My son, take through the coming years
> A purpose brave and high.

---

[31] Frances C. Muir, "Our Baby," (Henry Havelock Muir, died August 10, 1859) in John M. C. Muir, *Frances Cramp*, 16–18.

Marking Life's Experiences

To side with honour, virtue, truth.
Beneath God's searching eye;
The vows of early youth repeat
Within the sacred fold,
For wisdom's paths are pleasantness.
Peace marks them, as of old.

A mother's love would give thee health
And happy, prosperous days.
True friends, and every earthly good
The longing heart can crave.
There is one spot where tender thoughts
And precious memories twine.
Where joys are shared, and grief is soothed—
May such a home be thine.

Our [Fair] first-born, early called.
Had but two birthdays here;
We laid him down in dreamless rest,
With many a bitter tear.
When 'twas life's glowing summer-time,
Now autumn days are o'er,
The evening mists grow damp and chill,
But, on the farther shore.

Sometimes methinks that little form
For mother waiting stands,
Eager to give her welcome home,
With tiny, beckoning hands;
And there for thee, dear youngest-born,
A faithful watch we'll keep;
Earth's partings are so sad and long.
Heaven's meeting-time how sweet!

But life awaits thee, and the path
We may not always share
Shall be environed still with love,
With blessing and with prayer.
Youth has its happy heritage
Of sunshine and of joy;
May all the years fair fruitage yield,—

KEEPING THE FAITH

God keep and bless our boy.[32]

Tragedy struck the Muir family again in January 1890 when another son, George Francis Muir, died at thirty-four years of age. On this occasion, Frances, in her poem, seems to grapple with the unexplained loss and instead of claiming that it was God's will, she raises the question: why? There is no answer, though she concludes that this loss, too, must be met with the response of faith, and she holds to the sure promise of hope that one day they "will meet again."

> The New Year dawned,—listening within our home
> Methought its joy-bells had a plaintive tone,
> Memory recalled the tranquil, vanished days,
> The past was roseate with a sunset haze,
> And my poor heart in sad forboding turned
> Wishing Time's opening page might be unlearned.
> Alas! the unwonted dread, the shadowy fear,
> Soon found its echo, for the early year
> Numbered a few short days, when lo, a guest
> Unbidden came, and going, took our best;
> The cherished son, the brother loved so well.
> The warm, true friend,—Ah! what a funeral knell
> Was that which struck so many with dismay
> When his young life passed all too soon away.
>
> Why was *he* taken? there are pilgrim feet
> With dust-stained sandals, rest to such were sweet;
> To them life seems a rough and lengthened road.
> Their added years a sorrow laden load;
> But early manhood, with its promise fair,
> The hopes and joys it ever loves to share.
> The present happy, and the future bright
> With sunny day-dreams, decked in fancy's light;
> Alas! my son, my son, how could it be
> That cruel death in haste should summon thee,
> And leave us weeping at the close shut door,

---

[32] Frances C. Muir, "To my son Herbert Barclay Muir," on his twenty-first birthday, January 21, 1890, in John M. C. Muir, *Frances Cramp*, 52–54.

Marking Life's Experiences

From whence our loved ones can return no more.

No more! and must it be? thy mother's gaze
Bedimmed with tears, recalls the early days,
When a dear little one, with busy feet
Carefully tended, made home's music sweet—
And then a school-boy came, with graver face
And earnest purpose for the highest place.
While later years in life's exciting mart,
Bear honoured record of a faithful part.
The kindly friend, loyal and true as steel,
With silence for the faults he could not heal,
And ready always with a courteous grace,
To own a wrong or cover a mistake.

But in the home where happy brothers dwelt.
Loving, and much beloved, 'twas full content;
The Birthdays ne'er forgot, the Christmas-tide
Which came and went, to find him at our side,
The floral offerings to a sick bed brought,
The good-night kisses when my room he sought.
Ah, me, the change, to go and come at will
But listening always for a voice that's still.

His peaceful face when laid in dreamless rest
Was beautiful, and those who loved him best,
Entered that quiet room once and again
In tender farewell breathing the dear name.
Fragrance and beauty all around him lay.
Fresh blooming flowers were added day by day,
Friend after friend, a kindly message sent
Entwined with roses, or with lilies blent—
And one poor heart, stricken by sorrow, said.
Could we but keep him *thus*, our precious dead;
Then through the silence Hope's sweet message came:
A little while and you shall meet again.

Father in Heaven throughout life's changeful way
Thyself hath led, so now, as day by day
We miss our loved one, and the gathering night
Grows cheerless to our sad and fading sight;

We still can trust, for "what we know not now"
Faith's afterward suffices, to Thy will we bow;
Grateful for all the joy the past has known,
Counting the blessings which remain our own,
We wait the dawn, and watch its earliest ray,
"Till the day break, the shadows flee away."[33]

Conclusion

Tracing some of the experiences of the life of Frances Cramp Muir through her poetry in many ways leaves the impression that her life was quite ordinary. She has not been regarded as, and no doubt would not have wanted to be portrayed as, a "famous Baptist woman." Like many people, she knew both the happiness and the sadness that life brings. A person of Christian faith, she served the Lord through her commitment to church and to wider mission causes. However, like many women of her own era, much of her life was devoted to care for her family, and this brought with it joy and laughter as well as deep pain, sorrow, and loss.

Frances's poetry, while not remarkable for its poetic quality, is significant in that it offers some insight into the life and thought of a nineteenth-century Baptist woman. While she did not—perhaps could not at the time—follow her father into the pulpit or academy, in a sense, she used poetry as a tool for marking her own life's experiences. Yet it may be argued that these poems were not simply a way of remembering an event that occurred on a particular day. Rather, they were also a way in which she tried to reflect on Scripture or to encourage evangelism and to foster church fellowship. More personally, the poems offered a way of dealing honestly with grief and loss within the context of her own understanding of Christian faith. Writing poetry was, of course, also recognized as an acceptable way for evangelical women in the nineteenth century to express their faith. While they were barred from speaking in the pulpit, the verse which was put to music and "turned to song" was often taken to heart by congregations. In fact, these poetry "sung sermons" were often remembered far better than many of the pulpit diatribes.

In his book *Hymns at Heaven's Gate: The Use and Abuse of Hymns*, Roger Prentice, in whose memory this essay is written, wrote of the

---

[33] Frances C. Muir, "In Memoriam." George Francis Muir died January 13, 1890, aged thirty-four years. In John M. C. Muir, *Frances Cramp*, 50–52.

Marking Life's Experiences

importance of hymn singing. He believed it was not only important, but absolutely necessary for congregations to gather and, as part of their worship, to sing praises to God. Like Frances Cramp Muir, from time to time, he even wrote hymns for particular occasions. Hence, in concluding this exploration of Frances's life, and, in a way, as a remembrance of Roger, too, it seems most fitting to end this essay with one other poem written by Frances Cramp Muir, entitled "The Singing Church."

The verses were written as a reflection on a sermon that she heard at Olivet Baptist Church in 1881 and were based on the text "therefore the redeemed of the Lord shall return, and come with singing unto Zion" (Isaiah 51:11). In the poem, Frances reflects on different scenes from Scripture where the saints of old in captivity or on pilgrimage found themselves singing. In the final verses, Frances imagines one united chorus of praise as the Church on earth joins with the church above in singing praise to God. To such a scene, I can imagine Roger exclaiming, "Amen! Amen!"

The Singing Church

The Singing Church! through Time's long distant aisles
Reverberate her sweet and solemn strains:
The psalm of praise, the prophet's wondrous voice,
The angels' song by Bethlehem's hallowed plains.

With willing feet, she comes before the Lord,
Entering his gates with thankfulness and prayer;
And, through the ages, hallelujahs rise
From joyful souls who meet to worship there.

Is there a mourning one amid the throng,
Longing to flee away on dove-like wings?
A sacred song tells of His loving care
Who wept on earth, and yet was King of kings.

The Captive Church, with bowed and drooping head,
Sang of her Zion in a stranger-land;
And mountain-caves have treasured in their depths
The trembling tones of many a martyr-band.

Still sings the Pilgrim Church, and journeys on.
Crossing the path where ransomed footsteps trod,

KEEPING THE FAITH

The forward host with victory's cheer advance,
Seeing afar the city of their God.

And as the notes of fatherland beguile
The weary exile on his toilsome way,
So, wafted o'er the silent stream, is heard
Seraphic music from celestial day.

But listen! as the thrilling tones above
Responsive meet in one melodious strain,
A glorious choir resounds, "Worthy the Lamb!"
The church below repeats the sweet refrain.

Ye silent voices, speak of Jesus' love;
He waits to save,—begin the glad new song,
Learn while on earth the harmonies of heaven;
The Singing Church completes the ransomed throng. [34]

---

[34] Frances C. Muir, "The Singing Church," in John M. C. Muir, *Frances Cramp*, 36–37.

Acadia University and Maritime Connections

Praise to our alma mater, And glory for her place;
Her own embracing Charter enfolding faith and race,
She teaches, "Look higher, and find a noble call:
to all the world inspire that Truth can free us all."

Acadia has an answer for what we wish to be;
To friend and to our teachers we owe fraternity;
We come with expectation to learn and grow with grace
With every revelation where wisdom has its place.

The time will come to leave here, this caring, learning space;
Our hearts and minds enamour the knowledge we'll embrace
To make the world a better, encompassing, true shrine
Where one finds lab and letter disclosing truth sublime.

So raise your eyes where lofty, Vast mysteries proclaim,
And whispers tell us softly The wonders of a name:
The name is old Acadia Our *alma mater* true,
Omega and our Alpha, With garnet robed in blue.

Praise to our alma mater, And glory for her place;
Her own embracing Charter enfolding faith and race,
She teaches, "Look higher, and find a noble call:
to all the world inspire that Truth can free us all."

Text: Roger H. Prentice
Tune: Alexander Ewing, 1853

Lord God of all wisdom, we pray for Acadia University, that she may be faithful to the purposes of our Founders, continue to promote the search for truth and knowledge, and be an inspiration to others who follow. May we be a community of scholars sharing this ambition, caring for one another, and loyal to the truth revealed to us as thy disciples. Amen.

(University prayer written by Roger H. Prentice)

"Education Seasoned with Grace":
A Liberal Education at Acadia College*

Barry M. Moody

When the Baptists of Nova Scotia proudly gathered in Horton (Wolfville) on January 21, 1839, to witness the launch of their institution of higher learning, most of those assembled had only a scant understanding of what a college really was or should be. The few among the key participants in the founding who actually possessed a formal collegiate education would play an important role in determining the shape of Acadia-to-be,** but these men would never have the power to twist the college entirely to their purposes. The well-established social views of rural Nova Scotia Baptists, and their economic and social aspirations, would also do much to chart the future course of the college they so confidently thrust into the mainstream of the colony's development. The conviction that all must be, and be seen to be, to the glory of God and the building of His Kingdom here on earth was the third element underlying the college's founding. These three forces, and a handful of key men, would lay the basis of Acadia's approach to education in the nineteenth century.

Even a cursory examination of the story of the founding of Acadia College makes it abundantly clear that the developments of the fall of 1838 were dominated almost completely by that small but significant group of "new" Halifax Baptists who had fled from the Anglican Church in the rupture at Saint Paul's Cathedral in the mid-1820s.[1] Certainly there can be no doubt that Edmund Crawley, J. W. Johnston, James Nutting, and John Pryor played key roles in that (to some) unseemly rush to found an institution of higher learning in Wolfville. Of these four, Crawley was

---

*An earlier version of this essay was presented at "The Past and Future of Liberal Education" Conference at Mt. Allison University, Sackville, NB, 1990.

** For the first three years of its existence, the institution was known as Queen's College, but to avoid confusion, the term Acadia College will be used throughout this paper.

[1] See R. S. Longley, *Acadia University, 1838–1938* (Wolfville, NS: n.p., 1939), 15–31; George Levy, *The Baptists of the Maritime Provinces* (Saint John, NB: Barnes-Hopkins Ltd., 1946), 110–18.

Education Seasoned with Grace

without doubt the most important, and probably possessed the clearest idea of exactly where his child ought to be headed.[2]

Edmund Albern Crawley was born in England but had come as a child to Cape Breton, where his father served as crown surveyor. In 1816, young Crawley entered Anglican King's College, Windsor, where he received a thoroughly traditional classical education, one that would leave a permanent mark on him and a semipermanent mark on the future Acadia College. Graduating AB in 1820, Crawley entered the Halifax law firm of James W. Johnston, a man who had a great influence on him. With Johnston and others, he left Saint Paul's Cathedral in 1825 after a protracted struggle with Bishop John Inglish. Referred to by one of his admirers as "a lawyer subdued by grace," Crawley in 1828 began the study of theology and was ordained to the Baptist ministry in 1830.

It would be Crawley, as minister of Granville Street Baptist Church, Halifax, who would lead the movement for the founding of Acadia College in the fall of 1838. The extent of Crawley's personal ambition, and the lengths to which he would go to attain a college professorship, constitute a separate, although related, story, but what is clear is that he, unlike many of his fellow founders, already possessed a carefully defined picture of what constituted the proper course of study at any college. His years at King's had had a profound effect on him, and his departure from the Anglican Church, and affiliation with Nova Scotia Baptists, did not seem to have greatly changed his social or educational views. His own training had been firmly rooted in the classical tradition, stretching back through King's to Oxford and Cambridge Universities, and this would do much to mark both the man and the college he attempted to both found and shape.[3]

Even before the founding of Acadia, Crawley had expressed his views on higher education forcefully during the controversy over the reconstitution of Dalhousie College in 1838. He fully expected an appointment as one of the new professors at the institution, and in a strongly worded memorandum for the president-elect of that institution, the Rev. Thomas

---

[2] Barry M. Moody, "Crawley, Edmund Albern," in *Dictionary of Canadian Biography (DCB)*, vol. 11, University of Toronto/Université Laval, 2003–, accessed September 4, 2022, http://www.biographi.ca/en/bio/crawley_edmund_albern_11E.html.

[3] Robin Harris, *A History of Higher Education in Canada 1663–1960* (Toronto: 1960), 29–30.

123

McCulloch, he laid out what he viewed as the key elements of a classical education. He felt that a proper college needed four separate areas of instruction: logic and rhetoric, the classical languages, mathematics, and natural and experimental philosophy. Of these, the classical languages (which with characteristic modesty he claimed for himself) he deemed most important.[4]

McCulloch's caustic reply rightly pointed out that this was indeed the traditional King's approach; it would not do, however, in McCulloch's opinion, for Dalhousie. He wrote: "If Dalhousie College acquire usefulness and eminence it will be not by an imitation of Oxford, but as an institution of science and practical intelligence."[5] McCulloch wanted not Latin and Greek, of questionable usefulness in the Maritime context, but geology, botany, minerology, and zoology.[6]

This disagreement between Crawley and McCulloch had no time to mature beyond the theoretical stage, however. It was abruptly terminated in the fall of 1838 when the board of governors of Dalhousie decided to appoint only Presbyterians to the vacant professorships.[7] Crawley was left with a program but no college. Such a temporary problem was soon rectified by a special meeting of the Nova Scotia Baptist Education Society on November 15, 1838, with the decision to found a Baptist college in Wolfville.[8] Not surprisingly, Crawley was chosen as one of the two professors of the new institution, along with his fellow Haligonian, former Anglican and King's graduate John Pryor.

When the course of study of Queen's (Acadia) College was announced in January 1839, it followed exactly the shape of Crawley's proposed program for Dalhousie— classical languages, natural philosophy, moral philosophy, rhetoric and logic, and mathematics.[9] The familiar

---

[4] For a general discussion of the development of the classical tradition at North American liberal arts colleges, see George P. Schmidt, *The Liberal Arts College: A Chapter in American Cultural History* (Westport, CT: Rutgers University Press, 1957), 43–75.

[5] Quoted in D. C. Harvey, *An Introduction to the History of Dalhousie University* (Halifax, NS: Dalhousie University Press, 1938), 50.

[6] Ibid., 51.

[7] Ibid., 55–56.

[8] Acadia University Archives, minutes of the Nova Scotia Baptist Education Society, November 15, 1838; Longley, *Acadia University*, 25–31.

[9] *Christian Messenger* (January 4, 1839).

King's course of instruction had merely made its way down the valley from Windsor to Wolfville. The "Address of the Committee of the Nova Scotia Baptist Education Society to the Members of the Baptist Churches and Congregations, and other persons friendly to Education," published in late 1838 and probably written by Crawley himself, made clear the committee's thinking at this early stage of Acadia's development. It read in part:

> And if the improvements, enterprize, and wealth, which character-ize this age of the civilized world, are to be transplanted in any just proportion to our shores, it will be effected fully as much by raising the scale of intellectual cultivation, as by exercising the labours of industry, or developing the natural resources of the country.
>
> That this degree of cultivation must be attained by the usual courses of Collegiate instruction, is a principle which the experience of other countries had conclusively decided.... [We must] increase the facilities towards attaining a liberal education to the standards of other countries.[10]

Certainly, if Crawley had had the entire say in the matter, the young Acadia College would have had only the "usual courses of Collegiate in-struction," as he phrased it. However, Crawley did *not* have the entire say, much as he would have liked to. The founding of the new college had not been because of the actions of a single individual or group, but rather as the result of a number of forces, ideas, and individuals coming together from rather diverse backgrounds. Although influenced by many, no one individual or philosophy was able completely to dominate the institution in these early, formative years.[11]

For the rest of his very long and sometimes problematic association with Acadia, Crawley, with his King's-shaped philosophy of classical ed-ucation, would play an important role in the development of the institu-tion, but other forces were also present from the very beginning, forces which did much to thwart and modify Crawley's design, creating in the process a much more "Nova Scotian" college than what he might have had in mind. Without those changes, and the support of the broader Baptist

---

[10] *Christian Messenger* (November 30, 1838).

[11] Barry Moody, "Breadth of Vision, Breadth of Mind: The Baptists and Acadia College," in *Canadian Baptists and Christian Higher Education*, ed. G. A. Rawlyk (Kingston and Montreal: McGill-Queen's Press, 1988), 3–29.

community that they made possible, Acadia would not have survived the nineteenth century.

Until a bare month and a half before Acadia's founding, Crawley and the Halifax Baptist clique had steadfastly opposed such a development, throwing their considerable weight fully behind the Dalhousie idea. The failure of Crawley's plans for an influential role in the "new" Dalhousie forced an accommodation with the "country" Baptists, who had all along refused to lend their support to a Halifax-centered, "godless" institution.[12] Forced now to seek their aid in founding his college, Crawley trimmed his sails accordingly, and other ideas and personalities entered the picture.

The predominantly rural and lower-class nature of the majority of Baptists of Nova Scotia clearly altered somewhat the thrust of Crawley's views of classical education. A new emphasis on practicality, the utilitarian aspects of education, was now added to the mix. If one were, in fact, to educate the sons of farmers, fishermen, and small shopkeepers, as well as the scions of the elite families, the usefulness of such an exercise would have to be clearly demonstrated. Such had been the demand of some Baptists for a number of years.[13] That this might carry them somewhat away from the strict definition of "liberal education" was neither understood by most of them nor of concern if it were. "Arts becoming a gentleman" held little appeal for most Nova Scotians, Baptists or otherwise.[14] A literal translation of the Latin *artes liberales* would, quite unbeknownst to them, have been nearer the mark—"arts befitting a freeman," or citizen. That the nature of a freeman had changed considerably since the days of the Roman Empire is all too apparent; the definition of an education befitting a freeman would have to change as well. It is precisely because many Baptists saw in the fledgling Acadia the opportunity to secure for their sons and grandsons (and later their granddaughters) an education suitable to their background and useful in fulfilling their aspirations that they were

---

[12] See Crawley's letters to the editors of the *Novascotian*, reprinted in the *Christian Messenger* (September 12, October 5, October 12, and October 19, 1838), and Crawley to the Baptists of Nova Scotia, *Christian Messenger* (October 26, 1838).

[13] Barry Moody, "The Maritime Baptists and Higher Education in the Early Nineteenth Century," in *Repent and Believe: The Baptist Experience in Atlantic Canada*, ed. B. Moody (Hantsport, NS: Lancelot Press, 1980), 88–102.

[14] One of the meanings of "liberal arts" in *Webster's New World Dictionary*.

Education Seasoned with Grace

prepared to struggle so hard, and at times sacrifice so considerably, to see Acadia established and maintained.

From the very beginning, there existed usually-healthy tensions between the classicism and "pure" liberal arts bequeathed to the institution by its upper-class Halifax founders and the earthy practicality that was the legacy of its lower-class rural "parent." This latter influence was articulated as early as 1828 in the prospectus for Horton Academy, in many respects the forerunner of Acadia. It read, in part:

> That a principal object to be observed in the management of the Institution being to adapt the course of study to the state of society and the wants of the people, and to place the means of instruction as much as possible within the reach of all persons, it is considered primarily necessary to attend to those branches of Education which are of more general use, at the same time that a wider range of literary acquirements shall be open to those who may have the ability to seek them, or to whose prospects in life they may be more suitably adapted.[15]

In 1861, the new professor of classics at Acadia explored these contending forces in his inaugural address. He argued against the idea of merely imparting knowledge and information, saying that the true purpose of the college was to "train the mind: to exercise all its various faculties; to draw forth all its power, so that a man shall be master of himself and be able to use to the highest advantage every faculty which God has given him.... All the branches of collegiate education are therefore not items of knowledge to be imparted, but exercises for the purpose of disciplining the mind." Once the student has acquired an education, *then* "the acquirement of the knowledge of future duties can be begun with the certainty of success and he can go forth to plead, to teach, to lead, to discover."[16]

By as early as 1841, such subjects as mechanics, hydrostatics and pneumatic geology, chemistry, electricity, and magnetism had shouldered their way into the curriculum to take their place beside Cicero, Sophocles, Tacitus, and "Lectures on the Genius and Grammar of the Classical

---

[15] "Prospectus of the Nova Scotia Baptist Education Society," printed in *Memorials of Acadia College and Horton Academy for the Half-Century 1828–1878* (Montreal, 1881), 233.

[16] "Inaugural Discourse by James DeMille, MA," *Christian Messenger* (July 3 and July 10, 1861).

127

Languages."[17] Thomas McCulloch would doubtless have nodded his head in approval over this introduction of "practical intelligence," or what Sam Slick would have called "cypherin' and figgerin'."

For the rest of the century and beyond, Acadia College would add new courses, explore new avenues, and respond to changing needs with remarkably little expressed fear that she was compromising her convictions. French would be taught as early as 1841[18] and "agricultural chemistry" was discussed in the 1840s and 1850s (but not introduced due to shortage of funds).[19] A professor of modern languages was hired in 1856,[20] the president arguing that "so much of French is now incorporated with English literature, and the commercial relations of the two countries are becoming so common, that a course of education without some provision for an acquaintance with that language is very imperfect." Manuscript and printed sources relating to the early history of the colony were collected in the 1840s, along with "interesting relics of war, husbandry, or domestic furniture left by the Aboriginal or French and other early inhabitants."[21] Later in the century, surveying and navigation, biology, modern English literature, industrial arts, teacher training, and many others entered and departed from the program as interest, money, and personalities dictated.[22]

The Acadia curriculum, then, was almost from the beginning a combination of the traditional and the practical, reflecting the duality of Acadia's founding fathers. All subjects, the utilitarian and the theoretical, both Greek and navigation, were intended to serve a common end—the elevating of the mind and the expansion of its abilities. In 1847, one observer,

---

[17] *Christian Messenger* (March 19, 1841) outline of the four-year program at Acadia College. As early as 1840, a collection of geological specimens had been started, the beginning of a very extensive natural history museum at Acadia. Ibid., November 27, 1840.

[18] Acadia Archives, papers of the Nova Scotia Baptist Education Society, E. A. Crawley to J. W. Nutting, September 1841.

[19] *Christian Messenger* (December 24, 1852), "interested Spectator" to editor; ibid. (May 5, 1853), Aliquis to the editor.

[20] *Christian Messenger*, (October 21, 1857), editorial; ibid. (November 11, 1857), J. M. Cramp to editors.

[21] *Christian Messenger*, (June 5, 1846), Isaac Chipman and S. T. Rand to "The Alumni of the Institutions at Horton."

[22] See the various Acadia College catalogues, which were published on a regular basis from the mid-1860s onward.

Education Seasoned with Grace

in commenting on the closing exercises of the college, wrote that he was very impressed with "the sound instruction in the higher College branches, connected with that careful analysis, that thorough tutoring and discipline of all the mental powers so essential to any just scheme of liberal Education."[23] Two years later, a member of the board of governors explained what was being attempted at Acadia:

> The manner of instruction pursued aims very directly at the formation of sound habits of study, and the growth of the mental instruction, together with a discovery of laws of investigation, and principles of science, rather than a disorderly and cumbrous accumulation of facts. With this understanding, that the acquisition of mental power, and attainment of the true instruments of investigation, whether associated with ripening faculties, or with habits of study, lays far more truly an adequate foundation for progress in knowledge, than when the ruling aim is to gormandize facts in crudity and confusion, as if for the purpose of disgorging them at shortest notice, and without digestion. Seeking primarily and preeminently to perfect in the student's mind the framework, whether of his mental structure or of his knowledge, that is nevertheless, it is believed, no improper neglect of the external covering, or of that department of instruction which aims more expressly to procure adaption for bringing knowledge into contact with the transactions of life.... Indeed the belief is that whether for a life of mere abstract speculation, or of one of more extended intercourse with the world, the primary requisitions are the same, and are to be secured by similar training; while the supplementary influences may require to differ.[24]

This duality was forced on Crawley by his absolute need of support for the college's founding from practical rural Baptists. It would be maintained because of the ongoing necessity for that support. Unlike Dalhousie College, by the end of the century,[25] Acadia was unable to build a solid endowment base for its operations, and unlike many colleges and

---

[23] *Christian Messenger* (July 16, 1847), editorial.

[24] Ibid. (March 9, 1847), Executive Committee member of the Nova Scotia Baptist Education Society to the editors.

[25] Harvey, *Dalhousie University*, 101–103.

129

universities in Canada, it received little in the way of government support. Only by prodigious, ongoing efforts was Acadia College able to survive, and this was accomplished largely by annual appeals to the Baptists and Baptist churches of the Maritime provinces.[26] If the college lost touch with its constituency, if its usefulness could not be readily discerned by the hardnosed and tightfisted farmers, fishermen, merchants, and lumbermen of the Maritime Baptist churches, the college would be in serious straits indeed. This salutary influence maintained that duality observable from the beginning of the college's life, allowing a careful balancing of traditional classical education and practical, "useful" subjects. Acadia would see no contradiction in this.[27]

In his struggle for ideological control of Acadia, Crawley would have to contend not only with the general attitudes and assumptions of rural Nova Scotia Baptists, but also with specific individuals who would greatly alter and modify his approach to the proper course at a college. Isaac Chipman, John Mockett Cramp, and Artemus W. Sawyer, among others, added new dimensions to Acadia's definition of "liberal education," not always in ways of which the purists approved.

Isaac Chipman was the first of the new forces that would so greatly influence the institution. A native of the Annapolis Valley and a graduate of Horton Academy, Chipman had received his advanced education in the United States and returned to Wolfville in 1841. He would devote the rest of his tragically short life to the welfare of Acadia College. Chipman in many ways represented a new generation of Nova Scotia Baptists, better educated and ambitious, but also pious and committed. As the son of an important Baptist minister, and scion of one of the most influential families of Kings County, Chipman's appointment to the faculty of Acadia was a shrewd move in the effort to garner support for the fledgling institution.

---

[26] See repeated references to this in the minutes of the board of governors, Acadia College, 1852–1900, Acadia University Archives. Also, see the annual report of the college to the Baptist Convention, published annually in *The Baptist Year Book of the Maritime Provinces*.

[27] In fact, some argued that even a modest endowment fund, such as that proposed in the 1850s, would place the college too much out of the control of the ordinary people of the region. See the debate between William Hall and "CT" in *Christian Messenger* (February 18 and March 4, 1853).

However, it is doubtful that Crawley could have foreseen the long-term consequences of such an act.[28]

Chipman brought to Acadia an amazing energy, a burning commitment, and one of the most inquiring minds in the history of the institution. It is clear from a study of his years at Acadia that, unhampered by the confines of the classical tradition (in which he was nonetheless well versed), he considered all knowledge fascinating and worthy of investigation. He was intrigued by science, especially geology. In 1845, in a characteristic rush, he established a course in astronomy[29] while at the same time collecting the local manuscripts and "relics" mentioned above. He pressed for the production of a history of the Maritime Baptists and guided his best friend, Silas T. Rand, into his linguistic studies and missionary work with the Micmac people.[30] In many respects, it could be said that Chipman's work legitimized the study of the world immediately around Acadia—the people, the geology, the flora and fauna, the history of the Maritime region. It was not necessary constantly to look to the Ancient World, to the glories of Greece and Rome; the modern world provided an exciting, challenging study at their doorstep.

Chipman's prodigious efforts on Acadia's behalf, his popularity with the students, and his infectious enthusiasm for learning all made his approach to, and understanding of, education acceptable to the people of the Baptist denomination. His death by drowning in 1852, in the service of the college, only strengthened this acceptance. And above all, he was one of their own, a product of their own community, their own denomination, and they trusted him. Chipman was thus able to have a very considerable influence on the thinking and direction of Acadia College; in particular, he helped make the study of the sciences a legitimate and respectable part of the college curriculum.[31]

---

[28] See Longley, *Acadia University*, 39–41, 45–48; I. E. Bill, *Fifty Years with the Baptist Ministers and Churches of the Maritime Provinces of Canada* (Saint John, NB: Barnes Co., 1880), 736–38.

[29] Acadia Archives, papers of the Nova Scotia Baptist Education Society, Isaac Chipman to J. W. Nutting, September 5, 1845.

[30] See the Isaac Chipman correspondence in ibid. for the activities of this most energetic man.

[31] See, for example, *Christian Messenger* (May 19, 1848), Obed Chute to editors. Also Moody, "Breadth of Vision," 25–26.

John Mockett Cramp, Acadia's second president (1851–53, 1860–69), also had a significant role to play in modifying Crawley's classicism and in redefining Acadia's approach to liberal education. Born and educated in England, he was an experienced minister, writer, newspaper editor, and college administrator before coming to Nova Scotia in 1851. He would spend the rest of his life associated with Acadia College, leaving a very deep impression on that institution.[32]

Although he was the first published scholar among Acadia's faculty, Cramp was no slave to educational traditions. In his inaugural address at Acadia, he warned that the institution would have to be thoroughly modern, or disappear. He observed:

> It is especially incumbent on us to bear in mind that the age is remarkably progressive, and that all institutions must keep pace with it, or sink in public estimation. The range of study is extending every year, as the boundaries of science expand, so that the instructor finds it necessary to incorporate additional branches in his course, and the student is compelled, if he would avoid the reproach of ignorance, to spend much time in making acquisitions for which there was no demand in the days of his predecessors; while the ancient standards of learning still retain, and must continue to retain, their place and pre-eminence.... Nova Scotia and New Brunswick are shaking themselves from the dust, and rousing up the energies of their sons. They ask for railroads—and they will assuredly have them. Their agriculture is to be improved by science. Their mineral wealth is to be profitably explored. Their ships will sail in all waters. Their resources and capabilities, not yet half developed, will be ascertained, and brought into useful operation. Now, in order to the accomplishment of these and other beneficial results, the talent of the provinces must be sought out in every direction, and carefully cultivated. There will be abundant employment for men of ability and skill, both in originating improvements and in directing the agencies by which they may become available to the public; and if such men are trained in the provinces, patriotism will inspire them with ardour, and their efforts will be carried on with zeal which strangers would emulate in vain. It is obvious, therefore, that a

---

[32] *Dictionary of Canadian Biography*, vol. XI, 209–10; T. A. Higgins, *The Life of John Mockett Cramp, D.D. 1796–1881* (Montreal: Drysdale & Co., 1887); Longley, *Acadia*, 66–81.

Education Seasoned with Grace

solemn responsibility rests on our Institutions of learning, and that such arrangements as the exigencies of the times call for much be provided.[33]

Probably Cramp's greatest contribution to the intellectual development of Acadia was to be found in his emphasis on the importance of the freedom of inquiry. He had an almost obsessive fear of tyranny, and that lay at the heart of much of his writing and in the many causes that he championed. The tyranny of slavery, of alcohol, of Roman Catholicism, of despotism, of ignorance—these were all bound together in his mind. And despotism could be overcome only by knowledge and a thinking mind.

This was no narrow-minded cleric, however strong his many convictions might be. He urged his students and fellow Baptists to pursue truth wherever it might lead, for the truth could never take them away from God, the source of all truth. Any subject, any approach that aided in the search for truth could rightly be included in the college program, whether or not it might fit traditional definitions of education. Cramp's address to the graduating class of 1866 sums up well what he thought the students and the faculty ought to be doing at a college:

> Your object [in coming here] was to learn how to learn, and how to use your learning. You looked for an introduction to the prime sources of knowledge, ancient and modern, and for directions as to the manner in which your future researches might be prosecuted, with reasonable prospects of success. You hoped to obtain a general acquaintance with the laws which the Great God has impressed on matter and on mind, by which all beings are uniformly and constantly governed. You sought discipline. You desired to form habits of thinking,—to acquire correct taste,—and to be able to express your thoughts in a style neither diffuse or feeble on the one hand, nor rugged or obscure on the other, but distinguished by clearness, precision, and force.
>
> ...[I]t may be well to remind you that wherever you may go you will find society in an advanced and advancing state.... He who would sway the minds of his fellow-men must give proof that his

---

[33] J. M. Cramp, *The Inaugural Address, Delivered by the President, 20 June, 1851* (Halifax, NS, 1851), 8–9.

KEEPING THE FAITH

own mind is well furnished and that he has gained the habit of self-improvement, or he will not be able to maintain his position.[34]

With this in mind, Cramp at Acadia was a staunch defender of all inquiry, especially of science. He was unafraid of the new theories or Darwin and other contemporary scientists, and warned that Baptists and other Christians could not afford to hide, pretending that such discussions and investigations were not taking place. Ultimately, he argued, there could be no contradiction between true discoveries of science and the tenets of Christianity, since they came from the same Source. He bluntly stated: "The works and the word of God must be in full harmony."[35] Science and Christianity would illuminate each other, leading to a greater and more precise understanding of both. By consistently championing the cause of science, and urging his college and denomination to be unafraid of honest inquiry, Cramp did much to ensure that at this crucial time Acadia did not retreat into a narrow denominationalism that might well have stifled true learning and academic freedom,[36] making a significant contribution to the development of Acadia's definition of a "liberal" education.

The extent to which Cramp was prepared to go to expand learning and defeat ignorance is revealed in his espousal of what were termed the "partial course" and the "English course." Within a year of his arrival in Wolfville, Cramp was advocating for a shortened course of study for prospective ministers who lacked the necessary educational background in the classics.[37] Earnest and able young men were barred from the college program while "churches are anguishing for want of Pastors, and Sinners are perishing for lack of gospel light."[38] It was far better, in his opinion, to

---

[34] *Christian Messenger* (June 20, 1866), J. M. Cramp's address to the students, June 6, 1866.

[35] Ibid. (June 12, 1867), Cramp to the graduating class.

[36] In addition to the above addresses by Cramp on the subject, see *Christian Messenger* (July 22, 1868), Cramp to editor. For efforts to secure a professor of natural science, see ibid. (September 2 and 23, 1868), Acadia Archives, minutes of the board of governors, vol. I, minutes for 1868, 1869. For William Elder's appointment, see Longley, *Acadia*, 84. For Acadia's response to the challenges of science, see Moody, "Breadth of Vision," 24–28.

[37] *Christian Messenger* (July 30, 1852), Cramp to editors; *Christian Messenger* (April 14, 1853), Cramp to editors.

[38] *Christian Messenger* (May 5, 1853), editorial.

Education Seasoned with Grace

have an educated clergy without Latin and Greek than a clergy with no education at all, or worse, insufficient clergy for the demand.

In 1859, the same concerns were expressed by Cramp in the non-theological field. On his urging, the board of governors announced the establishment of a two-year "English Course," which would terminate with the awarding of a diploma. Cramp was eager to adapt at least some aspects of the Acadia program to meet the needs of the people of the Maritimes. Many young men had little or no grounding in Latin and Greek, and thus did not qualify for entry to Acadia or most other British North American colleges. Such students could "pursue their studies in the English branches of education only." The two-year program encompassed the study of algebra, modern history, rhetoric, geometry, logic, moral science, political economy, chemistry or mathematics, evidences of Christianity, geology, and intellectual philosophy.[39] The classics would remain important at Acadia College for the rest of the century, but educating a broader segment was becoming of greater significance.

The presidency of Artemus W. Sawyer (1869–1896) offers another example of the way in which Acadia's concept of a liberal education was constantly being modified in the light of changing circumstances and leadership. Sawyer was American born and trained, and like his predecessors in the presidency, an ordained Baptist minister. During his lengthy term at Acadia, in spite of his own commitment to the classics, a number of significant changes were made in the Acadia curriculum, and much heated discussion took place concerning the nature of a "proper" education.

Sawyer came to Acadia the same year that William Elder assumed the newly created chair of Natural Sciences. The chair was made possible by a special fund collected by Maritime Baptists, which heralded a new phase in the growth of the importance of the sciences at Acadia, challenging some of the previous assumptions about the nature of the college curriculum.[40] At the annual convocation ceremonies in the spring of 1870, Elder, in a one-and-a-half-hour oration, gave a spirited defence of scientific inquiry. "Experiment and exploration," he claimed, "had opened up wide fields of research, and had contributed vast resources for the welfare and happiness of the human family."[41]

---

[39] Ibid. (June 15, 1859).

[40] Longley, *Acadia*, 84.

[41] *Christian Messenger* (June 15, 1870): 186.

Elder's lengthy comments seem to have touched off the most intense debate on the nature of education yet indulged in by Acadia and the broader Baptist community. For much of the rest of the decade and beyond, there was a significant reevaluation of curriculum, program, and philosophy at Acadia.[42] Sawyer—even-tempered, practical, and broadminded—was able to preside over these discussions and supervise the subsequent alterations with apparent ease. Although the debate was occasionally heated, there were few serious ruptures in the Acadia/Baptist community as a result.[43] Sawyer had to balance the insistence by some on the retention of the classical elements with the demands made by others that Acadia come to terms with the new age. On the one hand, "Outis" could argue in the press that

> the secret of mental education is not the storing of the mind, but the making of it.... We live in an atmosphere artificial beyond precedent, and dense with the dust and vapour of scientific novelties. Such an atmosphere is friendly neither to culture, nor to philosophy or truth. "The spirit of the age," this tyrannous, unsated, and insatiable thirst for novelty, refused to take its eyes off this atmosphere of phantasmal wonder.... But now the itch for novelty will exempt nothing from change, not even these eternal truths; and accordingly it is asserted that nothing is wanted but new experiences (and these

---

[42] For examples, see *Christian Messenger*, June 22, 1870; July 6, 1870, W. H. Newcomb to editor; July 27, 1870, the first of a long series of letters from William Elder; October 11, 1871, and every issue for the next two months, contained a very extensive debate between "Modern Culture" and a number of other writers. April 16, 1873; May 24, 1876; *The Athenaeum*, April 1875.

[43] Probably the most serious revolved around the establishment of a "Chair in Didactics" in 1883, and the appointment of Theodore Harding Rand to fill it. See *Correspondence: Anonymous and Otherwise, Concerning the New Chair at Acadia College* (Halifax, NS, 1883); Margaret Conrad, "'An Abiding Conviction of the Paramount Importance of Christian Education': Theodore Harding Rand as Educator, 1860–1900," in *An Abiding Conviction: Maritime Baptists and Their World*, ed. Robert Wilson (Saint John, NB: Acadia Divinity College and the Baptist Historical Committee of the United Baptist Convention of the Atlantic Provinces, 1988), 171–74; Barry Moody, "'The Trail of the Serpent': The Appointment of a 'Professor of Didactics' at Acadia College, 1883," in *Historical Identities: The Professoriate in Canada*, eds. Paul Stortz and E. Lisa Panayotidis, (Toronto: University of Toronto Press, 2006), 107–30.

arise every hour) to make it possible that two straight lines may contain a space, and that twice two may be five. The mere statement of a thing being fixed is regarded as a challenge to upset it....

In these modern days, empirical sciences have filled the minds of men, and are polarizing all thought in one direction. They cannot help us in this matter of culture, since they deal not with the emotional nature, and far better instruments already exist for the culture of rational powers. The Modern Languages are equally devoid of any power to supply the want of emotional culture, and are inferior to the classics as a means of linguistic discipline.[44]

A writer calling himself "Modern *Culture*" argued that

the world moves on. History, Modern Science, and the Modern Languages, will soon have crowded their honoured predecessors from the Curricula of every respectable College, into the land of forgetfulness....

It is time we were done with the past in education, except so far as to study the actions of men. These are times of progress, and the spirit of the age demands a change. He is a blind man who does not read the doom of effete systems and methods of education already written on the wall.[45]

Men are beginning to see that the four years that are required to be devoted to study, may just as well be made of some practical service to a young man as to be consumed in that vague process of *mental culture*, to accomplish which does not demand that anything shall be learned at all,—all it requires is that the party shall study.[46]

An examination of the catalogues of Acadia College during the 1870s and 1880s reveals the gradual and sometimes subtle shifts that were taking place. Increasingly, the emphasis was on the sciences, modern languages, history, and English literature, although the classics clearly maintained a strong presence. However, by 1888, it was possible to elect "Modern

---

[44] *Christian Messenger*, November 29, 1871, Outis to editor.
[45] Ibid., October 25, 1871, Modern Culture to editor.
[46] Ibid., October 11, 1871.

Languages" in place of Greek, although Latin was still required of all students.[47]

With such changes, Sawyer seems to have had little difficulty. In fact, he appears to have encouraged them. The faculty that he hired during his term of office indicates that he had little fear of such modern trends. Acadia's first professors of modern history and English literature were added during his tenure, along with men trained in the German universities and in the educational philosophy and methods of the 1870s and 1880s.[48] What Sawyer did dislike was the growing trend toward specialization. He believed fervently and argued strongly that a general education, with a judicious mix of classical and more modern subjects, was the proper educational foundation for any young person, male or female. In his address commemorating the fiftieth anniversary of Acadia's founding, he pleaded for less specialization, not more. He particularly distrusted the North American move toward electives. He felt that a common program, carefully selected and shared by all students, provided the best type of curriculum for a small liberal arts college.[49]

Despite the reservations of Sawyer and others, Acadia, by the early 1890s, had developed a program that was substantially different from that pursued a scant fifty years or so before, and, in fact, was substantially different from that then in use at most other Canadian colleges.[50] Although the freshman and sophomore years were carefully controlled, considerable freedom reigned in the last two years of study, where choices from a number of more "modern" subjects were possible.[51] The sciences were firmly entrenched, and a decade later an entirely separate program, with its own degree (bachelor of science), signalled the defeat of those who had always argued for a general education based on the classics.

In spite of the considerable and revealing debate about the nature of the academic program, at no stage in Acadia's development in the nineteenth century was it ever assumed that this was the sole reason for a

---

[47] See various catalogues of the college between 1870 and 1890.

[48] Longley, *Acadia*, 85–88.

[49] See Sawyer's address in *Jubilee of Acadia College, and Memorial Exercises* (Halifax, NS: Holloway Brothers, 1889).

[50] Robin Harris, *A History of Higher Education in Canada* (Toronto, 1960), 125–26, 147.

[51] Longley, *Acadia*, 89; Catalogues of Acadia College for the early 1890s.

Education Seasoned with Grace

college's existence. From the beginning, those who directed and supported Acadia College had seen a higher purpose for their institution. Any education divorced from religion, any attempt to understand God's world without comprehending God's Word, and any institution which did not lay as much emphasis on the moral man (and later woman) as on the intellectual person was bound to fail. A strong sense of "Christian education" was thus the third important force which shaped Acadia's liberal arts tradition.

Acadia College was not founded with the unanimous and whole-hearted support of the Baptist community of the Maritimes. There were many reservations, expressed and unexpressed, about the dangers of elevating human knowledge to such heights. Might it not lead to human conceit, the placing of mere intellect above God's grace? Until the end of the nineteenth century, the successive revivals that took place at Acadia would be looked upon by many as proof of God's approval, and did much to remove the earlier prejudice against the institution, and higher learning in general, but the reservations were never fully removed.[52]

In addresses to graduating students, letters to the editor, student orations, public speeches, and private reflections, an emphasis on the spiritual aspects of education was sounded time after time. One writer to the Baptist press expressed it well when he commented, "All education whether collegiate or other, theological or secular, which does not enlighten the mind as to the nature, scope, power and value of Faith as taught by the Word and Spirit of Truth, is totally deficient of the essential element of true knowledge."[53] In 1872, the professor of natural science spoke of the necessity of understanding a "God-made, God-governed and God-redeemed world."[54] At Acadia there could be no thought of putting "liberal education" and religious experience into separate compartments. Each infused, enriched, and illuminated the other.

What was viewed as a special characteristic of Acadia was early recognized as an important aspect of life and learning at that institution. In

---

[52] Moody, "Breadth of Vision," 12–14; see A. C. Chute, *The Religious Life of Acadia* (Wolfville, NS: Acadia University, 1933).

[53] *Christian Messenger* (August 15, 1866), A. B. to editor.

[54] Ibid. (November 6, 1872), William Elder's reply to an address from his students.

his inaugural address in 1861, the new professor of classics, James B. DeMille,[55] pointed out that

> there has been one influence present here, which though not generally considered as a part of a College, is yet pre-eminently a characteristic of this institution.... Founded by praying men, its very stones were hallowed by their prayers....
>
> Men came here to be illumined by the light of Education, and lo! They saw the light of the sun of Righteousness. They came for earthly knowledge and obtained that heavenly knowledge which is life eternal.
>
> They came to study and they learned to pray.[56]

The influence of the Maritime Baptist concept of Christian education is to be found not so much in what was taught, but rather how it was taught. There is little in the Acadia curriculum in the nineteenth century that could be classified as biblical studies. There were no theological courses as part of the bachelor of arts program. (A course in "Evidences of Christianity" was as close as they seem to have come in this area.) The quality of the professors and the atmosphere of the college, were the key elements, not the subjects taught. The true Christian spirit was to suffuse the whole process.

Buttressed by what Theodore H. Rand called "an abiding conviction of the paramount importance of Christian education," Acadia could with confidence and no sense of fear face the new subjects that came its way in the nineteenth century.[57] In 1874 President Sawyer spoke of the great importance of having education seasoned with grace, and so conducted that science and religion should not be considered as antagonistic forces, but rather as different methods of reading and understanding the purposes of God. Hence those institutions which make religion the foundation of the

---

[55] *Dictionary of Canadian Biography,* vol. X.

[56] *Christian Messenger* (July 10, 1861)

[57] Margaret Conrad, "'An abiding conviction of the paramount importance of Christian education': Theodore Harding Rand as educator, 1860–1900," *An abiding conviction: Maritime Baptists and their world,* ed. R. S. Wilson (Hantsport, NS, 1988), 155–95.

Education Seasoned with Grace

structure and all branches of human knowledge the materials with which to build, should [receive our complete support.][58]

Acadia's early concept of a liberal education clearly was influenced by a number of forces coming together in a unique combination. It was a concept rooted firmly in the classical tradition, tempered by practicality, and overlaid by the demands of evangelical Christianity. Acadia's approach to the search for truth was perhaps best summed up by its second president, J. M. Cramp, when he told the graduating class of 1862:

> all your inquiries, unite freedom with reverence;—the freedom of the unfettered explorer—the reverence for the authority of God. Search diligently, availing yourselves of all helps. Decide impartially, according to the evidence. Dare to differ from others, whatever results may follow, if truth and conscience forbid agreement. But always submit to the claims of truth, though human pride may deem them somewhat exacting. [59]

[58] Ibid. (September 2, 1874): 274–75.
[59] Ibid. (June 11, 1862), Cramp to the graduating class.

A Nova Scotia Baptist Family:
Four Generations of Leadership in Church and Academy

Howard John Whidden

This paper looks at the roles of four members of the Whidden family of Nova Scotia in the formation and development of the Baptist denomination. It begins with John Blair Whidden, whose conversion and baptism in 1821 during the great tide of evangelical revival in Nova Scotia led to the forming of a new Baptist congregation in Antigonish and the carrying of the Gospel message throughout the eastern mainland of the province. It continues with his son, Charles Blanchard Whidden, who, as a key member of that congregation, also engaged in provincial and Maritime Baptist affairs, particularly as a supporter of Acadia College, which was founded in 1838, fifteen years after the Antigonish church was formed.

In the next generation, Howard Primrose Whidden, an Acadia graduate and ordained, like his grandfather, served in the pulpit and then moved to lead two of Canada's Baptist universities, Brandon and McMaster, through periods of growth, travail and divisions in the denomination. His son, Evan MacDonald Whidden, also began his career in the pulpit and then moved to Brandon, and then Acadia, where he laboured in the trenches of theological education as professor of church history and sometime dean.

It is impossible to know what specific beliefs JBW and CBW held, but one can speculate that they were the evangelical certainties of the era, perhaps tempered, as the years passed, by influences from the emphasis on education that were hallmarks of Nova Scotia Baptists in the mid-nineteenth century. Acadia's founders, it must be stressed, specified that there were to be no religious tests for admission, and of this determination, HPW and EMW were the beneficiaries, heirs, and proponents.

The paper ends in 1968 when, after 130 years, Acadia severed its affiliation with the Maritime Baptist Convention; Brandon had preceded it by thirty years, and McMaster by eleven. And in that year, EMW retired after thirty years in the Acadia School of Theology.

A Nova Scotia Baptist Family

The First Generation

The minute book of Antigonish Baptist Church begins: "A Baptist Church formed by the Rev'd David Nutter July 1823 with the following named members viz John Whidden, Harriet Whidden.... Brother John Whidden was chosen Deacon."

A few pages later, the following was recorded:

This is to certify, that on the 4th day of November 1832 Mr. John Whidden of Antigonish was publicly, and solemnly set apart to the work of the ministry, as an itinerant preacher of the Baptist denomination by the imposition of hands, in the Baptist meeting house, and at the request of the Baptist Church of Antigonish. By this solemn act he is duly qualified to preach the gospel, to administer ordinances, and perform marriage services, and every duty devolving on a regular minister of Christ.

We commend him to the great Head of the Church—to the churches of Christ—and to the confidence of all to whom he is called to administer hoping that he will ever continue a faithful Minister of Jesus Christ.

This is signed by Edward Manning, T. S. Harding, and Robert McLearn, pastors of the churches in Cornwallis, Horton, and Rawdon, all prominent leaders of the denomination in the first half of nineteenth-century Nova Scotia. Thus, John Blair Whidden began his ministry as an itinerant evangelist in Antigonish and Guysborough Counties in eastern mainland Nova Scotia.

JBW was born November 21, 1791, at Stewiacke, Nova Scotia, the son and seventh child of Simeon and Dorothy Blair Whidden, Simeon being the youngest of four brothers who, with their father James, came in 1760 to Nova Scotia from New Hampshire as New England Planters. James died in 1800 as the result of a logging accident; John lived with an older sister's family, and then in 1807, at the age of sixteen, settled in Antigonish. Here he worked as a carpenter and bought a farm at the west end of the village, a property today owned by John Whidden, a great-great-grandson. On December 4th, 1816, he married Harriet Elizabeth Symonds, a Presbyterian like himself. To quote from his obituary in the minutes of the nineteenth session of the Baptist Convention of Nova Scotia, New Brunswick, and Prince Edward Island, "Having been brought

143

under concern in reference to his soul, and failing in obtaining any light or relief from any human source, he was led back to his Bible and the throne of grace, and ultimately found joyful deliverance. Himself and wife, with another brother were afterwards the first persons scripturally baptized in the village of Antigonish."

John Blair Whidden's baptism was in 1821, Antigonish Baptist Church was formed two years later, and his ordination as an itinerant preacher took place nine years after that, well on in the great wave of evangelical revival which spread over Nova Scotia starting in the 1770s and from which rose the Baptist church in this region.

Church minutes for December 5th, 1846, state that "the Lord in his mercy appeared for us under the ministry of the Rev. W. C. Rideout," and in a week eighteen people under the age of twenty were baptized, including three of JBW's own children and the future wife of one of them. The minutes for December 8th go on to state that "at a church meeting this day Bro John Whidden was called to take pastoral care of the church one half of his time." During the other half, he presumably carried on as an itinerant preacher in the Canso and Guysborough areas, and with his work as a farmer and carpenter; his obituary notes that "he built a small place of worship almost wholly at his own expense, which is now, by the payment of a few pounds at their own request, in the service of the Church and congregation of that place." Except for a period between 1858 to 1859, JBW was in pastoral charge of the Antigonish church until his death in 1864 at the age of seventy-two.

The process of building a Baptist church in Antigonish was not an easy task. To begin with, the area had been settled in the late eighteenth century predominantly by Roman Catholic Scots whose descendants were very much in the majority in the nineteenth century, and, in fact, still are. In addition, the minority non-Catholics had the Presbyterian church and Church of England as well as the Baptist church to choose from. Building membership was entirely a matter of evangelism. Presumably, this is where JBW shone, as he continued preaching in the Canso and Guysborough areas. Baptist congregations continued to form, though the great period of revivalism and evangelism was coming to a close in his last years; in fact, Baptists reached their acme in numbers in the century and a half between 1831 and 1981, representing, in 1861, 18.8 percent of the population of Nova Scotia.

Between 1821 and 1864, eighty people are listed as having been baptized into the Antigonish church, including nine of JBW's own family, but

A Nova Scotia Baptist Family

the church then had to contend with two more realities: the huge continuing wave of out-migration from Nova Scotia, and ever-present worldly temptations. Of the eighty, twenty-one were removed or dismissed (resigned) from membership, some of whom were noted as being received in other Baptist congregations in Canada or, more likely, the United States, and others who presumably just left town. In addition, there were eleven who were excluded for sins of the faith as well as the flesh, and, of course, some died. It is difficult to firmly establish the size of the congregation, though it is noted, "20th Dec. 1846 Lord's supper dispensed this day church members present 35," and "17th July 1847 Church meeting this day—17 male members present."

The first mention of the Antigonish church in minutes of the Maritime Baptist Convention is in 1858, where the statistics of Nova Scotia churches state that it had twenty-seven members; in the 1860 minutes, John Whidden is listed as the ordained minister, and the church is noted as making a donation to the convention of just over one pound. In 1858, according to the church minutes, "Rev. Albert F. Porter took the pastoral care of the church," and in July 1859, the minutes state that "Bro Whidden resumed charge of the church"; he continued in charge until his death, which occurred July 19, 1864. Why he resigned is unstated, but clearly, judging from Porter's short tenure, the Antigonish church had its difficulties. The obituary in the 1865 minutes of the Maritime Baptist Convention is fulsome in its admiration of JBW:

> His praise is truly in all the churches in the Eastern part of Nova Scotia. Father Whidden was not distinguished for brilliant talents, but for something far better; brilliant piety, a guileless heart, and an eminently devoted Christian and ministerial life....He preached most successfully from house to house....Of his blameless and benevolent life and Christian faithfulness, most pleasing testimony was afforded in this village, where he spent the greater part of his life and died,—even many persons, Roman Catholic and Protestant, coming in during his dying hours to gaze on his countenance, and receive a word from one of their best friends, and a man of God....As might be expected, his life was pre-eminently a life of prayer,—of secret prayer no doubt; he was accustomed also, for 25 years, to maintain family worship *three* times a day, and a sister in his church recently remarked that she would go to a meeting to hear Father Whidden *pray*, if for nothing else.

Comment, after such an encomium, would be difficult.

KEEPING THE FAITH

The Second Generation

If JBW could be considered a pioneer in the Nova Scotia Baptist world, his son could be said to have been a builder. Charles Blanchard Whidden, born in 1831, was the ninth of eleven children of John and Harriet, and the youngest son. He was baptized in December 1846 on the same day as his future wife, Eunice Caroline Graham; that was a bumper month for the Antigonish church, with eighteen baptisms bringing the total membership from forty-nine to sixty-seven.

In addition to taking over the family farm, CBW become a merchant, and trade became his life's focus. Over his lifetime, he built a successful retail and wholesale business under the name C. B. Whidden & Son which, over the years, owned twenty-two sailing vessels in trade with Newfoundland and the West Indies, which was perhaps not surprizing as his father-in-law and three of his brothers-in-law were ship captains. The Whidden firm actively canvassed Antigonish County for local produce and products to carry abroad and sold imports at the retail and wholesale levels.

CBW first appears in the Antigonish church minutes at age twenty in 1851, being appointed clerk in place of his older brother, who had gone to the US. The minutes from 1856 record a resolution to pay him 40 shillings per year for tending to fires and lights, a resolution renewed for the following year. In 1869, a Sunday school was established, and he was appointed as one of the teachers. A hint as to his life's path, though, comes in the 1870 entry; the amalgamated accounts for heating and lighting for 1868 to 1870 show that the church was in debt to him for $20.52, there having been a shortfall in what he had been paid. It was resolved to pay him sixteen dollars for fuel and light in 1871, and to pay him from donation excesses over expenditures until the debt was retired. Family lore has it that he was always very generous to the church and to Acadia College; that he carried a debt of more than a year's cost for fuel and continued to supply the same gives some early substance to that lore.

The minutes of March 4th, 1871, mention Acadia for the first time, recording that an appeal had been received "from the Governors of Acadia College apportioning amount of Seven Dollars $7.00 as our share for yearly expenses." After some weeks of dithering, a committee of two was formed to collect what they could, that being six dollars. Those of May 30th, 1871, state that "a P.O. order of $6.00 was (purchased) and forwarded to A. D. Barss Esq. as our donation and a receipt for the same was duly received."

146

A Nova Scotia Baptist Family

A number of points are clear from entries of this period. First, the Antigonish church was still struggling: it was without a pastor from time to time, although several early attempts were made to find someone whom they would share with Canso, and then to obtain a pastor of their own. Secondly, Acadia, also living on the edge financially, saw itself as a partner of Baptist churches in the Maritimes through the convention, and therefore could "apportion" support. Thirdly, though pressed for money, the congregation did step up to assist Acadia, thus showing that the church was forward-looking in supporting higher education and theological training.

From about 1870 on, the minutes show the rapid transformation of the Antigonish church from a loose gathering of the baptized into an organized entity. From meetings held annually several times a year, or not at all, there were at least monthly "conferences." Members who missed meetings were asked to correspond with the clerk. Ad hoc committees were formed and reported. A Communion service was drawn up for use by the church. Special collections were taken up for a destitute "Sister" and for the Barney's River church. Delegates were chosen to attend Eastern Association gatherings. In short, Antigonish Baptists were becoming thoroughly structured, just as the Maritime Baptist Convention was, as shown by the increasing length and complexity of its annual convention minutes. Even so, the congregation went through a number of pastors in the last quarter of the century; whether Antigonish was more fractious than other churches is unknowable, nor can it be discerned what influence CBW exerted in these matters.

From family sources, it appears that this was the period which marked CBW's rise from local merchant to businessman, one whose ships began to trade and carry Antigonish County goods internationally. It was a great age of Canadian economic growth and, on a much smaller scale, he followed the same path from humble roots to business success as did the great financial, commercial, and railway tycoons of Toronto and Montreal.

CBW appears often in the Antigonish minute book as a mover or seconder of motions. In 1872, he was appointed to a committee formed to find a location for a new church. The site chosen was a lot owned by CBW which he offered in return for the lot occupied by the present building; the motion to accept was seconded by CBW, backed by his wife and nephew, and passed unanimously, a piece of business on which we shall refrain from comment. After the three-hour Christmas service of 1875, the congregation reassembled for the sale of pews (the cushioning of which was to conform with the platform desk) in the newly completed building, and voted to sell the shell of the old, the proceeds of which would be used to buy a lot for a parsonage. The Antigonish Baptist Church had clearly reached maturity, a fact recognized by Acadia, which raised the annual allotment to ten dollars.

In the 1870s and 1880s, the family was very much involved in church affairs. CBW was often a delegate to Eastern Conference meetings and to the Maritime Baptist Convention, culminating in his presidency of the convention in 1891, to which his wife, Eunice, was also a delegate. His cousin and then his eldest son, David Graham Whidden, served successively as church clerk. His second son, Charles Edgar, was a delegate to the convention and also served as clerk; all three served on various committees, not the least of which organized and fundraised for a new parsonage, for the building of which CBW received the contract, resigning from the building committee in favour of his son just prior to the motion. I prefer to interpret this as an indication that the small size of the congregation limited the number who were capable of undertaking such a project, and that there was no inclination to look outside the congregation for another builder who would undoubtedly be Catholic. The parsonage was completed in 1884, with an overrun of $800, which CBW offered to carry at 6 percent interest. The next year he presented a list of fourteen members who agreed to make specified lump-sum payments to erase the remaining debt of $435. Of that sum, he, his two older sons, and his mother-in-law pledged a total of $240. The offer was accepted.

In the winter of 1875 to 1876, CBW and his wife lost three young children to diphtheria in a two-month period, but nothing of this appears in the minutes. From 1882 to 1886, he served as the liberal-conservative member of the legislative assembly for Antigonish County, surely a vote of confidence in his ability and his support for Antigonish from that most Catholic of counties.

From 1883 to his death, nineteen years later, he was a governor of Acadia. His obituary in the Maritime Baptist year book, while not so baroque as that of his father, heaped praise upon him.

> Of Brother Whidden it could be truly said, "I have fought a good fight, I have kept the faith." He had long been a pillar of strength, spiritually and financially, in this church; and of late years especially, he had stood under his financial obligations with unswerving fidelity and a large generosity. He was a member of the Board of Governors of Acadia College, and as a far-seeing man his counsel was

A Nova Scotia Baptist Family

invaluable. He was a very generous contributor to the funds of that institution.

It further notes that "he also did much for the development of the resources of his native county. He ever took an active interest in all things relating to its social and moral well-being." His second son and business partner, Edgar, followed him in managing the firm and was on Acadia's board for a term. (I have to comment that a look through the board minutes from his time as a member shows that he was by no means a star in that theatre; he probably deserved a C+ for attendance and a B for his service on committees, but his descendants always have believed that he indeed merited an A for philanthropy.)

CBW was a layman of a type much desired and not unusual in congregations of the time: engaged in the spiritual life of the congregation, involved in the wider church, energetic in his participation, possessed of some means, and fully prepared to use his money in the support and advancement of his denomination. This was not uncommon in the latter half of nineteenth-century Canada, when wealth became more widely spread through commerce, industry, and finance amongst people who saw philanthropy as a duty. His fellows were to be found across the country in many congregations of all denominations, with the Masseys of Toronto being the most notable; in the records of my own Anglican parish of St. John's in Wolfville, there are several such.

The Antigonish Baptist Church continued in operation for some time after CBW's death in 1902, but, finally, the inevitabilities of the times and location prevailed. In the mid-1930s, those Whiddens remaining in the town, along with the other Baptists of the congregation, closed the doors and joined the congregation of the United Church of Canada down the street.

The Third Generation

Of CBW's three sons, it was the youngest, Howard Primrose Whidden, who made the Baptist church his life. Because of the death of three of his brothers, there were nine years between him and his next oldest sibling, Charles Edgar, and he grew up in a time of newly gained family prosperity. HPW was born in 1871 and baptized at the age of eleven in 1883. He attended school in Antigonish and then Horton Academy, the secondary school arm of Acadia College, and then became part of Acadia's Class of 1891, graduating at the age of twenty. He thus spent five or six of his most

149

formative years in Wolfville under Acadia's influence. I see this as important in developing his life-long approach to his faith and his interpretation of it. Acadia, while Baptist owned and operated, so to speak, had been explicitly founded to be open to students of any denomination, in contrast to Nova Scotia's Anglican and Roman Catholic institutions of higher learning, and this undoubtedly was a foundation for his broad-church outlook.

Early on, Howard Whidden made the decision to make the church his life. The April 5th, 1890, minutes of the vestry of the Antigonish church state that "the clerk reported having mailed to Bro Howard Whidden a licence to preach the Gospel as voted by the members of the church"; he is listed as a licentiate in the 1891 and 1892 annual reports, and is reported in May 1892 to have preached morning and evening to a larger-than-usual congregation. His path in life was thus set at age nineteen, a year before his graduation in 1891, the year of his father's presidency of the convention. Acadia then did not have a formal theological training program, so from 1892 to 1894, he attended Newton Theological Institution and McMaster University, obtaining a BTh from the latter, while at the same time, 1892 and 1893, lecturing on public reading and speaking at McMaster. His letter of dismissal from the Antigonish church was issued in 1894, the year in which he married and embarked on a two-year pastorate in Morden, Manitoba.

HPW and his wife, Katherine Louisa Ganong, from a New Brunswick Baptist family, and whom he met at Acadia, settled in Morden, Manitoba, then a village and watering spot for the railway, where he became pastor. In 1896 and '97, he did further studies at Newton and Chicago. From 1897 to 1900, he was pastor in Galt, Ontario, (now part of Cambridge) during which time he again lectured on public speaking and reading at McMaster; from 1900 to 1903, he was back in Manitoba as professor of biblical literature and English at Brandon College. In 1904, he was called to the large First Baptist Church in Dayton, Ohio, where, over an eight-year period, C. G. Stone and F. Joan Garnett say, he "was honoured by positions of responsibility in the Ohio and Northern Baptist Conventions being frequently sought after for important commissions." He was certainly successful enough for Denison University, an Ohio Baptist institution, to grant him in 1907 an honorary doctorate of divinity. From Dayton, after a sixteen-year grounding in both pulpit and lectern, he was called in 1912 to become president of Brandon College, to which he moved with his wife and their six children, beginning a twenty-nine-year period at the helm, successively, of the two Baptist institutions in which he had already served.

Brandon College was at that time an affiliate of McMaster University, which granted degrees to Brandon graduates. It was to some extent a feeder school for McMaster, where it was common for both graduates and faculty to move on. HPW accepted the post after being assured that the arts department would continue to be supported. This was central to his concept of higher education; throughout his years in office, he fought tenaciously to maintain the liberal arts and sciences as the core of both institutions, and to maintain cordial relations with the greater community, a priority for him throughout his time at Brandon, which stood the college in good stead.

Stone and Garnett quote his words from his first report to the board and convention: "In our staff of twenty-one we have a group of men and women carefully chosen because of their Christian ideals, their ability to influence for good the young people in attendance as well as their skill in presenting ably and efficiently the subjects they profess to teach. Only in this way is it possible to conduct a Christian college so as to secure the results desired by the good people who are naturally interested in and supporters of our educational enterprise." One notable aspect of this concern for the greater society was manifest in the excellent department of music, which served both Baptist churches and the community at large.

The outbreak of war in 1914 had a great effect on Brandon, not only for the four years of its duration, but also the future. In common with many other Canadian universities, a Canadian Officers' Training Corps was established with an accompanying university battalion; by 1917, 280 students had trained and enlisted, among them two nursing sisters and HPW's son Evan. Programs for patriotic work were formed, and the war effort became a central part of college life. Brandon was connected to the formation of Khaki College, set up in England by Sir Arthur Currie, the commander of the Canadian corps, at the instigation of the YMCA and Canadian academics, which from 1917 to 1919 provided university courses for overseas troops. All of these were a natural response for HPW, who saw patriotism and duty to God, king, and country as just and right.

Not surprizing for someone coming from a New England Planter and United Empire Loyalist Nova Scotia background, he also saw it as his duty to accept, when prevailed upon by many diverse groups in the Brandon area, to stand for parliament in support of the Unionist government of Sir Robert Borden in the "conscription" election of 1917. He was a prominent choice, and his views were certainly those of Borden, who came from a similar background and with whom he had a connection, as his uncle and Borden had been law partners. He won with a large majority and served as an MP until 1921.

In 1919, more than forty returned men were enrolled (of a total of 418 students), among them the presidents of the Student Association, the YMCA, Athletic Society, Ministerial Society, Student Volunteer Band, and Literary Society. With this influence, change was inevitable; a new postwar culture in the student body sharpened the need for expansion, and money was raised for a gymnasium in 1918 and a science building in 1922.

Fundraising was a continual concern, and the college was often in debt to the bank. Costs had risen during the war, and contributions from the Baptist Union were small; campaigns for current funds among the churches were conducted almost annually. In addition, HPW was able to get contributions for buildings from the city, and several wealthy contributors initiated a campaign to raise $100,000; additionally, the college had sold twenty-year bonds, with interest payments to come from an endowment fund, in order to consolidate debts of $115,000. Financial pressures never abated, but in this Brandon was most certainly among the majority of Canadian institutions of higher learning.

In commenting on HPW's time at Brandon, Stone and Garnett make observations on three important areas. First, they point to the able leaders from western church, business, and professional fields who became members of the college's board of directors and who were instrumental in fundraising, some of whom were very large donors themselves. Secondly, they were quite laudatory of the first-rate faculty members at Brandon and of the high quality of those appointed by HPW, all of whom gave strong support to his ideals of a Christian college as described in his first report to the board. Finally, Brandon continued as a liberal arts and science institution with community connections.

Brandon and HPW did not escape charges of liberal theological teaching from ultraconservative and fundamentalist elements of the Baptist church. The opposition appears to have been rather like volcanic mountains gently smoking for long periods, occasionally erupting in great, noisy clouds of ash and flows of vitriol. Essentially in the academic arena, these were battles between supporters of Baptist-run liberal arts and science institutions of higher learning and those who wanted institutions in which all curricula, including the sciences, were informed by conservative doctrine; in short, to be Bible colleges. While this problem emerged for

A Nova Scotia Baptist Family

HPW at Brandon, it was later at McMaster that he faced it in an existential struggle.

The Baptist Union appointed a commission to cooperate with the senate of Brandon in making a thorough review of curriculum and methods of instruction in the theological department. HPW wrote a statement affirming that "every teacher was loyal to the great principles of the Christian life and truth, emphasizing in their experience and teaching the divine Saviorhood and Lordship of Christ," a statement which, though not satisfying some, gave no grounds on which to quarrel. The commission met, consulted, and examined; its report in January 1923 concluded "that the Baptists of Western Canada are to be congratulated on having an educational institution in its midst of the character of Brandon College" and went on to pay a stirring tribute to the work and influence of the retiring president, Dr. Whidden.

In 1923, HPW submitted his resignation in order to become chancellor, as the president was then called, of the mother institution, McMaster University in Toronto. It was expected, says Charles M. Johnston in volume one of his history of the university, that "Whidden's new career would be a successful one, given his administrative talents, his capacity to inspire urban congregations, and his connections with politicians and educators across the country." Recently appointed executive-committee member of the board of governors E. Carey Fox and the new chairman of the board, Albert Matthews, met and interviewed HPW at the Lakehead and were enthusiastic in their support. Both Fox and Matthews, later lieutenant governor of Ontario, were prominent Toronto Baptist businessmen who supported McMaster and HPW throughout his chancellorship, and, without doubt, were crucial in the continued success of both.

The new chancellor arrived in Toronto and found himself embroiled in the same morass that he had hoped had been put to rest by the commission report on Brandon. The pot was stirred by the Rev. T. T. Shields of Jarvis Street Baptist Church, who wrote, in the context of McMaster's support to Brandon, that to "aid and abet the destructive work of Brandon College is nothing short of treason to Christ and His gospel." A powerful antagonist, an indefatigable, seemingly bigoted, unscrupulous, and persuasive preacher, and corrosive fundamentalist populist, he made HPW's life a misery for nearly five years. Shields attacked the pernicious influences of the University of Chicago (where many Baptist clergy, including HPW, had studied), various faculty members, HPW, and McMaster itself for being liberal, unsound, and/or modernist, all synonyms for anti-Christian.

153

His views on what Brandon and McMaster should be were the very antithesis of those held by HPW, and he went to every Ontario Baptist Convention church which would have him to thunder them. Shields also took every opportunity to be quoted in the press; he started his own paper, and even twenty-five years later, his sermons were still printed in the right-wing *Toronto Telegram*. McMaster's travails were played out in the public forum, to the bemusement of other universities; Shields came within striking distance of bringing down McMaster as a Baptist institution. Charles M. Johnson devoted a long, detailed, and eyebrow-lifting chapter to this struggle.

By harnessing resources from faculty, board, and as many pulpits as possible in the Ontario Baptist Convention, McMaster was prepared when the Shields forces struck at the convention meeting in October 1926 by moving the dismissal of L. H. Marshall, a prominent theology faculty member. In debate, Marshall, far better than HPW on his feet before the assembly, rounded on Shields, and finished up by saying, "The bigoted intolerance that has been displayed is at complete variance with the historic Baptist position simply because it seeks to strangle that reasonable liberty which is the birthright of every true disciple of Jesus Christ." He then asked that the divisive, disruptive, miserable campaign be brought to a close. The university, its officers, and its instructors were endorsed by a vote of 708 to 258. Shields went off bearing grudges and turned to the Baptist-run University of Des Moines, where he succeeded in taking control of the Baptist Bible Union of Iowa and the university with the aim of freeing it from the taint of modernism. In 1929, with many of the University of Des Moines's faculty having resigned or been fired, the students rose against Shields with, as Johnston says, "a barrage of eggs directed at the administration building in which Shields had taken prostrate refuge while urgently telephoning the police"; the university closed and was eventually turned into a medical school.

McMaster had won its battle, but divisions among the Baptists of Ontario were not reconciled. Marshall struck at the very heart of the disagreement amongst Baptists then and since—what is reasonable liberty? In essence, these were long-running and still-entrenched divisions reflecting those in the wider North American Baptist world, between urban and rural, broadly educated and less so, liberal and conservative, and the wealthier and the less so, which tended to be manifest in the distrust or welcoming of broadly and highly educated clergy. The stigma of elitism continued to dog McMaster as it endeavoured to increase support in the convention so that it could expand, and its theology graduates who had gone on to further study at Rochester or Chicago often found that pulpits south of the border were more welcoming than many in Ontario—to the detriment of the latter. And two generations of Whidden children blanched and trembled at the utterance of the name T. T. Shields.

The late George Rawlyk, however, made the point that McMaster's and HPW's positions on evangelism and Baptist tenets in relation to higher education were at odds with traditional Baptist opposition to modernism. Paul F. Armstrong, in his working paper "The Achievement of George Rawlyk," MIRCS Institute, discusses Rawlyk's interpretation of nineteenth-century Baptists as Henry Alline's "heirs," concluding that "the immediate contention of Rawlyk that Whidden betrayed radical evangelism seems unavoidable."

Armstrong quotes Mark Noll, an American evangelical historian, who wrote, "What matters is the common path away from spiritual authenticity and communal interdependence, which Rawlyk felt characterized much of nineteenth-century Canadian Baptist life, toward mechanistic spirituality and individualistic self-assertion." The break between the traditional and modern happened in Upper Canada over McMaster, but not in the Maritimes, or at least not until later, and in a less cataclysmic form. The governors of McMaster and Brandon, including many well-to-do urban businessmen who were instrumental in enabling both institutions to succeed and grow, were never in sympathy with imposing on higher education the traditional redemptive evangelism embraced by a large segment of western and Ontario Baptists; this was entirely representative of HPW's views, formed as they had been by his years at Acadia and Chicago, and his experience in the large Dayton First Baptist Church.

In a similar vein, Tom Mitchell, the former Brandon University archivist, described how Brandon's unequivocal support for World War I, the Union Government, and HPW's tenure as the member of parliament came back to bite the college in 1938. At the height of the Depression, the very time western Baptists were unable to continue their support, Brandon's labour movement, still seething from the conscription laws of 1917, made it impossible for the city to give financial aid to the college when it was bankrupt. It is clear that HPW was willing to burn bridges with fundamentalist Baptists at McMaster when his vision of academic freedom was at stake, but not that he understood how deeply his election to the Unionist government in 1917 was resented by the City of Brandon's industrial working class.

155

KEEPING THE FAITH

Beginning in 1923, overlapping the Shields wars, and coming more sharply into focus afterwards, was the question of moving McMaster from Toronto. The university occupied one large building with an attached chapel on the south side of Bloor Street just east of University Avenue; the original buildings are still there and now house the Royal Conservatory of Music. As it was hemmed in on three sides by the Royal Ontario Museum and the University of Toronto, and with no chance of extending existing facilities, the necessity of moving the institution was finally accepted; even the student body campaigned for more and larger facilities, particularly for sciences and athletics. The alternative, eventual absorption by University of Toronto, could not even be contemplated. A move to Hamilton, which HPW and the board supported, had been mooted for some time, and Hamilton city fathers as well as various local groups were anxious to make a deal. The city offered to donate to McMaster a site of more than fifty acres on which to build a new campus, and to raise half a million dollars as a contribution. The university hoped that about three times that could be raised from Baptist sources in Canada and the US in addition to the proceeds from selling the Toronto properties. At the 1927 meeting of the Baptist Convention of Ontario and Quebec, Jarvis Street Baptist Church was evicted from the convention, and the removal proposition authorizing a fresh start for McMaster was accepted.

Though HPW might have seemed to have triumphed, the way forward was by no means smooth. Preparations for the creation of a new campus in Hamilton ran straight into the beginning of the Great Depression, which understandably made fundraising a nightmare, as the pool of possible donors—the city, wealthy supporters, and the congregations of churches—were all detrimentally affected. Nonetheless, after three years of planning, canvassing for money, and construction, the university opened for the fall term of 1930 with four buildings: a women's and a men's residence, an arts and administration building, and Hamilton Hall, the science building paid for by the city. There was also a refectory and a residence for the chancellor funded by E. C. Fox and Cyrus Eaton, the Baptist Nova Scotia-born American industrialist, McMaster graduate, and long-time friend of HPW. Eaton had bought him a car in his Brandon days; after one near collision with a bull during his first driving lesson, his sons refused to let him try again, and to the end of his career he always hired a student to drive him.

The 1930s, while difficult, were a decade of strengthening McMaster's academic position; outstanding new faculty were hired, science

156

A Nova Scotia Baptist Family

programs were expanded to the point that there was some worry the arts were being left behind, and the student body increased. The new McMaster was a reflection of HPW's concept of what a Christian university could be: open to all and non-proselytizing, but with a strong moral and Christian foundation. A measure of his success came as HPW was elected as a member of the Royal Society of Canada, a real source of gratification, as were the five more honorary doctorates bestowed upon him.

In the late 1930s, McMaster's expansion was put on hold as war loomed again. In 1941, at the age of seventy, HPW, becoming somewhat forgetful, retired on the advice of his son Evan. He and my grandmother moved to Toronto, and he took on the task of editing *Canadian Baptist* for a number of years. He died in 1952, aged eighty. *The Globe and Mail*, in his obituary, noted that at Brandon, "he gave vigorous leadership to the struggling college," and that "during his term in the House of Commons, Dr. Whidden's special interests were immigration and the furtherance of scientific research." Other printed appreciations, unidentified, went on to say that he "lived an active life of great service to his fellow-men," that in higher education he "wielded a wide and constructive influence," and that in his field, he had been recognized as one of the ablest men of his time. Though by no means as orotund as the obituaries of his father and grandfather, these tributes described a man who had made a positive impact on his church and country.

In 1948, the science programs of McMaster were organized under a separate division which could receive provincial grants, and, in 1957, the final break was made with the Baptist convention. The divinity college alone retained a Baptist connection and carried on to deal with the struggles within the convention.

The Fourth Generation

Evan MacDonald Whidden was born in 1898 in Galt, Ontario, where his father was the minister of the South Water Street Baptist Church. He was the third of eight children of Howard Primrose and Katherine Louisa Ganong Whidden, though two of his next youngest brothers died in early childhood. He attended primary school in Dayton, Ohio, and when, in 1912, the family relocated to Brandon, enrolled in Brandon Academy which was affiliated with Brandon College.

Evan Whidden entered the college in 1916, and in March the following year, he enlisted in the Canadian Field Artillery, where he served,

157

until July 1919, in Winnipeg, Petawawa, England, France, Belgium, and Germany, the latter two subsequent to the Armistice of November 11th, 1918. He was in action at the front for just the last week of the war and told me that his only war wound was a bite from his horse. In his last four months, EMW was attached to Khaki University in England. He returned to Canada in time to reenter Brandon in the fall semester of 1919.

From his graduation in 1921 until 1936, his path took him back and forth between the pulpit and the student life. He was the student pastor of the Baptist church at Estevan, Saskatchewan, and then at Shaunavon. He did graduate work at McMaster and was pastor in Raebow and Palmerston, Ontario, receiving his MA degree in 1925. EMW then went to the Yale Divinity School while also acting as pastor of a nearby church, and he was granted a BTh in 1928. From then until 1935, he was the minister at Tabernacle Baptist Church in Winnipeg, resigning in order to do doctoral studies for a year in Edinburgh and a summer in Wiesbaden before accepting a position at Brandon College as professor of theology and dean of arts. When Brandon severed its connection with the Baptist Church in 1938, EMW went to Acadia as professor of church history, where he remained for thirty years, also serving as dean of theology from 1953 to 1963.

When he became dean, EMW was the longest serving member of the department, which, by the mid-1950s, was staffed with a very talented and diverse faculty that remained intact into the late 1960s. Amongst EMW's proudest achievements was the creation of a position for Dr. Charles Taylor, who developed a program of clinical pastoral training, including prison ministry, which became nationally recognized.

The overall tasks facing EMW and the School of Theology faculty in the 1950s and 1960s were very similar, though on a smaller scale, to those his father faced at McMaster: increasing enrollment; strengthening the faculty; focusing on a broad, liberal course of study; and keeping the fundamentalists at bay. On the larger front, there was the increasingly pressing question of Acadia's future as a Baptist institution. These topics were addressed over a fourteen-year span in various issues of the School of Theology *Bulletin* and elucidated the position of the school and its faculty and were, to some extent, responses to continual onslaughts from a fundamentalist element in the Maritime Baptist Convention, especially after their establishment of a bible school in Moncton.

The January 1955 edition of the *Bulletin* leads with an article on the dearth of pastors in the Maritime convention; membership numbers had increased for a decade, and ten new churches had been established, but even though sixty-one new pastors had been ordained and thirty-four others received into the fellowship, fifty-six had moved outside the Maritimes and fifty-three more had retired or died. As a result, "rapidly growing sects are continually riddling the membership of pastorless churches." In the same decade, of the forty graduates of the school, thirty-two served in convention churches and only three had left the region. Twenty-one new students, however, enrolled that academic year, and this was a hopeful sign. Of those whom the convention had ordained, 80 percent were university trained while fewer than 50 percent of those received from other conventions were. Here lay a driving factor for the school: the desire to maintain and increase the cadre of a university-trained pastorate. Against that desire lay the core of opposition to the school from fundamentalist, "anti-modernist," elements which simmered unceasingly in the convention. Over the next decade, enrollment, with an increasing number of women, remained steady at around sixty, by no means enough to fill the pulpits of Maritime churches.

Over that decade, the *Bulletin* contained a number of "Here I stand" articles by members of the theology faculty, all decidedly liberal. In the January 1956 issue, EMW outlined his position in "Theology at Acadia."

> Obviously there is theology in the Scriptures. Just as obviously the methods which God used in giving us the Scriptures did not include those which produced for us anywhere in the Bible a final comprehensive summary of all its truths.... It is partly for that reason that throughout the Christian era men and churches have attempted to create summaries of the Faith in the form of creeds and confessions of faith.... Need it be said that there have been a great number of theologians in Christian history, and further, that great religious leaders as well as great theologians have often fathered great theological systems, parties and schools.
>
> Six things may be said about these schools of thought. First, deliberately or not, each has tended to become the Christian Faith for the mass of its followers, instead of an interpretation of that living faith with its source in the Scriptures. Second, more often than not, the systems have been marked by some form of excess, however unintentionally. Overemphasizing some things or leaving out others, systems have lost Biblical balance and the balance of general truth. Third, since it is the creation of man, each system bears the mark of fallible man. When churches demand its acceptance, they are "teaching as their doctrines the precepts of men." Matt.15:9.

KEEPING THE FAITH

Fourth, each great system will be found to contain very much truth, and some of them more truth than others. Fifth, generally speaking it is not disagreement on what are the main Christian doctrines which marks the difference between schools. Revelation, God (including the doctrine of the Trinity), man, sin, Christ, salvation and the Christian life, the work of the Holy Spirit, the Church, and the last things—these are the perennial themes of theology. Systems vary in their interpretations of these themes and in the choices made to give these or those special emphases. And sixth, the great systems have remained to this day, or they tend to perpetuate both their errors and their truths in revised systems. Hence, if for no other reasons, theology must be taught to students to save them from error inherited from this system or that.

But all teachers at Acadia stand within three concentric circles—the circle of Protestantism; the evangelical circle within Protestantism; and the Baptist circle within the evangelical circle....

It would be both untrue and unworthy to say that any man teaching at Acadia must be fastened to any one of those inherited systems of theology which reach out from the inner to the outer one of those circles. That would put him in bondage to man instead of God.... But it is for any man at Acadia to be an honest interpreter and to try to teach a student to be so....

It is our task to see to it that our students are not misled, but rather enriched from every source that can be found. No man then should expect Acadia theology to be bound either by the old simply because of its age or by the new because of its novelty, no matter who propounds it; but to be for the best theology; taking the living Scriptures as sufficient authority in all matters of faith and practice, understood typically in the light of God's manifestations in nature and man's history.

This would seem to provide a good statement of EMW's beliefs as a Baptist educator and the framework upon which he sought to provide theological education at Acadia. In the March 1956 edition, EMW asked the following, in an article titled "Were the Founders of Acadia Right?"

Why did they say "Decided religious tests in our churches; no religious tests in our college?" Could the answer be other than that they knew that each man lives in more than one society, each of which has its own native principles of life? There is the church with its

160

A Nova Scotia Baptist Family

own appropriate principles, including that of a protected oneness in matters of faith. There is the college with its own appropriate rules, including the freedom to examine all things. There is the state with its own appropriate marks, including that of containing in its protection all free societies within its bounds.

"No religious tests" at the new college meant in principle that men as religiously unmarked citizens could come to consider what the whole past had said, and what the future might say.

This he qualified by acknowledging that, at the time, few students coming to Acadia, though some might not be Baptists, would not be Christian. Again, he stated the case for a school of theology as part of the university and free from convention control. In January 1958, he continued to make the case more explicitly:

All of this is not to suggest that the School of Theology thinks of itself as advanced and seeking license; or that it desires to work out some dire theological revolution. Its members know themselves as bound to the majestic truth of the Scriptures, and as interpreters thereof.... And finally we are to teach all as best we can, what types of healing rays are needed for the deep sores of our day, and how with success to direct those rays by means of the instruments of mind and hearts. Here is suggested our responsibility to the Light of the World and to our people.

The pressure on the School of Theology in the late 1950s and early 1960s was part of an examination of the structure of Acadia itself in changing times. Watson Kirkconnell wrote in the January 1960 issue of the *Bulletin*: "For better or for worse, Acadia is now the only Baptist University in the British Commonwealth." The Baptist convention still appointed all members of the board of governors, but for decades the alumni association had nominated half, none of whom had ever been rejected by the convention. McMaster changed its structure, setting up a related but independent divinity college in order to secure the huge provincial grants required to maintain and expand its extensive science programs. Acadia received $50,000 from the Nova Scotia government, a pittance by comparison, but in line with grants to Dalhousie.

Kirkconnell goes on to say,

The affection and good will of Maritime Baptists toward Acadia seem to be strengthening with the years. Part of this betterment in relations has been due to the untiring and devoted efforts of Dean Whidden and his colleagues in the School of Theology. Part of it has come from reciprocal efforts of the Convention's committee on relations with Acadia University. Part of it come from the helpfulness of Convention officials, Convention pastors and a host of men and women of good will.

The April 1964 issue of the *Bulletin* contains the transcript of a discussion with EMW and Dr. M. R. Cherry, his successor as dean, chaired by Prof. Charles Taylor and entitled "The Church and Higher Education." Essentially, they agreed that Acadia was of great benefit to Baptists of the Atlantic provinces, as here would be trained the rank and file of the lay leadership of the church. EMW stated that the great majority of Baptist leaders in North America would agree with Acadia's charter that neither students nor faculty should be required to meet religious tests, but also that Baptist-sponsored colleges and universities should be staffed by persons of moral and religious character.

EMW also argued for the School of Theology's continuance as part of the university where theology students would be exposed to the whole gamut of learning and opinion which would face them out in the world. Without a university connection and training for its students, the School of Theology would be in danger of becoming a mere Bible college. "I think that because of the magnitude of the Scripture...our students should be trained in a university atmosphere...that they might be saved from narrowing the Scripture truth to some special school—in other words, the Scripture has a universal outlook and so does the university discipline seek to have a universal outlook." Prof. Taylor summed up EMW's and Dr. Cherry's comments thus: "The church-related college provided the opportunity for the relation of the Christian faith to other disciplines, and so helps young people to a more meaningful acceptance of the Christian faith. And, on the other hand, it constantly challenges the Christian educator to articulate the faith in terms relevant to his generation."

However, similar forces to those that had brought change to Brandon and McMaster soon came to rock Acadia. This academic world in which EMW lived and worked, and which he sought to strengthen and defend, came crashing down in the 1967 meetings of the Atlantic Provinces Baptist Convention at which the de facto status quo, in place since Acadia's founding, was rent asunder when the convention passed a resolution requiring that all faculty espouse Christian principles. Uproar ensued in the university and in the press. The provincial government could not fund

A Nova Scotia Baptist Family

Acadia on such a basis; Acadia could not exist without government funding. Some members of faculty daydreamed that, through the alumni association, they might get control of the board. Great pressure was put on Premier Robert Stanfield by prominent Baptists to keep the lid on, so to speak. Acadia's charter was altered: convention could now appoint 40 percent of the governors, removing Baptist control, the alumni association would appoint 40 percent, and 20 percent would consist of faculty and student representatives along with members appointed by the government. Following the McMaster model, the Acadia Divinity College was created with its own board of governors, but the granting of degrees and approval of faculty appointments and curricula continued to rest with the university. The theology faculty fought hard for these safeguards, desiring to maintain the high standards and liberal bent of the school within which they taught in the face of the rightward march of the convention majority. The ADC opened on August 1st, 1968.

EMW had retired as dean in 1963 after ten years in the office. Dr. Earl C. Merrick, in the January 1964 *Bulletin*, commented,

> He brought to the task of shaping a new era for the School of Theology a rich store of scholarship, directive judgement and patience, plus a unique vision of the role that graduate training for the ministry must play in the proclamation of the Gospel. It is a considered judgement to say that every idea that Dr. Whidden brought to the years of his service, is written somewhere, visibly or invisibly, into the structure and future of the present School. He has put them there by the very quality of his leadership, his faith in the nature of truth in the large, his personal witness to the graciousness of the Gospel and his untiring passion for careful definition of the ways of its revealing.

No one could have written a finer tribute.

EMW continued to teach church history until he retired in 1967, and was then prevailed upon to teach for another year, living at the Revaron Lodge, as my mother had gone to England to look after her mother. He finally left the School of Theology, quite worn out, in May 1968, a few months before it disappeared to be reborn as the Acadia Divinity College. He lived in England for a year, recovering by doing gardening therapy, then went to Cornwall, Ontario, to live in a beautiful old stone house on the St. Lawrence River belonging to my mother's family. For four years he ministered in two rural churches southeast of Ottawa, and then returned to Cornwall, where he died in 1980.

Evan Whidden never came back to Wolfville. Acadia had changed utterly, and I think he had no wish to come to grips with those changes, nor to discuss the past or present with former colleagues. In a submission to a board of governors committee set up in the late 1950s to consider the future of the university, he suggested an institution that continued Acadia's character, a residence-based community which fostered graduates who had developed discernment, with a solid academic base and sound moral principles. He warned against growth which favoured one discipline over others, and especially against allowing the professional schools' tail to wag the arts and science dog. He foresaw a student body of perhaps 1,500 on the basis that more would undermine the sense of community which had been his experience at Brandon, McMaster, and Acadia, which he valued. He was hopelessly wrong, as, ultimately, the very opposite of this came to pass. I think he would be appalled by what appears to be the bottom-line culture of present management, the consequential widespread self-interest of many faculty, the bitter divide between the two, and the lack of self-discipline among many students. The more the university touts its traditional values, standards, and "experience," the less able, it seems, it is able to provide them.

I have no basis on which to judge what his opinion of the divinity college program would be, though he would surely be pleased with its success. I do think, though, that, were he here today, he would make his home with the Canadian Association of Baptist Freedoms. "The Atlantic Baptist Fellowship Its Aims and Purposes," an article from 1977 by Dr. Reginald Dunn, a former student of EMW, describes an association in which I'm sure he would feel at home. And I believe that the Rev. John Perkin's "Reflections of the Centrality of Christ, and Soul Liberty of Conscience in our Times" in the fall 2021 issue of the CABF *Bulletin* would receive his complete approbation. It is here that many of his esteemed former students gathered, and here, I think, that his vision lives. I am equally sure that the move of the Atlantic Baptist Convention to a prescriptive fundamentalist position, which led to the founding of the CABF, was and would be to him a source of deep and lasting disappointment.

A Nova Scotia Baptist Family

Conclusion

Today, the frameworks and certainties in and upon which each of these four characters lived their lives are changed utterly, as one might expect. The Antigonish Baptist Church is gone. Acadia, Brandon, and McMaster are no longer Baptist affiliated. The standards by which each had lived are largely passé; the number of adherents in most denominations, including Baptists, continues to drop; and Christianity itself seems to be facing minority status in our society. Those churches which appear to be thriving are those which require less thinking and more certainty. Within the next two generations of Whiddens in direct descent there is only one regular church-goer.

I doubt whether HPW and EMW would be comfortable with the theology of JBW, though I'm sure they would admire his faith, industry, and determination in spreading the Gospel. But all of the four unstintingly spent their lives contributing to the development of their faith, and that they are little remembered now is in the normal run of things. I think that JBW and CBW would rejoice that the Baptist denomination, which they strove to establish and to build, lives today in Canada's Baptist conventions; likewise, I am sure that HPW and EMW would be glad that the principles and openness which they struggled to maintain and foster are found today alive and well in the Canadian Association for Baptist Freedoms.

Epilogue

It was my great pleasure to have been asked to add to this memorial volume for the Rev. Dr. Roger Prentice. In my father's final years at Acadia, Roger took several of his courses and often mentioned how greatly he enjoyed them and benefited from them, and how much he appreciated his teaching style. Roger had also written a biography of my grandfather's best friend at Acadia, the Rev. Dr. John Howard MacDonald, after whom my father was named and whom he succeeded as professor of church history at Acadia, and so I was confident that Roger would be completely at home with what I had to say about both forebears. He was very laudatory about the biographical monograph I wrote about the first half of my father's life and suggested that I do a second volume to cover his Acadia days; the last part of this essay does that in some small part. I was thinking chiefly of Roger as my reader while I was writing, and therefore am saddened that he will never see it. I hope that other readers will find it of some interest.

It was suggested that I write about members of my family, four generations of whom served, in various ways, the Baptist Church in Canada. Certainly, in the Maritimes there are many families whose members were, and are, Baptists and who have, over the years and generations, given much to the denomination, so mine is by no means unique. Nonetheless, I have attempted here to give an outline of what engaged my father, grandfather, great-grandfather, and great-great-grandfather in strengthening the spreading of the Gospel over a century and a half, and how that task and focus changed over time.

This is not an academic research paper, so rather than providing a formal bibliography and footnotes, I will list here my sources. First are the minutes of the Antigonish Baptist Church from 1823 to 1900, held in Acadia's Esther Clark Wright Archives, a small gold mine worthy of study, and the minutes of Acadia's board of governors. Online, there are the minutes of all the annual meetings of the Maritime Baptist Convention, also worthy of scholarly historical attention, and most of the bulletins of the Acadia School of Theology from 1953 to 1966, all to be found through the ECWA website.

The principal texts I have relied upon are *Brandon College: A History, 1899—1967* by C. G. Stone and F. Joan Garnett; *McMaster University*, volumes one and two, by Charles M. Johnston; and *Acadia's Fifth Quarter Century* by Watson Kirkconnell. There have also been family letters and records and newspaper clippings, usually with no date or attribution.

As an Anglican, I think I can write reasonably objectively, if not particularly knowledgeably in detail, about Baptists over the 140 years that I have covered here, but should the sound of axes being ground in the background be discernable, I hope that it is not distracting. I am very grateful to Catherine Fancy, archives coordinator, for her help in accessing ECWA records; Patricia Townsend, archivist ECWA, for her suggestions on sources and clarifications of some aspects of Baptist history and Ann Myers of the ECWA staff.

Shepherding Soldiers:
Maritime Baptist Chaplains of the First World War

Carol Anne Janzen and Zachary Cooper

In 2017, to prepare for the centenary commemorations marking the ending of World War I, I secured a Canada Summer Jobs grant enabling me to employ a student research assistant "to compile, record and report the history of Canadian Maritime Baptist clergy who enlisted as chaplains in the Canadian Armed Forces between 1914 and 1918."[1] The successful applicant for the research position was Zachary Cooper, who was, at the time, a student at Acadia University majoring in history. Zachary worked diligently in the Vaughan Memorial Library over the summer of 2017; while I was the titular director of his research, he was aided in the day-to-day searches by Roger Prentice (who was working on his own projects in the same room) and Patricia Townsend, the university archivist. Roger took a keen interest in our project since it meshed so closely with his own profession and personal interest in Canadian military history; with his chaplain's heart, he also became a mentor and an encouragement to Zachary. Most of the research and many of the insights presented in this paper are Zachary's work. Together, we offer this short essay in gratitude and tribute to our dear friend, Rev. Dr. Roger Prentice.

Much has been written from various perspectives on the conflagration that has been called the Great War, or, more commonly, World War I; in more recent years, more attention has been given to Canada's role in this transformative event. This paper concerns merely a drop in the ocean of historical records of this war—the role of seven chaplains who came from a tiny corner of what was then a British Empire that spanned the globe.[2]

---

[1] Carol Anne Janzen, application to Canada Summer Jobs program, February 3, 2017. At the time, I was on faculty at Acadia Divinity College and director of the Charles J. Taylor Centre for Chaplaincy and Spiritual Care, one of the Centres of Excellence at Acadia University.

[2] Caveat: there is some indication in the annals of the war years of the *Maritime Baptist* that there may have been other servicemen who became chaplains once they were overseas; for instance, "His many friends are extending a warm welcome to Capt. (Rev.) C. W. Corey, who has returned to his native province

KEEPING THE FAITH

These seven chaplains were all leading ministers in the denomination that was then called the Maritime Baptist Convention, and now carries the name Canadian Baptists of Atlantic Canada.

Duff Crerar's comprehensive work *Padres in No Man's Land: Canadian Chaplains and the Great War* provides an excellent overview of the Canadian socioreligious background for this specialised field of ministry.[3] His focus, however, is largely an institutional one, tracing the development of the role of chaplaincy as it developed in Canada. This essay will explore how these seven individuals fit into this dramatic context. Their particular contributions will serve to highlight some of the general themes which marked Christian spiritual support during the war. The chaplains drew from a common well of patriotic duty and Christian convictions but, through the viewpoints of their contemporaries and their own writings, appear as individual men who emphasized distinct aspects of life and ministry. Maritime Baptists a century ago held to a vision of the Dominion of Canada as an ideally Christian society with her institutions serving the ultimate purpose of advancing the Kingdom of God.[4]

At the beginning of the twentieth century, Canada's place in the world was intimately shaped by its relationship to the British Empire.[5] Thanks to Halifax's position on the Eastern Seaboard and its roots as a garrison of the Royal Navy and New Brunswick's Loyalist heritage, the Atlantic Provinces, despite their diversity, retained a strong cultural connection to British culture. So, when the powder keg in the Balkans erupted into a declaration of war with Germany, the call for sons of the empire to enlist was readily answered by men from all walks of life, including those in the ministry. The denominational paper *Maritime Baptist* regularly noted the enlistment of serving ministers into the armed forces, whether

---

after service at the front. He enlisted in the ranks in British Columbia, but after reaching England he received appointment as Chaplain. His ancestral home is at Havelock, N.B." *Maritime Baptist* (October 24, 1917): 9.

[3] Duff Crerar, *Padres in No Man's Land: Canadian Chaplains and the Great War*, vol. 16, in McGill-Queen's Studies in the History of Religion, ed. G. A. Rawlyk (Montreal & Kingston: McGill-Queen's University Press, 1995).

[4] W. A. Robbins, BYPU column, *Maritime Baptist* (October 6, 2015), speaking of national destiny.

[5] Or, proper to those times, "her"; e.g., "Now [Rev. G. A. Lawson] lays down the work that he may be free to serve his country in the day of her peril." *Maritime Baptist* 11/20 (May 17, 1916): 9.

168

Shepherding Soldiers

as officers,[6] members of the ambulance brigade (which seemed to be a popular role for those not admitted to chaplaincy),[7] or as regular troops.[8]

Within the general call to service in this great patriotic effort was the recognition of a special role for Baptist clergy—that of chaplain. Given the established position of the Anglican church in Canada, the Baptist cause

---

[6] "Rev. C. G. Pincombe, pastor of the Main Street church, Marysville, who is an English army veteran, has been granted a commission with the overseas contingent...his experience compensating for the fact that he is somewhat past the usual age limit." *Maritime Baptist* (June 9, 1915): 9. "Rev. C. G. Pincombe, formerly pastor of the Main Street church, Marysville, N.B., has been appointed Adjutant of the 73rd Highlanders, Montreal." *Maritime Baptist* (August 18, 1915): 9. "He will have the rank of Major [of one of the companies of the 104th]." *Maritime Baptist* (November 3, 1915): 9. "Capt. E. J. Brooks [former pastor at Falmouth, NS] has been promoted to the rank of Major." *Maritime Baptist* (September 13, 1916): 9.

[7] "Rev. F. C. Burnett, who resigned his pastorate at Arthurette, N.B., to go to the front with the First Expeditionary Force, is now in France and serving with the Ambulance Corps, of which he is a member," *Maritime Baptist* (March 31, 1915): 9. "We have been informed that Rev. E. O. Steeves, who has been pastor for Nictaux for three years, has volunteered for overseas service in connection with the Ambulance Corps. This will be at least four Baptist ministers from these provinces who will soon be engaged in this service of saving life upon the battlefield," *Maritime Baptist* (September 8, 1915): 9. "Rev. J. H. Puddington, pastor at Pugwash, N.S., has volunteered for overseas service. If no appointment as chaplain is available, he has expressed his willingness to go as a member of an ambulance corps," *Maritime Baptist* (October 6, 1915): 9. "It was with a shock of surprise and real regret that the church and community [of Liverpool, NS] received the resignation of Rev. J. B. Anderson, who has joined the Army Medical Corps," *Maritime Baptist* (October 27, 1915): 12.

[8] "Rev. A. K. Herman has also joined the forces, but in what capacity we have not yet learned.... Pastor T. R. Russell of the Granville Mountain field has enlisted in the 219th Battalion," *Maritime Baptist* (March 22, 1916): 9. Of returning troops, this was written, "Rev. T. F. McWilliam, who recently landed at Halifax, enlisted as a private in the ranks and has passed through some of the heaviest fighting," *Maritime Baptist* (January 29, 1919): 9. "Since the beginning of the war Brother [Rev. C. W.] Corey has been in khaki, enlisting first as a private in a combatant battalion. Later he was given an appointment as chaplain, and still later entered the service of the Military Y.M.C.A. For some time he has been stationed in St. John," *Maritime Baptist* (April 16, 1919): 9.

in this regard required initiative and purpose. At the annual meeting of the Central Association of Nova Scotia in June 1914, it was reported,

> Rev. J. D. Spidell, ably supported by Rev. W. F. Parker, President of the Convention, spoke of the difficulty of securing the appointment of Baptist ministers as chaplains to the Canadian forces. After considerable discussion it was moved that a memorial be sent to General Hughes with a view to securing the appointment of Baptist chaplains, in view of the fact that a good proportion of the soldiers are Baptists.[9]

As it transpired, over the course of the war, seven ministers serving among the Baptists of Atlantic Canada were admitted to chaplaincy positions with Canadian armed forces. This essay will introduce these men and provide a brief glimpse into their service.

The seven ministers who are the focus of this paper are: George Albert Lawson, John Howard MacDonald, William Fowler Parker, Frederick Seely Porter, Joseph Dimock Spidell, William Andrew White, and James Clement Wilson. Both John Howard MacDonald and William Andrew White rose to prominence both within their denominational circles and on the national stage and have received historical attention; the others continued to be actively involved within the limits of the denomination.

Brief Biographical Sketches— In Order of Their Chaplaincy Appointments

John Howard MacDonald (1863–1946) was the first Maritime Baptist minister to receive a chaplaincy appointment.[10] Attached to the 26th battalion of the 2nd CEF in November 1914, MacDonald had previously served in New Brunswick as a militia chaplain with the 71st York Regiment. After a stretch at the western front with the 5th and 6th field ambulance units, in early 1916 MacDonald was moved to an administrative position at the Canadian Chaplain Service's London head office. When war broke out, MacDonald had been editor of the *Maritime Baptist* for less

---

[9] *Maritime Baptist* (July 28, 1914): 13.

[10] His military records are to be found in: Library and Archives Canada, Personnel Records of the First World War—Canadian Expeditionary Force (CEF), RG 150, Accession 1992–93/166, Box 6744—2, Item Number 148521, "MacDonald, John Howard."

Shepherding Soldiers

than a year. He continued his literary flair overseas by sending regular letters to the paper's readership until his move to London. He eventually became assistant director under Col. John Almond, attained the rank of lieutenant-colonel, and was decorated with membership in the order of the British Empire. After demobilization, MacDonald's prominence in Baptist spheres only increased; he was called to the Wolfville pastorate and became president of the convention in 1920. In 1923, MacDonald became professor of church history at Acadia University.[11]

William Fowler Parker (1855–1942) was the eldest Maritime Baptist chaplain, and second appointed.[12] As president of the convention in 1914, Parker lobbied for temperance, Belgian relief, and his denomination's presence in the chaplaincy. In August 1915, Parker received a commission to the 64th Battalion, which conveniently mobilized in Sussex, New Brunswick, his home and pastoral field. While engaged in hospital work in both England and France, Parker kept *Maritime Baptist* readers informed of his experiences. In the Etaples hospital bombings, May 1918, Parker's right leg was severely injured by German shrapnel. After a period of rest in Toronto, he returned to Sussex with a long-term position as postmaster.

Steeped in a lineage of Baptist ministers, **Frederick Seely Porter** (1880–1974) was conducting a successful ministry at Germain Street Baptist in Saint John, New Brunswick, when he was made chaplain of the 104th Battalion in April 1916.[13] Noted for his "coolness under shellfire," Porter "enjoyed good health throughout his period of active service" and was promoted to major. Porter also contributed to the *Maritime Baptist*, emphasizing the war's political and historical significance alongside the day-to-day work in the field. Once home, Porter took an administrative position

---

[11] MacDonald's illustrious career has received detailed treatment in Roger H. Prentice, *"The Cardinal"; A Chronicle of the Rev'd John Howard MacDonald, FRGS, CBE, DD;* ACBAS Booklet Series #3 (Wolfville, NS: Acadia Centre for Baptist and Anabaptist Studies, 2016, 2018).

[12] His military records are to be found in: Library and Archives Canada, Personnel Records of the First World War—Canadian Expeditionary Force (CEF), RG 150, Accession 1992–93/166, Box 7595—35, Item Number 555737, "Parker, William Fowler."

[13] Ibid., Box 7909—51, Item Number 582541, "Porter, Frederick Seely."

KEEPING THE FAITH

with the Canadian Bible Society (secretary for the Maritime Provinces and Newfoundland).[14]

Before sailing from Halifax in the summer of 1916, **Joseph Dimock Spidell** (1871–1955)[15] made waves in his long Kentville pastorate. A powerful orator, Spidell transferred those abilities to recruiting drives and an ambitious, yet unsuccessful, Tory candidacy in the 1916 provincial election. His persistence in promoting patriotism among the Baptists paid off with a chaplaincy appointment in England. From his lack of printed letters, we have little insight into Spidell's personal war experience, but he did serve in France without injury. After demobilization, Spidell returned to the pulpit in Liverpool, Nova Scotia.

The ancestor of many notable African-Canadians, **William Andrew White** (1874–1936) helped recruit for, and served overseas with, the No. 2 Construction Battalion as the segregated unit's chaplain.[16] For sixteen months, White kept a detailed regular diary of his life in uniform which covered everything from weather conditions to recreation to sermon outlines. White's chaplaincy spurred his transition between two lengthy ministries: twelve years before the war at the Zion Baptist Church of Truro and from 1919 until his passing at Cornwallis Street Baptist Church (now New Horizons Baptist Church) in Halifax (both churches were members of the African United Baptist Association of Nova Scotia).[17]

---

[14] *Maritime Baptist* (September 24, 1919): 9.

[15] His military records are to be found in: Library and Archives Canada, Personnel Records of the First World War—Canadian Expeditionary Force (CEF), RG 150, Accession 1992–93/166, Box 9195—46, Item Number 244286, "Spidell, Joseph Dimock."

[16] Ibid., Box 10307—29, Item Number 307048, "White, William Andrew."

[17] For a more detailed biography of this outstanding African-Canadian, see Barry Cahill, "White, William Andrew," *Dictionary of Canadian Biography*, http://www.biographi.ca/en/bio/white_william_andrew_16E.html, accessed August 1, 2022. Two documentary films have been made about him: *Captain of Souls: Rev. William White* (1999) and *Honour before Glory* (2001).

172

Shepherding Soldiers

George Albert Lawson (1872–1939) left one of the largest Maritime Baptist churches to become chaplain of the 145th Battalion.[18] The denominational paper described him as "tall and smiling, one great length of earnestness and sincerity."[19] First Baptist Church Moncton, New Brunswick, had recently rebounded from a building fire with a new stone edifice, but their fragile minister's health did not enjoy a corresponding boost. Nevertheless, Lawson continued his journey to the front but barely lasted a month in France. Shell shocked so badly that he lost his voice,[20] Lawson spent the waning months of the war in recovery and eventually continued serving as a pastor in the United States.[21]

James Clement Wilson (1879–1966) had only been in Doaktown, New Brunswick, for a few months when he enlisted in the 132nd North Shore Battalion as lieutenant.[22] During his service, he was encouraged to accept the chaplaincy; after a period in England, he went to France, and in the fall of 1918 was appointed education officer for the unit to which he was attached.[23] While silent toward *Maritime Baptist* readers during his tenure in England and France, Wilson made his opinions known to Lt. Col. MacDonald. Hailing from the Free Baptist tradition, Wilson diverged from the ecumenical, optimistic Social Gospel of his superior. Studying and ministering in the US after the war, Wilson eventually obtained a job

---

[18] His military records are to be found in: Library and Archives Canada, Personnel Records of the First World War—Canadian Expeditionary Force (CEF), RG 150, Accession 1992–93/166, Box 5469—25, Item Number 521572, "Lawson, George Albert."

[19] *Maritime Baptist* (September 30, 1914): 4.

[20] *Maritime Baptist* (August 28, 1918): 9.

[21] "Rev. G. A. Lawson began his ministry with the Union Square church, Somerville, Mass., on Sunday, September 14th. As in all the Baptist churches in Boston and vicinity, a goodly proportion of the worshippers hail from the Maritime provinces, so the new pastor will feel quite at home." *Maritime Baptist* (October 1, 1919): 9.

[22] His military records are to be found in: Library and Archives Canada, Personnel Records of the First World War—Canadian Expeditionary Force (CEF), RG 150, Accession 1992–93/166, Box 10457—3, Item Number 320516, "Wilson, James Clement."

[23] *Maritime Baptist* (June 4, 1919): 16.

KEEPING THE FAITH

as postmaster in the place of his upbringing, Grand Manan Island, New Brunswick.

Themes

Recruiting

One of the primary functions served by chaplains in the military establishment was as recruiters. Even before Kentville Baptist pastor Rev. J. D. Spidell was appointed to a chaplaincy post, he received special appointment under George Cutten, president of Acadia, and busied himself around the Annapolis Valley and elsewhere.

W. A. White's involvement with the historically recognized No. 2 Construction Battalion, the first African-Canadian battalion, has been well documented.[24] The *Maritime Baptist* included the following news item in March 1917: "Rev. W. A. White, pastor of Zion church, Truro, has been appointed chaplain of No. 2 Construction Battalion, and expects soon to go overseas. This battalion has been recruited from the coloured communities in all parts of Canada, Mr. White (now Capt. White) having been employed for some time as a recruiting officer."[25]

Initially, since military chaplaincy was not an organized profession as such, the job requirements were multifaceted. Officially, they were required to conduct regular parade services and supervise the social life and spiritual well-being of the troops. Unofficially, at least until their departure overseas, chaplains functioned as liaisons between the military and home communities. The credibility that churches of all mainline denominations held within their communities transferred to broad events such as "recruiting Sundays." The pride of a church who offered up her sons for military service was located not within a theology of militarism but as a contribution to greater society. A report from the resolutions committee of the United Baptist Association of New Brunswick in the denominational paper included the information, "One resolution called for the loyal support of all in the righteous struggle in which our Empire is engaged, and expressed a hope that peace might be secured only when such a peace would be consonant with justice and liberty."[26] The *Maritime Baptist* noted the

---

[24] M. S. Hunt, *Nova Scotia's Part in the Great War* (Halifax: Nova Scotia Veteran Pub. Co.,1920), 148–53.

[25] *Maritime Baptist* (March 21, 1917): 9.

[26] *Maritime Baptist* (September 29, 2015): 5.

174

Shepherding Soldiers

enthusiastic approval of the appearance of the residing president, Rev. William Parker, in uniform to open the convention assembly in October 1915, and continued with approval, "The applause was in part for the uniform, for this Convention always gave quick response to the patriotic appeal. But it was as much for the man, who is loved and honoured for his Christian zeal and earnestness, as well as for the pure patriotism which finds expression in his present work."[27] A steady routine of open-air preaching to audiences of various religious sentiments required a strong and convincing oratorical skill, which equipped preachers to be effective recruiters. Before his commission as a chaplain, "Rev. J. D. Spidell of Kentville, has received appointment as a recruiting officer. This is a gratifying recognition of his eminent ability as a campaign speaker, and we venture the assertion that the Militia Department will not have any more effective recruiter in its employ."[28] Dr. Barry Moody has noted the commonalities between evangelical revival meetings and recruitment campaigns. Much like an altar call, the pinnacle of a Gospel preacher's appeal, the recruitment appeal was an "altar call" to lay down one's life for the cause of King and country.[29]

Temperance and Moral Reform

Temperance and the push for prohibition gripped the attention of Maritime Baptists through this era. "No religious group in the Maritimes could match the depth of commitment or dedication to the anti-liquor crusade as that displayed by the Baptists."[30] And, after the war effort, no other topic garnered such sustained attention from Maritime Baptists.[31] It was only natural that this vociferous struggle found its way into discussions about the myriad perils young soldiers faced, many of whom had never

---

[27] *Maritime Baptist* (October 20, 1915) Convention Special: 4.

[28] *Maritime Baptist* (November 24, 1915): 9.

[29] Barry M. Moody, "Educating for War and Peace at Acadia University: The Great War Generation," in *Cultures, Communities, and Conflict: Histories of Canadian Universities and War*, eds. Paul Stortz and E. Lisa Panayotidis (University of Toronto Press, 2012), 26–50.

[30] C. Mark Davis, "I'll Drink to That: The Rise and Fall of Prohibition in the Maritime Provinces, 1900–1930," PhD Thesis McMaster University, 1990: 60.

[31] E. R. Forbes, "Prohibition and the Social Gospel in Nova Scotia," *Acadiensis* 1/1 (Autumn 1971); Davis, "I'll Drink to That."

KEEPING THE FAITH

before left the East Coast. Denominational consensus purported that beverage alcohol was a scourge more dangerous to Canadian troops than the German enemy. A recurring fear on the home front and a reported hindrance to enlistment was the Canadian troops' exposure to readily available alcohol once overseas. In March 1914, mere months before the war's outbreak, Minister of Militia Sam Hughes reassured the Canadian Social Service Congress that "we have done away with the wet canteens in our various training camps."[32]

Though Hughes held the line by making Valcartier a dry camp, overseas, English liberality prevailed. News of Salisbury's "wet canteens" provoked outrage at home while chaplains grappled to either rein in or mitigate their boisterous charges who were eager to explore the surrounding towns in periods of sedentary monotony.[33] Mark Davis sees "the reform enthusiasm unleashed by World War I" as a key factor in the successful crusade for total prohibition.[34] H. R. Grant, the Presbyterian general secretary of the Nova Scotia Temperance Alliance, regularly updated Maritime Baptist readers with anti-liquor developments in the province, nation, and empire—with the highest ranking total abstainer being King George V himself![35] Nationwide prohibition on "manufacture and sale of intoxicating beverages" was declared March 1918.[36]

As the war extended from months to years, these home front expectations for "personal conduct" met the grim reality of war. In reality, Canadian chaplains of other denominations—such as senior chaplain for the London area, Anglican major D. V. Warner—were less squeamish about what were considered "ordinary pastimes of mixed society, such as men are accustomed to have at home—dancing, cards, music, etc."[37] Providing "suitable and wholesome recreation," outlets for education, along with

---

[32] Col. the Hon. Sam Hughes, Minister of Militia, "Supervised Control of the Young," Social Service Congress: Ottawa, 1914, Report of Addresses and Proceedings (Toronto: The Social Service Council of Canada), 320.

[33] MB, September 2, 1914; Crerar, Canadian Chaplains, 37–8.

[34] Davis, "I'll Drink to That," 170l.

[35] See H. R. Grant, Maritime Baptist, "The War and Temperance: A Total Abstinence Campaign," (May 5, 1915): 5, and Grant, "The War Campaign for Total Abstinence" (May 19, 1915).

[36] Forbes, "Prohibition," 27.

[37] D. V. Warner, "Chaplain Service in the London Area," Maritime Baptist (March 27, 1918): 5.

Shepherding Soldiers

spiritual care showed that chaplains in the field had a well-rounded conception of ministry.[38]

The Maritime Baptist chaplains were, by and large, influential men of their denomination and home communities. In a complex ethical framework, the inherent patriotism in the chaplains' Anglo-dominant society intertwined with deep personal concern for the well-being of the young men they were often personally recruiting as soldiers. Due to the hazards of alcohol and moral licentiousness, vice was considered a more dangerous enemy than the German forces, so chaplains took it upon themselves to shepherd souls as well as to encourage the fight.

Laying aside the war's theological and psychological effects, overseas service still marked a professional shift for each of the chaplains. Only three of the seven returned to pastoral ministry in the Maritimes; none returned to lead their prewar congregations in spite of their former congregations' hopes. In the absence of personal diaries and/or correspondence, one is left with curiosity as to the lasting psychological impact of the Great War on these men, who were so determined to serve God and country before they enlisted. This topic merits further attention and research into the effect the war had on not only these individuals but also on the churches some of them eventually served. The impact of the war on wider society may be gauged by considering how the churches and their pastors reacted to postwar challenges. The unique role of these "shepherding soldiers" in the war, both as active spiritual guides as well as recruiters to the forces, gave these early pioneer Baptist chaplains a challenging task and their stories (with much more yet to be told) will undoubtedly cast more light on church-state relations and the wider recognition of the Baptist contribution to the chaplaincy role. The contribution of those involved in chaplaincy was an issue that was of particular interest to Roger not only in his research, but in his active witness and service at Acadia.

---

[38] Ibid.

Worship, Preaching, and Ministry

May our music sound our praise,
May each note proclaim God's love;
And our faith be in each phrase
Like His angels from above.

(Acadia Vesper Hymns, No. 54 RHP)

The litmus paper for worship is the "sense of direction" of what is being offered to God as our worship...The direction is from us towards the Divine. Everything that the congregation, the readers, the choir, and the Minister does, is for God's glory. The readers read on behalf of the congregation, the choir sings on behalf of the congregation (not to entertain them or even to elicit a "good feeling") and the Minister, as the prophetic voice, speaks so the congregation may recognize our relationship as a sacrificial communion with the Almighty.

R. H. Prentice, "The Ideal of Baptist Worship"
(Wolfville, 2019, p. 21)

Worship as Theatre

Robert Ellis

I met Roger Prentice at Regent's Park College in Oxford when we were both research students there. His work was in Baptist history, mine was in systematic theology—but we shared a common trajectory, both of us headed for ministry. Roger was a very good friend to me and to my wife, Sue, and we have many happy memories of spending time with him doing things serious and more frivolous. Roger did friendship very well, and his availability and ability to listen made him a kind of unofficial chaplain among our peers. He had the gift of asking a simple, direct question which could make one stop and think. As a pastor, he could function in spiritual director mode, too: probing experience to name God. It is one of the many ways in which the purposes of pastoral care and the leading of worship overlap, and Roger was adept at contriving ways to make people reflect deeply on spiritual things without approaching things "front on," so to speak.

A particular memory of Roger in Oxford for me relates to the stage. There had been dramatic productions at college before, but Roger's production and direction gave them an impetus and organization not known then for some time. I have no recollection of any of the preparatory phases (casting, budgeting, etc.), but I do remember happy times of rehearsal, the exhilaration of performance, and the community created among those who participated. Roger was the energy at the heart of this experience. In particular, I recall productions of very different plays: Christopher Fry's *The Firstborn* focuses on Moses and the leading of Hebrew slaves to freedom; Robert Bolt's *A Man for all Seasons* was a version of Sir Thomas More's stand against Henry VIII and for individual conscience. These plays had certain similarities and clear religious themes, but Terrence Rattigan's *French without Tears* and Tom Stoppard's *The Real Inspector Hound* were quite different. What a privilege it was to experience this range of drama in a relatively short student stint, and to share in turning the college's Helwys Hall into a theatrical auditorium.

On a visit to Acadia in 2002, I was delighted to be present for a performance of one of the Passion plays Roger produced each year in the chapel there. I saw evidence of the same processes at work as the cast

KEEPING THE FAITH

eddied around him, first-night nerves turning to after-show highs. Some years later, Sue and I were among those who received a short story from Roger with our Christmas cards. I have to confess that I found these a little too quaint for my tastes, but Roger evidently took great pleasure in creating characters and storylines which conveyed his message about the "true" meaning of Christmas, and he built up quite a corpus of these stories. As with the Passion plays, Roger used these narratives to communicate deeply held convictions. As with some of the dramas mentioned earlier, he put to use theatrical and narrative forms as vehicles for engaging audiences or readers and challenging them to think about important aspects of human living. Indeed, even the more apparently frivolous college plays put performers and audiences on their mettle: *French without Tears* is set in a school for adults wanting to cram-learn French for business use; *The Real Inspector Hound* has critics drawn into a play which they are watching—both of these had resonances for those preparing for Oxford examinations!

Anyone who has been present during a service of worship led by Roger will hear echoes of some of these interests. Many of the aspects of theatre, including its narrative interests shared with novels and short stories, illumine what is happening in worship—and Roger could lead worship in very dramatic ways. For instance, he had a clear sense of presence while leading worship, a strong sense of his "role" and "costume," and very clear ideas about the way in which its "plot" should unwind. This essay will reflect upon the ways in which worship might be regarded as "theatre." The purpose of such a comparison is not mere whimsy, but an attempt to cast a little light on what we do when we worship, and, in so doing, to honour and celebrate our friend, who straddled these spheres with such enthusiasm and aplomb.

Worship as Dialogue

Unless we are watching a drama performed in mime, theatrical performance involves dialogue—the exchange of spoken words between two or more participants. This dialogue serves multiple aims. It develops plot and also (along with actions, of course, and sometimes in tension with them) it reveals character. Dialogue can also add emotional variation and even provide basic information about setting. It shares many of these features with other aspects of drama.

182

Worship as Theatre

Dialogue is a key element in our relationships as human persons. We are able to express ourselves with some precision and to offer interpretations of our actions and behaviour. We ask questions, give answers, and make observations. Sometimes we just pass the time. In drama, dialogue is rarely just "shooting the breeze," however. It serves the playwright's purpose. Generally, it moves the play along, relating in some way to the overall plot or to what the audience needs to know about the characters.

The same goes for the words of our worship. They serve a purpose, or often several. But, primarily, worship is a dialogue between the one worshipped and the worshippers, between God and God's people. Understanding worship in this way immediately opens up a sense of expectation. Worship is not just us speaking into a void, or an experience akin to leaving a message on some heavenly answering machine; nor even to a monologue carried on before a silent hearer.[1] We speak and God speaks, too. In fact, God speaks first, initiates all that we do in worship. As Luther put it, "Worship is at once a dialogue and an act of praise.... The event which we call worship consists simply in this, that our well-beloved Lord himself speaks to us by his Holy Word, and we, for our part, speak to him by our prayers and our hymns of praise."[2] The whole act of worship is a "conversation" that continues through the whole service, such that we should examine every order of service to make sure that it facilitates this divine-human dialogue.[3]

More traditional service orders in Baptist churches, and the kind that Roger would have used most comfortably, made this dialogical structure clear. We think of it as part of our reformed tradition, but it is, in fact, present in most forms of Christian worship in some way and seems to flow naturally from what is sometimes called the biblical "call and response" pattern. A call to worship uses the words of Scripture, God's words, to summon the congregation. The people respond with a hymn of praise and prayers of adoration and confession. A prayer of invocation may be

---

[1] R. S. Thomas's wonderful poem "Folk Tale"; see *Collected Poems 1945–1990* (London: Dent, 1993), 517.

[2] A sermon of Luther quoted in J. D. Benoit, *Liturgical Renewal: Studies in Catholic and Protestant Developments on the Continent* (London: SCM Press, 1958), 59.

[3] See Christopher J. Ellis, *Approaching God: A Guide for Worship Leaders and Worshippers* (Norwich: Canterbury Press, 2009), 37.

183

included not because we need to ask God to be present, but in order to alert us and open us to God's presence. Through the words of Scripture, God speaks again, and the sermon, when effective, is a further means for God to address the congregation collectively and individually.

The sermon represents a particularly interesting aspect of this dialogue. All preachers are painfully aware—as they have wrestled with the text in their preparation, cast around for illustrative material, and considered how best to connect this particular congregation's needs with the angularity of a particular text—every sermon contains a large number of human words. No sermon is perfect, most much less than perfect. And yet we believe that God's word is spoken in and through human words. The sermon can be understood using many images and metaphors, some more obviously theological than others. In certain respects, a stress on the verbality of a sermon is unfortunate, leading some to an incorrect estimate of the authority of the preacher or to a flawed propositional view of Scripture's authority. Rather, a more sacramental understanding of preaching which stresses an encounter that cannot be "reduced" to words, or in which words are recognized as a second-order response, has much to be said for it. Nevertheless, the central Christian doctrine of incarnation also offers a way in to understanding how words work in preaching. The human words of the preacher are, by grace alone, sometimes, and wonderfully indeed, divine words. Sermons may have two "natures." This is not something that can be controlled by the preacher, though our work on techniques of preparation and delivery might relate to it in some way. In terms of our thinking about worship as dialogue, preaching occupies a place similar to almost all other words used in worship. They are, in some sense, human words, yet God might be hoped to speak through them, to be present and encountered in them. The congregation might then respond in song and offer prayers for themselves and the world. More song is followed by a blessing—and here God has the last word, as God had the first.

The back-and-forth dialogue of worship begins and ends with God's speech. But a Trinitarian understanding of worship requires us to be much more subtle. For because we do not know how or what to pray, God's Spirit is at work within us, forming our words and shaping our response.[4] God provokes *and* enables our response. God, so to speak, writes God's own script and ours. Even the words in worship that we think of as our

---

[4] Romans 8:26.

184

Worship as Theatre

own, as the human words in the divine-human dialogue, have (or should have) a divine origin.

C. S. Lewis, appropriately for our purposes, makes a similar point in story form.

> An ordinary simple Christian kneels down to say his prayers. He is trying to get into touch with God. But if he is a Christian he knows that what is prompting him to pray is also God; God is, so to speak, inside him. But he also knows that all his real knowledge of God comes through Christ, the Man who was God—that Christ is standing beside him, helping him to pray, praying for him. You see what is happening. God is the thing to which he is praying—the goal he is trying to reach. God is also the thing inside him which is pushing him on—the motive power. God is also the road or bridge along which he is being pushed to that goal. So that the whole threefold life of the three-personal being is actually going on in that ordinary little bedroom where an ordinary man is saying his prayers. The man is being caught up into the [life of God].[5]

Much of our understanding and expectation of worship seems one-dimensional—or rather, Unitarian—beside such a rich view. But as James B. Torrance suggests, a proper view of worship sees it as "the gift of participating through the Spirit in the incarnate Son's communion with the Father."[6] When our worship becomes (or is imagined as) monologue, we have slipped into what Torrance calls a Unitarian mode.

The dialogue of worship, as in a dramatic script, reveals character. The words of Scripture and (hopefully) sermon show something of God's character and concerns; our words articulate our concerns and longings. But we often use words shaped by hymn writers and liturgists, and there is an ideal element to them—they dress us in our Sunday best, as it were. These words might be regarded as aspirational—they show what we would *like* to be (or like to like to be, perhaps). This is one reason why prayers of confession should still find a place in our worship, even in an age when speaking of sin has become unfashionable and guilt is viewed as destructive rather than constructive. Confession grounds us. Here our dialogue

---

[5] C. S. Lewis, *Mere Christianity* (Glasgow: Fount, 1977), 138–39. See also James B. Torrance, *Worship, Community, and the Triune God of Grace* (Carlisle: Paternoster, 1996), 32–34.

[6] Torrance, *Triune God*, 18.

185

KEEPING THE FAITH

becomes most honest and vulnerable. Here we truly bare our hearts and show ourselves for what we are: people who need grace.

There is also a further aspect to dialogue in worship that we should note. As worshippers, we also talk to one another. Worship has God as its centre and focus, of course, but if we speak only of the "vertical" dimension and ignore any "horizontal" element, we have missed something important. When we sing and pray, when we say "this is the Word of the Lord" after Scripture is read, if and when we recite (or sing—for most of ours are in hymnody) statements of faith, we are also speaking to one another. We are finding agreement, support, what some academics might call "warrants." In so doing, we are creating community, a community based upon common language, belief, purpose. There are very few moments in worship when we speak to one another explicitly—during the sign of peace, perhaps, and some responses—but everything we direct to God is also, indirectly, addressed to one another.

Here the sermon has to be mentioned again, showing itself to be a many-faceted feature of our liturgies. For preachers speak their own words praying that God will speak through them: this has been memorably described as "truth through personality,"[7] an axiom that should encourage and caution us in equal measure. But the preacher who has properly "exegeted their congregation"[8] will not only be seeking to discern what God is saying to them at any given moment, but also trying to articulate what they are saying—to God and to one another.

> Preaching is more than speaking to a congregation, however sensitively, it is speaking for and with a congregation as well. Preaching attempts to articulate the concerns, questions, commitments, and celebrations, of the whole faith community.... The sermon is not a monologue, but an unfolding conversation of the people of God—

---

[7] Phillips Brooks, *Lectures on Preaching: Delivered before the Divinity School of Yale College, January and February 1877* (New York: Dutton & Co, 1877), 8. See below for a further discussion of this idea.

[8] See Leonora Tubbs Tidsdale, *Preaching as Local Theology and Folk Art* (Minneapolis, MN: Fortress, 1997), 54–88.

186

a conversation about and with God, and about their struggles to know and be faithful to God.[9]

The preacher puts the congregation's hopes and fears into words, enunciates their own issues of faith and practice, sums up their dilemmas, and so on. In saying these aloud, they can be owned, faced, put alongside Gospel words. Other elements of worship may work in a similar way. The congregation is able to make the words of the preacher and the words of all the worship (the vast majority of which have been selected by others) their own through a helpful process in which their own words are anticipated and vocalised.

Even less-formal services can be illumined by this metaphor—the secret is to maintain dialogue and not slip into monologue. The words of worship also propel its "plot," and we now turn to the narrative of worship.

Worship as Narrative

Speaking of worship as dialogue will not raise many eyebrows. But speaking of its "plot" may seem stranger to some. Yet I contend that much contemporary worship has "lost the plot," and I think Roger would have agreed!

The terms narrative and plot are, for our purposes, at least, mostly interchangeable. If we speak instead of a "narrative arc," we might be placing a greater emphasis on the sequence or the shape of a plot: the notion of an arc directs our attention to the flowing of the narrative into a crisis or climax and then a resolution and conclusion so that some kind of equilibrium is restored.[10] The plot unfolds with its scenes and characters; the narrative arc emphasizes the way in which the movement of the plot raises and resolves tension within it. Most of the drama we watch requires just this arc, building and releasing narrative tension. Even nonfiction writing requires something similar; both a biography and an exposé, for instance, require something more than a flat sequence of events in order to engage and maintain interest.

---

[9] David Schlafer in Henry Eggold, *Preaching as Dialogue*, quoted in Jolyon Mitchell, "Preaching Pictures," in *A Reader on Preaching*, eds. David Day, Jeff Astley, and Leslie J. Francis (Abingdon: Routledge, 2016), 154–65.

[10] Walter Bruggeman sees a similar pattern in the Psalms: *The Spirituality of the Psalms* (Minneapolis, MN: Fortress, 2002).

Sometimes a contrast is made between plot-driven and character-driven writing in fiction, drama, or film. This can be overdone, but most readers will recognize a spectrum of different styles. Dialogue propels plot and shows (or sometimes deliberately occludes) character. Narrative gives the shape in which we encounter characters and their development, the changing nature of their relationships. Technically, Roger Standing explains, a narrative is

> The sum total of devices and procedures that are used to shape and develop the story into a finished work. These include various strategies like plot development and characterisation. It may not follow strict chronological sequence and can also be selective by passing over some things while concentrating on others.[11]

Services of worship are inherently dramatic in various ways, but they certainly require a sense of movement, a "going somewhere." The strongest services are coherent and cohesive sequences, with a narrative arc which holds all elements together. The alternative is a sequence of elements which do not fit together and which might even clash with one another or, in a sense, "be in the wrong kind of tension"! Such elements might be dropped into any service of worship without much difference being made. I am not speaking here of the generalised form of worship—the praise-confession-Scripture-sermon-response sequence—but of the particular content of such components in any actual worship service. Choosing one's favourite song rather than one which "fits" may be the most obvious example.

The Scripture passage(s) at the heart of the service ideally engender the themes reflected in all parts of the liturgy. In terms of narrative structure, the service should begin and end with "equilibrium" (though given authentic worship's propensity to disturb the comfortable, we use that word with some caution). We might typically regard the Scripture passages as providing the crisis that requires some response and recalibration. The sermon will deepen this crisis and also begin its resolution, a resolution continued in prayers and responsive music. Before we have reached the Scriptures, the opening praises and prayers are already picking up its themes and (usually subtly) preparing us for what is to come.

---

[11] Roger Standing, *Finding the Plot* (Eugene, OR: Wipf & Stock:, 2012), 49–50.

There has been an interest in recent years in "narrative preaching," and even when preaching does not take the form of a narrative, understanding it in such terms helps a preacher understand the sermon's shape and direction. A pioneer in the field was Thomas Lowry, and the "Lowry Loop" is often referenced. The loop understands the sermon as a sequence passing through a number of points, labelled here §1 to §5.[12]

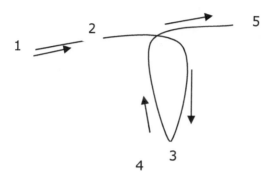

As we move from §1 to §2, the equilibrium is upset and tension established; from §2 to §3, this tension is intensified through analysis; at the point of severest difficulty, a clue to resolution is identified, and from §3 to §4 we find some release as Gospel is heard; as we proceed from §4 to §5, a new equilibrium is possible as we continue.

It is illuminating to compare this diagram, intended to illumine the narrative nature of preaching, with one offered in the British Baptist worship resource *Gathering for Worship*. The editors of the book and authors of this introduction to worship do not speak of narrative, but they do offer a diagrammatic representation of what they call the "flow" of worship through the movement of God's gathering and sending us. "As God gathers and sends us, our worship takes form and shape. It becomes a journeying into God and a journeying with God into the world. In the movement

---

[12] This diagram was taken from Peter K. Stevenson, "Preaching and Narrative," in *Reader on Preaching*, 102.

of gathering and sending worship can be seen as dynamic encounter with the Triune God."[13] The diagram they offer[14] is this:

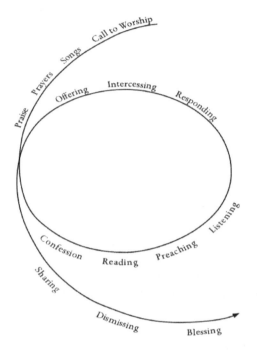

The resemblance between these two diagrams is not merely superficial. They both indicate a narrative arc. The continuous line of the worship's "gathering and sending" dynamic is an indication of its natural flow; the loop created at its centre indicates (in the language of the Lowry Loop) the disturbance of equilibrium and its reestablishment. The continuous line suggests that there is a natural flow from one element to the next, a natural flow (I suggest) which finds its heart in the word of Scripture.

---

[13] *Gathering for Worship* (Norwich: Canterbury, 2005), eds. Christopher J. Ellis and Myra Blyth, 4.
[14] Ibid., 6.

The editors of *Gathering for Worship* say something similar. "Baptists have not insisted on a set sequence of component parts in a service. Rather, they have been concerned that the community is attentive to scripture."[15] This attentiveness to Scripture is (or should be) the core element of worship. But even when the order of the various elements is varied—and they are keen to allow enough freedom to the Spirit (or the local congregation at any rate!) not to prescribe exactly what elements must be included—the arc should be retained. The worship is still going somewhere; still flowing from its beginning to its end with coherence. So, they say that "the precise order in which prayers and songs and readings take place needs to serve the specific context and situation of the congregation. The diagram seeks to demonstrate that the actions/media used within worship (i.e., singing, praying, reading, teaching) are secondary to the dynamic flow of God's Spirit gathering, transforming, and sending."[16] For their term "dynamic flow," we might substitute "narrative arc." Worship needs this sense of narrative direction in order to be coherent and satisfying. To *work*.

Worship as Acted Drama

In describing my earliest acquaintance with Roger, I told of his direction of several college plays. These were performed in a dining hall converted to theatrical use; later, Roger would direct a series of Passion plays in the chapel at Acadia—again repurposing a building, turning the chapel into a theatre. However, for all the drama of a dining room, there is something inherently theatrical about any chapel, any place designed for the offering of public worship.

Plays performed in theatres, in chapels, or in dining rooms are acted-out dramas. They are not mere "readings." Even the term "performance" is not sufficiently broad. Readings are also performed. Worship is acted. People move in physical space. There is choreography, however simple, and it is embodied; voices alone, however inflected, cannot convey the whole. I am not thinking here just of the minster raising hands in blessing, or even of congregants sharing the peace. The whole experience is performance and happens in a performance space.

---

[15] Ibid., 7.
[16] Ibid.

Since the era of classical drama, those reflecting upon stage work have stressed the interdependence of mind and body in acting: emotional expression and physical movement are conjoined. Much more recently, the nineteenth-century theorist Delsarte even prioritised physical movement over speech in acting.[17] While we might want to hold speech and movement, orality and physicality, together, it is impossible to imagine theatre without these elements of movement through and in physical space as well as the spoken word.[18]

Worship shares these characteristics. Our question should not be whether everything that happens—all words spoken and all movements and gestures by leaders and worshippers—is part of the performance of worship. Instead, the question should be whether all the words spoken and the movements and gestures of leaders and worshippers form together a coherent whole. Do they propel the narrative arc? Do they enhance or distract from the flow of the worship from its start to its completion?

We will come to consider performance space in a moment, but two other aspects require comment. The first is costume. A key part of the credibility of the actor in the eyes of the audience is that they appear in costume, dressed as the character whom they portray, not as themselves. The costume may be quite ordinary, but it fits with the staging and that of the other characters. It serves the overall purpose of storytelling and plays its part in the work of the narrative arc.

Roger had clear ideas on the "costume" of those who lead worship in Baptist (and all other) churches. He dressed in full regalia, a representative of the tradition for whom gown and cassock, clerical collar and tabs, were an important feature of the staging of worship. This "costume" reminds the congregation that the person leading worship is playing a role and is not simply standing before them as an individual. The items worn may have their own symbolic meaning, though the main significance of items

---

[17] Christopher B. Balme, *The Cambridge Introduction to Theatre Studies* (Cambridge: CUP, 2008), 22.

[18] Of course, there have been "performances" where one person speaks with little or no movement—we might think of Alec McCowen's rendition of Mark's Gospel which toured for some years—but such performances are accompanied by gesture and facial movements even when the actor remains in one place on the stage. Even if conceding that such performances do not include "movement," they are remarkable in part because they are the exception that proves the rule.

Worship as Theatre

such as the collar is more historical than theological, and of gowns as academic than ecclesiastical. Nevertheless, the whole taken together indicates
something theologically significant about the person and role of the minister leading worship.

Traditionalists decry the trend toward more casual dress generally,
and, in particular, among those leading worship. Often now in a British
Baptist church, the minister leading worship will be dressed casually—
sometimes in jeans and a T-shirt. In this, there is no differentiation by
"costume" from other members of the congregation. Such trends doubtless
reflect both general social patterns away from formality and deference, and
also those "in-house" church trends, like the charismatic movement, which
mirror the more general societal changes.

Yet despite what I have said earlier about staging and costume, it
seems to me that the case of ministerial dress is not quite so clear-cut for
contemporary Baptists. My observations about distractions above may be
pertinent here. The question is whether, given the general trends of society, certain kinds of dress may distract the congregation rather than assist
them. I confess that I find jeans and T-shirts distractingly over-casual: they
represent a hurdle which I must overcome in entering into the worship
experience. If they are complemented by general junk scattered around the
front of the church, I find this very unhelpful. This isn't to say that I cannot
overcome the hurdles, but that I recognize them *as* hurdles. However, I
am also fairly sure that for some others, especially on a worship set that is
contemporary and informal, the full regalia of cassock and tabs might also
be distracting, anomalous, or even strange in unhelpful ways. Decisions
about costume seem to me now to need to be made locally. What will help
this particular congregation worship?

Airing this might also push us back to the question of buildings and
space. Cathedrals might be seeing an increase in their congregations, but
not everyone will find this arrangement of space and particular pageantry
conducive. We sometimes hear of the difficulty of getting people with no
church background, or perhaps with a bad experience of church life, across
the threshold of a church building. It may be that some worship spaces are
more challenging than others—that those worship spaces that will work
for such people will deploy their symbols more subtly but nonetheless still
intentionally with a sense of liturgical purpose. Having informal space or
less formal costume does not mean being messy or badly thought-out. The
question is not whether or not a space looks like a church. It's whether a

193

space helps us to worship, leads us into an awareness of the presence of God, and assists the flow of worship as it takes us from call to dismissal.

The other aspect worth comment is the audience or congregation. Our modern experience of drama in the West is shaped by the theatre's proscenium arch and the invisible fourth wall.[19] As Diderot put it in 1758, "Imagine a wall across the front of the stage, dividing you from the audience, and act precisely as if the curtain had not risen."[20] This fourth wall is a posited, invisible barrier—it allows the audience to see in at the actors and the action, but the actors (act as if they) cannot see out. In practical terms, lighting often makes this a reality. This separates the audience from the action and turns them into spectators rather than participants. Even when the actors temporarily remove the fourth wall, as when they enter or exit the stage through the audience, or even, as in Richard Bean's *One Man, Two Guvnors*, a member of the audience is invited onto stage for some slapstick part of the action, or when a TV character addresses the camera directly, somehow the effect of this metatheatre is to reinforce the barrier between audience and performers by drawing our attention to the fact that we are watching a play.

At first sight, this seems like a clear contrast to worship, where the congregation is participating in an experience led by another(s). Of course, most of us have been in services where worship feels like a *performance* of this kind—that word may even be used pejoratively to describe the experience. The congregation is here, the leaders are there, and they speak at us rather than to us or with us. Some not at home in the cathedral, for instance, might remark that this is how Choral Evensong feels to them— a sung musical concert rather than an act of worship. But there are different ways of participating, and when we become wholly passive at Evensong, we might miss an opportunity to reflect upon, and be moved by, the music which says as much about us as about the worship itself.

Similarly, while convention inhibits actors from breaking the fourth wall by speaking with the audience or even referring to their existence, it is a poor dramatic performance which does not in some way "feed off" the presence of the audience. In a comedy like *French without Tears*, audience laughter indicates their participation in the unfolding story. But in the

---

[19] See Elizabeth Bell, *Theories of Performance* (Los Angeles: Sage, 2008), 203.

[20] Denis Diderot, *On Dramatic Poetry*, quoted in *The Methuen Drama Dictionary of the Theatre*, ed. Jonathan Law (London: Bloomsbury, 2011), 194.

Worship as Theatre

climactic drama of the final scenes of *A Man for all Seasons*, the actors do not need audible gasps to sense that the audience is with them. To attend a Shakespeare play is not merely to go and watch something that other people do. It is to become involved in that action as we identify with characters, feel their dilemmas and joys, are moved by their fallibility and poor choices, laugh at their grandiose behaviour—all of which helps us see ourselves and our world in new ways. What goes for Shakespeare goes elsewhere, too. Bolt's Thomas More asks us questions about our convictions and what they mean to us, and so on.

Nevertheless, it must be conceded that there appears to be a difference of degree here: congregations who join responsive prayers and sing songs and affirm "this is the Word of the Lord" are more obviously participating than theatrical audiences. There are theatrical parallels, perhaps. Pantomime and stand-up comedy are among the examples of greater obvious audience participation, of a thinner fourth wall.

Worship as an Event in a "Performance Space"

Just as all words and movement either add to or hinder the narrative arc, so the "stage" upon which worship is performed is not mere space—filled or cluttered with this and that, as if a stage play might work around debris left over by the previous people occupying the area, or the detritus of the actors' belongings (though doubtless some experimental theatre has appeared to be just this!). The stage is carefully designed and lit, given constraints of budgets and logistics, to create an effect. This effect is subordinate to the aim of the performance. The effect created by the stage design is calculated to assist the telling of the story, to create opportunities for the actors to move meaningfully. Just as the actor performs as someone else, the space is also "performing" as a different space. This is no longer the dais in the college dining hall, it is now Thomas Cromwell's home or Pharaoh's throne room. It is something else, just as the drama of worship transforms the space of the church into something else—or something more than a postcode. Max Herrmann, pioneer of theatre studies in Germany, put it like this:

> [A]rt is a spatial art. This should not be understood in the sense that the representation of space could be an end in itself in theatre.... In the art of theatre we are not dealing with the representation of space but with the execution of human movement in theatrical space. This space is however never or hardly ever identical with the

real space that exists on stage.... The space that theatre creates is rather an artificial space which only comes into being through a substantial transformation of actual space, it is an experience by which the stage space is transformed into a different kind of space.[21]

In order to transform the stage space, theatre directors import props and furniture. Somehow, while it may not really look like Pharaoh's throne room, it has to *suggest* that place to the audience. A drape, a magnificent seat, some spangled item, a neatly placed flunky, with the characters present and the dialogue they share, tell the audience where they are now. Not in a dining hall or in London's West End, but in ancient Egypt.

Something similar is happening in church. A cross, a table, a pulpit or lectern, a banner. Stained glass perhaps, with Gospel scenes. Bread and wine, an open Bible, perhaps a candle flickers. Such appurtenances transform the space: no longer a nondescript rectangular building in a side street, rather now the gateway of heaven (to use rather old-fashioned language). Each of the items in the stage set and the props play their part. As on the theatre stage, clutter must be minimised—not because we are house proud, but because it risks distracting; not telling the story, but instead breaking the space.

Audiences engage in something which every reader of fiction also adopts. They willingly suspend disbelief and enter into the experience offered to them. They *know* they are in a college dining hall or a West End theatre; they are not daft. However, they give themselves to the experience. We might even say that for a while they accept the illusion as a reality, they proceed *as if* they are in Egypt, and not just off the Central line tube station. Items which distract from this, which point to the illusion, which make it more difficult to willingly suspend disbelief, must be minimised.

Again, something similar is happening in worship. Worship of the highest quality, where the narrative arc is strong and the sense of flow absorbing, draws the congregation into the experience. This can happen with minimal staging in terms of the set and props. A congregation meeting in a school hall might simply have a cross on a table as the only space-transformative clue. But the experience is likely to be more immersive if there is more to help the congregation make the switch from school hall to

---

[21] Max Herrmann, "Das theatralische Raumerlebnis" [The Experience of Theatrical Space], *Zeitschrift für Ästhetik und allgemeine Kunstwissenschaft* (Beiheft), 1931, 25: 152–63, quoted in Balme, *Cambridge*, 48.

Worship as Theatre

heaven's gate. The removal of clutter will be a good start: those coats and electrical cords should go, what furniture is necessary should be neat and not attract the eye; instead, the eye should be caught by symbols which move us into the worship, alert us to the presence of God, help us to suspend disbelief (in various ways!), readying us to be part of the Gospel drama which will unfold.

While set and props can be simple, we see here what an advantage there might be in a building which has the opportunity for more durable and larger-scale symbols. The cathedral congregations growing in recent decades in England have something here, with their built-in (quite literally) sense of the numinous and their rich symbolic layers. But Baptist churches can also offer some of this. Our forebears wanted simple buildings, eschewing stained glass imagery and all symbols. We might share their desire not to distract, but also worry that the baby was thrown out with the bathwater. Baptist churches built in the last 150 years have often been more symbol-rich. And the school hall need not be wholly bare in these terms either—even the now-ubiquitous projector can be used to deploy imagery which assists the worship experience now that we've evolved beyond the overhead projector's obsession with words.

We spoke earlier of the proscenium arch, which helps to create the "fourth wall" illusion. It is thought to make it easier for the audience to imagine the reality of the action in the play, and there are practical advantages with everyone in the audience facing in, more or less, the same direction on tiered seating to improve sight lines and make blocking and lighting the action easier for the director. But not all stages are set up in this way, and the director might prefer a different layout which would enable them to mediate a different kind of experience and different understandings of the nature of that experience. When the setup is "in the round," the audience sits on all sides of the stage, with actors always entering and exiting through them. This offers a different kind of immersive possibility. Because the audience can more clearly see one another, there is a constant reminder that what is being watched is *theatre*. Similarly, traverse staging positions the audience on both sides of a long rectangular stage, rather like a fashion show catwalk. This limits scenery considerably but has other possibilities which the director may feel are important. A thrust stage offers a cross between the traverse and proscenium arch, with the stage protruding out into the audience from the arch, allowing backdrops and scenery, but also allowing the actors to move into the audience and permitting the audience to see one another face-to-face. More radical

KEEPING THE FAITH

is the promenade staging where, perhaps outdoors, the actors move around. They may walk among a standing audience, or the audience may follow the actors along the road.

These different types of staging each reflect different understandings of theatre and different kinds of dramatic experience. In the same way, the designs of churches' worship spaces might be considered as varying kinds of performance space—with each kind suggesting something distinctive about the experience of worship. The design of this space is fixed in certain ways when a church is built, and to some extent subsequent generations are mitigating its less desirable (to them) aspects in their adaptation and use. However, even when we adapt and reshape, what we end up with is not simply a functional space: wittingly or otherwise, it says something about what we think worship is. A few examples may be helpful.

The traditional chapel of the Welsh valleys has a high central pulpit (yes, six feet above contradiction), central organ pipes, and pews in straight lines. The deacons sit on the "big seat" around a modest Communion table under the pulpit, and the baptistry is neatly out of sight underneath it. Plain white walls, opaque glass, high ceilings for acoustics, a gallery. Everything maximises the use of space in an economical way, and directs our attention to the Word. There is an implicit statement about authority and leadership. There are no visual aids as such, but everything that can be seen acts as one!

Another church in a wealthy Victorian suburb has a clock tower and looks, at first glance, as if it might be a parish church. It has a cruciform shape with short transepts and a chancel up a few steps. The baptistry is open against the back wall, the large Communion table central, the pulpit still high but to the side, balanced by a free-standing lectern opposite it. Again, there are straight rows of seats, though they are chairs rather than pews and can be reconfigured if desired. Stained glass windows with biblical scenes add colour, with the ceiling painted a rich red. There is confidence here, a different aesthetic, and the sacraments are more explicitly valued; the Word is still prominent even if the Lord's Supper appears to be the climax. The size and shape suggests mystery and distance, the otherness of God.

The next building doubles as a community centre: an older, small chapel has had a new suite of rooms built on to its side, changing the original building's orientation. Folding doors screen off the sanctuary from the multipurpose hall now adjoining. There is an organ, though it is no longer often used, and the remodelling has created space for a band alongside the

Worship as Theatre

dais. There is a portable pulpit and a larger (but still portable) table, a modern cross on the wall, and a couple of tapestry hangings, with a baptistery which is sometimes open and sometimes not—the dais rolls back and forth according to need. All these make clear statements about worship's specialness but nevertheless, being imaginative and flexible, those who conceived the alterations did not think worship should be something that happens in a separated, special place. Despite the screened "special" end, it is necessarily connected with the quotidian. Here "church" may be about resources being used carefully and making connections. While worship embraces symbolism and Word and sacrament, there is a more down-to-earth feel, immanence with transcendence.

Another more modern church is not large but has a clever use of perspective. There might be an oddly shaped roof or window, and the architect has ensured that the eye is led to the main front wall where a dramatic cross accentuates the height of that wall and further draws the eye. The pulpit is off centre and not particularly large, there is a wide table in the centre and rich curtains behind. There is probably an open baptistry—perhaps with "running" water. There is bright colour in abstract stained glass and in banners and paintings around the side and rear walls. The congregation will not sit in straight rows, but in an arc across the building on comfortable upholstered chairs. By rearranging seats, there is space for other things to happen: dance and drama become viable, allowing a new wholeness of response. Some of the confidence is back, but now fellowship is a crucial part—the people do not just look at the front but at one another. Colour, comfort, and art, suggest that an older more "Puritan" view of worship has been superseded.

The school hall requires dedicated people who come in early every Sunday to set out seats and arrange the "set"—in some ways this is more like an actual theatre, because the "scenery" is not so fixed, as it was in the earlier examples, however flexible. The sight lines have been chosen carefully so that the clutter which can't be moved is behind the congregation. A simple table draped with a deep-coloured cloth is central at the front, with a candle burning upon it; on it there is a cross to one side and an open Bible on the other. Against curtains behind it have been placed several banners made by members of the congregation which change with the seasons. A screen is used for song words, Scripture readings, and for images which help orient the congregants to the theme of the service. A simple lectern has a fall with an appliqué semiabstract pattern suggesting the Holy Spirit, adding further colour and focus. The band is neatly arranged to one side. Here worship is clearly part of ordinary everyday activity, and yet the arrangement of the props seems to sanctify this ordinariness. Symbol and colour and sight lines are used to good effect to help a congregation which needs a little more assistance in willingly suspending their "disbelief."

As in a theatrical performance, where we worship and how that space is arranged are significant contributing components of the experience. The space in which we worship is not a neutral, meaning-free one. It is a performance space, with its scenery and props, its sight lines and acoustics (about which we have said nothing), colour and shape. All of these things help or hinder worship. How we work with and in them and adapt them also say something about what we think worship is—and by implication, whom we think God is.

The Role of the Worship Leader

> If I may be allowed to conjecture what is the nature of that mysterious power by which a player really is the character which he represents, my notion is, that he must have a kind of double feeling. He must assume in a strong degree the character which he represents, while he at the same time retains the consciousness of his own character.[22]

So opined James Boswell in 1770, reflecting on the actor's task. The actor, Boswell suggests, represents a character while also retaining his own identity. The leader of worship is also, in some sense, inhabiting a role. We might even say "playing a part" while still remaining themselves.

Whether ordained or not, any worship leader in a Baptist setting is invited or "called" to occupy this role by the congregation. It is never a task undertaken off our own bat or undertaken for our own satisfaction. I have already referred to the use of special clothing to "cover" the personality of the individual, but there is a sense in which such garb also indicates what Boswell calls "the character which [s]he represents." Similarly, I have already quoted Phillips Brooks's definition of preaching as "truth through personality,"[23] a definition offered in his Yale *Lectures on Preaching*. Brooks

---

[22] James Boswell, "Remarks on the Profession of a Player," *London Magazine* (August 1770): 397–98; (September 1770): 468–517. Quoted in Balme, *Cambridge*, 17.

[23] Brooks, *Lectures on Preaching*, 8.

Worship as Theatre

argues that the truth of preaching is not merely abstracted as if "written on the sky,"[24] nor simply a matter of oratorical skill. Instead, it must be mediated through the preacher's "character, his affections, his whole intellectual and moral being. It must come genuinely through him."[25]

In this tension, between having one's personality "covered" and preaching a truth inevitably and properly mediated through one's personality, we find the role of the preacher and worship leader, and it is similar to the tension Boswell identified for an actor. Acting techniques quite often emphasize the desirability of an actor finding similar emotions and responses from their own experience to help them portray their character in a play. This is the essence of the "method acting" advocated by Konstantin Stanislavsky (1863–1938), who "sought 'inner realism' by insisting that his actors find the truth within themselves and 'become' the characters they portrayed."[26] Even when the actor tries to be another person, they draw upon their own experience and emotional range in so doing. Similarly, the preacher draws upon their own experience in articulating the Gospel; and the worship leader will also be a worshipper and draw upon their experience of worship (at first and second hand as they become a more practised listener) in planning and leading worship.

In an authentic liturgy there will be something of the leader's personality which is obvious to the congregation that knows them, but it will not be the most significant thing about the worship, it will not dominate. Speaking of the "role" of leading worship, we immediately see a similarity with acting. The worship leader plays a part. That part is a representative one. At times, during the worship they will "represent" God in ways which those in traditions with a priestly understanding of ministry might find more comfortable than we usually do. Perhaps this is most obvious for us in the blessing, but it is present elsewhere in the liturgy too. The worship leader, however, represents the other side of the dialogue, too. The leader in prayer—praise, confession, intercession—and in seeking to articulate the congregation's questions while preaching most clearly is representing the congregants. In doing so, the leader strives to be mindful of a whole range of sensibilities regarding worship, just as he or she is also looking to

---

[24] Ibid., 5.
[25] Ibid., 8.
[26] "Stanislavsky, Konstantin," in *Methuen Drama Dictionary* 479.

be aware of the different stages of spiritual maturity and intellectual engagement from the congregation.

All this is demanding. It is not easy to lead worship well. In inhabiting the role of the worship leader, that person is not just drawing upon his or her own knowledge of themselves and others but also tacitly agreeing not to please themselves first of all. They are there to lead others into worship and to put the needs of those others before their own. In this sense, also, they "cover" their personality with its preferences and foibles, even though that personality still figures in the liturgy in a way which is hopefully meaningful.

Those who do succumb to the temptation to give their own preferences and enjoyment the highest priority risk falling into a more serious error. In a culture which so often whirls around celebrity and stardom, worship leaders, too, can become intoxicated with even the meagre suggestion of a celebrity status within the sanctuary. Perhaps the ubiquitous microphone now makes this an even greater risk. Worship leaders should not be the centre of attention, just as preachers should not use illustration or rhetorical flourish to become the stars of their own sermons. The actor may be a star, a celebrity; might sign autographs and make special guest appearances. And here the similarities between acting and worship leader must break down.

"Decently and in Order": Form and Improvisation in Worship

One of the growth areas in modern drama and comedy in recent decades has been improvisation. In improvisational theatre, "text and action are created anew each night. What remains constant is the general format and the types of scenes employed. Such examples remain, however, exceptions."[27] These approaches remain largely experimental and "edgy"—the majority of regular theatre-goers might never see (or want to see) such a performance. But it is more common and mainstream elsewhere. The film director Mike Leigh has a well-known method whereby he asks actors to rehearse and shape their own script within the overall requirements of a given scene.

> Leigh always begins his project process without a script. He usually starts from a basic premise or storyline which is developed through

---

[27] Balme, *Cambridge*, 134.

lengthy improvisation by the actors. He begins working with each actor on a "on to one" basis.... The actor, with the help of Leigh, builds an elaborate alter ego, mapping out the character's life in fine detail.... Once these individual characters are formed separately, Leigh gradually brings the actors together for a series of useful improvisations.... None of the actors know anything about the film or theatre piece other than their own place in it.... Leigh writes an outline of scenes which then can become a general outline for the final film or play. The actors improvise specifically around these scenes, while an assistant takes notes. The best lines and moments are then distilled and scripted, and shooting can at last begin.[28]

Leigh's approach encourages freshness in the performance and also helps the actors to inhabit their parts credibly and own the material as their own. Improvisational comedy can work in similar ways, with performers working within preconceived, overarching structures, but unlike Leigh's repeated rehearsals and refinement before a fixed final product is produced, the comedy is new every show and never the same twice. Shorter form improv comedy has been made mainstream by such TV shows as *Whose Line Is It Anyway?* while longer forms might improvise shorter scenes within a larger storyline or thematic unity. Somewhat anarchic in feel, such theatre is popular with a wide range of audiences.[29]

This notion of improvising within certain fixed points has an immediate resonance with much contemporary worship in Baptist churches, though not all of it would have been approved by Roger Prentice! Ellis and Blyth's introduction to *Gathering for Worship* notes that freedom is the "gifting of the Spirit, who gives life and freedom to the gathering people of God, enabling them to worship in Spirit and in truth (John 4:24). Where the Spirit is, there is freedom (2 Cor. 3:16)."[30] Those antagonised by all charismatic-influenced worship will often complain that it does not comply with Paul's injunction that "all things should be done decently and in order" (1 Cor. 14:40). But while improv comedy can be anarchic and

---

[28] "Mike Leigh's process and techniques," in *Acting Hub*, online at https://www.actorhub.co.uk/383/mike-leighs-process-and-techniques

[29] If you fancy having a go, you might start here: "How to improvise stand-up comedy," *Wired* (April 2014), online at https://www.wired.co.uk/article/improv-stand-up

[30] Ellis and Blyth, *Gathering*, 5.

KEEPING THE FAITH

subversive, worship which is not entirely scripted but allows space for the Spirit's leading need not be. Those who quote the Pauline text often ignore the verse immediately preceding it: "So, my brothers and sisters, strive to prophesy, and do not forbid speaking in tongues, but all things should be done decently and in order."

There should still be the narrative arc which brings coherence to the whole, and which gives the *flow* of the worship its forward momentum from a particular call to worship to a particular conclusion. Like the improvised drama, the worship can still have its shape, can still have "scenes" which accomplish certain elements of the narrative, facilitate elements of the dialogue. But not everything in the scene must be scripted to achieve this end. That said, there is some skill involved in managing this process, in keeping the non-scripted content propelling the overarching arc—though one might also recognize, as any preacher who has abandoned a script or veered off it in profitable ways does, that sometimes the Spirit can surprize and lead us in new directions in the moment. It is also one thing to plan but be open to this leading, and quite another to presume that the Spirit will make up for the lack of seriousness with which we have approached the service. Many years ago, as an undergraduate, I attended a Pentecostal service. The leader began by saying he'd had a busy week and "left it all to the Spirit." It soon became apparent that the Spirit must also have had a busy week, and left it all to him.

Seriously, this freedom within constraints is recognized in *Gathering for Worship*.

> At the same time, we worship God in the freedom of the Spirit. Given this potential for spontaneity and variation, this book seeks only to indicate the core shape and dynamic flow of worship from which planning may begin. As music, readings, prayers and other symbolic actions emerge in the process of preparation, so the shape will grow from a pattern on the page to the full expression of worship in the congregation...[so that] the inner dynamic of gathering and sending are deliberately given prominence.[31]

---

[31] Ibid., 7.

Worship as Theatre

Conclusion

The notion of worship as theatre does not always work. Like all such metaphors, it strains or fails at various points. However, the resonances are many and illuminating. Indeed, at times they are so strong that we might even say we have gone beyond metaphor and that worship *is* theatre in important respects. I believe that thinking about worship in these terms can help us understand more fully certain aspects of worship and what it means to lead it and participate in it well. Roger Prentice was a devotee and a fine practitioner in both spheres. Perhaps in his person we saw them meld creatively and understand our worship a little better as a result. He would certainly be pleased with such an outcome.

A Homiletic Hermeneutic for the Rewriting of Hymn Texts

J. Daniel Gibson

The world in consciousness is ever-changing, mysteries of being human are variously understood...images of salvation may be different, even the ways in which we grasp images of revelation may alter from age to age.[1]

There is a clear, mutually supportive relationship between preaching and the singing of hymns, the Word spoken and the Word sung. There is a rich treasury of Christian hymnody which has been used to reinforce the faith of believers and for education and evangelism. This heritage of church music has been a growing, changing entity. Each generation and age has made its own contribution in style and language, and as new hymns were added, others were quietly discarded through disuse. Some hymns, however, retained their places of usefulness and honour within the body of hymnody. They have been retranslated from one language to another. They have also been retranslated within the same language so that they can continue to speak to new generations through words and images that are contemporary and therefore meaningful.

Arguably, the revision of hymns has been necessary in the past and continues to be needed. Our present task is to discover and recommend consistent principles through which the necessary revisions can be made with maximum gains in a variety of competing objectives. Hymns that have been judged beautiful and worthy for hundreds of years deserve the best treatment possible so that they will continue to serve the church for years to come. Otherwise, a great hymn, because of poor revision, will fall into disuse and be lost forever. This essay will present three clearly identified concerns which must be addressed before any revision may be attempted. Then, a hermeneutic for hymn revision will be proposed.

---

[1] David Buttrick, *Homiletic: Moves and Structures* (Philadelphia: Fortress Press, 1987), 269.

A Homiletic Hermeneutic for the Rewriting of Hymn Texts

Three Questions and Considerations

1. Is it true? In any translation, retranslation, interpretation, or revision, we come back to this basic question asked by David Buttrick. While Buttrick was referring specifically to the interpretation of a text, the principle applies equally well to hymn revision. He says of the preacher,

> "Truth" and "efficacy" are two different kinds of judgments. In speaking of God, the question we must ask of interpretation is "Is it true?" and not "Is it helpful?" Though grace may triumph efficaciously through all kinds of error (thank God!), we should not presume upon grace. So, responsible preachers worry about being true to a text.[2]

Sometimes change is both true and helpful. But first it must be true. To change truth into untruth simply to make it more palatable or pleasing to the hearer is never acceptable; but to reinterpret it so that its larger truth is heard is to be commended. In the case of Jesus' statement about resurrection (John 11:25–26), the preacher rightly tells the whole truth, that when Jesus spoke these words he was referring to *one man* (*Lazarus*); but through that one man, Jesus proclaimed his good news to *all people*. If this is true of Gospel and Scripture and sermons, it may also be applied to the issues of rewriting hymn texts, since they are dedicated to the same message. The primary concern will always be, "Is it true to the Gospel?"

For many Christians, the Scriptures are given the place of authority in matters of faith and practice, against which experience, tradition, and personal revelation are tested. Believers ask, "Is it true to the Scriptures?" This is a very difficult issue on which to satisfy the many differing stances. Buttrick, in his discussion on the nature of Scripture, believes that those who assert the inerrant literalism of the Bible take an unyielding stance, which he describes as "an extravagant position, seldom ventured by the church 'fathers' or by the framers of Reformation faith."[3] On the other extreme are those who regard Scripture as a human invention, helpful in parts, but unreliable and prone to error. Some follow the Zwinglian tradition that if something cannot be specifically found or endorsed in the

---

[2] Ibid., 270.
[3] Ibid., 264.

207

KEEPING THE FAITH

Bible, it is not acceptable, while others hold to the Lutheran tradition that anything is acceptable if not expressly forbidden in the Bible.

So, the question "Is it true to the Scriptures?" will elicit responses which differ significantly according to the doctrine of Scripture held by each individual or faith community. An important consideration is that words of a Scripture text and the message of Scripture may not always seem to be the same. Martin Luther points out emphatically that Scripture is often idiomatic language, and to translate idiomatic language literally is to lose much of the meaning. He advocates translating the text into equally idiomatic language so that the full truth of the message (and the Gospel) is clearly spoken for all to hear:

> Here, in Romans 3 [28], I knew very well that the word *solum* is not in the Greek or Latin text; the papists did not have time to teach me that. It is a fact that these four letters *s o l a* are not there. And these blockheads stare at them like cows at a new gate. At the same time they do not see that it conveys the sense of the text; it belongs there if the translation is to be clear and vigorous. I wanted to speak German, not Latin or Greek, since it was German I had undertaken to speak in the translation. But it is in the nature of our German language that in speaking of two things, one of which is affirmed and the other denied, we use the term *solum (allein)*, along with the word *nicht* [not] or *kein* [no]. For example, we say, "The farmer brings *allein* grain and *kein* money"; "I have *allein* eaten and *nicht* yet drunk"; "Did you *allein* write it, and *nicht* read it over?" There are innumerable cases of this kind in daily use. In all these phrases, this is the German usage, even though it is not the Latin or Greek usage. It is the nature of the German language to add the word *allein* in order that the word *nicht* or *kein* may be clearer and more complete. We do not have to enquire of the literal Latin, how we are to speak German, as these asses do. Rather we must enquire about this of the mother in that home, the children on the street, the common man in the marketplace. We must be guided by their language, the way they speak, and do our translating accordingly.[4]

---

[4] "Word and Sacrament," vol. 35, *On Translating: An Open Letter, Luther's Works*, ed. E. Theodore Bachman (Philadelphia: Muhlenberg Press, 1960), 188–89.

208

A Homiletic Hermeneutic for the Rewriting of Hymn Texts

All proclamation must be true to the Gospel and to the fullest interpretation of Scripture. This will affect the manner in which preachers prepare their sermons, the way hymn texts are evaluated, and the attitude of those who would revise. The end product is to be true, and all other considerations become secondary. It does not matter if the sermon or the revised hymn is aesthetically pleasing or grammatically perfect unless it is first clearly shown to be true. God is a God of truth, and nothing less than truth is acceptable in Christian preaching and singing.

2. By what authority do we proceed? The whole question of authority is always before us in the interpretation of Scripture and the preparation of text to be preached to the faith community or sung by them. Buttrick asks, "For the preacher, where is authority—in text, in interpretation, in imagination, in the congregation—where?"[5] The authority of every preacher and the authority of every believer is to be found in relationship to Christ. We do not presume in our own right to have authority, but we respond to the call of God (the call of Jesus in the Gospels) which is confirmed in the community of faith. The authority of the preacher is assigned rather than assumed. Like the women at the tomb, who were the first to see the risen Christ and were the first commanded by him to "Go and tell..." (Matthew 28:10), every preacher is constrained to continue the telling or proclamation of the Gospel first assigned to the women. We tell openly and honestly all that has been revealed to us, and we claim it to be true, for we believe it to be true. Paul Scott Wilson adds that

> the authority to preach is an office given by the entire church, in accordance with Scripture, usually through laying on of hands at ordination, only after the candidate has been thoroughly tested with regard to call, character, theological knowledge, and ability to interpret the Scripture correctly.[6]

While there is no guarantee of perfection in the work or wisdom of any human preacher, the combination of divine call and ecclesiastical confirmation is the best source of authority possible. So, the claim to know the mind of God is both preposterous and proper—preposterous because

---

[5] Buttrick, *Homiletic*, 243.

[6] Paul Scott Wilson, *The Practice of Preaching* (Toronto: United Methodist Publishing House, rev. ed., 2020), 136.

KEEPING THE FAITH

we cannot possibly know God as well as we are known; proper because we are granted the knowledge and experience of much of God's will for us and the world. We feel ourselves to be personally present in the narratives of our Lord's ministry and his death and resurrection, and there is authority in our feeling and experience of Christ. Beyond this revelation, we can relate our own joy at having received forgiveness and our experience of the Spirit. The preacher dares to walk on holy ground and speak for God. We are thus commissioned to preach the Gospel—to tell the truth as it has been revealed to us. This means that we must constantly wrestle with the limits of authority.

For the hymn reviser, this sense of authority is no less important. While it may be easy to justify a change of wording which simply updates an out-of-date term, there are more serious questions to be raised about the author's original intent. Is the proposed change faithful to the original intent of the author? There are three distinct levels of answers to this question.

First, what did the author *mean* to say? It is impossible for any person fully to know the mind of another. When we say that we know what someone meant, we *presume* that we know. If we are able to discuss in detail with the author the intent and meaning, we can still only presume that we understand. Even the author, looking back, may not be sure what was meant at the time of writing. People's feelings and opinions change, and with these changes come different interpretations of their own actions and speech. "[The poet] Klopstock was questioned regarding the meaning of a passage in his poem. He replied, 'God and I both knew what it meant once; now only God knows.'"[7]

Second, what did the author *actually* say? There is no certainty that the words used by an author relate perfectly the intent of the author, even if that intent is certain. Words are used to convey ideas and messages, but words are limited in that by themselves they can never fully describe the idea or become the message. Marshall McLuhan's 1964 proposition *that the medium is the message*, when applied to linguistics, affirms that the choice of words used to deliver a message cannot help but modify the message. The author's choice of words will always affect the way the hearer

---

[7] Cesare Lombroso, *The Man of Genius* (1891), part 1, ch. 2, as quoted in *Bartlett's Familiar Quotations* (online version), licensed from Little, Brown and Company, Inc., 1980.

A Homiletic Hermeneutic for the Rewriting of Hymn Texts

receives the message, and this may or may not be in keeping with the author's intent. Words are best studied in context, that is, in relationship to the rest of the text. Just as Scripture texts are understood and interpreted in the context of the larger passage and larger message, the words of hymn texts need to be studied as part of the entire hymn. For example, a metaphor taken out of context may not be effective or may even be misinterpreted. Looking for the actual meaning of the words is further complicated by the fact that any given text or writing may have more than one meaning, which may be evident in the original, the modern understanding, or both.

> Anyone who has ever penned a poem and then listened as friends (or those not so friendly) interpret the words knows that meaning may well be wider than an author may suppose. Words are obviously not lexically narrow in definition, they tend to connote; thus we speak of polyvalent meaning. Someone reading a poem you have written may come up with surprising meanings that you, as poet, did not anticipate. In some cases, you may object, perhaps on the basis of intent, saying "No way!," but at other times you may turn inward and admit that, yes, the words you wrote may well reach beyond your own awareness, that unwittingly your poem has evoked more meaning than you knew. So, when we write, we may pen a system of words that, detached from our consciousness, claims a wider range of meaning than we once intended.[8]

Third, what is (or was) the author's *attitude* about the use of the hymn? This is a major consideration, because it raises the whole issue of ownership from an emotional and spiritual perspective. (This is also a separate legal issue, to be discussed hereafter.) Who *owns* a hymn which has been written for the glory of God, or the work of evangelism, or the edification of the church, or the strengthening of a believer's devotional life? Some will insist that this is purely a legal issue of intellectual property rights. Others will say that a hymn dedicated to God is now God's alone, and the Spirit will guide believers toward its best and most fitting use. Yet others will say that hymns designed for worship in church become the property of the church universal and every believer who feels drawn to sing them.

---

[8] Buttrick, *Homiletic*, 270.

211

KEEPING THE FAITH

The evidence of the lives and ministries of many early hymn writers is that they were not concerned about legal issues of ownership—copyright was a later innovation and has been practised with much more fervour in America than England. The accepted practice in the early days of the English hymn was that new hymns were meant to be shared. As a new hymn was introduced, a visitor would remember it—perhaps even copy it down—and take it back to his or her own church, where it would be added to the small but growing collection of hymns. This is much the same way the original copies of the Gospels and other New Testament writings were passed on—shared and copied by many early churches so that all could benefit equally. The early hymn writers were pleased and honoured that their hymns were deemed worthy of wider distribution, and many actually encouraged the practice. Some, such as the Wesleys, however, discouraged their copiers from making any revisions. In the preface to their *Collection of Hymns for the Use of the People Called Methodists* of 1780, John wrote:

> Many gentlemen have done my brother and me (though without naming us) the honour to reprint many of our hymns. Now they are perfectly welcome so to do, provided they print them just as they are. But I desire that they would not attempt to mend them: for they really are not able. None of them is able to mend either the sense or the verse. Therefore, I must beg of them one of these two favours: either to let them stand just as they are, to take them for better for worse: or to add the true reading [the original text] in the margin, or at the bottom of the page; that we may be no longer accountable either for the nonsense or for the doggerel of other men.[9]

For the Wesleys, there were two issues. They regarded their hymns as a vital part of the great evangelistic effort to which they and others were wholeheartedly committed, and the more their hymns were used, the more souls would be won for the Kingdom. But they were deeply concerned that the message would be compromised by alteration. This would reduce the usefulness of the hymns for evangelism and Christian lifestyle, and was therefore vigorously opposed. Their desire to limit "mending," as they called it, was for the sake of the larger ministry of the hymns. From this

---

[9] John Wesley, *A Collection of Hymns for the Use of People Called Methodists* (London: John Mason, 1830), preface. https://en.wikisource.org/wiki/A_Collection_of_Hymns,_for_the_Use_of_the_People_Called_Methodists_(1830)

212

A Homiletic Hermeneutic for the Rewriting of Hymn Texts

we can find reason to appreciate and commend those who have dedicated their works to the Saviour and the church, and who desire to see them bear fruit as widely as possible, and for a long time to come. We must also appreciate their concern that the gifts they had freely given not be abused by thoughtless or unworthy change.

Other hymn writers, such as William Merrill ("Rise Up, O Men of God!"), were less interested in the broader ministry of their hymns, preferring to keep them as written, and bound to their original purpose, even after it was pointed out that the change of a few words could enlarge the scope and potential usefulness of the hymn dramatically. This raises the question of whether the need of the larger group outweighs the author's preference. Most hymnal editorial boards have decided that if the revision of a few words can expand the usefulness and the life of a hymn, then it is proper to proceed for the sake of the wider proclamation of the Gospel. This, presuming there are no legal restrictions, will be done regardless of the author's preference. In short, hymns, once offered to God in worship, may be retranslated and amended as needed to ensure their continued service to God.

We do not revise a hymn to suit ourselves or our own biases, but we do so under the authority given to us, who are called to speak for the living God, and to represent God's interests in our age. So, the only acceptable starting point for the hymn reviser is to approach the task at hand with honour and sensitivity. God's truth and message warrant only the best of our human talents and abilities and attitudes. But more than that, they demand an openness to the leading and the inspiration of the Holy Spirit. This is God's message, not ours, and not even the original author's; we all are the messengers entrusted with the task of making God's message clear and understandable and appealing for today. "We must seek a model that will relate contemporary interpretation to both original meaning and, somehow, original intending."[10]

3. Is it legal? This is a consideration which is often overlooked by preachers and hymn revisers. Preachers are used to searching for new ideas and interpretations to incorporate into sermons. We borrow thoughts and themes wherever we can find them, realizing that each generation rediscovers the same texts and themes over and over. No modern preacher has

---

[10] Buttrick, *Homiletic*, 274.

ever preached a sermon with a text and theme never before heard. But while sermon texts and themes are used again and again, they are seldom copyrighted. How can one copyright a theme which is thousands of years old and which was originally delivered by a prophet or apostle on behalf of God? The particular style or treatment of a theme or text in a sermon can be copyrighted, but many preachers have been hesitant to do so, preferring to allow others free access to the sermon in hopes that it will be found profitable for the spread of the Gospel. It is always assumed, however, that reasonable credit will be given.

Church music and hymns, however, are now almost always copyrighted when published. The theology and the message, of course, are the property of all people who embrace them, but the wording used by the hymn writer, usually in poetic form, is regarded in society and in law as artistic property. Copyright laws vary from country to country but usually relate to the life of the author plus a number of years (normally fifty). Sometimes copyrights are renewed by estates and others well after this period. During all this time, it is illegal to copy or publish the work of that author without being granted permission. It is also illegal to change even one word in a copyrighted hymn without permission of the author. In the copyright analysis published by the Royal Canadian College of Organists, we read, "Adaptation—no one may make changes to a copyrighted work without permission. This includes, but is not limited to, changing words, harmonizing or reharmonizing, making a choral or instrumental arrangement, or changing a music line."[11]

In recent years, copyright licensing agencies have offered umbrella programs which, for a set annual fee, authorize churches and institutions to use copyrighted works of authors and publishers who participate in the licensing program. This permission is sometimes presumed to include the right to make minor alterations in those works. But it does not; the only permission granted is to use the original work in its exact form, with no alteration allowed, not even a change in punctuation. Those who revise hymns must be sure that what they are proposing is within the law. Churches and pastors are not exempt. As a spiritual matter, God is not glorified by the use of stolen property. There is an obvious tension between the belief that hymns offered to God are the property (spiritually) of God's

---

[11] Alan C. Whitmore, "Copyright and the Church," *Organ Canada: The Triannual Journal of the Royal Canadian College of Organists*, 11/2 (July 2, 1998): 7.

church, and the fact that certain laws have been passed to protect the rights (legally) of human artists and writers. We must work within that tension.

A Proposed Hermeneutic for the Revision of Hymns

The revision of hymns is not a new thing. It is a task which has confronted editorial boards since the first hymnals were published. More than 100 years ago, an editor wrote,

> The most arduous labours of the Committee were in connexion with the texts of the hymns. Wherever common use has endeared a particular reading to the Church, the Committee have not deemed it expedient to revert to the original form: e.g. "Hark, how all the welkin rings," the original of "Hark, the herald angels sing."[12]

What is new and exceedingly relevant is the recent development of computer and copier technology now within reach of most churches, pastors, and musicians.

Learning and applying all the theories of homiletics does not guarantee that a preacher will become a great preacher, though it should produce a more competent preacher. Similarly, applying all the theories of homiletics to hymn text revision will not guarantee perfect results, though it will eliminate many of the failings and inadequacies attendant to such revision. In both cases, the product will have the benefit of the best help available and will be more reliable for having been subjected to an appropriate hermeneutic.

Homileticians themselves do not agree on every point, but there is a strong enough consensus to warrant our confidence and trust as we are provided with clear direction and process in the preparation and revision of sermons. Wilson provides a graphic representation of the process of sermonic preparation, which he calls the hermeneutical square.[13] In it he identifies four steps: what the text says, what the text means, what experience says, and what the preacher says. This basic outline, with one addition, will be adapted for the proposed hermeneutic for hymn-text revision. He suggests that in following these steps, the preacher will at each stage

---

[12] *The Book of Common Praise: Being Hymnal of the Church of England in Canada.* (Oxford: University Press, 1908), xii.

[13] Paul Scott Wilson, *The Practice of Preaching* (Toronto, ON: United Church Publishing House, 1995), 127.

ask the questions and do the research necessary to find the answers. Each step, when completed, leads to the next; the process is incomplete if any steps are skipped.

The proposed hermeneutic for the revision of hymn texts takes a similar form, although the steps are appropriately modified to relate to the process at hand. Many of the conclusions sought and the questions asked to reach those conclusions are the same in spirit and content as those asked by the preacher preparing a sermon. The major difference is that the preacher starts with a text from Scripture, which already has a certain level of authority and standing with the faith community; otherwise it would not be used. The hymn reviser starts with the text of a hymn which, though loved and given a level of standing with the faith community, has been alleged to contain in its words one or more problems which have lessened its appeal or usefulness to the community. This means that though the result sought may be identical—the proclamation of the Word—the approach taken will be modified according to the text at hand.

A Hermeneutic for Hymn Revision

1. What do the words say? Of the preacher's task of retranslating Scripture, Buttrick says, "Spread out on a page, are words from long ago and distant lands. Preachers are supposed to decipher meanings, not for an ancient age, but for *now*."[14] The person who has been asked, or feels compelled, to revise a hymn also has a text spread out. This text may not be as ancient; in fact, even some modern hymns need revision. But the first task is the same, to find out exactly what the words say. For the hymn, this step may have already started with the identification of the offending words. What do they say, and what is it about them which has caused some question or offence? Just as Scripture words must never be lifted from their context, but must always be viewed as part of a larger statement, the rest of the hymn must be analysed to see what all the words of the hymn say, not just the few problematic ones. As quoted earlier, the hymn "Make Me a Captive, Lord," declares:

> My heart is weak and poor
> 'Til it a master find;

---

[14] Emphasis in original. Buttrick, *Homiletic*, 263.

A Homiletic Hermeneutic for the Rewriting of Hymn Texts

It has no spring of action sure—
It varies with the wind.
It cannot freely move
'Til Thou hast wrought its chain;
Enslave it with Thy matchless love,
And deathless it shall reign.

Those words deemed problematic because of their out-of-date imagery are highlighted. They must be analysed to ascertain exactly and literally what is being said. But this must be interpreted in the context of what the other lines of the verse say, as part of the whole hymn.

2. What did it mean to the writer? This is the issue of original intent. The writer obviously felt that there was something to say and used these particular words to say it. But how can we, with our modern understanding of words and language, understand what the words meant to the writer, whose world and worldview were different from ours? David Buttrick has wondered, "Can we get at the psychological state of the writer?"[15] This involves trying to reconstruct the situation and the experience of that author, to see his or her world through eyes of that moment in time, to set aside some of the advantages of modern technology and life, and feel the surroundings as they were then. For instance, many Victorian-era hymns seem preoccupied with death. Children's prayers and hymns had ideas such as "if I should die before I wake," which seem jarring to us. To the authors and writers, and the parents and children of that time period, however, death was a very real prospect, at any age and at any time; the poetry and hymns of that period reflects this very real part of life. To know what the author means in the words, we must comprehend and appreciate the Christian experience of that time, and what it felt like, day by day, without modern medicine to protect from the many epidemics which decimated the population, especially the children. When we are sure we understand what the author meant, we are ready to ask the next question.

3. Was the intended message valid at the time of writing? This is the extra step added to Wilson's previously discussed hermeneutical square. When the preacher deals with a Scripture text, there is the happy presumption

---

[15] Ibid., 275.

217

that the message intended by the human writer *and* the Lord of the Word was valid. The fact that particular Scriptures were included in the canon gives us some reassurance of their validity and reliability. The same assumption cannot be made of hymns, for though they may be greatly loved and have high standing with the faith community, they are not on par with Scripture in authorship or authority. (The exception is those hymns which are direct quotations from Scripture, as Calvin restrictively taught that *all* hymns should be.)

So, it is possible and probable that the hymn reviser will come across words in a hymn clearly stating something which should never have been said, like the original third verse of Mrs. Cecil Frances Alexander's "All Things Bright and Beautiful," which reads,

> The rich man in his castle,
> The poor man at his gate,
> God made them high and lowly,
> And order'd their estate.

At the time these words were written, this type of Calvinism strongly influenced mainstream Christianity. As well, many still accepted slavery as being God-ordained. Since that time, however, the vast majority of the Christian faith community has rejected this theology as being unbiblical and un-Christian. To Christians today, there is bewilderment that words like these could ever have been written. So, in answer to the question, the conclusion would be that the intended message was not valid even at the time of writing.

4. Is the message still valid? What does Christian experience say? If the message was not valid at the time of writing, then it is highly improbable that the message will be considered acceptable and valid in our age. Such cases will most often result in replacing the offending words or phrases with a new and different message which meets the needs of the faith community. For those instances in which the original message was valid for its time, we must decide whether the message still has meaning for today's world. Is the approach to Christian mission identical to what it was centuries ago? Would the message of impending death lurking around every corner be as appropriate to our time, or does it need to be updated to reflect the state of medical science now taken for granted? Or have we become too reliant on modern medicine to the detriment of our reliance on God's tender mercy? As we decide whether a message is still needed and appropriate for today, we come to the final step of the proposed hermeneutic.

5. How can it best be reinterpreted for today's community? The preacher tells the story or retranslates the message of the Word of the Lord. In preaching, there are almost limitless options for style and methods of delivery. Words can be chosen which will paint a picture, or tug at an emotion, or explain a difficult concept with a few simple words. The preacher can take as long as needed to deliver the sermon, and even has the option of adding some spontaneous comment at any time during the delivery. The hymn reviser, though, is limited to just the few words which need alteration. Unlike much modern poetry which is free verse, most hymns were written according to some very firm rules of poetry, stressing but not limited to rhythm and rhyme. Added to this is the fact that hymns are sung to musical tunes which have become closely associated with the words and may have been composed with *those* words in mind. This creates even more difficulty in finding the perfect balance of message and meaning and poetic flow. New words which may say perfectly in modern language what was meant by the original author may fail as poetry or as musical lyric because the em-*pha*-sis is on the wrong syl-*la*-ble. The result is very unpleasant and unmusical. When all the verses have six lines, one verse cannot be altered with the addition of a seventh line! This means that the hymn reviser will primarily revise according to message and meaning, but will then have to address all the issues of prose and poetry to ensure that the alteration will fit seamlessly into the flow of the original. A well-revised hymn will not have alterations which announce their own presence with poor matching of poetic quality.

The preacher delivers a sermon. It is an event in time and space, and the preacher is seen and heard as part of the message. It is impossible to preach a sermon anonymously. It is possible for the hymn reviser to remain anonymous, but this removes part of the authenticity of the message. It is no longer the pure message of the original author. Some of the words have been amended, and therefore some of the message is altered. The source of the revision should always be identified so the faith community may know who it is that has had a share in producing the gift of a hymn for all to sing and proclaim. The inclusion of the name of the reviser(s) as a footnote on the page would be very helpful.

KEEPING THE FAITH

Conclusion

Since it is certain that the call for hymn revision is going to continue to become more pronounced as groups and individuals focus increasingly on issues of language and imagery, it is essential that pastors and church musicians be given the skills necessary to undertake the task. The identification in this thesis of the many current issues of language usage—gender, inclusiveness, archaic language—will help those facing these issues to know that others have faced them already, and that significant analysis has been done to assist in understanding the implications of retaining or changing particular words.

By careful application of this proposed hermeneutic for hymn revision, many of the great hymns of the faith can be reclaimed for a new age. It would be a tragedy if such hymns were rejected and forgotten simply because a few words and images had become outmoded. The authors of these hymns were inspired to tell stories, teach doctrine, and share the Gospel as they wrote their verses and poems, which were eagerly embraced by the faithful. It is to be hoped that others who are equally inspired will carefully, even lovingly, make the alterations needed to bring these hymns back to life again and again.

A Postscript on What Preachers Can Learn from Hymn Writers and Musicians

It has become evident that similarity of focus and intent between preaching and hymn singing leads very naturally to the value of sharing information and technique between two related disciplines. This essay has demonstrated that the discipline of homiletical hermeneutics may and should make a significant contribution toward the renewal of great church music, specifically hymns. This appendix will present observations concerning some practical aspects of preaching which would benefit from the church musician's training and experience.

First, as noted in the introduction, both David Buttrick and Paul Scott Wilson make emphatic reference to the *voice*; that is, the voice of God or the voice of the Word being spoken. Wilson goes on in a later chapter of his book to explain that this voice of God, heard through the sermon, depends very much on the voice of the preacher, and that no education in homiletics is complete without training the human voice to prepare it for the awesome responsibility of presenting God's voice. He says,

220

"Voice is one of the first things people notice, and it can mean the difference between people listening or not. Even our reading of Scripture should capture attention."[16] James Forbes puts it even more bluntly: "A preacher who doesn't respect the word enough to strive for excellence in leading the congregation to hear it, doesn't deserve the opportunity to present his or her manuscript as if such words are somehow more important than the Bible."[17] Wilson advises every aspiring preacher to learn simultaneously the skills of delivery with the skills of sermon preparation, and encourages preachers to seek out a musician who can give valuable voice coaching.[18] The voice is an instrument for which training and practice are required. The preacher's voice is one of the gifts of God which accompany the call to preach, and it is a gift which matures with us.

A second and closely related aspect of the voice and the message is the musical quality of preaching. The best and easiest illustration of this is found in the unique and effective preaching style common to many African American churches and preachers. One is immediately aware that the words preached are not merely spoken, they are almost sung. This style uses the flow and cadence of free verse poetry, but adds to it the richness of musical motion and expression. The particular raising and lowering of the voice, not just in volume, but also in pitch and tonal quality, has become a recognized trademark of these preachers. As the sermon starts, the voice is fairly restrained and the words come clearly and with control. Then, as momentum and excitement build, the voice is transformed until, at the climax, which may last a considerable time, the whole congregation is swept into the event. This often becomes antiphonal, with listeners joining in to respond, sometimes word for word, with identical musical cadence, to the voice they have absorbed into their own being. Not every preacher can or should adopt this culturally unique voice, but every preacher should be aware of the powerful effect that speech as a musical event can offer to preaching.

The third lesson to be learned, particularly from hymn writers, is to make every word count. Sermons may run to several thousand words. Hymns seldom exceed a couple of hundred words. This gives the preacher

---

[16] Wilson, *Practice of Preaching*, 268.

[17] James Forbes, *The Holy Spirit and Preaching* (Nashville, TN: Abingdon Press, 1979), 70.

[18] Wilson, *Practice of Preaching*, 268.

the potential to use far more words than are necessary to say what needs to be said. Fiction writers during the Victorian era filled page after page with detail about the decoration of "the room where the murder took place," and readers happily read these details for hours. It was an accepted part of the culture of communication at that time. In preaching, there is a danger that the sermon will become so full of detail, with word definitions and explanations of lesser points, that the main point(s) will be hopelessly lost in the mix. Preaching to our modern mind and mentality requires the ability to say what needs to be said in fewer rather than more words, and with great care shown in choosing the words which will best deliver the message. The hymn writer, on the other hand, knows from the beginning that the entire message or story in the hymn must be delivered in relatively few words. As a result, words which are rich in imagery and emotion and feeling will be chosen. These words will strike responsive chords in the hearers and singers, which will prompt them to fill in the details from their own experience or memories or feelings. The preacher might say of Psalm 23, "*I sincerely want to become one of the sheep who follow the Lord, because He will feed me from the greenest pastures, and make sure that I always have enough to eat, especially in the dry season when good grass is hard to find.*" The hymn writer Dorothy Ann Thrupp says, "*Saviour, like a shepherd lead us, much we need Thy tender care.*" In these words, rich images are seen and felt, being drawn from the experience and lives of the singers. The word *Saviour* connects us with God in a personal way. *Shepherd* is full of images of what a shepherd does; very little detail is needed. In the choice and flow of the words, the whole line has emotional elements of yearning and pleading, and the word *tender* has emotional power which always evokes a response. The combined result is that in one dozen words we are brought face to face with feelings and memories and expressions which are embraced instantly, but which would take hundreds and hundreds of words to describe. Good preaching uses words skillfully and takes advantage of the power of individual words to paint pictures which fill the listeners' minds with images.

Fourth, preachers can borrow from hymn writers the desire to tell a story. Narrative preaching is currently undergoing a strong revival. It is not a new discovery, but represents the rediscovery of the very first means of passing on the essence of a society's history and beliefs. The oral tradition, which we view as an image of the elders and children of the tribe sitting around the campfire, has the old men and women telling the stories of when they were young, and the events that their parents and grandparents

A Homiletic Hermeneutic for the Rewriting of Hymn Texts

passed on to them. The stories became the heritage of the people long before the invention of writing and recorded history. Jesus was a master storyteller, skillfully weaving stories which drew the listeners right into the plot and often left them squirming when he put in a surprizing, unexpected ending. A quick look at any hymnal will reveal that many hymn writers are storytellers at heart. Their songs take us on a short but meaningful adventure and then deliver us safely to a new location. In the preface to the hymnal *Sing Joyfully*, Karen Burton Mains says that music and the words in a hymn have the power to transport us momentarily into the presence of the divine:

> Within its [this book's] binding and pages are contained the doctrines of the faith culled through the ages and saturated with the devotion of those saints who have been members of the church triumphant. Music by its very nature evokes the soul's response. If we allow it, music can lift our hearts to attend to God; singing heartily, suddenly we discover that for a moment, brief but powerfully, we are absolutely preoccupied with the divine.[19]

Good sermons embody this sense of adventure. They take us somewhere in our minds and hearts and deliver us safely a little closer to the Saviour. The words which paint the picture or map out the journey are by design a neat package which starts where we presently are, whisks us off on the adventure, and leaves us better off than we were. Great hymns have always attempted this and sermons must also.

Finally, hymns attempt to evoke a response in the singers. If it is a hymn of praise, it is more than a list of reasons why our God is worthy of praise; we are called to join in the praise. If it is a devotional hymn, we are drawn into an attitude of contemplation and prayer. If it is a hymn of challenge, we are given clear indications of what is desired of us as servants of the Lord. If it is a teaching hymn, we are encouraged to learn more and more. In every case, there is a presumed response built into the hymn, either stated openly or skillfully touching the subconscious yearnings of the singer. A sermon which does not have a presumed response built into it is just a lecture. Preaching which does not attempt to move the hearers from where they are to where God wants them is just a talk. In every real

---

[19] *Sing Joyfully*, eds. Jack Schrader and Karen Burton Mains (Carol Stream, IL: Hope Publishing, 1989), preface.

KEEPING THE FAITH

sermon, the voice of God is calling to his people—perhaps as a pleading voice, or a demanding voice, or a reconciling voice—but always as a voice asking for a response. Why bother preaching if there is no anticipated movement toward God?

In fine preaching and great hymns we have the very best of friends who share each other's interests, hopes, and dreams. They are made for each other by divine choice and purpose, and they serve God best when used to complement and support each other. The union of the spoken Word and the sung Word is like the coming together of God's children, male and female, generously offering the unique characteristics of both genders to become God's complete people. John Greenleaf Whittier's hymn "O Brother Man," which itself is in serious need of updating, reminds us that in the final analysis, all our worship and preaching and singing must be validated in our living.

> To worship rightly is to love each other,
> Each smile a hymn, each kindly deed a prayer.

"Someone's in the Kitchen with Martha": Outlines for a Eucharistic Homiletic

Barry Morrison

In this brief paper, I will sketch the outlines of what I call "a Eucharistic homiletic." The field of homiletics has gained a great deal from a variety of disciplines—rhetoric, drama, linguistics, and literary and narrative theory, to name a few. Another worthy partner is the field of liturgical theology. Like neighbours who have lived next door for years but have rarely been into each other's homes, homiletics and liturgy may have much yet to learn about one another and, in the encounter, strengthen the community in which both reside.

In some traditions the sermon has been treated as a kind of hors d'oeuvre—a morsel on which to nibble while awaiting the main course— still real food, but not enough to count as a meal; rather, something on which to whet the appetite in anticipation of the Eucharistic feast. In other traditions, the sermon has taken the place of the feast and has become the main course in its own right. Other elements in the worship service are relegated to the status of mere preliminaries to the main event—the preaching of the Word or, in the language of some, the teaching.

In contrast to the minimalism of a morsel of bread and a sip of wine, the full-course sermon occupies easily a third, if not half the time of the gathering—about the same proportion of the preacher's work week, if we follow the homiletical recipe that calls for an hour of preparation for every minute in the pulpit. That's a lot of time in the kitchen for a little time at the table, particularly in those traditions where the Eucharist is celebrated infrequently—monthly, or even quarterly. Disconnected from communion, the sermon has developed its own raison d'être and has tended to become self-sufficient in its design. As a result, the cord binding Word and sacrament risks becoming frayed, if not broken.

Yet we still speak easily of the service of Word and sacrament, the service of the Word, and the service of the table. In practice, however, (particularly in the so-called Free Churches) "Word *and* sacrament" have often been replaced by "Word *or* sacrament," as if one could (and sometimes does) stand without the other. There is, for example, the practice of

KEEPING THE FAITH

an early morning Communion quite separate from the later preaching service. Likewise, some continue the practice of dismissing the congregation with a benediction before regrouping for communion, sometimes in a place other than that used for the main service of worship. In these settings, it would be uncommon for there to be any obvious continuity between pulpit and table.

If the dilemma is not perpetuated, it is at least sustained by the current state of specialization in the theological curriculum. While it is becoming more common to have the same person teaching both homiletics and worship, in many schools the disciplines remain separate. Perhaps this helps to account for the observation of David Greenhaw and Ronald Allen that "the relationship between the sermon and its context in worship has received relatively little attention from pastors and from scholars in the fields of preaching and worship."[1]

Preachers are often quite deliberate with regard to the overall liturgical context in which preaching takes place. The lectionary texts, the rhythms of the liturgical calendar, and national and local pastoral concerns are never far from the homiletical workbench, nor should they be. Less attention seems to be applied, however, to the immediate liturgical context in which the sermon is situated—the service of worship. Indeed, even when worship is designed with the sermon in mind, it is most often to undergird the theme of the sermon. While continuity and flow are important considerations, such an approach leaves little doubt that the sermon is, de facto, the main event.

Likewise, specialists in worship have applied themselves to the construction of a fitting liturgical environment for the gathered community. They, too, work within the rhythms of the liturgical year. Their hands are those of skillful artisans who weave patterns of praise and prayer by which we may discover ourselves in the divine presence and both hear and respond to God. Woe betide any liturgical Philistines who trample the courts of the Lord with references to *mere preliminaries*, as if the worship service existed simply to set the stage for the sermon. Indeed, some liturgists seem either to eschew the preeminence so often afforded the sermon or have been content to let the preachers look after that detail. Thus, while homileticians and liturgists are obviously in the same pond, it is less clear

---

[1] *Preaching in the Context of Worship*, eds. David M. Greenhaw and Ronald J. Allen (St. Louis, MO: Chalice Press, 2000), xii.

Someone's in the Kitchen with Martha

that they are always in the same boat. Like the Mary and Martha of the theological curriculum, one may complain about the other: "Lord, tell my sister to help me," yet it remains a matter of debate as to which one has chosen the better part.

Neither sermon nor liturgy, however, has the last word on a Sunday morning. Rather, both participate in a greater movement which leads to a higher goal: the thank-full response of heart, mind, soul, and strength to the gift and calling of God—the sacrifice of thanksgiving we name Eucharist. All our acts of worship, including the sermon, share in and contribute to this one action. The separation of Word and sacrament has often obscured their fundamental unity. Recovering this unity may yield insights that will inform our theology of preaching as well as our appreciation of the Eucharistic nature of worship—even when it does not include the sharing of bread and wine. As Charles Rice affirms, "Even in churches where the Eucharist is not celebrated every Sunday...placing the sermon between the reading of Scripture and the offertory, before the prayers, is one way of recognizing the function of preaching: to enable people to face the world and then to give themselves once more to God."[2]

Essentially, the entire service of worship preaches. The various movements of the liturgy enable the people of God to proclaim, confess, console, teach, heal, challenge, repent, promise, understand, and celebrate. To speak of worship as spiritual formation is to acknowledge the power of liturgy as well as the impact of the sermon. Coming from a Baptist background, my wife notes the sense of safety she finds in the Anglican liturgy. Unlike our Free Church home, where Sunday worship so often rises or falls on the strength of the sermon, the prayer book service, with its climax in the Eucharist, offers a depth of worship that does not depend on the accomplishments of the preacher. The liturgy itself, with prayers and readings and responses, becomes the preacher. It is as Mary Catherine Hilkert says: "The desire to hear the good news and prayerful listening to the proclamation of the word as well as participation in proclaiming the Christian story through singing or speaking the words of the psalmist—regardless of the quality of the preaching—are never in vain."[3]

---

[2] Charles L. Rice, *The Embodied Word: Preaching as Art and Liturgy* (Minneapolis, MN: Fortress Press, 1991), 21.

[3] Mary Cathering Hilkert, *Naming Grace: Preaching and the Sacramental Imagination* (New York: Continuum, 1998), 68, 69.

KEEPING THE FAITH

This is not to suggest that preachers in the more liturgical traditions are like Garrison Keillor's violists, who suddenly realize that they cannot be heard past the second row. Speaking of the place of the sermon in the liturgy, Charles Rice affirms "the crucial office of the preacher."[4] The liturgy would be incomplete without the proclamation of the Word in the local and global context of the day. Perhaps, however, it might help preachers to relax a little in the awareness that we do not come as virtuoso soloists. Rather, we are part players who sometimes carry the melody but who are also carried by it.

When it is set clearly in the context of the whole, the sermon serves to speak the biblical texts into the present situation or, as William Skudlarek articulates his central understanding of preaching, the sermon interprets "our concrete human situation by the word of God in such a way that people are led to turn to God in acts of praise and thanksgiving."[5] Thus the sermon is intended to engage the congregation in the dynamism of the liturgy, focusing the whole momentum of worship, from gathering, to giving thanks, to sending forth, on the needs and opportunities of *these* people in *this* place on *this* day, set in the larger context of the identity and mission of the church in the world. Again, Skudlarek identifies the goal of the sermon as Eucharistic: "We need to know why we should lift up our hearts. We need some reason to be able to answer the celebrant's 'Let us give thanks to God' with 'It is right to give [God] thanks and praise.'"[6] This is true whether the response to the Word involves coming to the table or not, for every sermon requires a response. The truncated liturgy that moves immediately from sermon to closing hymn surely does the congregation a disservice. The people at least need opportunity to offer thanks, to intercede for others, to celebrate and commit themselves to the sermon's glimpse of God's vision for life.

It seems reasonable, therefore, for the structure of the sermon to be informed by the shape of the liturgy. This does not necessarily mean that the sermon will be constructed according to the order of the liturgy—from gathering and praising to hearing and responding—although it would be interesting to explore those possibilities. Rather, the sense is of what Paul

---

[4] Rice, *Embodied Word*, 88.

[5] William Skudlarek, *The Word in Worship: Preaching in a Liturgical Context* (Nashville: Abingdon, 1981), 70.

[6] Ibid.

228

Someone's in the Kitchen with Martha

Scott Wilson refers to as a "theological grammar," those strong currents or tides that flow within the sermon and give it substance and depth regardless of what is happening on the surface.

A Eucharistic homiletic, then, is a way of thinking theologically about the sermon as integral to the impulse of the entire liturgy toward the giving of thanks, with all that that implies about the church's response of heart and mind and strength. What the sermon does for the text of Scripture—that is, in part, interpret the ways in which our story is woven into the biblical story—it can do for the Eucharistic prayer—that is, help us to understand our present situation as somehow caught up in the flow of God's redeeming grace and give us a reason to offer thanks.

Paul Scott Wilson reminds us that "a unity exists between preaching and scripture, which is one reason the word *sermon* in John Knox's *The Form of Prayers* refers to both the scripture reading and the proclamation."[7] Likewise, following William Skudlarek, Charles Rice, Mary Catherine Hilkert, and others, the sermon is not finished until we have come to the table.[8] In terms of its deep grammar, then, the sermon, which begins in the language of Scripture, will also be shaped by the language of the *anaphora*—the great prayer of thanksgiving—and especially by its movements of *anamnesis, epiclesis,* and eschatological hope. Why these three? Essentially because these movements are central to the formation, identity, and mission of the people of God.

In one sense, much of Scripture functions at the level of *anamnesis*—the call to remember God's nature and covenant love. Literally "calling back to mind," the *anamnesis* in the Eucharist prayer calls the worshippers to a multivalent remembering that includes both the Passion of Christ and also Christ's future coming. It is in the faithful reaching out in both of these directions that the present may be interpreted, endured, and faithfully lived. Similarly, when the sermon speaks the language of *anamnesis,*

---

[7] Paul Scott Wilson, "Preaching and the Sacrament of Holy Communion," in *Preaching in the Context of Worship*, 57.

[8] Although Wilson cautions against drawing too close a connection between the sermon and the prayers leading to communion, he makes the important observation that "in preaching, the Word takes shape, both in the course of preaching and throughout the week, in the lives of the people as they seek to live out the good news" (58). This taking shape of the Word surely includes, and perhaps begins with, the Eucharist.

KEEPING THE FAITH

the past is remembered as a present reality, the force of which will issue forth in thanksgiving and righteous living. Consider, for example, the "eucharistic" dimensions of the bringing of first fruits and tithes in Deuteronomy 26. The *anamnesis* begins:

> A wandering Aramean was my ancestor; he went down into Egypt and lived there as an alien, few in number, and there he became a great nation, mighty and populous. When the Egyptians treated us harshly and afflicted us, by imposing hard labour on us, we cried to the Lord, the God of our ancestors; the Lord heard our voice and saw our affliction, our toil and our oppression. The Lord brought us out of Egypt with a mighty hand and an outstretched arm, with a terrifying display of power, and with signs and wonders; and he brought us into this place and gave us this land, a land flowing with milk and honey. [vs. 5b–9]

This remembrance leads directly into the act of thanksgiving: "'So now I bring the first fruit of the ground that you, O Lord, have given me.' You shall set it down before the Lord your God and bow down before the Lord your God" (v. 10).

Noteworthy in the passage is the flow from remembrance to thanksgiving to the care of "the aliens, the orphans, and the widows, so that they may eat their fill within your towns." Only when the poor and marginalized have been included does the liturgy dare to ask God's blessing. How does the blessing come?—with the call to obedience to the covenantal promises: "This very day the Lord your God is commanding you to observe these statutes and ordinances; so observe them diligently with all your heart and with all your soul" (v. 16).

The sermon as *anamnesis* reminds us of what God has done and who God is.[9] It also reminds us who we are—both in our nobility and our frailty as God's people. When James Sanders employs the technique of dynamic equivalency as part of a prophetic hermeneutic, it is because the text is not simply about characters in the distant past. It is also about us. "We should look for persons and figures in it who might represent different folk today

---

[9] Neither does God forget. Another *anamnestic* movement that could be developed in this context is the plea for God to remember and have mercy. This is especially relevant when the sermon uncovers trouble and cries out in lament or issues the call for intercession.

Someone's in the Kitchen with Martha

dynamically."[10] Says Sanders, "I try to get whitey, myself and my brother and sister in the fine suburban situation, to take Ramses, Sennacherib, Herod, and Pilate as mirrors to see what it is we do to others when we do not even know we are doing it, bless us."[11] Above all, however, the *anamnestic* function of the sermon serves as a kind of *haggadah* recalling our basic identity as those named and claimed by divine grace. What Sanders describes of Judaism is suggestive of the basis of Christian identity as well: "By reciting the traditions, especially the basic tradition, Torah, Jews are reminded—no matter where they may be in the world, whether in times of crisis or when tempted to assimilate to the dominant culture, in times of ease when identity so easily slips away—that they are Jews.... Memory shapes identity."[12]

The second major movement of a Eucharistic homiletic is *epiclesis*. At the table/altar the Holy Spirit is called down "upon us and upon these gifts of bread and wine." A prayer from a Baptist order says, "Living God, fill us with your Spirit, that as we share this bread and this wine we may feed on the body and blood of Christ, and be empowered for service in your world."[13] The thrust of the *epicletic* movement of the sermon is empowerment and transformation, reminding us that this is God's work and not simply our own. Indeed, the entire liturgy assumes, even requires, *epiclesis* if we are to make so bold as to lift up our hearts in the first place. For who could confess without the confidence that God is present to forgive? Who could dare to speak of the reign of God without the conviction that even now God's Spirit hovers over the waters of a new creation?

Epiclesis is also about the work of identity as the people of God are called into the astonishing awareness that we share common claim with the prophet Joel's "sons and daughters" as well as with those still fearful ones who, on the evening of the first day of the week, were sent into the world with Jesus' words, "Receive the Holy Spirit" (John 20:19–23) As Paul Scott Wilson, Mary Catherine Hilkert, and others have shown, the

---

[10] James A. Sanders, *God Has a Story Too: Sermons in Context* (Philadelphia: Fortress Press, 1979), 20.

[11] Ibid., 19.

[12] Ibid., 21.

[13] The Baptist Union of Great Britain, *Patterns and Prayers for Christian Worship* (Oxford: Oxford University Press, 1991), 86.

sermon is about "naming grace," identifying the many ways in which the grace evident in the text of Scripture is also active today.

As such, the *epicletic* movement of the sermon invites the Sprit's renewing, forgiving, transforming work. The preacher will ask, "How does the word of this text summon up, assure, challenge, and enable our continuing transformation and restoration into the image of God? Why and how do we call on the Spirit?" The currents of *epiclesis* running through the sermon take care to speak plainly of the Holy Spirit as a real presence as we take consolation and courage and respond to the commission to live into the already/not yet reign of God.

This brings us, of course, to the eschatological dimensions of a Eucharistic homiletic. For even as the Communion liturgy looks forward to a day when "all your children shall be free, and the whole earth to live to praise your name,"[14] the sermon, too, will summon up a vision of that day for *these* people in *this* time and place. Paul Scott Wilson speaks of this in terms of the missional directions of the sermon,[15] which understand particular and local acts as harbingers of the divine commonwealth.

In a certain sense eschatological hope will always retain an element of the "not yet." Yet the missional movement toward the reign of God gives flesh and blood to a theological reality that impinges upon, challenges, and transforms our present reality. At the same time that Christian faith leans into the promise of God's future, that future also meets us on the road with the heartwarming news that God's *kairos* has already arrived. Capturing the power of this movement, Mary Catherine Hilkert writes, "Remembering God's fidelity in the past and calling on the power of the Spirit for the present and future empower the community to refigure their lives according to the gospel."[16]

With those on the way to (or was it from?) home at Emmaus, that eschatological hope, now the future present, has been made known to us in the breaking of the bread. Developing the eschatological elements of the sermon, the preacher will ask, "How does this Word send us out to be and become the Body of Christ in the world? How does this text help us to identify and cooperate with, in the power of the Holy Spirit, what God

---

[14] Ibid., 90.

[15] Paul Scott Wilson, *The Four Pages of the Sermon* (Nashville, TN: Abingdon, 1999).

[16] Hilkert, *Naming Grace*, 102.

Someone's in the Kitchen with Martha

wills and works for the life of the world? How is the continuing drama of redemption, which we celebrate in the Eucharist, being played out in and through us who seek to be doers as well as hearers of the Word?" In other words, what are the reasons and results of the hope that is within us?

Anamnesis, epiclesis, and eschatological hope—three movements of a Eucharistic homiletic in which sermon links "text and table." Perhaps it is just as well, when John tells the story in chapter 12, that he makes no mention of "the better part." Either/or gives way to both/and as contemplation and action, word and deed, love and labour are woven together in one movement of selfless adoration and praise. "Six days before the Passover Jesus came to Bethany.... There they gave a dinner for him. Martha served...Mary anointed Jesus' feet."

Bread for the Journey
John 6:26–35; 48–51

Just a few steps from the busy campus of Acadia University in Nova Scotia, Canada, the university garden offers an oasis of calm. You could walk through it in a matter of minutes; or you could wander along the paths at a more leisurely pace and explore the many indigenous Maritime plants that have been gathered there—all carefully catalogued and arranged according to their native environment. There are woodland plants, field plants, species found on rocky headlands; there is an herb garden full of plants the first inhabitants used for medicines and elixirs; there is even a waterfall that leads into a typical Maritime bog, complete with meat-eating pitcher plants.

One of the most interesting features is a drystone wall that was built by a team of Scottish stone masons. In Scotland, it would be called a "drystane dyke." If you've ever tried it, you know that building a wall is a rather more complicated task than simply stacking rocks on top of one another. It is both an art and a craft as the mason carefully turns each stone, assessing it for size and shape, to determine where it will best fit. It's a skill that's been handed down through many generations. Isn't it interesting to think that even a newly built wall embodies the wisdom of the ages?

That sense of continuity can be seen in another way as well. For when the wall has been finished, the mason carries away a stone from that project, and that stone is the first one laid in the next wall. What this means

233

KEEPING THE FAITH

is that the masons who built the wall in the Irving Gardens would have brought a stone from the last wall they built. And their next wall, wherever it is in the world, would have been begun with a stone from here in Nova Scotia.

This leads to an intriguing question: how many drystane dykes are there? Well, of course, in one sense, there are many. But in another sense, there is only one, as all those walls are interrelated, not only because they share a common craft, but because they are linked by those first and last stones. It is a kind of embodied metaphor in which, if we can entertain this more poetic dimension, there is only one wall in many places.

Why all this talk about drystane dykes? Because a similar metaphor may be applied to Communion. From the earliest days of the church, bread from one Communion service was carried over to the next, symbolizing the unbroken continuity of the sacrament from one celebration to the next, one place to the next, one day, one week, one month, one year, one generation to the next.

Can you get a sense of the interrelatedness here? When we gather around this table, we are sitting down with the many saints who have shared Communion here in days gone by; and not only the saints from this congregation. The communion this table represents spans continents and centuries, reaching all the way back to the time of Jesus and that night when he shared this special meal with his disciples. Can you see them? Peter and Andrew, Thomas and Nathaniel, Salome and Mary and Cleopas, and all the others, gathered around this sacred table.

The early church understood it in even grander terms. They saw this table as a bridge between two worlds, for here the earthly church was carried into heaven—or did heaven come down to earth?—and the church joined her song with the song of the angels. Did you know that the choir represents the choir of angels? That's right. It is as if they are members of a much larger choir, echoing the voices of those who sing around the throne of God.

An ancient Communion hymn which is still sung in many churches invites the worshippers beyond the world of sight and sound and into the realm of mystery. "Now let us who mystically represent the cherubim lay aside all earthly cares that we may receive the King of all, who comes invisibly escorted by the divine hosts." The cherubim are not to be mistaken for the chubby cherubs we see on Valentine cards. The cherubim are those great winged creatures whose golden images adorn the Ark of the Covenant, the mercy seat, which represents the very presence of God.

234

Someone's in the Kitchen with Martha

The invitation of the hymn, indeed, the invitation of this table, is to see beyond what we can see, to know beyond what we can understand, to experience ourselves as part of a far greater mystery than we can imagine.

This is the world into which John invites us in these verses where we hear Jesus saying, "I am the bread of life.... Whoever eats this bread will live forever; and the bread that I will give for the life of the world is my flesh." John anticipates our reaction. The crowds say, "How can this man give us his flesh to eat?" Rather than give in to their skepticism, Jesus presses the point: "Those who eat my flesh and drink my blood have eternal life...for my flesh is true food and my blood is true drink. Those who eat my flesh and drink my blood abide in me and I in them."

I remember one Sunday, in another part of the country, when a leader of the congregation chastised me after the Communion service. He said, "You shouldn't say Jesus said, 'This bread is my body.' You should say Jesus said, 'This bread represents my body.'" Was he right? What do you think? Does it make a difference—This is the body of Christ or This *represents* the body of Christ? Of course, he is right. This bread does represent the body of Christ. But at another level, I'm afraid he may have been missing the point. For if we tailor our language to fit our limited understanding, we risk missing the great, transformative experience to which Jesus invites us. Thomas Merton is quoted as saying that "when you hear Jesus say that you must 'eat my flesh and drink my blood' you are supposed to stop breathing for a few minutes. Instead we just argue about it."

And there is another reason the church has insisted on retaining Jesus' difficult language when she approaches this holy table; because if we settle for "this bread represents the body of Christ," we can too easily say, "Oh yes, here we remember something Jesus did a long time ago." And, of course, in one sense we do. But there is so much more to it than that. What does it mean when we hear the very words of Jesus: "This is my body"? It is much more than a simply memory. "I am here," he says, "and with this bread and wine I give you my heart, I give you my mind, I give you my life." His body becomes our body. The New Testament uses even more compelling language: who do we become by virtue of this bread and wine? We become the Body of Christ. At which point we are supposed to stop breathing for a few minutes.

This is an awesome thought. For even as Christ offers himself in the gifts of bread and wine, the invitation is for us to offer ourselves in return. The theological formula goes something like this: he became what we are so we may become what he is. Stop breathing again—for this is more than

235

KEEPING THE FAITH

poetry. In John Michael Talbot's musical rendering of the Lord's Supper, it means nothing less than this: that with this bread, we must be broken; with this wine, we must be poured out for the life of the world. That's what it means to be the Body of Christ, to be built into that great company through the ages who have trusted in Christ for their life and have gone out to live the life of Christ in the world.

Just think—as that last stone from the wall became the first stone in this one, and as the last stone in this one will become the first stone in the next, the song of praise that the church sings at the table has continued unbroken from that first evening when Jesus was at table with his disciples and said, "This bread is my body; this cup is my blood of the covenant." Those disciples went from that meal to the next, and someone from that next meal went to the next, and so on from day to day, week to week, month to month, year to year, across continents and centuries, until we have arrived here at this table to share Communion with one another and with the One who said, "Remember, I am with you always, even unto the end of the age."

Be present, be present, O Jesus, O good High Priest, as you were in the midst of your disciples, and make yourself known to us in the breaking of the bread, who lives and reigns with the Father and the Holy Spirit, One God, world without end. Amen.

(adapted from the Church of South India)

Silence and the Cadences of Worship

Paul L. Harris

As a tribute to Roger Prentice, in grateful remembrance of his friendship and in appreciation of his life as an ordained minister of Word and sacrament, this short essay offers a personal reflection on the subject of worship and the Word. The backdrop for these thoughts is the recollection of many hours spent alongside Roger in worship and, indeed, together reflecting on worship or viewing places of worship, both ancient and modern. Since we first met in Oxford in 1979, Roger and I spent many hours together in worship in Baptist church contexts, but also, through the years, in in other, mainly Anglican, services. Not only did we worship together, but we also had many conversations in person, and in later years many a dialogue on the subject by email.

Roger, as is well known, took liturgical worship in the Baptist context very seriously to heart (with a deep concern for due order, reverence, and liturgical propriety together with respect for long-held, deeply cherished tradition). As is noted elsewhere in this volume, Roger wrote on the subject of hymnody and Communion, and composed his own hymns for special occasions. He also penned Advent and Holy Week devotional material and, of course, he wrote the Passion plays which he directed while serving as a university chaplain at the Manning Memorial Chapel, Acadia.

Given the on-going conversations Roger and I had over so many years, it seems fitting that in his memory I might address (by way of personal reflection rather than in an academic essay) one particular theme which I know was important to him: the place of silence in worship. By addressing this theme in his memory, I am not seeking to add fresh thought to the already plentiful literature on the nature and meaning of silence. Rather, bearing in mind the many devotional and theological works which reflect on Christian spirituality and silence, my intention is simply to look at the importance of silence in creating what we might call the cadences or rhythms of worship. After a brief discussion of the way that silence may shape the cadence of worship, attention will be given to exploring silence in worship, especially in a Baptist context, and some of its ramifications in this digital age.

KEEPING THE FAITH

Silence and the Cadences of Worship

In musical terms, of course, cadence has to do with rhythm or the beat of the music or the song in question. In diction, cadence may also reflect the rhythm of a voice created by the inflection of speech. In music, the cadence or rhythm itself contributes to the overall experience of a particular composition. As music is sung or played, there are moments when a note is held longer or a verse is sung quietly or with a different tempo. In other words, an entire musical composition is not presented overall as just a flowing series of sounds or a single unending sound. Indeed, in a musical score there may even be a *fermata*, a pause, which in certain instances intimates a short interval of silence. It might be argued that in this way cadence creates interest and elicits meaning, thus evoking attentiveness to that which is being conveyed.

Just as silence may contribute to the rhythm of music, so, it may be argued, silence is critical to the cadence of worship. In fact, in worship it is essential that there are moments of silence in order to break through sheer wordiness and to disturb the monotony of seemingly endless verbiage—whether in preaching or in other verbal liturgical forms in worship. The rhythm of worship, of course, may be changed in other ways by interspersing hymns, chants, or songs between Scripture readings or by including instrumental music (not necessarily played on the piano or organ) to allow for meditation. However, it may be argued that silence creates a different kind of space for worship, and in this space the worshipper may be encouraged to a new openness to God as Holy Spirit. Significantly, it is often in these wordless moments that we glimpse the reality of God in a particular way, and for a moment encounter God in God's infinite majesty from a fresh perspective.

To argue for spaces of silence (or other nonverbal collective reflection) is not to deny the importance of scriptural teaching and exhortation, or public prayers of praise, thanksgiving, petition, and intercession. There is no suggestion that these elements of worship are not important or should simply be replaced by an empty silence or wordless void in the worship assembly. Moreover, arguing in this way for silence in worship does not mean advocating complete quiet simply for its own sake in worship. Such total silence may not anyway be possible, even if it were desired, given the particular context of those gathered at worship. The absence of all sound is not the point at issue. Rather, what seems crucial is the realization that worship is much diminished without the place of significant and

238

Silence and Cadences of Worship

intentional wordlessness as part of the overall rhythm. Indeed, the distinctness of a spiritually orientated, intentional "cadence"—where the spoken/sung voice in diction and intonation gives way to a different shape of sound—is a crucial factor in directing worship. In a genuine encounter with God during corporate worship, as much as in personal devotion, at some point and in various respects, "wordy" sound itself must eventually give way to wordlessness (silent or otherwise) as the only fitting response to the manifestation of the living God, whose Word has issued forth in the silence (see Psalm 50:1–6).

The Word and Wordless Encounter

To speak of the need for moments in our worship when words must fade into deliberate silence (or better, wordlessness) may sound strange to many Christians, especially those in a Baptist context. In our very wordy contemporary world, as we are seemingly bombarded by verbal input around the clock, we are led to believe that when confronted by unbelief, what is often needed is a stronger or more convincing argument, through a more focused and intensive expression in words. Furthermore, in Baptist life in particular there has been a tendency to claim that the exposition of Scripture in worship takes such primacy as though it is all that really matters. Yet while Baptist expositors have sometimes advocated pounding the pulpit (or its equivalent in the dynamic leading of corporate prayer), perhaps there is, in fact, something to be said for the sound of silence. After all, as Jesus taught in the context of personal prayer, we are not heard as a result of our "many words" (Matthew 6:7)! Paradoxically, there is even Jesus' injunction that we be persistent in prayer (Luke 18:1), while the apostle Paul also made the case on more than one occasion for being constant, even unceasing, in prayer (Ephesians 6:18).

Naturally, the centrality of Scripture in worship must never be neglected. Believers are urged in Scripture, in the language of the familiar old Collect, "to read, mark, learn and inwardly digest" the biblical revelation of God's Word. The word of the Gospel rightly proclaimed—through the inspiration of the Spirit—may indeed "hit home," as it were, and lead to a change of mind and heart. Yet throughout Scripture there are also stories of those who are recorded as having met God in the silence. For all his apparent face-to-face encounters with God, on one occasion Moses was reported as "seeing" God, strangely, according to the record, only from behind after the Lord had wordlessly passed by. In one of his close

239

encounters with God, we read of Elijah's experience of a "still small voice," a sound which was possibly—as some commentators claim—that of "sheer silence" (1 Kings 19:12 NRSV). There are other instances where we are led to presume that silence was part of the encounter with the Lord. In his meetings with different figures, especially those recorded in the Fourth Gospel, it takes very little imagination to conceive of various pregnant pauses in the dialogues Jesus had with individuals (whether Nathanael, John 1:47–51; Nicodemus, John 3:1–10; the woman at the well, John 4:8–26) or with others such as Mary and Martha (John 11) or with the disciples (John 14–17). Elsewhere, it is clear that there was sometimes movement and gesture with considerable nonverbal communication besides actual diction (Mark 7:32–37, Mark 8:22–26, John 8:2–11). It may be taken that silence was part of the encounter, and I would contend that this is a feature of the stories that we tend to dismiss at our peril, especially as we think about our devotion, and particularly our corporate worship, in our very wordy but also highly visual, digital age. It is surely not simply a curious, even throwaway aside that in the Book of Revelation, attributed to John the Divine, there was even reference, amid the endless praises of the myriads around the throne, to silence in heaven for about half an hour (Revelation 8:1)! Merely that strange allusion ought to give us cause for thought.

Silence, of course, has always been recognized as a vital part of devotion in the Judeo-Christian traditions and in the history of the church. Without silence, spirituality is wholly impoverished, and from the earliest centuries, Christians have valued time to be still and quiet before God. Early Christian writers such as the desert mothers and fathers spoke of those moments beyond words and in unhurried space between words when they were convinced of God's presence among them. Since the seventeenth century, those of the Society of Friends (the Quaker tradition) have gathered in silence. Other church traditions (Roman Catholic, Orthodox, Anglican, among others) have incorporated silence into patterns for daily and weekly worship. In doing so, there is the clear recognition that God is encountered in silence, at a deep, inner level of our being, as much as in word-based interaction on a cognitive level.

Obviously, as already indicated, this emphasis on silence in no way negates the place of the spoken word or other verbal forms of expression in corporate worship. Preaching is a vital element in promoting and encouraging Christian faith and belief. Yet there is a place for what we might call the "holy mute": a time even in corporate worship to be still and quiet in God's presence. There needs to be time to listen and wait rather than to do or even speak. As in the example above, scriptural references to encounters with God in the silence, as well as the teaching of other spiritual writings through the centuries, affirm the need to attend to silence as well as verbal recitation or proclamation in the cadence of worship. If such silence (or other nonverbal pause or interaction) is given a place in our worship together, those gathered for worship may be surprized to discover a deeper awareness of the reality of God in our midst.

The liturgical tradition of silence, including word-free but deeply symbolic acts—together with the consequent rhythms of space and time in worship—has been largely overlooked in many Baptist circles. Arguably, this aversion to symbolism and the frequent lack of any significant quiet space or, indeed, the absence of words in our tradition of Baptist worship has been to our detriment. If corporate worship is to be enhanced, worship leaders must recognize how worship may be shaped in order to incorporate silence and other nonverbal elements. This recognition and its implementation in practice are crucial, for it is often in those moments beyond words—and in unhurried space between words—that we are specially aware both that God, as it were, comes to us quite uniquely and closely within and also that God's Word encounters us at a deep level of our being.

To Mute or to Unmute: Shaping Worship in Silence

As already discussed above, sometimes in Baptist circles today, worship is conducted with silence left wholly aside. In an effort to engage the worshipping participant, many churches have resorted to digital visual presentations to accompany sermons. While these may have the potential to add to the listener's understanding, often they serve simply to detract from the spoken word or the silence, which is part of the dynamic of the worship experience. During the coronavirus pandemic, when there were restrictions on gathering in person, online meetings became commonplace. Sometimes local church services were prepared ahead of being "premiered" online, a practice commonly used by nationally broadcast services which "produce" worship services for TV and radio. Yet while prerecorded services may allow for a better "production," it not only raises questions about the nature of worship, but also highlights what is often a lack of silence in worship.

Of course, even "live" services are generally recorded for subsequent viewing later at one's convenience. These services may then be observed when it suits the viewer, or indeed may be watched again and again by anyone who accesses them, thus raising other issues over what constitutes or inspires authentic corporate worship. The worship service is actually over, but participants who so chose to do so may engage with the recorded service and so continue on in their worship in a personal and private way. The silences may remain a part of it unless they are eventually edited out, but the interaction of the viewer with the original worshippers through the screen may render these silences less meaningful, especially after repetition of it.

Although technological input (e.g., PowerPoint) and in-screen technical wizardry (e.g., imaging) had long been a part of worship for some, and the facility to watch online has been of enormous benefit when attendance was either prohibited or restricted, this modern-day revolution in worship presentation in many churches, precipitated in large part by the pandemic, has led to much rethinking about how we proceed in our worship. This has been particularly the case in the administration of the sacraments of baptism and the Lord's Supper which, by their very nature, seemingly demand a real presence on the part of the congregants to be valid in the sense usually intended.

While, arguably, churches using technology may well be seeking to present the Gospel in the contemporary era within the context of such corporate worship, there is a danger lurking that must be addressed. The danger is that worship is diminished with an overconcentration on simply words (whether spoken, chanted, or sung) or other word-based media such as text(s) on the screen, without an appreciation of worship in devout and humble wordlessness before the Lord. The preponderance of words, always a threat in such situations, has become an endemic issue whether the service is online or in person. One might humbly suggest that, on holy ground, one doesn't just have to do without sandals!

With the advent of online interactive gatherings for meetings or worship, one phrase has become commonplace: "You're on mute." Significantly, a word which previously had been used merely as an adjective to describe someone who was unable or unwilling to speak, or to describe a function button on a remote control or phone handset, is now often used as a verb. We speak of muting and unmuting with the understanding that we are referring to turning on and off the microphone in order to speak or to remain silent. In this context of online sharing, there has sometimes been much confusion and cause for hilarity as someone begins to try to

Silence and Cadences of Worship

contribute verbally to the gathering, only to hear a chiding chorus of voices: "You need to unmute yourself."

The emphasis on muting or unmuting by clicking on an icon makes for an interesting and fruitful reflection on speaking—or maybe deliberately not actually uttering words—to convey the truth of the Word for the church in the world. Reflecting on corporate worship, the question arises: should there be moments when even the leader of worship ought (proverbially) to be "on mute"? Indeed, the concept of muting ourselves may offer a useful paradigm for what is sometimes needed in worship. God speaks often into our moments of silence, but there is the risk that our wordiness will drown out the so-called "still small voice."

The difficulty, as we have already noted, is that since the kingdom message in the Gospels is about the communication of the faith as good news, there is often a very strong emphasis on expounding the truths of Christian faith through sermon or hymnody. All preachers or worship leaders are, of course, dependent on language, that of Scripture as well as the great liturgical heritage of our faith and that of the preacher's own devising under the Spirit of God. However, there is a sense in which, as we seek to articulate the truth of the Gospel authentically in the context of frail human words, more often than not, the mystery of God leaves us at a very real loss for appropriate language or that which is worthy of the Ineffable One.

Notwithstanding the importance of proclamation, it is also true that the absence of our words may allow for an awareness of God's reality in our midst. The emphasis on hearing the Word, while so important in congregational life, can prove to have unintended drawbacks, since it is possible that there might be, as a result, just too many words. Hence, in order for our worship to better reflect the richness of our faith in the God of infinite majesty, there is a real need for the person in the pulpit or on the rostrum to learn when to "mute" or at least to be on "pause."

The case being made here is for leaders in *corporate worship* to generate creative silence and empty (but certainly not vacuous) space primarily in the gathering for worship. The point is that the cadence in worship may be changed by a certain intonation of voice that leads into silence or possibly just a pregnant pause. Indeed, it may be argued that in worship, cadence is created by how the diction flows as much as by what is, or what is not, actually spoken (or chanted or sung) in terms of content.

On this premise, by attending to the cadences of the devotions and guided by the Holy Spirit, a worship leader might quite naturally lead the congregation into silence. It is possible, indeed, desirable, for a person leading in corporate prayer to allow for a period of quietness so that there is a creative, silent space for the Word to have its own impact upon those gathered (or even "tuned in" online). The silence, far from being awkward or out of place may, if rightly understood, even help to articulate the divine mystery. Indeed, the notion of being on mute might serve as a paradigm of due humility and awe before the mystery of the Trinitarian God.

The exclusion of significant silence has always been an issue for churches which favour a more free (purportedly, open and extempore) worship, but it has affected other churches, too. However, the need to consider silence as an important part of the cadence of worship has become particularly crucial as the church slowly emerges into the post-pandemic world, for one very clear reason. That reason is this danger: with the advent of online worship, the temptation is to fill every moment with words, on the presumption that silence "on air" or online is not conducive to the worship experience. This juncture is one where the case for silence and the consideration of other nonverbal elements to worship both need to be heard afresh.

What is needed, perhaps, is for worship leaders to always have a sense of our human inadequacy to speak wholly worthily of the things of God. This means that in preaching, we recognize our dependence, first and foremost, on the power of God as Holy Spirit to speak the Word to the human heart. The same may be said for the leadership of corporate prayer. However well verbal communication (along with actions, gestures, or facial expressions) may help participants, in their engagement with the Word, there is always a need for words to give way to a sacred, even if only fleeting, wordless encounter with God.

Sometimes, in church life, our focus on God's Word seems to achieve precisely the opposite to effective encounter with the Divine. Ill-chosen words or an abundance of nonstop words appear to get in the way of the Word, even hindering our true openness to God. Excessive or trite, even repetitive (thus ultimately unhelpful) words appear to mitigate the impact of the revelation of the eternal and end up being a distraction from, rather than a pointer to, the mystery of divine being. Hence, the challenge for a discerning preacher or worship leader is to be sensitive to the cadences of worship under the rhythms of the Spirit. It means noting those places in worship when speech (or its musical equivalent) should momentarily be on hold. The cadences of devotion surely include, occasionally, both the short or the long pause, clearly intentional, but without being overly

Silence and Cadences of Worship

dramatic, as in a performance mode. Such times and spaces for quiet, or indeed for sheer wordlessness, might be wisely fostered in corporate worship through timely inclusion of the "holy mute," as the congregation is nurtured to let go of its tendency toward overly wordy worship. Long, meandering, or tedious prayers or needlessly verbose (i.e., those that are highly "decorated," even "flowery") litanies, or high-sounding "pulpiteering" all tend to hinder rather than enhance heartfelt corporate worship.

There is also the peril of an overly simplistic dissemination of an often all-too-neatly "packaged faith" which does not do justice to the majesty of God, or point to the possibility of the alluring mystery of abiding with Christ. Both majesty and mystery are key elements at the heart of all our professed knowledge of God. It is my contention that the worship style itself, with the structured, creative rhythms of led devotions, not simply the content as such, ought to reflect that reality of God's mystery. The point here is that in corporate worship, what we might call a "holy mute" is surely the only appropriate response to, and rightful appreciation of, divine inscrutability, which draws us out of ourselves in worship.

Sacred Space and Silence

The widespread use of online worship coupled with the fact that many congregations today meet in wholly secular spaces (such as commercial buildings, schools, community halls, or other social venues) present another issue when considering the role of silence in worship. Namely, how does wordlessness in worship help to create a sense of what might be called "sacred space," or a place of assembly for corporate worship where an encounter with God might take place? In other words, how is the nonverbal a key dimension in determining any place as sacred space?

This is not to say that God may only be worshipped in a building that has been set apart, and so considered "holy." During the first centuries of the Early Church (and after temple and synagogue attendance also waned), the worship of fellowship groups and congregations was not initially in a designated sanctuary. It was only later, as the church became more established in society, that church buildings began to be constructed, fostering the notion of a designated sacred space. While even today Christians continue to make pilgrimages to certain places and may feel that some sites are especially "holy," there can be no sense in which God is confined by earthly structures of whatever kind! As Jesus made clear in his dialogue with the Samaritan woman at Sychar, the time was at hand when

245

geographic location (or a particular cherished shrine) no longer had any bearing on the authenticity of worship, for honorable worship is "in spirit and in truth" (John 4:24). God may, of course, be worshipped at any time or any place, but corporate worship does take into account other factors which might foster or hinder openness to God. Today, more than ever, given the common use of multifunctional buildings and the prevalence of online worship where people are even sitting in their own homes, consideration should be given to the way silence, combined with symbol and ritual within the cadence of worship, helps to create sacred space. Still, the question remains as to what exactly it is that makes a place (whether a church or not) a holy worship space for the congregants when such a place is given over on Sundays or other occasions for corporate worship.

Reflection on the principle of the "holy mute" before the Lord, yielding both time and space to God, perhaps helps here. It is essential to note that nonverbal elements have an impact on our readiness for the Word: God is, of course, never constrained by our context, but we can certainly prepare ourselves better to be open and receptive to the divine Word. These nonverbal elements have a significant bearing not only on what we say or don't say, do or don't do in our verbalized worship forms, but also on our gathering in worship whether in the normalcy of the dedicated sacred space or not. While many early Baptists shied away from any type of symbol which they believed smacked of ritual, later congregations have incorporated the symbols of an open baptistery and Communion table. Today, many Baptists have found it helpful to venture further into the use symbol in worship. Sanctuary candles, open Bibles, seasonal banners, or antependia (the latter being a particular favourite of Roger), together with services marking the Christian year. These nonverbal elements are crucial for establishing the cadences of worship and express—without words—the mystery and wonder of faith.

Rituals, Rites, and Silence

To speak of rituals or rites may seem rather incongruous in a discussion of corporate worship from a Baptist perspective. It is commonly held that early Baptists, as well as other Dissenters, separated from the Established Church not only because of matters of ecclesiology, but also because of the various beliefs associated with much ritual. Yet sacred symbol, beyond such things as an open baptistery or a Communion table in a church, as already noted, has an important place in Baptist worship and thus is

Silence and Cadences of Worship

reflected in various practices. In certain churches, there might be other traditions which shape the sacred space or even demarcate the environs of the gathered assembly in remarkable ways which are not necessarily always recognized in symbolic terms, as such. For instance, there are Baptist churches in Britain which maintain the practice of reverently bringing the lectern Bible into the church in order to call the congregation to moments of silence before the worship service formally begins. There are other churches which, after reading out the notices for the week, place the notice book in the offering plate as if to symbolically—even without words—offer the week of church activity to God. The processing in or out by a church choir is evidently becoming much less common in Baptist circles, but there are other patterns (e.g., introits or the doxology) which have retained their place at the beginning and ending of services, respectively. Though not prescribed, other contributory elements, nonetheless, have an impact on the space being created for corporate worship with or without words, including times of intentional waiting or quiet, as during the organ prelude or postlude (which Roger insisted on calling a "voluntary").

Other rites are, perhaps, less common in Baptist churches, but there is also the place for greeting one another or the sharing of the peace in fellowship (a kiss of peace, handshake in fellowship, or informal hug of greeting). Furthermore, the laying on of hands and the practice of anointing with oil are sometimes practised in Baptist life. These might also be considered, similarly, as conveying this sense of our acknowledgement of the holiness of God by making space for God to act in our lives—in this case in corporate worship of a particular kind—without being dependent on human verbal forms. The assumption is that in our worship, God is always at work communicating the mystery of the Word, even above, beneath, and beyond our mere words, no matter how well chosen and woven together the latter might happen to be.

The notion of the "holy mute," in the broader sense of the nonverbal aspect of worship, could be construed as having another dimension in the regular gathering of the congregation, namely, in the body language (or posture assumed) during the different parts of the service. The raising of the hands by a minister as an act of blessing or benediction on the congregation, or, in fact, members of a congregation raising their hands in praise, may each, in turn, be an important nonverbal element of corporate worship. This is something which naturally varies, depending on the tradition and composition of the congregation, including people of different cultures, backgrounds, temperaments, and physical abilities. The most obvious bodily gestures which might be a cause of some differentiation between congregations and, indeed, within any specific congregation, might be the encouragement of the posture of standing or kneeling for prayer.

Standing in worship has been commonplace through the centuries for hymns, or particular prayers, or the recitation of the creed, or the singing of the doxology, and, occasionally, for the Scripture reading (e.g., as with the Gospel reading, the Gloria, the canticles, and the creed, in the Roman Catholic, Anglican, or Episcopal tradition). The provision of kneelers is not part of the Baptist tradition, but one might question why , historically, that has been the case. For those who are able, the opportunity to kneel in prayer (as well as to stand at other points) could be the powerful use of one or another bodily posture which is enriching in worship and expressive of the nature of our relationship with God, albeit possibly divisive in terms of inclusion. In these and other respects, variation in bodily posture might be thought of as yet another expression of the "holy mute" for the congregation in terms of the cadences of worship. In all these respects, it could be argued that recognition is being paid to the fact that encounter with God, irrespective of actual word-based cognition of the same, is beyond our mere verbalized forms of expression as we gather *here and now* in worship together.

Conclusion

The initial impetus for this reflection on the place of silence in worship came from a quite ordinary online gathering for worship during the pandemic. Restricted from going to a service in person, I was "attending" an online service which was being live-streamed. It began, reasonably enough, with a warning that there would be significant periods of silence; the congregation was encouraged not to assume that such periods of silences were awkward, unexpected, or unplanned. The worship leader went on to explain that the silence would be deliberate, and thus there was no need to presume at all that it had come about owing to the worship leaders losing their place, getting confused, or forgetting what was due to come next in the liturgy! Happily, the service unfolded as planned without any seeming awkwardness. In fact, as it proceeded smoothly, there was, for me, at least, a deeply moving sense of being conscious of God's Word being encountered not only within the sanctuary from which the worship leader spoke, but also in the online "space." That incident made me think again about

Silence and Cadences of Worship

the importance of the "cadences of worship" in terms of speech/no speech and the sheer variety of both *verbal* and *nonverbal* forms of affirmation of the spiritual life of plumbing the depths, scaling the heights, and discovering the riches of our faith in true encounter with God.

Throughout the pandemic, I often sent Roger online links to various worship services (as he did, likewise, to me), and we regularly commented to each other about the perils of online worship. We both shared many questions and not a few hesitations over its rightful application for even non-Eucharistic, let alone Eucharistic, worship. Subsequently, I have reflected further about both the "movements in" and the "dimensions to" worship, and feel strongly that the notion of the "holy mute" as a key element within the cadences of worship is paramount. I think Roger would have agreed. He, too, appreciated silence and space in corporate worship, just as he always commended the actual use of the concluding sung "Amen" when sung at the end of some of the grander, more stately, majestic hymns of faith when appropriate. Notably, as Roger would concur, after the final amen there is the opportunity for another period of silence as the congregation remains seated for the duration of the concluding organ voluntary (with no applause afterward!).

It seems to me, that whether we are worshipping in a church building (or elsewhere) or sharing in worship online, silence and space, pointer and symbol matter. To press the "mute button" in worship in order to allow for encounter with God is not, of course, to suggest that there should be no verbal theological expression in worship, or that devotion should be completely wordless. Words convey meaning to the initiated when spoken, whispered, chanted, or sung. However, when thinking about the rhythms and movements of corporate worship, the place of silence, symbol, and sacred space may open the door to an experience of encounter with the divine which is wholly beyond our limited mortal expression and human language. As we explore this dimension together, we can surely, undoubtedly know for ourselves the reality of the experience intended by Roger's oft-repeated expression: *Dominus vobiscum.*

Four Dimensions of Christian Ministry
in the New Testament

Allison A. Trites

Many years ago, when I was a student at Regent's Park College, Oxford, I had an opportunity to attend a meeting of the Theological Students' Fellowship, a university group for theological students preparing for Christian ministry in the churches. The guest speaker for this occasion was none other one than the Rev. Dr. John R. W. Stott, at that time the rector of All Souls' Church, Langham Place, London, and one of the royal chaplains for Queen Elizabeth II. Dr. Scott gave a brilliant lecture based upon four Greek words found in the New Testament. In paying tribute and remembering my former student and lifelong friend the Rev. Dr. Roger Prentice, who served for so many years as the much-loved chaplain of Acadia University, I want to share these four key words with you about the spiritual leader's responsibilities. These words address four dimensions of a Christian leader. They include his or her relation to God, to the Christian community, to the world, and to oneself.

The first word is *eusebeia*—reverence (for God). Without this essential dimension intact, there can be no genuine ministry of any significance. This basic dimension is sounded again and again in the Pastoral Epistles. Clearly, this theme is important in 1 Timothy, where the writer insists on godliness as a nonnegotiable dimension of ministry: "Train yourself to be godly...godliness [*eusebeia*] has value in all things, holding promise for both the present life and the life to come" (1 Tim. 4:7–8).[1] Timothy was a young Christian leader who looked to his older, more experienced mentor Paul for guidance and direction.[2] He was told to offer "sound instruction"

---

[1] All scriptural quotations, unless otherwise noted, are taken from the *New International Version* (Grand Rapids, MI: Zondervan, 1984).

[2] Pauline authorship of the Pastoral Epistles has often been contested, particularly in the last 200 years. For a careful, balanced treatment of the complex issues involved see Lee Martin McDonald and Stanley E. Porter, *Early Christianity and Its Sacred Literature* (Peabody, MA: Hendricksen, 2000), 488–98.

Four Dimensions of Christian Ministry

and "godly teaching" (1 Tim. 6:3) and to keep away from people of corrupt mind "who think godliness is a means to financial gain" (1 Tim. 6:5). In contrast to this commercial exploitation of the Gospel, "godliness with contentment" is to be viewed as "great gain" (1 Tim. 6:7). This magnificent faith is to be cherished as a divine mystery: "Great is the mystery of godliness" (*eusebeia*), and it is thoroughly Christocentric in character:

"He [that is, Jesus Christ] appeared in a body,
was vindicated by the Spirit,
was seen by angels,
was preached among the nations,
was believed on in the world,
was taken up in glory." (1 Tim. 3:16)

This creed-like statement is presented as a brief summary of what belief in God and reverence for him should mean to the Christian leader. Clearly, it is not surprizing that in charging Timothy, Paul reminds him to "pursue righteousness, godliness [*eusebeia*], faith, love, endurance and gentleness" (1 Tim. 5:10, 11). Such a Christ-centered lifestyle was not perfunctory; it ruled out simply going through the motions. Timothy was solemnly warned against the godlessness that would characterize the last days, when people would be "lovers of themselves, lovers of money, boastful, proud, abusive, disobedient to their parents, ungrateful, unholy, without love, unforgiving, slanderous, without self-control, brutal, not lovers of God—having a form of godliness [*eusebeia*] but denying its power" (2 Tim. 3:2–5).

Similarly, Titus is given instruction in "the truth that leads to godliness" (*eusebeia*, Tit. 1:1). Reverence for God, with all that this entailed, was mandatory for the Christian leader: "You must teach what is in accord with sound doctrine" (Tit. 2:1). The purpose of the Christian leader's teaching and lifestyle was to "make the teaching about God our Savior attractive" (Tit. 2:10).

The second Greek word is *philadelphia*—brotherly love: "Be devoted to one another in brotherly love" (Rom. 12:10). Sometimes the disciples of Jesus were inclined to be self-seekers and tried to put themselves forward at the expense of their fellow disciples. James and John, for instance, asked to sit at the right and left hand of Jesus in glory (Mark 10:37), and thereby aroused the anger and resentment of the other disciples (Mark 10:41). In dealing with them, Jesus taught them that true greatness was to

KEEPING THE FAITH

be found in self-giving service (Mark 10:42–45; cf. Matt. 20:20–25; Luke 22:24–27).

Like his Lord, the apostle Paul also taught the indispensability of unselfish brotherly love; he declared that "about brotherly love [*philadelphia*] we do not need to write to you, for you yourselves have been taught by God to love each other" (1 Thess. 4:9). This kind of mutual caring was clearly an imperative for Christian living and, as such, was central to Paul's admonitions to the Philippian leaders: "I plead with Euodia and I plead with Syntyche to agree with each other" (Phil. 4:2). He asked his "loyal yokefellow" to intervene to "help these women who have contended at my side in the cause of the gospel, along with Clement and the rest of my fellow workers, whose names are in the book of life" (Phil. 4:3). The love and respect Christians had for one another was vital to the advancement of the Gospel, and Paul spoke forcefully of its importance in promoting the Christian message.

Similar exhortations appear in other epistles: "Let mutual love continue," the writer to the Hebrews advises (Heb.13:1,NRSV), and 1 Peter insists "now that you have purified your souls by your obedience to the truth so that you have genuine mutual love, love one another deeply from your hearts" (1 Pet.1:22, NRSV). This emphasis is pressed again in 2 Peter, where it is presented as an essential part of the Christian's character; here in 2 Peter 1:7, a close link binds together reverence for God (*eusebeia*) and brotherly love (*philadelphia*). A right relationship with God must be accompanied by a right relationship with one's fellow believers. When this connection was disrupted, as Luke tells us about a strong "clash" (*paroxysm*) between Paul and Barnabas, sparks flew (Acts 15:39). Later, this quarrel was patched up. Mark subsequently proved himself by being with Paul during the apostle's first Roman imprisonment (Col. 4:10; Philem. 24). We might note the fact that Paul asked for Timothy to bring Mark with him to Rome "because he is helpful to me in my ministry" (2 Tim. 4:11). The breech in brotherly love was healed.

The third key word is *martyria*—witness.[3] The Christian leader is called to bear witness to his or her personal faith in a world which is

---

[3] For a brief summary of the idea of witness, see Allison A. Trites, "Witness," *The Oxford Companion to the Bible*, eds. Bruce M. Metzger and Michael D. Coogan (Oxford: Oxford University Press,1993), 805–806. For a full-length treatment of the witness theme in the Bible see Allison A. Trites, *The New*

Four Dimensions of Christian Ministry

unbelieving, hostile, and skeptical. Going back to the Gospels, we have a wonderful example of a model witness in the person of John the Baptist. This witnessing role is highlighted in the Fourth Gospel.[4] John "himself was not the light; he came only as a witness to the light" (John 1:8). The prologue to the Fourth Gospel makes clear the purely instrumental role of John the Baptist in sacred history. He refuses to claim any salvific role for himself; rather, he points to Jesus, declaring, "Look, the Lamb of God, who takes away the sin of the world!" (John 1:29). He specifically rejects the idea that he is Elijah or the expected latter-day prophet (John 1:21). Modestly, he proclaims himself as only a "voice"; his task is simply that of a herald, making a public proclamation: "I am the voice of one calling in the desert, 'Make straight the way for the Lord'" (John 1:23). To sum up, in the Fourth Gospel we have an ideal picture of the quintessential witness—one who points to Jesus as the divine Saviour of the world. A true witness recognizes his complete unworthiness (John 1:27) and speaks boldly and plainly for his Master. Later in the Fourth Gospel, John's place is acknowledged when others say of him, "Though John never performed a miraculous sign, all that John said about this man was true" (John 1:41).

The original setting of a witness was in the law court. Here it was absolutely essential that the witness tell the truth, the whole truth, and nothing but the truth (Lev. 5:1). False witness was condemned and punishable (Prov. 19:5, 9); note the law of malicious witness (Deut. 19:16–19). False witnesses are noted in both the trials of Jesus and Stephen (Matt. 27:60–62; Mark 14:57; Acts 6:13). A truthful witness was expected to share what he had seen and heard, and that is clearly what the earliest Christians did: "That which was from the beginning, which we have seen with our eyes, which we have touched—this we proclaim concerning the Word of life.... We proclaim to you what we have seen and heard, so that you may have fellowship with us" (1 John 1:1–3; note the reference to "eyewitnesses" [*autoptai*] in Luke 1:2).

The original apostles were eyewitnesses and "ear" witnesses of Jesus. They could testify what they had actually seen and heard: "You also must

---

Testament Conception of Witness (Cambridge and New York: Cambridge University Press,1977).

[4] For a detailed and helpful exposition of witness themes in the Fourth Gospel see John R.W. Stott, *The Preacher's Portrait* (London: Tyndale Press, 1961), 53–70.

253

KEEPING THE FAITH

testify, for you have been with me from the beginning" (John 15:27). Yet the apostles were more than witnesses to the facts; they were also advocates who took Christ's side and pressed the saving significance of what they had witnessed: "The life appeared, we have seen it and testify to it and we proclaim to you the eternal life which was with the Father, and has appeared to us" (1 John 1:2). The apostles shared not only their experience of the historical Jesus but also the saving impression that the living Lord had made on them. In consequence of their life-changing encounter with Christ, they were charged with a divinely given task: "You will receive power when the Holy Spirit comes on you; and you will be my witnesses in Jerusalem, and in all Judea and Samaria, and to the ends of the world" (Acts 1:8).

According to Luke, this task was also given to Paul, the apostle to the Gentiles, on the road to Damascus, where God chose him "to see the Righteous One and to hear words from his mouth. You will be a witness to all men of what you have seen and heard" (Acts 22:15). The third account of the experience on the Damascus road similarly places emphasis on Paul's duty as a witness: "I have appeared to you to appoint you as a servant and as a witness of what you have seen and what I will show you" (Acts 22:16). In due course, this witness-bearing task was given to the disciples, and the first Gospel account indicates that the church has been left to fulfill the Great Commission (Matt. 28:16–20).[5] Christian leaders today pass on the apostolic witness and faithfully take Christ's side as his advocates. We stand squarely on the shoulders of those who have gone before us and bear testimony to what the Lord has done for us. True witness is not self-testimony, but witness to Christ. Like John the Baptist, it must be offered with humility and it must be truthful.

But Jesus has "weightier testimony" than that provided by John the Baptist or any human witness. The Father himself bears witness to him through Christ's "works" and through the Scriptures (John 5:30–40). Also, when the Advocate, the Holy Spirit, comes, Jesus declared, "He will testify

---

[5] On the relevance of the witness theme for the Church's evangelistic task today see Gerald L. Borchert, *Dynamics of Evangelism* (Waco, TX: Word Books,1976); Kenneth L. Chafin, *The Reluctant Witness* (Nashvillle: Broadman Press, 1974) and Allison A. Trites, *New Testament Witness in Today's World* (Valley Forge, PA: Judson Press, 1983).

Four Dimensions of Christian Ministry

about me" (John 15:26). We are to understand God has not left himself without witness!

The final key word is *enkrateia*—self-control.[6] For a spiritual leader, this is a necessary quality. As the book of Proverbs said so simply long ago, "It is better to have self-control than to conquer a city" (Prov. 16:32, NLT). The apostle Paul in writing to the Galatians insists that the fruit of the Holy Spirit includes, significantly, self-control (*enkrateia*, Gal. 5:23). It is essential that reverence for God, love for one's Christian brothers and sisters, and faithful witness to Christ be presented in a life that is balanced and self-controlled. The Pastoral Epistles make it clear that the elder must be a model Christian leader who is "blameless—not overbearing, not quick-tempered, not given to drunkenness, not violent, not pursuing dishonest gain. Rather he must be hospitable, one who loves what is good, who is self-controlled, upright, holy and disciplined" (Tit. 1:7). Christian truth must be presented by a strong, self-disciplined, and self-controlled leader.

Roger Prentice offered such a ministry in both the parish and the university setting. Reverence for God was always paramount in his preaching, teaching, and leadership in worship. Concern for his brothers and sisters, both laity and clergy, was always important to him. Witness for Christ led him to work with students in the Passion plays that he produced for many years in Manning Memorial Chapel at Acadia University. He was happy to encourage the Acadia hockey team, the Axemen, and pray with them before their games. And a strong sense of self-control and self-discipline marked his leadership throughout his ministry. We thank God for all four dimensions of his Christian life and ends with service.

---

[6] For the wider use of *enkrateia* see H. Baltensweiler, *The New International Dictionary of New Testament Theology*, ed. Colin Brown (Exeter: Paternoster Press, 1975), I, 494–97.

Engaging with Others in the Church and in the Wider World

A bell has called us to this place,
And we have said our prayers;
We seek Thee, Lord, to find Thy face
To calm our faithless fears;
The hymns and words we offer Thee,
May they express our love;
The parting benediction be
Kind words from Thee above.

We lift our eyes to serve Thee now,
So that Thy kingdom come,
For all the sweat found on our brow
Is prayer—'Thy will be done';
We lift our hands to do Thy work
Where're it may be found;
May we, with faith and love, be girt;
By these may Christ be crowned. Amen.

(The Acadia Vespers Hymns, No. 70. RHP)

The point of this presentation is to reflect upon the various motivations, responses, and reflections people have when they come to the foot of the cross in their lives. It is a confrontation which people have when they deal with important moral and ethical issues in their lives, and the purpose of God for us as we face the world. Will we face the world with or without, the cross as a part of our lives?

(R. H. Prentice, introduction to "A Passion Play: It Happened on Friday: The Passion of Our Lord," Acadia University, 2000)

Ecumenisms of Tomorrow:
Paradoxes for the Future of Faith

David M. Csinos and Lydia Hood

During the summer of 2021, we met Roger Prentice for lunch at a café in Wolfville, Nova Scotia. It was, at first, not an unusual occurrence. We would often call Roger when we knew we'd be driving to his part of the province, and we'd plan to meet to enjoy coffee or a meal together. This lunch, however, stands out to us. For one thing, we remember well how Roger and our then-six-month-old daughter spent most of the lunch making faces at each other from across the table. But what also stands out is that when we informed Roger that we had been invited to offer a presentation about the future of faith at the fiftieth anniversary celebration of the Canadian Association of Baptist Freedoms, he was quick to respond with, "Oh, good! The committee took my recommendation." Upon learning that it was Roger who recommended us, an ordained Baptist professor and a Roman Catholic layperson, to speak at this upcoming anniversary gathering, we asked him why he felt we had something to contribute. He looked at Lydia and said, "You pay attention. You ask good questions. And you see things that other people miss. CABF needs that kind of perspective."

What Roger was indicating was that he knew the value of receptive ecumenism. While ecumenism is a word thrown around to speak of various movements, efforts, and networks promoting Christian unity across denominational lines, receptive ecumenism is a particular way of going about this work. Paul Murray, a Catholic theologian at Durham University, describes receptive ecumenism as "concerned to place at the forefront of the Christian ecumenical agenda the self-critical question, 'What, in any given situation, can one's own tradition appropriately learn with integrity from other traditions?' and, moreover, to ask this question without insisting, although certainly hoping, that these other traditions are also asking themselves the same question."[1] Kimberly Hope Belcher defines it

---

[1] Paul D. Murray, "Receptive Ecumenism and Catholic Learning—Establishing the Agenda," in *Receptive Ecumenism and the Call to Catholic Learning:*

more simply as "a dialogue that prioritizes an ecumenical exchange of gifts over the weighing of different doctrinal positions."[2] Receptive ecumenism is about sharing the best of different Christian traditions with one another.

One of the gifts to be shared through receptive ecumenism consists of the particular perspectives that each Christian tradition can bring to one another, not only perspectives of their own tradition, but of one another's as well. As a Roman Catholic layperson who is privy to Baptist circles, Lydia has a unique lens for seeing and interpreting "Baptisty" things. This perspective is one of the many gifts of receptive ecumenism that, as Steven Harmon has pointed out, help "form communities of more faithful followers of Jesus Christ."[3] Being an outsider is not easy, but it offers its advantages when it comes to studying a people group. Sharan Merriam et al. argue that when it comes to researching cultures, being an insider has benefits, but so does being an outsider: "The outsider's advantage lies in curiosity with the unfamiliar, the ability to ask taboo questions, and being seen as non-aligned with subgroups, thus often getting more information."[4] By combining Lydia's position as an outsider—albeit an outsider with relationships and access to the inside—with Dave's position as an insider—albeit a more recent insider, or "external-insider"[5]—we are collectively able to offer a vision of the future of faith that is thicker, wider, and richer than either of us could have generated on our own.

Since it was Roger who so enthusiastically recommended that we present at the CABF anniversary celebration—a celebration he did not live long enough to see—we felt compelled to use this chapter as an opportunity to put into writing the insights we first shared at that event in June 2022. What we present is a hope-filled vision for the future of Baptist faith—and of Christian faith in general—especially as it engages with

---

Exploring a Way for Contemporary Ecumenism, eds. Paul D. Murray with Luca Badini-Confalonieri, 5–25 (Oxford: Oxford University Press, 2008), 12.

[2] Kimberly Hope Belcher, *Eucharist and Receptive Ecumenism: From Thanksgiving to Communion* (Cambridge: Cambridge University Press, 2021), 2.

[3] Steven R. Harmon, *Baptists, Catholics, and the Whole Church: Partners in the Pilgrimage to Unity* (Hyde Park, NY: New City, 2021), 16.

[4] Sharan B. Merriam, Juanita Johnson-Bailey, Ming-Yeh Lee, Youngwha Kee, Gabo Ntseane, and Mazanah Muhammad, "Power and Positionality: Negotiating Insider/Outsider Status within and across Cultures," *International Journal of Lifelong Education* 20/5 (2001): 411.

[5] Ibid., 412.

diversity and difference in a world that is simultaneously becoming more pluralistic and more entrenched in fundamentalism as a response to such pluralism. Like our own faith lives, this vision is informed by a variety of sources from several Christian traditions. While we draw from scholars and academic theologians to inform our work, we also rely heavily on human experience.

Practical theology as a field of study has long known that classic theological texts— such as Julian of Norwich's *Revelations of Divine Love*, Augustine's *Confessions*, or Karl Barth's *Church Dogmatics*—are not the only sources of insight for theological wisdom. So, too, are the lives of ordinary people of faith. Practical theologian Pete Ward says it well: "Christian practice itself is inherently and profoundly theological."[6] And so, in constructing our ideas within this chapter, we draw from stories of our own experiences and we honour Roger by using the stories he has shared with us about his life and ministry as key sources of insight. These ordinary experiences of faith are chock-full of theological wisdom. Although Roger was far from ordinary (we thank God for that!), his life was a theological text played out in real time throughout nearly eighty years of life and more than fifty years of ordained ministry.

This chapter smashes dichotomous and binary understandings of the world. It is an insider-outsider, Baptist-Catholic, practical-theoretical vision of the future of faith. As such, the ideas we share are nuanced, non-linear, and even downright contradictory at times. They are filled with what Pope Francis has called contrapositions, or different points of view that sit in tension without competing with or obliterating one another. "A contraposition involves two poles in tension, pulling away from each other: horizon/limit, local/global, whole/part, and so on. These are contrapositions because they are opposites that nonetheless interact in a fruitful, creative tension.... [C]reation is full of these living polarities.... [T]hey are what make us alive and dynamic."[7] Our chapter will proceed as a series of contrapositions, four paradoxes that we hope will shape the future of Christian faith as it is played in Baptist keys. These contrapositions are not sequential, nor are they exhaustive. In fact, they intersect, overlap, and

---

[6] Pete Ward, *Introducing Practical Theology: Mission, Ministry, and the Life of the Church* (Grand Rapids, MI: Baker Academic, 2017), 10.

[7] Pope Francis, *Let Us Dream: The Path to a Better Future* (New York: Simon and Schuster, 2020), 79.

bleed into one another in all sorts of ways, reflecting the messy, dynamic, and multifaceted cacophony that is human faith.

We Move Further into Our Faith by Entering the Faith of Others

Roger was a proud Baptist and a staunch ecumenist. In his ministry throughout Canada's Maritime Provinces, he developed a number of positive relationships with clergy from other Christian denominations who served in the same towns and cities in which he ministered. At one point, he formed a close collegial relationship with a local Catholic priest. The two clerics would regularly meet to talk about faith and pastoral leadership, and we recall Roger saying that at times they even preached in one another's pulpits.

This pastoral camaraderie has a bit of an "odd couple" feel to it. Steven Harmon has said that "within the whole church, Baptists and Catholics might seem to be ecclesiological and liturgical polar opposites...[;] these two traditions are arguably more dissimilar from one another than each is from almost any other Christian tradition."[8] This is a sentiment Roger may have felt too. We recall him telling us that he once remarked to this priest how strange it was that the two of them—clerics from such dissimilar Christian traditions—were able to work so well together. Why was it easier, he wondered, for this Catholic priest and this Baptist minister to work together than it was for them to work with clergy from denominations that were more liturgically or doctrinally similar to each other. The priest's answer was simple: "Because I know where you stand."

The priest's pithy response is an example of the paradoxical truth that we strengthen our own faith by entering the faith of others. That is, the more we encounter and experience how others live out their faith—whether they are part of another Christian tradition or another religion altogether—the more opportunities we have to move further into our own faith. Knowing where the other stands does not mean we try to sway that person closer to our religious tradition, but that we remain grounded in our faith tradition *while* learning more about those of others. In so doing, we can become stronger in our own faith.

---

[8] Harmon, *Baptists, Catholics, and the Whole Church*, 21.

Brian McLaren has called this sort of stance a "strong-benevolent faith." He describes it as

> a Christian identity that is both strong and kind. By *strong* I mean vigorous, vital, durable, motivating, faithful, attractive and defining—an authentic Christian identity that matters. By *kind* I mean something far more robust than mere tolerance, political correctness or coexistence: I mean benevolent, hospitable, accepting, interested and loving, so that the stronger our Christian faith, the more goodwill we will feel and show toward those of other faiths, seeking to understand and appreciate their religion from their point of view.[9]

Having a strong-benevolent faith means that, at the same time, we hold fast to that which makes us Christian (one could also name a particular stream of Christianity—Baptist, Catholic, Lutheran, Adventist, etc.) while at the same time being willing to deconstruct, interrogate, and assess the doctrines that we hold dear in order to reconstruct them in ways that better reflect our faithfulness to the love of God and the love of the world—human and nonhuman world alike—that Jesus named as the heart of the Gospel. It's difficult, humbling, and sometimes painful work. But what we build in the process is a faith that is even stronger than before.

McLaren's proposal for a strong-benevolent faith was born within a context of religious pluralism. But, as we already alluded, what he says about relationships among Christians and those of other religions also has implications for those within different Christian denominations. It was a strong-benevolent faith that allowed Roger and his priest colleague to work so well together; they knew where one another stood and yet both showed interest in each other's traditions and openness to allowing their own faith to be strengthened by experiencing these traditions.

Life has changed since the days when Roger and that Catholic priest forged a friendship across denominational lines. For the past number of years, our experiences have led us to suspect that a "new ecumenism" may be built not among different Christian denominations, but among members of the same denomination who hold opposing views. The increasing

---

[9] Brian D. McLaren, *Why Did Jesus, Moses, the Buddha, and Mohammed Cross the Road? Christian Identity in a Multi-Faith World* (New York: Jericho, 2012), 10–11.

polarization experienced in many parts of the world seems to have made it relatively easy for a Baptist and a Catholic who exist on the same side of the spectrum that spans the poles of liberalism/progressivism and conservativism/traditionalism (we use these terms knowing they are deeply flawed) to see eye to eye, to work together, and to simply get along. What has become more difficult is for people who exist within the same denomination but who hold to beliefs that rest on different ends of this spectrum to build relationships—for example, a more liberal-leaning Baptist and a more conservative-leaning Baptist.[10] A strong-benevolent faith allows us to encounter with curiosity the faith of those with whom we differ and disagree, whether they are members of a different religion or are part of our own denominations.

We have spoken of relationships across different traditions and within the same tradition. But what about those who are not part of any Christian tradition or any religion at all? Entering the faith of others is also a call to all Christians to see ourselves the way religious outsiders see us.

At some recent conversations at Dave's church in Nova Scotia, the pastor asked congregants to describe their view of their congregation. Here are some of the words they used: inclusive, caring, welcoming, generous, broadminded, Christocentric, globally aware, open. We both know that these are accurate descriptors of this imperfect but faithful community. But do people outside of the church know this? We aren't so sure.

The issue is that Christianity has a branding problem. Since some of Christianity's loudest voices are also the least Jesus-like, the church universal has garnered some far-from-stellar reviews among the wider public. About a decade ago, David Kinnaman researched how both young non-Christians and young former Christians perceive the church. The words comprising the lists he compiled are far from those on the lists of members of Dave's congregation. Here are some terms on Kinnaman's lists: hypocritical, antihomosexual, judgmental, sheltered, shallow, exclusive, antiscience, doubtless.[11] Clearly, the church has a tarnished reputation among

---

[10] Without explicitly building on his notion of a strong-benevolent faith, McLaren offered a similar observation during an online Faith Forward presentation in March of 2022.

[11] David Kinnaman and Gabe Lyons, *unChristian: What a New Generation Really Thinks about Christianity...and Why It Matters* (Grand Rapids, MI: Baker,

Ecumenisms of Tomorrow

some people. Baptists, sadly, are some of those at the heart of this branding crisis, thanks to churches and associations that claim the label of Baptist while spewing hatred and discord and living in ways that are antithetical to the Gospel. In the face of such negative depictions, some churches are dropping the term *Baptist* while others are describing themselves as "a different kind of Baptist."

However we might describe the church, it's imperative for Christians to recognize that how we see ourselves may differ from how the world sees us. Strengthening our faith and growing our faithfulness to the Gospel means we need to get out of ourselves and see ourselves how others see us. Only then can we do the work that McLaren calls for from strong-benevolent Christians: "We must be willing to critically revisit those central Christian doctrines we believe to be firmly rooted in the Bible. We must courageously and humbly uncover the ways our doctrines have been used to foster hostility and violence in the past, and then respond in faithful, ethical ways."[12]

*We Learn More about Ourselves by
Learning More about Others*

Lydia's parents were ecumenical before anyone in her family even knew what *ecumenical* meant. Much to the chagrin of their fellow Catholic parishioners, her parents sent Lydia to kindergarten at a private Baptist school. While most kindergarteners were striving to learn the letters of the alphabet, her class went one step further: as they learned each letter of the alphabet, they also learned a Bible verse that begins with that letter. For example: "B. Believe on the Lord Jesus Christ and thou shalt be saved. Acts 16:31." (If you're going to spend your kindergarten years learning Bible verses, you might as well go all in and memorize the King James Version.) Yes, at the delicate age of five, Lydia had twenty-six Bible verses under her belt. Encouraged by how much Lydia thrived at this private kindergarten, her parents subsequently chose to withdraw her three older brothers from public school and send all four of them to a private Christian Reformed school.

2007). David Kinnaman with Aly Hawkins, *You Lost Me: Why Young Christians are Leaving Church...and Rethinking Faith* (Grand Rapids, MI: Baker, 2011).
   [12] McLaren, *Why Did Jesus*, 100–101.

Lydia was in grade three when she first remembers feeling hostility about being Catholic from other students at this school. Some classmates told her that her family was not Christian because they worshipped Mary; therefore, they were destined for hell. That's a lot to take in at just eight years old. These misunderstandings about Catholicism continued to follow Lydia as she moved through grades. They stayed with her during her education at the University of Prince Edward Island, where she majored in religious studies and minored in Catholic studies. And they became even more obvious after a move to Halifax, Nova Scotia, to study at Atlantic School of Theology, where she continued her studies alongside other Catholics, but also Anglicans, United Church students, Pentecostals, Salvation Army officers, and others.

Dialogue with some classmates was nearly impossible when certain topics arose in class discussions. This was all too apparent when she took a particular Christian ethics class. If you're looking to add a bit of controversy to your life, join a class predominantly populated by United Church of Canada students, sprinkle in a few Anglicans, and finish it off with two Catholics. Stir in some student-led discussions about such issues as same-sex marriage, abortion, and gambling, and see what happens.

The official doctrines of these Christian denominations may differ on these very divisive issues, but the students in this classroom had their own views, some of which were out of step with their denominations. As Lydia listened to her United Church and Anglican classmates share their views on these matters—and on a host of other theological topics—they pushed her to think more about her own beliefs, how they aligned and diverged from official Catholic doctrine, and why she was a Catholic in the first place. Thanks to her Baptist kindergarten and Christian Reformed elementary school, it was not the first time she had been confronted with religious difference in the classroom. But it was different this time. As an adult, she had to listen carefully to concerns that people had with the Catholic Church and take them to heart. After all, the United and Anglican classmates who shared their negative views had become her friends.

These experiences of difference forced Lydia to wrestle with her commitment to the Catholic Church. She had to come to terms with why this fundamentally flawed human religious institution was the one that she continues to look toward for her spiritual nourishment. Of course, all denominations are flawed. All have fallen short in their human efforts to join

Ecumenisms of Tomorrow

God in God's divine mission.[13] So Lydia's story isn't terribly unique. We could swap Catholic for Presbyterian, Methodist, or Baptist and tell a similar story.

In retrospect, what Lydia was going through was what John Westerhoff named as a move from affiliative faith to searching faith, and, finally, to owned faith.[14] It's a transition from a faith based on common belonging, experience, and thought among a group (affiliative faith) through a period of asking oneself what in particular one believes (searching faith) and toward the maturity that comes with taking a stand and choosing the complexity of belief that is bound up with disagreement, doubt, and uncertainty (owned faith). Lydia could not have moved so deeply into her faith without her Baptist classmates in kindergarten, her Christian Reformed schoolmates a few years later, and her United and Anglican peers at Atlantic School of Theology. By learning what they thought and what their denominations believed and practised, she learned far more about her own faith than would have been possible in Catholic-only settings.

When Lydia completed her studies, she experienced a "full-circle" moment. During her undergraduate degree, she expressed to a visiting professor that she wished to pursue further studies in theology, listing several Catholic universities to which she was interested in applying. This professor, a convert to Catholicism, gently suggested a number of other universities, none of which were Catholic—or, at least, exclusively Catholic. Having devoted much of his life to living out receptive ecumenism, he told her all about the benefits that come with studying and living alongside other Christian communities. He was enlightened to the many advantages of exploring one's faith more deeply while honestly engaging with the beliefs and practices of other denominations, and he wanted her to experience it for herself. At the time, Lydia could not fully understand the paradox that one can learn so much about one's own faith by learning

---

[13] David Bosch is one of many missiologists who understand the purpose of the church as the participation in God's mission. See David J. Bosch, *Transforming Mission: Paradigm Shifts in Theology of Mission* (Maryknoll, NY: Orbis, 1991), 511. We appreciate how Pamela Couture draws from traditional Roman Catholic missiology to state that "God has a mission in the world; and that mission has a church." Pamela Couture, *Child Poverty: Love, Justice, and Social Responsibility* (St. Louis, MO: Chalice, 2007), 60.

[14] John H. Westerhoff III, *Will Our Children Have Faith?*, 3rd ed. (Harrisburg, PA: Morehouse, 2012).

267

about the faiths of others. But after living this paradox for herself, she came to see the profound wisdom in this contraposition.

We Honour Tradition by Continuously Reimagining Tradition

Tradition is central to the lives of both of our families of origin. We don't think we're unique in saying that Christian traditions have held particularly revered positions. For more than two decades, Lydia's family celebrated Christmas through a large Christmas Eve party that her parents would host for their extended families. Then, once the party began to wind down, she and each of her siblings would be allowed to open one gift from under the tree. Those who were old enough to do so would make their way to the cathedral for midnight Mass while the younger children would make their way to bed.

Whether going to bed early or after Midnight Mass, everyone knew what to expect in the morning: a stocking filled with practical items; Lydia's mother militantly watching them open their gifts and making sure all gifts were returned to boxes with the gift tags tucked inside so that thank-you phone calls and cards could be made; anyone who hadn't made it to Midnight Mass had to be at the church for the ten o'clock service; and, finally, they had their Christmas meal at noon.

This pattern was disrupted only once during Lydia's childhood: her younger brother decided that Christmas Day was as good as any to be born, so he (inconveniently) arrived on December 25 and was airlifted to the children's hospital, more than 350km away. The second disruption to Lydia's participation in her family's Christmas festivities happened when she was in her early twenties and teaching English in central France for the year. With some time off at Christmas, she decided to spend the holidays with a friend from her hometown who happened to be discerning the priesthood with a small religious community in the south of France. While the location was dreamy and the religious community was welcoming, Lydia distinctly recalls feeling as though it wasn't Christmas. There was no family party. There was no gift before bed. There was no stocking waiting for her in the morning. And her mother's stuffing was missing from the dinner table. It was an unsettling experience. She enjoyed spending time with her friend, and she relished the opportunity to travel to a new part of France, but something wasn't right. Without the traditions that marked Christmas in her family, it just didn't feel like Christmas.

268

Ecumenisms of Tomorrow

Did Lydia really expect her family's Christmas tradition to remain the same forever? The short answer is yes, she did. It all seems so foolish now, years later. Lydia's siblings were getting married, having children of their own, and trying to establish their own traditions. And yet there was a sense that her family was still trying to fit into the mould, albeit with disrupted patterns and more family members who were bringing and creating their own traditions.

Again, this is not an unusual situation. As families grow and change, they have no choice but to adapt their traditions or risk being stifled by them if they do not shift. For Lydia, her family had to examine its current reality, thank the past for the memories, and move forward. The first few Christmases with reimagined traditions were rocky—let's face it, change can be hard—but now her family enjoys Christmas even more, because each year they celebrate in ways that reflect the reality of their family's life and are inclusive of their ever-growing numbers. They've learned what Gary West, chair of Traditional Arts and Culture Scotland, once wrote: "Tradition, then, is a story, learned from the past, told in the present, but looking to the future."[15]

We all find ourselves in this predicament. We have all found ourselves unwilling to let go of a tradition, a belief, or a practice that we hold dear, one that has come to mark our lives and has become central to our identity. We believe, in many cases, that if we can maintain the status quo, tradition will help us weather the storms of change. Unfortunately, in holding too fast to tradition, we may end up going down with the ship. For those on the inside of our communities, holding too fast to unmovable traditions has made us stagnant. For those on the outside, it makes us divisive, excluding those who do things differently from us. The more we try to maintain the status quo in the midst of new members and changing demographics—like the in-laws who started coming to Lydia's family's Christmases—the more we communicate to others that they are not welcome. This may not be our intent, but it can certainly be a repercussion of our unwillingness to let go.

Roger—a staunch traditionalist—found himself in a similar predicament when he was chaplain at Acadia University. Roger was adamant that,

---

[15] Gary West, "About Traditional Arts: What Is Tradition?," *Traditional Arts and Culture Scotland*, accessed June 28, 2022. Available at https://tracscotland.org/about-traditional-arts/.

while Baptist, he was chaplain to the entire university, regardless of one's faith tradition. At one point, a group of Catholic students told Roger that they wished to have a Mass held in the chapel. Unfortunately, because it was not a Catholic chapel, the celebration of the Mass would require special permission from the diocese—each and every time. Well-meaning and purposeful tradition was getting in the way of the faith lives of Acadia's Catholic students.

Roger spoke with the local Catholic bishop about this predicament, asking if there was any way that a permanent exception could be made. The bishop said (and we're paraphrasing), "In special circumstances when there is no Catholic church nearby, the church can grant a community the ability to celebrate Mass outside of a Catholic chapel or church. This is what we do in military outposts, for example. What if we treat Acadia's chapel as an outpost? Then there's no reason why Mass can't be celebrated in the chapel this time or any other time that the Catholic community on campus would like it celebrated." Both Roger and the bishop knew that tradition needed to be adapted for the sake of inclusion.

Tradition was never meant to be stagnant. Tradition at its best is a living thing, always changing, shifting, and adapting as the inheritors of tradition have holy arguments[16] about how it looks, how it's practised, and what it means in one's current time and place. Sometimes the breath of the Holy Spirit comes and blows through our communities with gale-force winds, letting us know that it is time for us to take stock of our traditions and do some heavy decluttering, cleaning, and reorganizing.

The reexamination and reimagination of the traditions among our communities is not a condemnation, as if to say that those who came before us had it wrong. It is, in fact, a tradition unto itself, one that Emily Askew and O. Wesley Allen say is bound up with the continuation of the church apostolic: "Apostolicity...is a paradox of consistently holding onto the authoritative ideal of the past in order to reform constantly the

---

[16] Alasdair MacIntyre defines a living tradition as "an historically extended, socially embodied argument, and an argument precisely in part about the goods which constitute that tradition." Alasdair MacIntyre, *After Virtue: A Study in Moral Theory*, 2nd ed. (Notre Dame, IN: University of Notre Dame Press, 1984), 222.

practices of the past."[17] Reimagining traditions is an act of gratitude to those who have created, adapted, and passed on traditions before our time. It is a thanksgiving for how our forebears brought us to this place, and it is an invitation to journey together so we can continue to grow and to welcome others to join us on this journey.

Theologian Dorothy Bass writes that "a living tradition is not an inert entity passed from one generation to the next.... The historical extension of living traditions requires that others make those traditions their own." As we honour our inherited traditions by making them our own, we will make choices in our communities today, the fruit of which many of us will not see. It seems ludicrous that many of the ways in which we make our inherited traditions our own will not have a direct impact on us; but our efforts will make all the difference for our children and their children. What a responsibility we have for the future of Christianity!

We Become More Baptist by Becoming Less Baptist

Baptists are not known for their commitment to ecumenism. In fact, some see the words "Baptist" and "ecumenism" in opposition to one another, that to be ecumenical, to open ourselves to those who practise Christianity in different ways, is to put all that distinguishes us as Baptists at risk of deterioration. Thus, Baptists have often existed as observers—even encouragers—rather than as participants in ecumenical and interfaith engagement.[18]

It's no wonder, then, that Baptists can feel threatened by changes in society. LGBTQ+ advocacy, antiracism, truth and reconciliation, nonliteral views of Scripture, and even openness to evolutionary theory in some circles are all seen by some as potential blows to the health of Baptist orthodoxy—whatever that is deemed to be in a given congregation or association. Rather than being open to how our Christian faith might lead us to greater faithfulness as a result of societal change, the easy answer is to dig down and entrench ourselves in our current doctrine while at the same

---

[17] Emily Askey and O. Wesley Allen Jr., *Beyond Heterosexism in the Pulpit* (Eugene, OR: Cascade, 2015), Kindle loc. 1262.

[18] Harmon, for example, writes that "Baptists have a reputation as the 'problem children' of the modern ecumenical movement, and the stereotype is not without foundation. Baptists have been quick to declare other traditions to be false churches." Harmon, *Baptists, Catholics, and the Whole Church*, 69.

time erecting defensive structures that are reinforced whenever we face a new threat. What results are strongholds of what some Baptists deem to be orthodoxy amidst a diverse and changing world—a world in which other Baptists keep their fingers on the pulse of these changes in order to see how God might be at work within them.

The image we've painted here is certainly simplified. But it's a simplification that rings true. To be Baptist, in the eyes of several insiders and outsiders, is to hold firm to what is deemed to be traditional and fundamental to the faith. So perhaps it's no surprise to learn that Baptists have not been the first to jump into the pool of ecumenism and the neighbouring ponds marked by other kinds of diversity.

The truth is, however, that rather than seeing Baptist tradition as threatened by experiences of difference, Baptists actually hold an advantageous position in the quest to remain faithful to tradition and also to reimagine faithfulness in light of contemporary life. The advantage comes in the form of what Walter Shurden famously called the "four fragile freedoms,"[19] four distinctive elements that he has found to be central to Baptist identity:

* Bible Freedom: the ability to interpret and live out the truths of Scripture for oneself;
* Soul Freedom: the view that everyone is accountable to God directly and need not rely on creeds or clergy;
* Church Freedom: the responsibility to live out one's common faith through any polity, doctrine, or practise to which God is calling the community;
* Religious Freedom: the ability to practise (or not practise) religion without interference by governments.

Sadly, some people have manipulated these freedoms into excuses to bully, harass, and even oppress anyone who disagrees with them. But the incredibly good news is that it is actually these freedoms that offer us a way forward in faithfulness. These fragile freedoms empower individual Baptists and corporate Baptist faith communities with the freedom to dissent

---

[19] Walter B. Shurden, *The Baptist Identity: Four Fragile Freedoms* (Macon, GA: Smyth and Helwys, 1993/2013).

Ecumenisms of Tomorrow

that is so central to living traditions.[20] It affords them a faith filled with ongoing opportunities to practise, interrogate, and adapt that faith in the unending quest to be faithful to the way of life to which God has called us, which Jesus taught and modeled to us, and for which the Spirit empowers us. Through exercising Bible freedom, for example, Baptists can read Scripture in literary rather than literal ways, seeing how God is always pointing humanity toward more just, loving, and unified ways of living. Through exercising church freedom, Baptist congregations can choose to live their communal faith in ways that God is calling them, even if it is contrary to the doctrines and practices of larger, more prominent Baptist churches and more dominant Baptist associations. Baptist churches can pass and uphold statements of radical inclusion. They can worship through liturgies that are so filled with "smells and bells" that they might be mistaken for High Anglicans. They might include the communal recitation of the Apostles' Creed in an ordination service, as Dave's congregation did at the service for his ordination. All this is possible not in spite of what makes one Baptist, but *because* of it. All this is possible because of the freedoms that lie at the heart of Baptist identity.

At times, upholding the freedoms at the heart of Baptist identity means that we bend the rules. During an introductory course on Christian worship that Dave taught in 2019, he invited three seasoned ministers to be part of a panel titled "Is Ecumenical Worship Possible?": a Roman Catholic priest, an Anglican priest, and a Baptist minister (who, of course, was Roger). For more than an hour, these three clerics shared stories about times when they found themselves face-to-face with the challenge of ecumenical worship over their many years of ministry. They spoke of Catholic priests offering the Eucharist to Protestant ministers at a funeral Mass, of Baptists and Catholics preaching in one another's pulpits, and of many other times when official doctrine and liturgy were bent—and even broken—for the sake of Christian unity. At the end of the panel, Dave offered a summary of what the panelists shared that day: "Ecumenical worship is possible, but it often involves breaking the rules for the sake of loving one another."

---

[20] Steven Harmon has argued that the Baptist practice of dissent is a gift that Baptists can offer other Christian traditions. See Steven R. Harmon, *Baptist Identity and the Ecumenical Future: Story, Tradition, and the Recovery of Community* (Waco, TX: Baylor University Press, 2016), 49–52.

While some denominations may be less prone to affirming that summary and the stories that inspired it, the freedoms at the heart of Baptist faith provide Baptists with an advantage. After all, freedom to love God and love others without restriction from a particular interpretation of Scripture, a reliance on clergy and creeds, ecclesial regulations and procedures, and government imposition allows Baptists to bend and break the rules while leaning further into the very centre of their faith tradition. Perhaps this could be stated as a related contraposition, or a paradox within a paradox: "We follow the rules by bending (and breaking) the rules."

Exercising Baptist freedoms is not easy. This is why they are fragile. Choosing beliefs and practices that are faithful to the Gospel but wildly unpopular with our Baptist siblings may put us at odds with longtime allies. It may cause our congregations to decrease in membership. It may evoke hatred and violence. And it may mean following God as God calls us to live our faith in ways that don't look very Baptist—at least ways that don't look like what many people imagine Baptists to be.

The reality is that such choices actually lead us further into our Baptist faith. By taking seriously the *responsibility* that comes with living out our freedoms as Baptist Christians—and it is a responsibility—we affirm the heart of Baptist tradition. So, the future of Baptist faith may seem less obviously Baptist than its past—at least in more superficial ways. But at its heart, by being open to change through the exercise of its freedoms, it will become more thoroughly Baptist than ever before.

The Future of Faith

We are not fortune tellers or soothsayers. We do not know what tomorrow will bring. However, by digging into the experience of Christian faith as it has been lived out in contemporary lives—our lives as well as Roger's—it is possible to catch some glimpses of the challenges and opportunities that the church will face in its future.

In offering the four paradoxes we outlined in this chapter, we are doing nothing more than sharing our glimpses of a church filled with the complexities of human life. How we live into whatever tomorrow brings will depend on our ability to hold these contrapositions in tension:

* We will move further into our own faith by entering the faith of others.
* We will learn more about ourselves by learning more about others.

Ecumenisms of Tomorrow

* We will honour tradition by continuously reimagining tradition.
* We will become more Baptist by becoming less Baptist.

There are more contrapositions we can add to this list. But whatever we might add, it's crucial that we keep at the forefront of our minds the wisdom found within the *Back to the Future* film franchise (Dave's a big fan!). At the end of the third film, Dr. Emmett Brown returns to 1985 after spending a few years in the 1880s. Jennifer, the main character's girlfriend, shows Doc Brown a piece of paper that she received in the second film, when she went forward in time thirty years to 2015. Don't worry if you're a bit confused by the backstory; the main point comes in a bit of dialogue that ensues when Jennifer opens the paper. Showing Doc Brown, she says, "I brought this note back from the future and...now it's erased!" "Of course it's erased!," Doc responds. She looks back at him and asks, "But what does that mean?" Doc smiles and replies, "It means that your future hasn't been written yet. No one's has. Your future is whatever you make it. So make it a good one."

God calls all of us to join God in making a future that is good, a future marked by hope, justice, compassion, and love that extends to the whole world, human and nonhuman alike. No exceptions. It is that simple and that complex. It will not be easy to live into the paradoxes bound up with faithfulness to the Gospel of Jesus Christ. So, as we steer ourselves toward new horizons, may we remember the clues to God's good future that are embedded in the lives of the faithful who have gone before us, and may we keep our eyes open to the new thing that God is doing all around us.

State Neutrality and Religion in Europe: What's the Prospect?*

Malcolm D. Evans

What is the role of the state when it comes to matters of religious belief? Few questions have provoked greater controversy through the ages. In some ways, the very posing of this question assumes elements of a relationship between the state and religion which some might consider controversial, in particular that there is a distinction to be drawn between them that requires that there be a "relationship" at all. Yet the origins of the contemporary conception of the state lie in the idea that there should be some degree of separation between them to help create the space in which those of different faiths might be able to practice their beliefs without this posing an existential challenge to the governing authorities. The journey from the *cuius regio, eius religio* of sixteenth-century Europe[1] through the seventeenth-century Treaties of Westphalia[2] to the freedom of religion or belief as set out in the 1948 UN Declaration on Human

---

* This chapter has its origins in an address given to a conference on "State Neutrality and Religious Diversity" in March 2022 at Hasselt, Belgium, and a version has been published in the *Oxford Journal of Law of Religion*.

[1] In 1555, the Religious Peace of Augsburg permitted lay princes of the Holy Roman Empire to determine, in effect, whether their territories were to adhere to the Lutheran Confession or to the old (Roman Catholic) religion and for that choice to be respected by others. Those objecting to the choice had the right to emigrate.

[2] The twin treaties of Munster and Osnabruck were signed between France and Sweden respectively and the emperor in October 1648. The treaties extended to principle of *cuius regio, eius religio* to the Reformed (i.e., Calvinist) religion. They also permitted a degree of what would now be described as a degree of "free exercise" of a recognized religion other than that of the state, at least for a period of up to five years, after which they might be required to leave. For an overview, see Evans, *Religious Liberty and International Law in Europe* (Cambridge: Cambridge University Press, 1997), ch. 2.

Rights[3] and in contemporary international human rights law[4] has been a long one[5]—but where does that journey end, or, at least, where has it taken us?

This chapter looks at the jurisprudence of the European Convention on Human Rights on this topic, which has changed markedly over the last thirty years[6] and has become increasingly focused on the idea of "neutrality."[7] This, it is suggested, is a significant error which ought not be replicated elsewhere.[8] The chapter is not, therefore, an example of a Eurocentric approach to the topic, but quite the opposite: it is intended to highlight the shortcomings of the approaches which have been generated in the European context. Perhaps unsurprisingly, this European jurisprudence remains permeated by the same tension—some might say contradiction—which has bedevilled the approach to the freedom of religion or belief in Europe ever since the sixteenth and seventeenth century "settlements" at the conclusion of the Thirty Years War, or the wars of religion.

---

[3] UNGA Res 271A (III), adopted December 10, 1948.

[4] See generally Heiner Bielefeldt, Nazila Ghanea, and Michael Wiener, *Freedom of Religion or Belief: An International Commentary* (Oxford: Oxford University Press, 2016).

[5] See generally Noel D Johnson and Mark Koyama, *Persecution and Toleration: The Long Road to Religious Freedom* (Cambridge: Cambridge University Press, 2019).

[6] See generally *The European Court of Human Rights and the Freedom of Religion or Belief: 25 Years since Kokkinakis*, eds. Jeroen Temperman, T. Jeremy Gunn, and Malcolm Evans (Leiden, NL: Nijhoff/Brill, 2019).

[7] See Malcolm Evans and Peter Petkoff, "A Separation of Convenience? The Concept of Neutrality in the Jurisprudence of the European Court of Human Rights," *Religion, State and Society* 36 (2008): 205–23; Malcolm Evans and Peter Petkoff, "Marginal Neutrality—Neutrality in and the Margin of Appreciation in the Jurisprudence of the European Convention of Human Rights," in *European Court of Human Rights*, (n. 6), ch. 6. Ian Leigh, "The European Court of Human Rights and religious neutrality," in *Religion in a Liberal State*, eds. Gavin D'Costa, Malcolm Evans, Tariq Modood, and Julian Rivers (Cambridge: Cambridge University Press, 2013), ch. 2.

[8] For an alternative view, defending approaches based upon neutrality, see Julie Ringelheim, "State Neutrality as a Common European Standard? Reappraising the European Court of Human Rights Approach," *Oxford Journal of Law and Religion* (2017): 24–47.

KEEPING THE FAITH

In a nutshell, that tension, or contraction, concerns the very purposes of religious toleration and/or religious freedom[9] from a human rights perspective. As far as the European Court of Human Rights is concerned, is it predominantly about reducing tension within a religious or political community and so fostering civic harmony?[10] Or is it predominantly about permitting individuals to practice freely their religion or belief?[11] Obviously, neither is an absolute,[12] and each approach supports the other.[13] Nevertheless, the starting premise is important. The sixteenth-century Peace of Augsburg was largely focused on reducing tensions by permitting a limited degree of religious pluralism within the Holy Roman Empire by allowing some territories to be either Roman Catholic or Lutheran, coupled with a right for individuals to move to other territories where the dominant religion was more congenial to them.[14] This approach is largely premised on reducing communal religious tension rather than promoting individual religious freedom.

---

[9] The general literature on religious toleration is too vast and too well known to merit citation or engagement given the limited purposes of this chapter.

[10] See, for example, Serif v. Greece, no. 38178/97, ECHR 1999-IX, para 53; Metropolitan Church of Bessarabia and Others v. Moldova, no. 45701/99, ECHR 2001-XII, para. 115: Lautsi and Others v. Italy [GC], no. 30814/06, ECHR 2011, para. 60; Bayatyan v. Armenia [GC], no. 23459/03, ECHR 2011, para. 120; S.A.S. v. France [GC], no. 43835/11, ECHR 2014, para. 128; Centre of Societies for Krishna Consciousness in Russia and Frolov v. Russia, no. 37477/11, November 23, 2021, para. 40. November 2021 all of which stress the potential significance for the broader community of the exercise of the freedom of religion or belief by the individual. There are many other examples.

[11] See the foundational jurisprudential statement of principle in Kokkinakis v. Greece, May 25, 1993, Series A no. 260-A, discussed below.

[12] Thus, in the recent case of Ancient Baltic religious association "Romuva" v. Lithuania, no. 48329/19, June 8, 2021, para. 145, the court said it was "unable to accept that the existence of a religion to which the majority of the population adheres, or any alleged tension between the applicant association and the majority religion, or the opposition of an authority of that religion, could constitute objective and reasonable justification for refusing State recognition to the applicant association."

[13] In Ancient Baltic religious association "Romuva" v. Lithuania (n. 12), para 143, the court has said that it "has repeatedly emphasised that maintaining true religious pluralism is vital to the survival of a democratic society."

[14] See n. 1 above.

State Neutrality and Religion in Europe

The premise underlying human rights approaches to the freedom of religion or belief is very different, as the terminology itself suggests. These are rights which are to be enjoyed by the individual and exercised against the state; they mark out the limits of the legitimacy of state intrusion, or state-sanctioned intrusion, into religious beliefs and practices. This carries with it the potential to cause tensions rather than remove or mitigate them, which is the very reason why the exercise of such rights can be subject to limitations, including those "necessary in a democratic society" to protect the rights and freedoms of others.[15] But the bias is clear: it is predominantly about the rights of individuals, tempered by some limitations if necessary. Against this general background, it is illuminating to consider what remain the two foundational jurisprudential utterances by the European Court of Human Rights concerning the freedom of thought, conscience, and religion as set out in Article 9 of the ECHR.

Although the first judgment of the European Court of Human Rights was given as long ago as 1960,[16] it was not until 1993 that the court gave its first judgment concerning Article 9 in the case of *Kokkinakis v. Greece*, concerning the criminal conviction of a member of the Jehovah's Witnesses for proselytism. In what has become the "standard recital," routinely quoted or alluded to in virtually all cases concerning that article, the court said that:[17]

> As enshrined in Article 9, freedom of thought, conscience and religion is one of the foundations of a "democratic society" within the meaning of the Convention. It is, in its religious dimension, one of the most vital elements that go to make up the identity of believers

---

[15] The limitations on the exercise of the right do not, however, include the need to protect public order as such. On the scope of limitations, see Mark Hill and Katherine Barnes, "Limitations on Freedom of Religion or Belief in the Jurisprudence of the European Court of Human Rights," in *European Court of Human Rights* (n. 6), ch. 4, who, on pages 98–101, highlight the extent to which "neutrality" has emerged in practice as an alternative form of limitation, an insight of particular importance.

[16] This being Lawless v. Ireland (no. 1), November 14, 1960, series A, no. 1.

[17] Kokkinakis v. Greece (n. 11), para. 31. For the dangers which now lurk behind this being reduced to a ritual incantation, see Malcolm Evans, "Freedom of Religion or Belief in the European Court of Human Rights since the *Kokkinakis* case: 'Quoting *Kokkinakis*,'" in *European Court of Human Rights*, (n. 6), ch. 2.

279

and their conception of life, but it is also a precious asset for atheists, agnostics, sceptics and the unconcerned. The pluralism indissociable from a democratic society, which has been dearly won over the centuries, depends on it.

It immediately went on to observe that[18] "while religious freedom is primarily a matter of individual conscience, it also implies, *inter alia*, freedom to 'manifest [one's] religion.' Bearing witness in words and deeds is bound up with the existence of religious convictions." As a result, the real debate underpinning that very first judgment was whether the state had a legitimate role to play in the structuring of religious life in a country at all—some believing that religious life was so important that the state had to step in to protect believers from the dangers of proselytism,[19] others believing that it was so important that the state should not do so.[20] As is so often the way, the court steered a middle ground, accepting the legitimacy of the state engaging with matters concerning religious life by prohibiting "improper proselytism" but seeking to ensure it did so in a way

---

[18] Ibid.

[19] Famously reflected in the trenchant comments of Judge Valticos, of Greece, who, in his dissenting opinion (ibid., 28), in a passage still worth quoting in full, characterized the situation in the following way: "On the one hand, we have a militant Jehovah's Witness, a hardbitten adept of proselytism, a specialist in conversion, a martyr of the criminal courts whose earlier convictions have served only to harden him in his militancy, and, on the other hand, the ideal victim, a naïve woman, the wife of a cantor in the Orthodox Church (if he manages to convert her, what a triumph!). He swoops on her, trumpets that he has good news for her (the play on words is obvious, but no doubt not to her), manages to get himself let in and, as an experienced commercial traveller and cunning purveyor of a faith he wants to spread, expounds to her his intellectual wares cunningly wrapped up in a mantle of universal peace and radiant happiness. Who, indeed, would not like peace and happiness? But is this the mere exposition of Mr Kokkinakis's beliefs or is it not rather an attempt to beguile the simple soul of the cantor's wife? Does the Convention afford its protection to such undertakings? Certainly not."

[20] See the partly dissenting opinion of Judge Martens (ibid., 35), who said, "To allow States to interfere in the 'conflict' implied in proselytising by making proselytising a criminal offence would not only run counter to the strict neutrality which the State is required to maintain in this field but also create the danger of discrimination when there is one dominant religion."

State Neutrality and Religion in Europe

which respected the rights and freedoms of others.[21] On the facts of the case, it found Greece to be in breach of the convention when it convicted the applicant, a member of the Jehovah's Witnesses, for unlawful proselytism.

Twelve years later, its approach had changed subtly but significantly. In the case of *Leyla Sahin v. Turkey*, which concerned a ban on wearing head coverings in a Turkish university, the court, while quoting verbatim its famous phrases from the *Kokkinakis* case, went on to say,[22] "The Court has frequently emphasised the State's role as the neutral and impartial organiser of the exercise of various religions, faiths and beliefs, and stated that this role is conducive to public order, religious harmony and tolerance in a democratic society." In what is possibly an even more trenchant statement of this approach, in its Grand Chamber judgment in *Lautsi v. Italy*, the court observed that[23] "states have responsibility for ensuring, neutrally and impartially, the exercise of various religions, faiths and beliefs. Their role is to help maintain public order, religious harmony and tolerance in a democratic society, particularly between opposing groups.... That concerns both relations between believers and non-believers and relations between the adherents of various religions, faiths and beliefs." The judgments of the European court are littered with references to these two ideas—that of the primordial importance of the freedom of religion or belief by the individual to the flourishing of democratic society as set out in *Kokkinakis*, and the responsibility of the state to ensure that religious differences do not spill over into tensions which fracture the harmony of society, as reflected in *Leyla Sahin*, *Lautsi* and many others.[24] It is easy to see in these two contrasting strands of thought reflections of the differences of approach evidenced by the Augsburg/Westphalian and individualist human rights approaches to addressing questions of religion and belief—and their underlying rationales for doing so.

---

[21] Kokkinakis v. Greece (n. 11), paras. 48–50. On this aspect of the case, see Brett Scharffs, "*Kokkinakis* and the Narratives of Proper and Improper Proselytizing," in *European Court of Human Rights*, (n. 6), ch. 7.

[22] Leyla Sahin v. Turkey [GC], no. 44774/98, ECHR 2005-XI, para. 107.

[23] Lautsi and Others v. Italy (n. 10), para. 60.

[24] See, for example, the cases cited in n. 10 above. Barely a case concerning Article 9 (of which there are now several hundreds) fails to refer, directly or indirectly, to one or, more usually, both of these ideas.

These tensions have rarely played out in more tortuous a fashion than in the subsequent case of *S.A.S. v. France*, concerning the legitimacy of the French ban on the wearing of full-face coverings in public—in effect, the so-called "Burka Ban." In an agonizingly handwringing judgment in 2014, quoting all the above passages from *Kokkinakis*, *Leyla Sahin*, and many more cases of a similar ilk,[25] the court finally concluded that prohibiting the wearing of religiously inspired clothing which masked the face could be justified, accepting that the French government was entitled to take the view that[26] "the voluntary and systematic concealment of the face is problematic because it is quite simply incompatible with the fundamental requirements of 'living together' in French society" and that "the systematic concealment of the face in public places, contrary to the ideal of fraternity...falls short of the minimum requirement of civility that is necessary for social interaction." As a result, the court found that "the impugned ban can be regarded as justified in its principle solely in so far as it seeks to guarantee the conditions of 'living together.'"[27] This seems to permit the state to act in ways which are inimical to the religious freedoms of the individual when, in its assessment, doing so will lessen broader communal tensions. At least in 1555 under the Peace of Augsburg, those so disadvantaged were accorded the right to move elsewhere to a place where they might be better able to practice their religion and act in accordance with their beliefs, which appears not to be the case some 460 years later.[28]

---

[25] Though interestingly not *Lautsi*, which has rarely been cited in subsequent cases.

[26] S.A.S. v. France (n. 10), para. 141.

[27] Ibid., para 142. "Living together" is an English translation of the "vivre ensemble." See also para. 154, confirming that the ban was also proportionate under the circumstances of the case. Predictably, a vast and largely critical literature developed swiftly around this judgment. For a well-balanced exploration of its practical impact, see Megan Pearson, "What Happened to 'Vivre Ensemble?'": Developments after *SAS v. France*" 10 *Oxford Journal of Law and Religion* (2021): 185–205, https://doi.org/10.1093/ojlr/rwab017

[28] Cf. Myriam Hunter-Henin, *Why Religious Freedom Matters for Democracy: Comparative Reflections from Britain and France for a Democratic "Vivre Ensemble,"* (Oxford: Hart Publishing, 2020), which argues, in effect, that courts should adopt a broad, inclusive approach to what is required to achieve the "vivre ensemble" in order to ensure sufficient space for the exercise of the rights of individuals. The resonances of the tensions addressed by Peace of Augsburg are unmistakable.

State Neutrality and Religion in Europe

At least rhetorically, however, the difference is that when acting to reduce communal tensions, the state is not meant to be partial as between religions. This flows from the court's insistence that it is to be "neutral" and "impartial" on matters of religion or belief.[29] To continue the comparison with the position under the Treaty of Augsburg (slightly tongue in cheek), while in 1555 Lutherans might have been subjected to restrictions in a territory under the authority of a secular Catholic ruler simply because they were Lutherans (and vice versa), that would not be possible under the approach of the ECHR in the *S.A.S.* case. What would have to be shown is that placing restrictions on Lutherans rather than on Catholics would be the best way of ensuring the "vivre ensemble" within the territory in question. Then it might be "neutral" and "impartial"—though doubtless the Lutherans might well consider it to be neither.

It is this, then, that becomes the defining hallmark of the current European jurisprudential approach to the freedom of religion or belief: that the court is to take an "uber-Olympian" approach in which it divests itself of all interests other than its adoption of a disinterested attitude to the freedom. It seeks to solve the problem of religion by simply transcending it, and this is achieved (a) by refusing to take a view concerning the legitimacy of any particular form of religion or belief[30] and (b) by insisting upon the neutrality of states in relation to all forms of religion or belief.[31] It then adds for good measure that since there is no European consensus on such matters, states are to enjoy an increasingly broad margin of appreciation to craft their own solutions in accordance with democratic principles.[32] In

---

[29] See the cases cited above.

[30] For an early example of this, see Manoussakis and Others v. Greece, September 26, 1996, *Reports of Judgments and Decisions*, 1996-IV, para. 47: "The right to freedom of religion as guaranteed under the Convention excludes any discretion on the part of the State to determine whether religious beliefs or the means used to express such beliefs are legitimate."

[31] See, for example, Hasan and Chaush v. Bulgaria [GC], no. 30985/96, ECHR 2000-XI, para. 78; SAS v. France (n. 10), para. 127.

[32] See, for example, SAS v. France (n. 10), para. 155 ("In matters of general policy, on which opinions within a democratic society may reasonably differ widely, the role of the domestic policy-maker should be given special weight.... In other words, France had a wide margin of appreciation in the present case.") In 2017, the court said, in "Orthodox Ohrid Archdiocese (Greek-Orthodox Ohrid Archdiocese of the Peć Patriarchy)" v. the former Yugoslav Republic of

short, and possibly taking a cue from Pontius Pilate, the court moves from handwringing to handwashing. It simply does not want to get involved in how states settle these conundrums if it can help it, provided only that those solutions can be projected as being driven by objective concerns rather than religious partiality. Except that everyone knows this is not really true. As will be seen, it is not correct to say that the court refuses to take a view concerning various forms of religion or belief. In consequence, it is certainly not "neutral" in its approach. Indeed, the court's projection of neutrality is often at variance with its own jurisprudence and, as a result, what it *says* is not what it *does*.

The myth of neutrality

Although the European court routinely says that states should be "neutral" in relation to religion, they are not. Virtually all states have some corpus of law which affects the manner in which the state interacts with religion to some degree,[33] and the very fact of engaging in discussion concerning the relationship between religion and the state assumes the significance of the underlying concepts. After all, one does not enter a relationship, or govern through law a relationship, with someone or something the very relevance of which one rejects. One might disagree, disapprove, or even deny the reality of religion, in the sense of asserting that the concept is all nonsense, make believe, the "opium of the people," and so on. But what one *cannot* deny—if a state defines a position or crafts some form of relationship between itself and religion—is that the very process of doing so involves an acknowledgment that there is within society a phenomenon of religion which is present, important enough, and real enough to warrant the

---

Macedonia (no. 3532/07, November 16, 2017, para. 95), that "States enjoy a wide margin of appreciation in the particularly delicate area of their relations with religious communities." The margin of appreciation is, however, endlessly malleable. Cf. İzzettin Doğan and Others v. Turkey [GC], no. 62649/10, April 26, 2016, para 132 where the same general approach resulted in the State having in that case only "*some* margin of appreciation in choosing the forms of cooperation with the various religious communities" (emphasis added). On such inconsistencies and possible resultant dangers, see Stephanie Berry, "Avoiding Scrutiny? The Margin of Appreciation and Religious Freedom," in *European Court of Human Rights*, (n. 6) ch. 5.

[33] For discussion and examples, see text below at n. 76.

State Neutrality and Religion in Europe

political community's engagement with it. Irrespective of the nature and content of that engagement, this is not a position of neutrality; it may not be taking sides, but it is certainly taking a view. As a result, there is not the slightest prospect of a state being neutral, in this thinnest of senses, to the concept of religion. A state which engages in the regulation of its relationship with religion cannot be a state which is taking a neutral stance to the idea of religion—it is recognizing it as something to be engaged with.

Much the same can be said of the relationship between human rights and religion, which is as contested as the relationship between the state and religion, if not more so.[34] At some level, this is odd, given that religious thought has long been the inspiration for much of what is now human rights law,[35] and indeed international law itself.[36] Although some modern-era human rights documents expressly acknowledge religious underpinnings—for example, the 1960 Canadian Bill of Rights[37]—most do not, and the difficulties are well illustrated by the ultimately unsuccessful attempts to do so in the preamble of the Universal Declaration of Human Rights.[38] What is striking, however, is that while the recognition of those religious underpinnings has proven difficult to acknowledge, the idea that the freedom of religion should be recognized as a human right within such

---

[34] See, for example, Winnifred Sullivan, *The Impossibility of Religious Freedom* (Princeton, NJ: Princeton University Press, 2018).

[35] See, for example, Linde Lindqvist, *Religious Freedom and the Universal Declaration of Human Rights* (Cambridge: Cambridge University Press, 2017). For a provocative exploration of the relationship, see Samuel Moyn, *Christian Human Rights* (Philadelphia: University of Pennsylvania Press, 2015).

[36] See, for example, Norman Bentwich, *The Religious Foundations of Internationalism* (London: George Allen and Unwin, 1933); Mark W Janis and Carolyn Evans, *Religion and International Law* (Leiden, NL: Nijhoff/Brill, 2004); Martti Koskenniemi, Monica Garcia-Salmones Rovira, and Paolo Amorosa, *International Law and Religion* (Oxford: Oxford University Press, 2017); *Christianity and International Law*, eds. Pamela Slotte and John D Haskell (Cambridge: Cambridge University Press, 2021).

[37] S.C. 1960, c. 44.

[38] See Mary Ann Glendon, *A World Made New: Eleanor Roosevelt and the Universal Declaration of Human Rights* (New York: Random House, 2001), 154–55.

statements has been largely uncontested.[39] Indeed, its inclusion was long ago considered "an easy case," even if further normative development has been very difficult to achieve.

It is routinely—and rightly—pointed out that human rights protection is not limited to forms of religious belief but is to the freedom of "thought, conscience and religion," and there is no special privileging of religion within this. Indeed, the *Kokkinakis* case describes the right as a "precious asset" for "atheists, agnostics, sceptics and the unconcerned"[40] and the concept of "religion or belief" is itself to be understood in a broad, inclusive fashion.[41] Nevertheless, this runs the risk of downplaying the significance of the reference to religion by stressing that it is not *only* about religion, or forms of religious-like beliefs. To say that the right is "not just about religion" does not mean that it is "not really about religion," although this does seem at times to be the implication. International human rights law obviously does "protect" religion.

As with the regulation of relations between the state and religion, this has one irreducible consequence: irrespective of its meaning and content, the very fact that international human rights law requires that states respect the freedom of religion or belief means that states cannot be (or ought not to be) "neutral" about religion. Similarly, and just as it is not "neutral" with regard to the other rights which it sets out, or with regard to democracy, the rule of law and other foundational assumptions which underpin the political project on which it is founded, it also cannot seriously claim to espouse such a position in relation to the idea of religion. Both states and the court have an obligation to uphold the freedom of religion or belief. As a result, not only can they not *be* "neutral" in relation to religion, they are required *not* to be. They are enjoined to the "pro" freedom of religion or belief. This does not mean that court or states must be "for" religion at the expense of other rights, or accord it any greater priority or protection than they would any other right within the human rights

---

[39] Indeed, it was recognized as one of the four "fundamental freedoms" in the Atlantic Charter, the precursor to the UN. See Evans (n. 2), 173–74.

[40] Kokkinakis v. Greece (n. 11), para. 31.

[41] See Carolyn Evans, "Pre-Kokkinakis case law of the European Court of Human Rights: Foreshadowing the Future," in *European Court of Human Rights*, (n. 6), ch. 1, p. 15.

State Neutrality and Religion in Europe

canon. It certainly means that they cannot be "against" religion as such.[42] But it means more than this. It means that there must be an acknowledgement of its significance and steps taken to secure the enjoyment of the freedom. Hostility cannot be replaced by mere indifference. Despite what is said about neutrality, this truth finds reflection in a number of ways within the jurisprudence of the court.

As has been seen, the *Kokkinakis* case famously set out the essence of why the freedom is of such importance, and it is worth looking at that statement in more detail. It addresses two distinct, though related, issues. The first concerns the significance of the freedom of thought, conscience, and religion to society as a whole. It says that "freedom of thought, conscience and religion is one of the foundations of a 'democratic society' within the meaning of the Convention," and then goes on to make the point that "the pluralism indissociable from a democratic society, which has been dearly won over the centuries, depends on it."[43] This may seem little more than hyperbolic rhetorical overkill, but when this pronouncement, made by a European court in Strasbourg, is placed in its geographic, historic, and conceptual setting, it takes on a rather different hue. As has already been mentioned, the defining moment in the development of the modern concept of statehood and its relationship to religion lies in the Treaties of Westphalia and their embracing of religious pluralism as a means of addressing religious discord.[44] It is entirely true to say that in the Central European setting, the emergence of modern democratic society is intimately linked to the espousal of religious pluralism, incrementally and painfully contested—"dearly contested," if one wills. This is no flight of

---

[42] To that extent, there is need for care when engaging discussions concerning the so-called "freedom from" religion: there is no right to be free from religion as such. The negative aspect of the freedom protects the right not to be forced to identify with a religion or belief, not to be insulated from it. See, for example, Perovy v. Russia, no. 47429/09, October 20, 2020, para: 73. "The values of pluralism and tolerance and the spirit of compromise and dialogue are indispensable in a democratic society and do not provide any religious group or individual with the right not to witness individual or collective manifestations of other religious or non-religious beliefs and convictions" (this concerning a young boy present at a religious ceremony in his municipal school).

[43] Kokkinakis v. Greece (n. 11), para. 31.

[44] See text above at n. 2. See also Derek Croxton, *Westphalia: The Last Christian Peace* (London: Palgrave Macmillan, 2015)

fancy, but a grounded reflection of the European reality, and not to be dismissed lightly.

The second element of the *Kokkinakis* statement concerns the personal significance of the freedom, which is generally mispresented. The court says that the freedom of thought, conscience, and religion "in its *religious dimension*" forms "one of the most vital elements that go to make up the identity of believers and their conception of life."[45] It then goes on to recognize that the freedom is also "a precious asset for atheists, agnostics, sceptics and the unconcerned." There is in this a recognition of the particular nature of *religious* belief and the heightened role that it plays in the life of believers. Whether it accords a similarly heightened role to protected patterns of thought and conscience which are so precious to others is a matter which could be debated but is hardly germane. What matters is that there is a clear recognition of the "heightened" significance of religious belief in the lives of religious believers, and that this is something which the court—and the state—is to respect.

When analysed in this way, the *Kokkinakis* statement seems to seek to reconcile the tensions noted earlier in this chapter concerning the focus of the protection of the freedom of religion: whether the predominant focus is to be upon addressing communal tensions or upon securing individual freedoms. Its very structure intertwines them both, attempting to draw them closer together and reducing (while not eliminating) the potential tension between them. Whether it succeeds in this lies well beyond the scope of this chapter and need not be considered further. The essential point is that the very attempt to do this has significant consequences, the chief of which is that it is just not credible for the court, or the state, to say, in effect, that religion is "so vitally important to democratic society and to the life of believers that we have no opinion on the topic." If neutrality precludes hostility, it also precludes indifference.

This is reflected in the relatively recent recognition that the freedom of religion or belief entails positive obligations. It is not enough that the state does not infringe upon the right; in appropriate cases, it is necessary for the state to facilitate the enjoyment of the right.[46] Article 9 is a relative

---

[45] Kokkinakis v. Greece (n. 11), para. 31 (emphasis added).

[46] See, for example, Eweida and Others v. the United Kingdom, nos. 48420/10 others, ECHR 2013, para. 84; İzzettin Doğan and Others v. Turkey

newcomer to the list of rights which carry positive obligations,[47] and the extent of those obligations remains uncertain, though they can be extensive. For example, in the recent case of *Abdullah Yalçın v. Turkey (no. 2)*, the applicant was an inmate in a high-security prison who requested, and was denied, permission to offer communal Friday prayers in a room within the prison to be provided for this purpose, which he claimed was required of him as a Muslim. The court concluded that the government had "failed to demonstrate that the domestic authorities weighed the competing interests at stake by adducing relevant and sufficient reasons in a manner that was compliant with their positive obligations under Article 9 of the Convention to guarantee the applicant's freedom to manifest his religion in community with others, namely by offering Friday prayers in prison."[48] To put it another way, the prison authorities had not shown good reason not to provide a room for the purposes of communal prayer at which the applicant could attend.

This is as clear an example of a positive obligation as one might ever see and shows the potential breadth of its application. Not only is the state not to be hostile to religion or disinterested in religion in high-security prisons, but, given its importance in the life of believers, it is to take steps to facilitate its practice. If the state cannot be "neutral" to the significance of religion in prisons, why should it be "neutral" to the significance of religion in the community at large? In short, religion is important, and human rights law recognizes this. In the light of this, it might well be asked what the court really means when it enjoins states to be "neutral and impartial" in relation to the freedom of religion or belief.

What does it mean to be "neutral"?

It might be objected that whether the state is or is not neutral to the idea of religion is not the real issue and that what matters is how the state responds to the *fact* of religion when undertaking its functions as a state. This immediately raises the question of what the legitimate functions of a

---

[GC] (n. 32) para. 96; Abdullah Yalçın v. Turkey (no. 2), no. 34417/10, June 14, 2022, para. 35.

[47] For an earlier example, but not using the language of positive obligations, see Members of the Gldani Congregation of Jehovah's Witnesses and Others v. Georgia, no. 71156/01, May 3, 2007.

[48] Abdullah Yalçın v. Turkey (no. 2) (n. 46), para. 35.

state with regard to religion actually are, this being the question at the root of the problem facing the court in the *Kokkinakis* case.

The ECHR has sometimes described the state as the "organizer" of religious life within a country[49]—which is palpably untrue. While it is certainly the case that the state has the authority to exercise power over activities of religious believers and religious bodies, this does not make it the "organizer" of religious life as such. It can make things easier or harder for religious believers and religious organizations, but it cannot "organize" their beliefs or the exercise of them. Indeed, the ECHR has itself made that clear by stressing that it is not the role of the state to determine the legitimacy or content of any religious belief, since doing so would be incompatible with its duty of neutrality and impartiality.[50] For some, this is what neutrality is all about—not *involving* oneself in religious matters; in cruder terms, it is all about minding one's own business, it being understood that disputes concerning religious matters are not the business of the state.[51]

Yet for approaching fifty years, the idea of neutrality in relation to matters concerning religion was unknown to the ECHR. Indeed, it was generally accepted that states need *not* be "neutral" as between religions: they most definitely *could* have views and preferences, and those views and preferences were routinely left unchallenged by the commission and the court provided individuals were left free to be able to hold and practice their own beliefs.[52] Even today, the court has never said that an established state church is impermissible from a convention perspective, and it accepts that states are able to determine the nature of their relationships with

---

[49] See, for example, Leyla Sahin v. Turkey (n. 22), para 107; S.A.S. v. France (n. 10), para 127; Izzettin Dogan v. Turkey (n. 32), para 107. See also Lautsi v. Italy [GC] (n. 10), para 60, where the court referred to the state's role as "ensuring, neutrally and impartially, the exercise of various religions, faiths and beliefs."

[50] See, for example, Eweida and Others v. the United Kingdom (n. 46), para 81; Mockutė v. Lithuania, no. 66490/09, February 27, 2018, para. 118; Centre of Societies for Krishna Consciousness in Russia and Frolov v. Russia (n. 10), para. 40.

[51] This is reflected in the more general idea of the autonomy of religious organizations, which is beyond the scope of this chapter.

[52] See, for example, the inadmissibility decision in Iglesia Bautista "El Salvador" and Jose Orga Moratilla v. Spain, January 11, 1992, European Commission of Human Rights, no. 17522/90.

State Neutrality and Religion in Europe

religions and religious organizations based on their various histories, traditions, and political philosophies.[53] So why does the question of the state being neutral in relation to such questions arise at all?

The seeds of change came in the case of *Hasan and Chaush v. Bulgaria*—a little more than twenty years ago—where the court found itself dealing with a case in which the state had, in effect, become embroiled in a dispute between two factions concerning leadership within the Muslim community in Bulgaria by virtue of its decision not to register as grand mufti the person chosen by that community, but a rival. Famously, it said that[54] "facts demonstrating a failure by the authorities to remain neutral in the exercise of their powers in this domain must lead to the conclusion that the State interfered with the believers' freedom to manifest their religion within the meaning of Article 9 of the Convention." This is the only mention of the word "neutrality" in the judgment. In its earlier consideration of the case, the European Commission on Human Rights produced an Article 31 Report (under the older convention procedures, which were about to be superseded) used the word three times, concluding that[55] "the executive branch of government in Bulgaria failed in its duty to remain neutral when confronted with a division in a religious community and, exceeding its powers, intervened unlawfully in the internal dispute of the Muslim religious community." This is a very thin basis on which to build a principle of religious neutrality within the jurisprudence of the ECHR. *Hasan and Chaush* says that the executive must exercise its powers in a neutral manner. This is a remarkably uncontroversial observation and would be equally applicable to the exercise of executive powers in relation to almost anything. In this case, it was a violation of the freedom of religion or belief which provided the context, but in and of itself, it is not

---

[53] Sindicatul "Păstorul cel Bun" v. Romania [GC], no. 2330/09, ECHR 2013, para 138; Fernández Martínez v. Spain [GC], no. 56030/07, ECHR 2014, para. 130; İzzettin Doğan and Others v. Turkey (n. 32). paras. 112, 163; Magyar Keresztény Mennonita Egyház and Others v. Hungary, nos. 70945/11 and 8 others, ECHR 2014, para. 108. See also Francois Tulkens, "The European Convention on Human Rights and Church-State Relations Pluralism vs. Pluralism" (2008–2009) 30 *Cardozo L. Rev.* 2575.

[54] Hasan and Chaush v. Bulgaria [GC] (n. 31) para. 78.

[55] Fikri Sali Hasan and Ismail Ahmed Chaush v. Bulgaria, Report of the European Commission, no. 30985/96, October 29, 1999, para. 94. See also paras. 86 and 87.

KEEPING THE FAITH

saying anything of particular significance about the relationship between religion, religions, and the state. That all comes later, misrepresenting what *Hasan and Chaush* was really saying.

This is not the place to recount the development of the case law, which is well known. It suffices to say that through a series of landmark cases, the court seemed to arrive at the position that it was the duty of the state not only *to act* neutrally when exercising its powers in respect of religious bodies, but *to be* neutral and impartial in relation to matters concerning religion, and, finally, also to *be seen* as being so. And as with any observational phenomenon, neutrality, like beauty, is in the eye of the beholder: if one sees something which one thinks means that the state is endorsing or favouring a particular religion or belief, then to you, the observer, it is. Others may see it differently. This raises the question of whether it is appropriate for a court, in the exercise of its jurisdiction relating to the protection of human rights, to decide who is right or who is wrong, when what is really at issue concerns perceptions rather than facts or other matters capable of objective determination.[56]

The "road crash" case that best exemplifies the tensions inherent in the developing jurisprudence are the judgments of the chamber and grand chamber of the court in *Lautsi v. Italy*.[57] The issue at the heart of the case was simple enough: does the presence of a cross in a municipal school classroom mean that the state is not being neutral and impartial in matters of religion or belief? Well, of course, it does, unless you think that it doesn't. Or is it the other way around: it doesn't, unless you think that it

---

[56] In an early case concerning a child being required to attend what his parents considered to be a militaristic event, the court seemed happy to substitute its characterization of the occasion for that of the parents. See Valsamis v. Greece, December 18, 1996, *Reports of Judgments and Decisions* 1996-VI, paras 31–33. Cf the recent case of Perovy v. Russia (n. 42) in which the court felt there was no evidence to suggest that any real negative consequences had resulted from a seven-year-old boy being present at a "one off" religious ceremony organized at a school. However, the court is clear that it will not challenge an applicant's view concerning whether their wearing of particular forms of clothing or symbols is or is not a manifestation of their religion or beliefs. See Eweida v. UK (n. 46), paras. 81–82; S.A.S. v. France (n. 10), paras. 55–56.

[57] See generally *The Lautsi Papers: Multidisciplinary Reflections on Religious Symbols in the Public School Classroom*, ed. Jeroen Temperman (Leiden, NL: Nijhoff/Brill, 2012).

292

State Neutrality and Religion in Europe

does? And therein lies the difference between the approach of the chamber and of the grand chamber in that case: for the chamber, the presence of the cross embodied the state endorsement of Roman Catholicism, and so its presence breached the rights of the applicant;[58] for the grand chamber, the cross was just "there," passively doing nothing other than just being there, and so its presence did not amount to a violation of the applicant's rights.[59] Setting aside questions of metaphysics and the mystery of religion for a moment, it seems fairly obvious that it was, in fact, doing both. It literally depends on who was looking at it. Ultimately, the grand chamber is telling the applicant that it does not see what they are seeing. And like it or not, that is taking sides.

Such debates are currently commonplace in the UK, as they are elsewhere, with contentious discussions taking place concerning the removal of statues and other commemorations of historical figures which are now associated with slavery, colonialism, and empire. Taking something away is at least as much of a symbol or symbolic act as leaving something alone, as those toppling the monuments of others have known since the dawn of recorded history. In the university city of Bristol, a jury refused to convict those who admitted to pulling down a statue of the slave trader Edward Colston and throwing it into the waters of Bristol dock of criminal damage. The now empty plinth is a very powerful statement indeed, as would a wall from which a cross had been removed. There is not a lot of space for "neutrality" here. [60]

The problem with the chamber decision in *Lautsi* was that it seemed to suggest that neutrality and impartiality involved cleansing the public space of the trappings of religion on the grounds that those trappings

---

[58] Lautsi v. Italy, no. 30814/06, November 3, 2009, paras. 56–57.

[59] Lautsi and Others v. Italy [GC] (n. 10), para. 72: "Furthermore, a crucifix on a wall is an essentially passive symbol and this point is of importance in the Court's view, particularly having regard to the principle of neutrality. It cannot be deemed to have an influence on pupils comparable to that of didactic speech or participation in religious activities."

[60] See R v. Graham and Others [2022], Bristol Crown Court, unreported, January 9, 2022. The incident involved a statue of Edward Colston. Daubed with paint, the statue is now in a local museum, lying horizontally as "fallen." See also the controversy concerning the Rustat memorial at Jesus College, Oxford, permission of which to remove was denied by a court (*Re the Rustat Memorial, Jesus College Cambridge*, [2022] ECC Ely 2).

might cause offence.[61] This has only to be stated to be seen as untenable. There is no right to be insulated from things which cause offence; indeed, the court has made it very clear for very many years that there is freedom to say things which may cause offence.[62] If causing offence alone is not sufficient to require someone not to speak, how can it be sufficient alone to justify the removal of a cross, or of a statue? One cannot have a classroom in which there both is and is not a cross, plinth on which there both is and is not a statue. There must be a choice as to which it is to be. Perhaps what neutrality means here is "stepping back" from preconceptions of what things may or may not mean, to help create a space for debate. It can be a tool to facilitate public discourse on contentious matters within the democratic space, but it does not describe or dictate the outcome.

Neutrality and Sovereignty

There is a relationship between neutrality and choice. The ECHR, like all international human rights instruments, seeks to hold in tension two fundamental pressures: that of the "universal" and the "local." How does one hold firm to the universal values of human rights protection while at the same time respecting the social norms and practices which characterize a particular society? Human rights are enjoyed in a context, and an application which is shorn of context is likely to result in poor application, or to be no application at all. Rights are not enjoyed in a vacuum, and the local matters when determining what the enjoyment of—and violation of—a right looks like.

For the international lawyer, the local is bounded by the bands of statehood. While everyone may share a common humanity and human dignity, we do not all share a common polity. As a result, an individual's experience of their rights, and of rights protection, is shaped by the

---

[61] See also Leigh (n. 7), p. 62, who argues that this "would be tantamount to the Convention-sponsored imposition across the continent of secularism in the name of neutrality."

[62] Handyside v. the United Kingdom, December 7, 1976, Series A no. 24, para. 49, confirming that the freedom of expression is "not only to 'information' or 'ideas' that are favourably received or regarded as inoffensive or as a matter of indifference, but also to those that offend, shock or disturb the State or any sector of the population. Such are the demands of that pluralism, tolerance and broad-mindedness without which there is no 'democratic society.'"

collective judgments of the political communities of which they form a part, and an approach to rights that pays no heed to this is an approach which is doomed to fail. This does not mean that the individual is to submit to the whims and impositions of the political majority or the politically dominant. The entire point of human rights law is to ensure that this does not happen. However, human rights protection needs to be respectful of collective decisions properly taken when seeking to ensure the protection of rights and freedoms. Under the EHCR, this used to be the territory of the margin of appreciation,[63] and now, perhaps, of subsidiarity.[64] Neither removes the obligation on the state to protect the rights of those subject to its jurisdiction, or to be subject to scrutiny. But it may very well affect what such protection looks like.

There is no magic here. For example, what a person wears may legitimately give rise to fears or concerns in others, and where that is proven to be the case, then its wearing might properly be restricted in order to protect the rights and freedoms of others. But this does not justify an *a priori* assumption that the wearing of something which identifies you as having a religious belief has such an effect. Many may find it difficult to understand why the state might be thought to be in some way endorsing a particular religious belief simply because one of its employees wears something which betokens their faith: if an employee wears a jacket with a designer label or logo, does that mean that the employer is endorsing or supporting the designer or the manufacturer? But if a state, through democratic means, considers it inappropriate for its public servants to wear religiously inspired clothing or symbols, then it may be that this point of view just has to be respected, even if others consider it irrational.[65]

---

[63] See text above at n. 32 and see Andreas Follesdal, "Appreciating the Margin of Appreciation," in Adam Etinson, *Human Rights: Moral or Political?* (Oxford: Oxford University Press, 2018), ch. 8.

[64] The principle of subsidiarity has recently been introduced into the preamble of the European Convention on Human Rights by virtue of the entry into force in August 2021 of Protocol 15 to European Convention on Human Rights (June 24, 2013, ETS no. 213). The influence of subsidiarity on the jurisprudence of the European Court of Human Rights has, however, already been evident for many years now. See Alastair Mowbray, "Subsidiarity and the European Convention on Human Rights," *Human Rights Law Review*, 15 (2015): 313–41.

[65] This would appear to be the best approach to the early and much criticized case of Dahlab v. Switzerland (dec.), no. 42393/98, ECHR 2001-V, in which the

The limits of this approach appear to have been stretched to breaking point by the court in the *S.A.S* case, mentioned above, concerning general restrictions on full-face coverings in the public space.[66] Ultimately, this reflects a choice made by the state concerning how it wishes to approach the manifestation of religious belief, democratically and within its sphere of sovereignty, and which has been subject to challenge and scrutiny from a human rights perspective. Whatever one might think of the outcome, the central point is that it underlines the extent to which the state has a choice. It does not have to be neutral on this. It can choose a more (or less) secularized state environment—and this has consequences for the exercise of rights. Provided the choice of that "environment" is the product of an exercise of public reason, then it is reasonable that it should provide the context in which the exercise of the freedom of religion or belief is examined. For example, many, if not most, schools in some European countries are religious or faith-based in one way or another. In other European countries, none are permitted within the public education system, or indeed at all.[67] Both approaches are both justifiable and unjustifiable, non-transposable, and neither is neutral.

This does not amount to an argument in favour of the seemingly hands-off approach famously adopted by Judge Martens in the foundational *Kokkinakis* case questioning the legitimacy of the state involving itself in matters concerning the freedom of religion—as if it were off limits in some ways.[68] Nor does it endorse the equally problematic approach taken by another dissenter in that famous case, calling for the state to stand in solidarity with the church against those who seek to seduce its adherents into other ways.[69] Neutrality eschews such extremes. It is not the role of the state to proselytize. But it does not demand indifference and neither

---

dismissal of a nursery school teacher for wearing a headscarf was upheld, despite there being no evidence of its either having caused harm or even being objected to by children or their parents.

[66] See text at n. 25 above.

[67] See, for example, *Religious Schools in Europe: Institutional Opportunities and Contemporary Challenges*, eds. Marcel Maussen, Floris Vermeulen, Michael Merry, and Veit Bader (London: Routledge, 2018).

[68] See n. 20 above. One is reminded of the famous—infamous—comment made by Alistair Campbell, reminding the then-prime minister Tony Blair that "we don't do God."

[69] See n. 19 above.

State Neutrality and Religion in Europe

does it eschew preference, provided that this does not stand in the way of the exercise of religious freedoms by others. Systems which are secular, laic, separatist are all understood to be compatible with the idea of neutrality. It follows as night follows day that so too must a system which accepts a connection between religion and the state, and, as has been seen, this is indeed the case.[70] It is difficult to see how neutrality can do otherwise without surrendering its claim of being neutral. But where does this leave "neutrality"?

The Partial but Neutral State

The essence of neutrality under the European Convention on Human Rights does not lie in the nature of the relationship between the state and religion or belief but in the manner in which the state approaches the exercise of the right.[71] If the state, whatever its pattern of religion/state relations, fails when exercising its functions as a state to be "neutral" between different religions, then there is a breach of the obligation of neutrality. This, in essence, is what occurred in *Hasan and Chaush*, the starting point of these debates and discussions. The case concerned the refusal of the Bulgarian authorities to recognize the decision of the majority within the Muslim community concerning their choice of leader and their preference for another, which, in effect, prevented the chosen leader from acting as such. It is easy to see why the key statement of principle was couched in the language of neutrality, but it might easily have been viewed as a question about the unlawful exercise of executive authority—for that is what it was—without referring to neutrality at all.

Despite what the court has said, states are not required to be neutral and impartial as between religions or belief systems when framing their laws. They are, however, required to act in a neutral and impartial way when implementing the framework which they have put in place—indeed, the rule of law itself demands this. The question of the compatibility of that framework with the freedom of religion or belief is a different question. In other words, neutrality means that the state must be impartial in

---

[70] See n. 53 above.

[71] See Julie Ringelheim, "Rights, Religion and the Public Sphere: The European Court of Human Rights in Search of a Theory," in *Law, State and Religion in the New Europe*, eds. Lorenzo Zucca and Camil Ungureanu (Cambridge: Cambridge University Press, 2012), 290.

KEEPING THE FAITH

the application of laws and the exercise of its power, but the legal framework itself need not be impartial, provided its partiality does not prevent the effective exercise of the freedom of religion or belief by all those subject to the jurisdiction of the state in question.

When it comes to the content of that legal framework, neutrality is a something of a chimera. While it is not the role of the court to determine the truth or otherwise of a particular form of religion or belief, or to prevent individuals from adhering to beliefs of their choice, it is just not true to say that the state is unable to hold a view concerning certain forms of belief, and to be able to reflect its view in its approach to them.[72] Two relatively recent judgments of the court, though there are many others, can be used to illustrate this.

The *Ancient Baltic Religious Association Romuva v. Lithuania*[73] case concerned a refusal to register the applicant association of pagan believers as a nontraditional religious association, which the court found to be in breach of the convention. The key point, however, is that relevant law, like so many others in Europe, has different criteria for recognition and registration,[74] and the legitimacy of this was neither challenged by the applicants nor questioned by the court. The case turned on whether those responsible for the decision (in this case, the members of the Lithuanian Parliament) had acted "fairly" and in accordance with sufficiently well-

---

[72] See, for example, Leela Förderkreis e.V. and others v. Germany, no. 58911/00 and others, November 6, 2008, where the court upheld the legitimacy of the state warning young people of the dangers of becoming associated with the Osho movement. This was distinguished in the recent case of Centre of Societies for Krishna Consciousness in Russia and Frolov v. Russia (n. 10), para. 41, on the ground that in this later case, "the exclusion of new or minority religious movements had been embedded in the set-up of the project from its inception"; that is, it had not examined the case in sufficient depth to warrant speaking out against it. The court does not say that it could not do so.

[73] Ancient Baltic religious association "Romuva" v. Lithuania (n. 12).

[74] There were three categories—traditional religious associations, nontraditional religious associations recognized by the state, and other religious associations. Traditional and nontraditional associations enjoy special privileges from those enjoyed by other religious associations. The applicant was a religious association but wished to become a nontraditional association. Nine traditional associations were automatically recognized as such by law (ibid., paras 4–5 and 56–57).

State Neutrality and Religion in Europe

established criteria when assessing whether the association complied with the relevant legislative requirements, and whether they had been improperly influenced by prejudice and bias (or worse) when doing so. The court concluded that "the members of the Seimas who voted against the granting of State recognition did not remain neutral and impartial in exercising their regulatory powers."[75] In other words, it was the application of the process, rather than the underlying approach to registration, that resulted in a violation. The law itself, which was manifestly far from being neutral as between different forms of religion or belief, was not seen as being in any way problematic.

Many other cases have upheld, expressly or implicitly, the legitimacy of registration frameworks which on any objective analysis are "not neutral" as regards religions, since they make it far more onerous for some to achieve a given legal status, and with it rights and opportunities as a religious organization, than others.[76] This can only be justifiable if the law permitting this is not itself considered to violate the freedom of religion or belief of the followers of such religions. And it seems clear that this is not necessarily the case. Of course, some such laws *may* do so, if they have the effect of preventing the effective exercise of the freedom of religion or belief. But that does not turn on whether those laws are or are not "neutral"— even if the outcome can be described that way.

Similarly, the recent case of *De Wilde v. Netherlands*[77] offers a timely reminder that states are entitled to determine that some forms of religious belief—like some forms of nonreligious views or belief[78]—are just not

---

[75] Ibid., para. 147.

[76] See, for example, Religionsgemeinschaft der Zeugen Jehovas and Others v. Austria, no. 40825/98, July 31, 2008, para. 96–98, where the court accepted that requiring some, but not all, religious organizations to wait ten years before being able to seek registration may be acceptable under certain circumstances. See also Savez crkava "Riječ života" and Others v. Croatia, no. 7798/08, December 9, 2010, paras. 85–93; Magyar Keresztény Mennonita Egyház and Others v. Hungary (n. 53), para. 100; İzzettin Doğan and Others v. Turkey [GC] (n. 32), para. 163, 175; and many others.

[77] Hermina Geertruida de Wilde v. the Netherlands, no. 9476/19, November 9, 2021.

[78] See ECHR Article 17, which provides that "Nothing in [the] Convention may be interpreted as implying for any State, group or person any right to engage in any activity or perform any act aimed at the destruction of any of the rights and

worthy of respect in a democratic society and so do not engage the freedom of religion or belief at all.[79] In this case, the belief system in question was "Pastafarianism." It is widely asserted that "Pastafarianism" is not actually a religion, but rather a parody of religion:[80] but if some people mistake the parody for the real thing, or find spiritual meaning in the parody, then who are we to deny them?[81] The European court decided that the state was indeed entitled to make such a judgment and to refuse to recognize the legitimacy of the system of belief.[82] It hardly needs to be pointed out that

---

freedoms set forth herein or at their limitation to a greater extent than is provided for in the Convention." In Norwood v. the United Kingdom (dec.), no. 23131/03, ECHR 2004-XI, it was said that "the general purpose of Article 17 is to prevent individuals or groups with totalitarian aims from exploiting in their own interests the principles enunciated by the Convention." As a result, the Convention offered no protection to those whose "words and images on the poster amounted to a public expression of attack on all Muslims in the United Kingdom. Such a general, vehement attack against a religious group, linking the group as a whole with a grave act of terrorism, is incompatible with the values proclaimed and guaranteed by the Convention, notably tolerance, social peace and non-discrimination."

[79] Cf. in December 2016 the UK Charity Commission determination that the Jedi Temple could not be registered as a charity since it did not display the characteristics of a religion for the purposes of charity law (Charity Commission for England and Wales, The Temple of The Jedi Order—Application for Registration, Decision of the Commission, December 16, 2016, para 14). However, they also made it clear that "the Commission...is not concerned with the truth or otherwise of the beliefs in question but will not recognize as a religion everything that chooses to call itself a religion" (para. 8).

[80] Hermina Geertruida de Wilde v. the Netherlands (n. 77), paras. 30–31.

[81] One might recall the ending of the musical *The Book of Mormon*, in which a group chose to find enlightenment in the rather different contents of the "Book of Arnold."

[82] Hermina Geertruida de Wilde v. the Netherlands (n. 77), paras. 54–55: "In these circumstances, and in particular in view of the very aims for which the Pastafarian movement was founded, the Court does not consider Pastafarianism to be a 'religion' or 'belief' within the meaning of Article 9 of the Convention. Consequently, the wearing of a colander by followers of Pastafarianism cannot be considered a manifestation of a 'religion' or 'belief' within the meaning of Article 9, even if the person concerned submits that he or she chooses to do so out of a conviction that is genuine and sincerely held.... It follows that Article 9 can apply neither to the 'Church of the Flying Spaghetti Monster' nor to those who claim to profess its doctrines."

State Neutrality and Religion in Europe

this is not really being "neutral"; it is the state taking a view concerning the legitimacy, integrity, and worth of a purported belief system and acting accordingly. Rightly, this decision had been subject to challenge and scrutiny before the European court, but the view of the state prevailed. One might say that Pastafarianism "is cooked"—at least in the Netherlands, it seems. Of course, others elsewhere can take different views, just as they have of many other religious groups throughout the course of European history. And that can hardly be described as being neutral.

Conclusion

It may be that it would be better to think less about the word and more about its meaning. States *are* entitled to make judgments about the ordering of religious life within their jurisdictions. These judgements are entitled to take account of a whole range of factors and do not have to be neutral in the sense of impartial. States can (as they do) have preferences. But the manner in which those preferences are expressed in law and in practice must not encroach upon the ability of others to follow their own religions or beliefs in accordance with their constitutional and convention rights. Difference is justifiable, but discrimination in the enjoyment of the right is not. Likewise, when implementing a legislative framework which meets these criteria, the state must ensure that it does so fairly and without bias or discrimination—let us say neutrally. This is what the ECHR requires of states, and it is a very great deal.

This certainly leaves much to the discursive space within each state to work out what this means in practice, but this is as it should be. It is not about "injecting" neutrality into the protective system, it is about examining the protection of the freedom of religion or belief in a neutral way, which is a very different and more positive and productive approach. Neutrality is central to the engagement of the state with religion, religions, and belief. But it is a tool, not an outcome; a means, and not an end. Otherwise, it becomes, at best, a means of avoiding and, at worst, one of rejecting one's responsibility to respect, protect, and fulfil the freedom of religion or belief—the vital asset of democratic society.

This also stands squarely in the light of European thought concerning the relationship between religions and the state, which has slowly developed over the last 500 years, replacing exclusion with inclusion but in a variegated manner reflecting the local political communities which they address. The framers of the Peace of Augsburg might well be shocked at the patterns of religious belief in Europe today, but they would probably recognize the tools used to accommodate them. What they would never recognize, however, is the idea of neutrality toward religion—and neither does European human rights law, if properly understood.

Religious Freedom in the Post-Nation-State: The Canadian Experiment

Mark Parent[1]

Along with the various countries that are members of the European Union, the country of Canada has often been labelled a postnational state. In an interview with a reporter from the *New York Times Magazine* only six days after his election as prime minister, Justin Trudeau claimed that Canada was the world's first postnational state: "There is no core identity, no mainstream in Canada. There are shared values—openness, respect, compassion, willingness to work hard, to be there for each other, to search for equality and justice. Those qualities are what make us the first postnational state."[2]

Trudeau's description of Canada as a postnational state did not elicit much attention at the time. In an article written some two years later, Canadian novelist Charles Foran observed that Trudeau's remarks "failed to cause a ripple," noting that when he mentioned his assertion to Michael Bach, Germany's minister for European Affairs at the time, Bach was "astounded," insisting that "no European politician would say such a thing...the thought was too radical."[3]

Part of the reason for this lack of reaction to Trudeau's comments is that others have made the same assertion about Canada, long before he did. Almost forty years earlier, in a speech to the Royal Society of Canada, Northrop Frye noted "there is no Canadian way of life, no hundred per cent Canadian, no ancestral figures corresponding to Washington or

---

[1] I am indebted to Earle Illsley, who helped with research for this article, although the conclusions are mine alone.

[2] Guy Lawson, "Trudeau's Canada, Again," *New York Times Magazine*, 2015.

[3] Charles Foran, "The Canada Experiment: Is This the Worlds First 'Postnational' Country?," *The Guardian*, 2017.

KEEPING THE FAITH

Franklin or Jefferson, no eighteenth-century self-evident certainties about human rights, no symmetrically laid out country."[4]

Such comments are not without their critics, with pundits claiming that it would be more accurate to label Canada as a "plurinational" or "multiversal" state rather than a postnational one.[5] However, the term "postnational" has seeped into public discourse in a way that other descriptors have not, and so, in spite of the fact that the word "post" says more about what Canada isn't rather than what it is, it is worth examining how and why Canada can be labelled a postnational state. Moreover, since the formation of the nation-state in Europe in the mid-1600's was so integrally connected with religion and religious freedom, the question must be asked and examined as to what impact a postnational Canada has, and might have, on religion and on religious freedom.

The Nation-State

The Peace of Westphalia, the name commonly used for the treaties of Munster and Osnabrück signed in 1648, is often credited with bringing into being the modern nation-state. However, as important as it was at the time, it is only in retrospect that such a claim can be made, as the Peace of Westphalia simply marked the end of the political ideal of the Holy Roman Empire. In fact, the concept of national sovereignty known as the "Westphalian construct" has origins earlier in the German nationalist sentiment, which allowed the Protestant reformer Martin Luther to challenge the theological hegemony of the Roman Catholic Church. Moreover, key characteristics that define the modern nation-state were not fully articulated until after the Peace of Westphalia.[6] Indeed, the Peace of Westphalia did not even mark the end of the religiously inspired wars which spanned

---

[4] Northrop Frye, "National Consciousness in Canadian Culture," in *Divisions on a Ground : Essays on Canadian Culture*, ed. James Polk (Toronto: Anansi, 1982). Frye presumably feels that the roles of Canadian political figures such as MacDonald, Laurier, and Cartier are not equivalent to his American triumvirate.

[5] Thibault Biscahie, "Beyond the Mosaic: Justin Trudeau and the Postnational Chimera," *London Journal of Canadian Studies* 34/3 (2019).

[6] Derek Croxton, "The Peace of Westphalia of 1648 and the Origins of Sovereignty," *The International History Review* 21/3 (1999).

the fifteenth to eighteenth centuries beginning with the Oldcastle Revolt of 1413 and ending with the Toggenburg War of 1712.

Nevertheless, with the demise of the Holy Roman Empire, which was based on a common religion, a new political ideal had to be forged. The Westphalian construct is used in international studies to demarcate the end of one political system and the genesis of another. In the new political system, which grew out of the Peace of Westphalia, the concept of a nation held together by common ethnic, cultural, and religious ties was fused with state sovereignty, resulting in the modern nation-state.[7]

The Nation-State and Religious Freedom

With the birth of the nation-state, the role of religion was radically redefined. The first stage in this redefinition was the expansion of religious freedom beyond that of the Roman Catholic faith. The Peace of Augsburg in 1555 brought hostilities between Lutherans and Roman Catholics to an end by establishing the principle *cuius regio, eius religio*.[8] At first, this principle applied only to Roman Catholicism and Lutheranism but, in time, was extended to Calvinistic expression of Protestantism and then, due to the Anabaptist movement (the third wing of the Protestant Reformation), to other Protestant groups as well, especially in countries where Protestant Christianity was the official faith.[9]

The second stage in the redefinition of the roles of religion and political power coincided with the growing influence of the nation-state. Religious power increasingly became subservient to state power while remaining important as one of the main components of the concept of

---

[7] Max Weber defines the state as a community that successfully monopolizes physical force within a given territory. Max Weber, Hans Heinrich Gerth, and C. Wright Mills, *From Max Weber: Essays in Sociology* (New York: Oxford University Press, 1946). This results in the concept of citizenship as being one of exclusion where one can only be a citizen of one country and where there is a sharp distinction between citizen and noncitizen.

[8] Latin for "whose land, his religion."

[9] Daniel-Rops claims that as result of the Peace of Augsburg, religious identification began to be subservient to political identification. Henri Daniel-Rops, *The Protestant Reformation*, trans. Audrey Bulter (London: J. M. Dent and Sons, 1961), 506.

nationhood—the glue that held the nation-state together.[10] Religion supported the formation of good citizens, fostered a stress on the good, and infused the citizen with the sense of self-sacrifice and self-discipline needed to secure the power of the state to wage war and punish crime.

In the eighteenth century, with the new delineation first in economics and later in politics of the "public sphere" and the "private sphere," the relationship between politics and religion entered a third stage. The public sphere, according to philosopher Charles Taylor, is a "common space" where ideas and discussions which impact the economic and well-being of society takes place.[11] It enabled society to come to a consensus on political and economic life, thereby providing a new basis for the national understanding and economic activity that did not depend on religious affiliation or participation. Religion was slowly removed from the public sphere and confined to the private sphere, the sphere of family and marriage, where it was seen as the guarantor of moral values.

The concept of the separation of church and state enshrined in the American Constitution codified this diminution of religious influence in political life. By birth, one was a member of a given country, a citizen with rights and obligations, but one entered, through free choice, into a voluntaristic association with religion, similar to other voluntary clubs and associations, albeit with religion given pride of place due to the historical influence of Christianity in Europe and North America. Little wonder that the Baptist movement, which emphasized the principle of "soul liberty" (i.e., the concept that no one can make a religious choice for anyone else), flourished in the United States.

This process of the withdrawal of religion from the workings of the state was far slower in Canada than in the United States. Colonized first by the French under Samuel de Champlain when a permanent settlement was established at Quebec in 1608, the early traders included many Huguenots who adhered to a form of Calvinistic Protestantism. However, a

---

[10] Samuel Huntington in his influential book *The Clash of Civilizations* would disagree, claiming that at the larger "civilizational" level, religion still functions as the primary differentiator. See Samuel Huntington, *The Clash of Civilizations and the Remaking of the World Order* (New York: Simon and Schuster, 1996), 42.

[11] Charles Taylor, *Modern Social Imaginaries* (Durham, NC: Duke University Press), 83f.

Religious Freedom in the Post-Nation-State

vacuum of leadership in France, which allowed for the growing influence of Roman Catholic Cardinal Richelieu, meant that the Compagnie des Cent-Associes, the commercial entity that spearheaded colonization efforts, was given a charter for trade on the condition that it "was to settle only French Roman Catholics in the colony."[12]

Meanwhile, English colonization efforts outside Quebec refused to recognize the Roman Catholic Church for reasons articulated by John Locke and others,[13] and so the stage was set for religious conflict when French colonies in Quebec were ceded to England with the Treaty of Paris in 1763, which ended the Seven Years' War. Concerns about the growing specter of self-government in the American colonies, however, resulted in the British parliament enacting the Quebec Act 1774, which guaranteed the freedom of the Roman Catholic Church and restored its right to impose church tithes in the newly formed territory of Quebec.

The almost complete dominance of Roman Catholicism within the French-speaking areas of what was to be the country of Canada helped ensure a stronger role for religion in public and political life than might otherwise have been the case. Thus, when Canada become a separate country in 1867, the Constitution Act passed in the British Parliament recognized state support for religious school systems, both Protestant and Roman Catholic, in the four provinces of Quebec, Ontario, New Brunswick, and Nova Scotia, which made up the country of Canada at the time.[14]

---

[12] Terrence Murphy and Roberto Perin, *A Concise History of Christianity in Canada* (Toronto ; New York: Oxford University Press, 1996), 3.

[13] See John Locke, "Two Treatises of Government and a Letter Concerning Toleration," in *Rethinking the Western Tradition*, ed. Ian Shapiro (New Haven: Yale University Press, 2003).

[14] Canadian historian E. R. Norman cautions that while their historic backgrounds differ, in their attitude toward the separation of religion from political life, the United States and Canada were more similar than they were different. There was no constitutional separation of religion and state in Canada, he admits, but there was de facto separation due to the influence of Protestant separatists in Great Britain and the proximity of the United States. In opposition, David Seljak takes a more measured approach, concluding that a robust separation of church and state did not take root in Canada until after World War II. Edward R. Norman, *The Conscience of the State in North America*, Cambridge Studies in the History and Theory of Politics, (Cambridge: Cambridge University Press, 1968),

KEEPING THE FAITH

Religious freedom in Canada in the first hundred years of its history, thus, clearly favoured Christian expressions of religion, with Protestant forms dominating in English Canada, and the Roman Catholic Church in the province of Quebec. This began to change in the 1960s, and change abruptly and dramatically. What is suggestive about this change is that it coincided with the growing depiction of Canada as a postnational state.

The Post-Nation-State

Following World War II, the nation-state in Europe was seen not as a bulwark against religious violence, which had become a concern of the past, but as a political entity that was divisive in itself, fanning the flames of nationalist interests. The formation of the United Nations in 1945, while acknowledging the legitimate sovereignty of the nation-state, nevertheless called for accountability to larger principles of international law. Scholars such as Jurgen Habermas, who was born in Dusseldorf in 1929 and scarred by the German experience of World War II, began to envision a global community, a new political entity to supplant the nation-state.[15] The philosopher Immanuel Kant was pressed into service of this new political ideal, being depicted as the first philosopher of the postnational state.

While Kant's 1795 essay "Perpetual Peace: A Philosophical Sketch" is seen as a seminal text, in it he expressly recognizes the legitimate sovereignty of the nation-state.[16] Kant's postnational-state contribution, then, is not based on his "Philosophical Sketch," but instead on his substantive attempt to base moral and ethical principles on reason alone, rather than any religious framework.[17] While it is debatable whether Kant accomplished this,[18] he is nevertheless embraced by scholars of globalism as

---

9. David Seljak, "Secularization and the Separation of Church and State in Canada," *Canadian Diversity* 6/1 (2008), 8.

[15] See Andrew Linklater, *Critical Theory and World Politics: Citizenship, Sovereignty and Humanity* (London, New York: Routledge, 2007), 5.

[16] See Immanuel Kant, *Perpetual Peace*, ed. Nicholas Murray Butler (New York: Columbia University Press, 1939).

[17] See Kant, *The Metaphysics of Morals*.

[18] Paul Tillich claims that Kant's role in the Protestant tradition can be seen as analogous to the role of Aristotle played in the formation or Roman Catholic theology. See Paul Tillich, *A History of Christian Thought: From Its Judaic and*

308

providing the philosophical underpinnings for a political entity based on universal values and principles common to the human creature which transcend national borders and allow for the creation of a new political entity—the post-nation-state.[19]

This dream of a post-nation-state coincided with economic globalization, which flourished after World War II and which came to view the nation-state as an impediment to economic growth.[20] Thus, the European Economic Community was formed in 1957. Originally an economic union, it slowly but steadily morphed into a political union with the formation of the European Union in 1993.

The European experience gives rise, then, to two definitions of the post-nation-state. The first is what I call an "imagined" community based upon global ethical values. The second is an "institutional" definition in which some nation-state power is transferred to other political units, be they subnational or, more commonly, as in the case of the European Union, supranational.[21]

In opposition to the European example, in Canada, the "imagined" post-nation-state came to prominence after, rather than before, the "institutional" definition. The French-English divide in Canada meant that Canada, from its very inception, could not function as a nation-state like other nation-states. Lord Durham, sent over from Great Britain in 1838

Hellenistic Origins to Existentialism, ed. Carl E. Braaten (New York: Simon and Schuster, 1968), 361.

[19] See William and Robert Fine Smith, "Kantian Cosmopolitanism Today: John Rawls and Jürgen Habermas on Immanuel Kant's Foedus Pacificum," *King's Law Journal* 15, p. 5.

[20] There was 4100 percent growth in world trade volumes from 1950 to 2020, and world trade values ballooned by almost 300 times from 1950 levels. https://www.wto.org/english/res_e/statis_e/trade_evolution_e/evolution_trade_ wto_e.htm#fnt-1.

[21] With the formation of the EU, Canadian scholar William Lawton asserts that "power is thus shifting away from national capitals in both directions: above and below. While this does not mean the end of the nation-state, it does signal a 'post-nation-state' ideal." William Lawton, "The Crisis of the Nation State: A Post-Modernist Canada?," *Acadiensis* 22/1 (Autumn 1992), 134.

KEEPING THE FAITH

to look at future governmental adjustments in British North America, re-ported that he "found two nations warring in the bosom of a single state."[22]

The political accommodation to this problem was the devolution of political power to the respective future provinces of Canada, a political re-ality that was enshrined in the Act of Union in 1841, which united Upper and Lower Canada, and later the Confederation Act of 1867, when Nova Scotia and New Brunswick joined this union, and the country of Canada came into being. Indeed, Northrop Frye wryly remarked that because of the necessities of this devolution of political power, Canada never really became a nation but skipped over this stage of political development.[23] A more accurate depiction, however, would be that of Lord Durham, where Canada became an amalgam of two smaller nation-states coupled within one larger nation-state.

By the time of its first centenary, in 1967, this political compromise had begun to crumble due to two main factors. The first of these was the collapse of the religious hegemony of Roman Catholicism within the prov-ince of Quebec coupled with the less visible but still dramatic collapse of Protestantism in the "rest of Canada."[24] The second factor was a growing

---

[22] Durham Report: John George Lambton Durham and Gerald M. Craig, *Lord Durham's Report : An Abridgement of Report on the Affairs of British North America*, New ed., Carleton Library Series, (Montreal: McGill-Queen's University Press, 2007).

[23] Frye, "National Consciousness in Canadian Culture," 15.

[24] The Quiet Revolution in Quebec, where the power of the Roman Catholic Church was quickly displaced by the state, has been well chronicled. See David Seljak, "Why the Quiet Revolution was 'Quiet': The Catholic Church's Reaction to the Secularization of Nationalism in Quebec after 1960," *CCHA, Historical Studies* 62 (1996). Geneviève Zubrzycki, *Beheading the saint: Nationalism, religion, and secularism in Quebec* (University of Chicago Press, 2016). Less well chronicled has been the collapse of the United Church of Canada, a church union which was supposed to rival, in English Canada, the role of the Roman Catholic Church in French Canada. The decline of the United Church of Canada took place at ap-proximately the same time as the Quiet Revolution and "decisively closed the chapter on the decades in which Canada's largest Protestant denomination had striven...'to establish a certain kind of Christian Canada.'" Kevin N. Flatt, *After Evangelicalism: The Sixties and the United Church of Canada*, McGill-Queen's Studies in the History of Religion (Montreal: McGill-Queens University Press, 2013), 254. See also Gary R. Miedema, *For Canada's Sake: Public Religion, Centennial Celebrations, and the Re-making of Canada in the 1960s*, McGill-

310

consensus in the province of Quebec that the two-nation comprise resulted in the slowed-down but nevertheless inevitable loss both of the French language in the province of Quebec and its distinctive Quebecoise culture.[25]

Increasingly, there were calls in Quebec for further independence from the "rest of Canada."[26] To blunt this move toward independence, an official policy of multiculturalism was adopted, and Canada became one of the leading nations in accepting immigrants. In addition, the Constitution was repatriated from Great Britain in 1981. Within this new Constitution, pride of place was afforded to the Charter of Canadian Rights and Freedoms adopted in 1982. As a result of the new Charter of Rights, the Supreme Court of Canada was tasked with not only ruling on the division of powers between the national and provincial governments, but also on whether federal or provincial statutes were compatible with the charter itself.[27]

The Charter of Rights and Freedoms, therefore, much like the United Nations Declaration of Universal Human Rights in 1948, helped facilitate the rise of the second definition of what constitutes a post-nation-state—an imagined political entity based on universal values. What originally was a widening of the Canadian nation to include diverse ethnic groups and religious experiences under Prime Minister Pierre Trudeau in the 1970s and 1980s, morphed, under his son Justin Trudeau, into a full-blown declaration of post-nationhood, as evidenced by his comments in *The New Yorker* magazine in 2015.

Queen's Studies in the History of Religion (Montreal: McGill-Queen's University Press, 2005), 205.

[25] In 1967, the same year as the Centenary celebration, the Mouvement Souveraineté-Association by Quebec politician René Lévesque was established to press for greater provincial autonomy in the form of sovereignty association, leading in time to the full-blown Quebec Independence Referendum of 1980.

[26] Used to designate the provinces of Canada, aside from the province of Quebec.

[27] To facilitate its adoption by the various provinces, the charter contains a clause which allows provinces to opt out of Supreme Court charter challenges for a period of five years, after which it must be reviewed.

KEEPING THE FAITH

The Post–Nation–State and Religious Freedom

Although not as dramatic as the impact on religion of the rise of the nation-state, the two definitions of what is meant by the term post-nation-state both have had, and are having, significant influences upon religion and religious freedom in Canada. The "institutional" post-nation-state has had an effect in the past, as it now affects, religion and religious freedom in Canada in two different ways. The first is due to the globalization of the economy, which, in its present consumeristic phase,[28] transforms even religious commitments into consumeristic choices. Increasingly, Canadians "church shop" to find the religious community that meets their needs. More importantly, they form syncretistic amalgamations of religious beliefs that depend on no religious institution but provide an individualized form of spiritual satisfaction—a personal religion if you will. This has resulted in a growing menu of religious options and a growing acceptance of how Canadians express their religious (i.e., spiritual) beliefs. [29]

The second way in which the institutionally defined post-nation state has affected religion and religious freedom in Canada has been through the devolution of political and economic power from the national to the subnational level. The concept of nationhood has been expanded in Canada to include the province of Quebec, which was recognized as a nation by the Canadian Parliament in 2006,[30] as well as various indigenous groups

---

[28] For the growth and dominance of consumer capitalism see Lizabeth Cohen, *A Consumer's Republic: The Politics of Mass Consumption in Postwar America* (New York: Vintage Books, 2003); Susan Strasser, "The Alien Past: Consumer Culture in Historical Perspective," in *The Advertising and Consumer Culture Reader*, ed. Joseph and Matthew McAllister Turow (New York: Routledge, 2009); Gary Cross, *An All Consuming Century: Why Commercialism Won in Modern America* (New York: Columbia University Press, 2000).

[29] I examined the phenomenon of being "spiritual but not religious" in my book *Spiritscapes: Mapping the Spiritual & Scientific Terrain at the Dawn of the New Millennium* (Kelowna, BC: Northstone, 1998).

[30] The motion in English reads, "That this House recognize that the Québécois form a nation within a united Canada." Hansard; 39th Parliament, First Session; No. 087, November 27, 2006.

who, in the new Oath of Citizenship adopted June 21, 2021, are referred to as "First Nations."[31]

On the one hand, this expansion of nationhood has resulted in the expansion of religious freedom primarily due to the recognition and rediscovery of various indigenous faiths and spiritual traditions. While much work needs to be done in this regard, as expressions of indigenous religion were discouraged and repressed for many years,[32] advances have been made and expressions of indigenous religious traditions have been adopted by non-indigenous people as well. The town of Wolfville, Nova Scotia, the home of Acadia University, for example, opens each session with a shortened form of the seven sacred teachings based on Anishinaabe religious tradition.[33]

In contrast, religious freedom has been curtailed in the province of Quebec, which recently invoked the notwithstanding clause in the Canadian Charter of Rights and Freedoms in order to pass a government bill (Bill 21) that bars public officials in positions of authority from wearing overt religious symbols while at work. In 2021, this bill was used to remove a Muslim schoolteacher, Fatemeh Anvari, from teaching a grade 3 classroom for refusing to stop wearing a hijab while she was teaching. While Ms. Anvari did not consider it her full-blown Islamic duty to wear the

---

[31] Government of Canada, "Canada's oath of citizenship now recognizes First Nations, Inuit and Métis rights," news release, June 21, 2021, https://www.canada.ca/en/immigration-refugees-citizenship/news/2021/06/canadas-oath-of-citizenship-now-recognizes-first-nations-inuit-and-metis-rights.html.

[32] Census Canada collects data on religious affiliation every ten years. In the 2001 Census, the topic-based tabulation categorized Aboriginal Spirituality with Pagan, Wicca, Pantheist, Scientology, Rastafarian, New Age, Gnostic, and Satanist options. In 1991, Aboriginal Spirituality was not listed at all.

[33] While the current mayor claims that the religious background of the sacred teachings is "not on anyone's radar" and therefore the statement is viewed in secular terms, the former mayor, Jeff Cantwell, who instituted the practice, did so because of what can only be termed as a religious epiphany which he had during a concert when the Indigenous songwriter and artist William Prince performed at Acadia University's Convocation Hall. Jeff Cantwell email to Mark Parent, July 1, 2022.

hijab, nevertheless, she refused to compromise on her dress since it formed part of her identity and was her form of "resistance" to Bill 21.[34]

Clearly, there has been, and continues to be, some impact in the "institutionally" defined post-nation-state in which economic and/or political power is pushed upward or downward to supra- or subnational entities, but it would be wrong to read too much into its influence. Global capitalism has had the effect of consumerizing religious choices and opportunities in countries which make no claim to postnational status, such as the United States. Moreover, the Quebec example, I would argue, is more of a case of the province seeking to become a type of nation-state rather than a postnational one.

Of greater interest, then, is the way in which the post-nation-state, as an "imagined" community, has influenced religion and religious freedom. It was the imagined post-nation-state that Prime Minister Justin Trudeau was referring to in his 2015 interview, as, immediately after claiming that Canada has no "core" national identity, he went on to provide a list of values which he claimed all Canadians have in common. Instead of a nation based on the "warm relations of membership," Canada, according to Trudeau,[35] was based on a "cool adherence to a scheme of abstract duties and rights," to use philosopher Roger Scruton's terms.[36]

This "imagined" post-nation-state has had, and is having, an impact on religion and religious freedom in Canada in two main ways. The first is through the redefinition of religion as purely an interior concern, shorn of any institutional framework or authoritative teachings. The second is through the selection of values which Canadians are supposed to hold in common as members of the world's "first postnational state."

The interiorization of religion can be seen as merely another chapter in the subjection of religious power to political power, which was the result of the establishment of the modern nation-state.[37] I would argue, however,

---

[34] Colby Cosh, "Quebec teacher fights tyranny by refusing to take off article of clothing," *The National Post* (Toronto) 2021.

[35] Trudeau's claims cannot be universally applied to all Canadians. Indeed, in the last federal election, he won with 32.2 percent of the vote, the slimmest share of overall electoral support in Canadian history.

[36] Roger, Scruton *The West and the Rest: Globalization and the Terrorist Threat*, retrieved from https://www.kobo.com.

[37] Bruce Kapferer claims that in the nation-state, the religious is always subjected to the political. See Bruce Kapferer, Kari Telle, and Annelin Eriksen,

Religious Freedom in the Post–Nation–State

that the interiorization of religion in the postnational state of Canada is far more substantive. The Baptist movement, for example, while often depicted as interiorizing religion and making it, as philosopher Charles Taylor claims, "irrelevant to great segments of modern life,"[38] always emphasized the social implications of Christian faith and through the "gathered" community of the local church, affiliated with other local churches and sought to influence public life for the better. The examples of Martin Luther King Jr. in the United States and Tommy Douglas in Canada, both Baptists and both social justice proponents, the first in racial equality and the second through the establishment of the Canadian public health system, give lie to to the idea of Baptist irrelevancy. The interiorization of religion in the post-nation-state is different. It is akin to Whitehead's famous comment that "religion is what the individual does with his own solitariness."[39]

The primary vehicle for this redefinition of religion has been the Supreme Court of Canada (SCC). An important case, in this regard, concerned four orthodox Jews who were co-owners of units in luxury condominiums in the city of Montréal. To celebrate the annual nine-day Jewish religious festival of Sukkoth, the four appellants to the Supreme Court set up "succahs" on their balconies for the purposes of fulfilling the biblically mandated obligation of dwelling in such small, enclosed, temporary huts. The bylaws and co-ownership contract, however, prohibited decorations, alterations, and constructions on the balconies due to safety concerns without prior permission by the condominium's board of directors. The individuals were asked to remove the balcony succahs, and a compromise of building a communal succah in the building's garden space was proposed by the board, on authority of the Canadian Jewish Congress, which noted that personal succahs were not a mandatory obligation of the Jewish

---

Contemporary Religiosities: Emergent Socialities and the Post-nation State (New York, Oxford: Berghahn Books, 2010), 90.

[38] Charles Taylor, *Dilemmas and Connections: Selected Essays* (Cambridge, MA: Belknap Press of Harvard University Press, 2011). "A Catholic Modernity," 171.

[39] Alfred North Whitehead, *Religion in the Making*, Lowell Institute lectures, (Cambridge: Cambridge University Press, 1927), 6.

faith.[40] This compromise was rejected by the appellants, and so the board of directors asked the Quebec Superior Court to permit an injunction to prohibit the construction of the succahs. This order was granted by the Quebec Superior Court and affirmed by the court of appeals.

When the case reached the Supreme Court, however, the decision of the lower court was overturned on the grounds of religious freedom. In the explanation for such a decision, the majority judges defined religion as the sincere belief of an individual "irrespective of whether a particular practice or belief is required by official religious dogma or is in conformity with the position of religious officials," concluding that "this understanding is consistent with a personal or subjective understanding of freedom of religion."[41]

While at first blush the SCC's decision demonstrated support for religious freedom, law professor Margaret Ogilvie argues that the reverse is true since by ignoring the advice of religious experts and defining religion on such a personalistic basis, the Supreme Court thereby assumed the role of arbiter as to what qualifies as religion, so that religion "can become whatever they [the SCC] want it to be, and indeed, be nothing in particular," meriting "protection or not" solely on a whim.[42]

Ogilvie's criticism that the Supreme Court, in interiorizing religion, strikes a blow to religious freedom is echoed by indigenous scholar Nicholas Shrubsole, who, in a book on indigenous religious freedom in Canada, examined a 2018 Supreme Court case brought by the Ktunaxa Nation against the proposal by a company to build a ski resort on land known as Qat'muk and traditionally claimed by the Ktunaxa people. Consultations were held by the company and agreement seemed to be within reach when the Ktunaxa Nation "decided that accommodation was impossible because the project would drive Grizzly Bear Spirit from Qat'muk and therefore irrevocably impair their religious beliefs and practices."[43]

The Ktunaxa Nation appealed to the Supreme Court which decided that, though the belief in the Grizzly Bear Spirit, as well as the belief that

---

[40] Margaret H. Ogilvie, "And Then There Was One: Freedom of Religion in Canada—The Incredible Shrinking Concept," *Ecclesiastical Law Journal* 10/2 (2008): 198.

[41] *Syndicat Northcrest v. Amselem*, (2004) 2 SCR 551, 2004 SCC 47.

[42] Ogilvie, *Freedom of Religion*, 197.

[43] *Ktunaxa Nation v. British Columbia*, (2017) SCC 54.

the ski development would drive the Great Bear Spirit from the land, were "valid" religious beliefs, the development could proceed because it did not undercut the Ktunaxa's Nation's "freedom to believe in Grizzly Bear Spirit or their freedom to manifest that belief."[44] Shrubsole concludes that this ruling completely misunderstands the conceptual meaning of land in North American indigenous religious beliefs and practices and stands as a key example as to why "indigenous religious freedom is so difficult in Canada today."[45]

The interiorization of religious beliefs by the SCC also explains comments made by former chief justice of the Supreme Court Beverley Mclaughlin in a lecture delivered in 2002 at McGill University. In this lecture, Mclaughlin expounded on the relationship between law and religion, noting that both functioned as ultimate sources of authority, but that in the end, while "due recognition must be given to the dignity of individuals and communities bound by a religious worldview and ethos," such recognition must not compromise "the integrity of the rule of law and the values for which it stands."[46] Law, therefore, is tasked, in Mclaughlin's words, with carving out a "space within itself" for religious "ultimate commitments." Setting aside her rather novel concept that law serves in a quasi-religious fashion as a source of ultimate authority, it is clear that law triumphs, in her view, as an ultimate commitment over religion. The only logical way by which McLaughlin can make the claim that the Supreme Court of Canada succeeds in resolving the "paradoxical task"[47] of balancing the authority of law and religion as two forms of ultimate commitment is by redefining religion as that which one does in one's solitude.

Another example of how the interiorization of religion affects religious freedom can be discerned in the closure rules that were enacted by the provinces and the federal government during Covid lockdowns. In British Columbia, all religious gatherings were prohibited at the same time

---

[44] Ibid.

[45] Nicholas Shrubsole, *What Has No Place, Remains: The Challenges for Indigenous Religious Freedom in Canada Today* (Toronto, Buffalo, London: University of Toronto Press, 2019), 192.

[46] Beverley McLachlin, "Freedom of Religion and the Rule of Law: A Canadian Perspective," in *Recognizing Religion in a Secular Society: Essays in Pluralism, Religion, and Public Policy*, ed. Douglas Farrow (Montreal: McGill-Queen's Press, 2004), 28.

[47] Ibid., 16.

that Alcoholics Anonymous meetings were allowed, often in the selfsame religious buildings, and liquor stores operated with only minimal restrictions. Roman Catholic priest and commentator Raymond De Souza described this shutdown as an example of an infatuation with power by the chief medical officer of the province of British Columbia, Dr. Bonnie Henry.[48] However, it could just as easily be argued that government officials, such as Dr. Henry, view religion as an "interior" activity, with religious gatherings being ancillary and thus disposable.

This leads closely to the second way in which the "imagined" post-nation-state affects religion and religious freedom, which is through the choice of the values which are deemed to be common to all. The nation-state sought accommodation with religion by assigning religious authority to certain moral values. The state was seen to be in charge of moral values dealing with economic issues, but in the sphere of family life and marriage, religious institutions still held a great deal of sway. The post-nation-state, however, founded upon common values set by the state—albeit supposedly commonly and freely held by all citizens—takes control of these values as well.

The radically different decisions of the Supreme Court of Canada regarding the Trinity Western School of Education in 2001 and the proposed Trinity Western Law School in 2018 provide an interesting insight into the way in which postnational state values can override religious ones. In 2001, the Supreme Court of Canada was tasked with deciding whether Trinity Western University, a private university in British Columbia affiliated with the Evangelical Free Church of Canada, could provide the first four years of an education degree. Trinity Western applied to the B.C. College of Teachers to ensure that students who took such training would be approved to teach in B.C. schools. The College of Teachers refused to grant this permission, as Trinity Western enforced a student "code of conduct" which barred the student from sexual activity outside the bonds of Christian marriage, which was interpreted as excluding same-sex marriage. The case went to the Supreme Court, which overruled the College of Teachers and decided in favour of allowing Trinity Western to train public school teachers, as the majority judges noted that "absent concrete evidence that training teachers at TWU fosters

---

[48] Raymond De Souza, "Government overreach on COVID measures has been about power—not the pandemic," *National Post* (Toronto), October 23, 2021.

discrimination in the public schools of B.C., the freedom of individuals to adhere to certain religious beliefs while at TWU should be respected."[49]

Not even twenty years later, though, when a similar case came before the Supreme Court regarding the possibility of Trinity Western University providing training toward a law degree which would be recognized by the Law Society of British Columbia (LSBC), the Supreme Court made a complete reversal and ruled that because of the Trinity Western University "code of conduct," the decision of the Law Society of British Columbia to bar such graduates from practicing law would stand.

Explaining their decision, the majority judges dismissed freedom of religion claims and did not even bother with ascertaining whether law graduates of Trinity Western would result in lawyers who were at odds with Canadian law on same-sex relations. Rather, the judges attacked the very existence of "code of conduct," stating that "the LSBC's decision prevents the risk of significant harm to LGBTQ people who feel they have no choice but to attend TWU's proposed law school. These individuals would have to deny who they are for three years to receive a legal education. Being required by someone else's religious beliefs to behave contrary to one's sexual identity is degrading and disrespectful."[50]

A more recent example of the way in which the post-nation-state's usurping of the setting of moral values affects religion and religious freedom is found in a report commissioned by the Ministry of National Defence on Racism and Discrimination within the Canadian Armed Forces. This report features a section on "Redefining Chaplaincy," in which the writers of the report assert that chaplains should not be employed who are members of any religious group which does not fully support women in ministry, or LGBTQ2+ rights, or which is monotheistic and thus discriminatory against pagan and polytheistic faiths.

Carefully avoiding the fact that this would probably result in the dismissal of the overwhelming number of current chaplains serving within the armed forces, the report concludes the section on chaplaincy by noting that

> the Advisory Panel has observed that there are varying degrees of misogyny, sexism and discrimination woven into the philosophies and beliefs of some mainstream religions currently represented in the cadre of chaplains in the CAF. This Advisory Panel does not seek to evaluate

---

[49] *Trinity Western University v. College of Teachers*, 2001 SCC 31.

[50] *Trinity Western University v. Law Society of Upper Canada*, 2018 SCC 33.

or categorize these religions in this report. Rather it is pointing out that the Defence Team cannot consider itself supportive of inclusivity when it employs as chaplains members of organizations whose values are not consistent with National Defence's ethics and values—even if those members express non-adherence to the policies of their chosen religion.[51]

Another value which has resulted in tension with some religious groups, although not enshrined in legislation, and thus not enforceable by the Supreme Court of Canada, is abortion rights. In February 2012, prior to his election as prime minister, Justin Trudeau went so far as to state that he would be willing to support the separation of Quebec from Canada "in order to defend abortion rights and same-sex marriage in Quebec."[52] He followed this up in 2014, as liberal party leader, with an insistence that all liberal MPs would have to be proabortion and pro-same-sex marriage, going against a longstanding tradition in Canadian politics that on issues of personal conscience, MPs could vote their conscience.

In 2018, this new emphasis on abortion rights was used by the government to ban any nonprofit group that did not support abortion rights from receiving Canada Summer Jobs and Youth Service funding. This affected several religious charities which had traditionally received such funding to help with the staffing of summer youth programs.[53]

Conclusion

With the exception of Quebec, the "institutional" post-nation-state, at least in the Canadian experience, has resulted in greater religious diversity and religious freedom in Canada, both in the increased form of varied expressions of spirituality as well as in the rediscovery of indigenous spirituality.

The impact of the "imagined" post-nation-state on religious freedom, however, is not as clear-cut. While support for same-sex marriage and gender

---

[51] Government of Canada, Minister of National Defence Advisory Panel on Systemic Racism and Discrimination, Final Report, January 2022: With a focus on Anti-Indigenous and Anti-Black Racism, LGBTQ2+ Prejudice, Gender Bias, and White Supremacy (Government of Canada, 2022), 42.

[52] Paul Tuns, "Justin Trudeau on abortion," *The Interim* (Hamilton, Ontario), July 27, 2015.

[53] Staff Reporter, "Trudeau bans anti-abortion groups from summer jobs funding," *BBC World News*, January 18, 2018.

and abortion rights is present in many countries, in the postnational state of Canada, such values are seen to be "core" values. They are values that supposedly bind Canadians together in the absence of any other shared identity; values that the Supreme Court of Canada has been more than willing to enforce, even if they go against "fundamental freedoms," such as freedom of religion, listed in the Canadian Charter of Rights and Freedom.

For some, this is clear proof that religious freedom is eroding in Canada. Professor Shannon Ishiyama Smithey, after examining Canadian Supreme Court decisions, concludes that "despite support for religion in the Charter, judicial decisions have tended to reduce rather than foster religion in Canadian society."[54] While legal scholar and advocate Janet Epp Buckingham notes that the Supreme Court decision to rule as unconstitutional the Lord's Day Act in 1985 too often simply resulted in the exclusion of religion from the public square.[55] Meanwhile, columnist Chris Selley, writing in the *National Post*, one of Canada's two main newspapers, asserts, "Religious freedom is certainly imperiled in Canada nowadays."[56]

At times, however, such criticisms seem to reflect not the loss of religious freedom, but the loss of religious privilege by the once-dominant Christian majority, as given voice by former professor and politician F. L. Morton, who claims that "the right to freedom of religion prohibits government policy from accommodating the beliefs of Christians, but requires it to accommodate the beliefs of non-Christians. Sunday-closing laws are declared unconstitutional, but Sikhs must be exempted from RCMP dress regulations."[57]

In opposition to such a perspective, one could argue that the emphasis on the value of diversity, a value which came out of the official government promotion of multiculturalism in the 1970s and which has become part of the core Canadian postnational values, has been a boon to religious freedom,

---

[54] Shannon Ishiyama Smithey, "Religious Freedom and Equality Concerns under the Canadian Charter of Rights and Freedoms," *Canadian Journal of Political Science/Revue Canadienne de Science Politique* 34/1 (2001), 103.

[55] Janet Epp Buckingham, *Fighting Over God: A Legal and Political History of Religious Freedom in Canada* (Montreal: McGill-Queens University Press, 2014).

[56] Chris Selley, "Pro-lockdown or anti-lockdown, Canadians need to guard their freedoms," *National Post* (Toronto), April 2, 2021.

[57] F. L. Morton, "The Charter of Rights: Myth and Reality" in *After Liberalism: Essays in Search of Freedom, Virtue, and Order*, ed. William Douglas Gairdner (Toronto: Stoddart, 1998).

allowing members of non-Western-based religious groups[58] to find a home in Canada.

Nevertheless, I would argue that the growing role of the "imagined" postnational state to decide on values, once considered part of the purview of religious institutions, poses a threat to all religious traditions. This threat can be easily discerned simply by contrasting two statements on Canadian values, the first by former chief justice Beverley Mclaughlin, and the second by Prime Minister Trudeau.

In a speech given in 2004, McLaughlin listed as common Canadian values many of the same things which Trudeau did in 2015, with one key difference; as she stated, "We believe in the principle that the state should recognize the equal freedom of all citizens, and that it should remain neutral as to their conceptions of the good."[59] Presumably, McLaughlin saw the various conceptions of the good as being formed by individuals influenced, in large part by their respective religious traditions.

In 2015, however, the newly elected prime minister made it clear that the postnational state would not be neutral in conceptions of the good, but would take the leading role in their formation, thus depriving religious traditions of much of their previous role and potentially putting religious freedom at risk when the values of religious traditions do not align with the values of the postnational state.

Another concern, closely allied to this, arises out of the defining of religion as an interior activity. When religion is defined in such a manner, the possibility of the postnational state running rampart over the institutional and/or community aspects of religious faith is of concern.

Moreover, it is doubtful whether religion can ever be interiorized to the extent that the Supreme Court of Canada feels it should be without losing its essence. Indeed, the concept of religion as a separate aspect of human life has been shown to be a Western emphasis which does not translate well to non-

---

[58] Sikhism, Hinduism, and Islam are the fastest growing in Canada today. Louis Cornelissen, "Religiosity in Canada and its evolution from 1985 to 2019," Statistics Canada (Ottawa, 2021).

[59] McLaughlin, ADM Forum, Government of Canada, Ottawa, Ontario, October 26, 2004.

Religious Freedom in the Post–Nation-State

Western faiths.[60] I would argue that it does not translate well to Western religious traditions either.

---

[60] See Jack Miles, *Religion as We Know It: An Origin Story*, 1st ed. (New York: W. W. Norton & Company, 2020). Brent Nongbri, *Before Religion: A History of a Modern Concept* (New Haven, CT: Yale University Press, 2013).

May our music sound our praise,
May each note proclaim God's love;
And our faith be in each phrase
Like His angels from above.

Acadia Vesper Hymns, No. 54, vs. 3 RHP

We sing to thee, "amen,"
So be it: amen;
For it is our chorus:
Let it be, "Amen." Amen.

"Lord our hearts are open,"
Acadia Vesper Hymns, No. 24, RHP

Index

Acadia University 22, 23, 25, 28, 30, 31, 36, 37, 91, 93, 123, 163, 172, 233, 255, 269, 313

Acadia Divinity College 31, 39, 42n55, 164,

Acadia Centre for Baptist and Anabaptist Studies (ACBAS) 33

African United Baptist Association of Nova Scotia 173

African-American churches 221

Anglican(s) 11, 24, 25, 26, 59, 61, 63, 72, 74, 83, 87n18, 123, 124, 125, 150, 151, 167, 171, 177, 227, 248, 238, 248, 266, 267, 273

antiphonal 221

Amherst, First Baptist Church 5, 30, 31

Atlantic Baptist Fellowship (ABF) 32, 39, 42, 165

Annapolis Royal 6

Baptist College in Montreal 22, 23, 73n31

Baptist Missionary Society 92n1, 93

Book of Common Prayer (1662) 44, 51, 52, 54, 55, 56, 57, 59, 61

Brandon College 36, 151, 152, 154, 158, 159, 167

Bristol Academy 45

Brown University 25

Buchan, John 11

Buttrick, David 206n1, 207, 217, 220

cadence(s) 221, 238, 239, 241, 243-249

Canadian Armed Forces 168, 171, 319

Canadian Association of Baptist Freedoms (CABF) 11, 40, 42, 165, 260

Canadian Baptist Overseas Mission Board (CBOMB) 41

Canadian Bill of Rights 285

Canadian Council of Churches 42

Case, Shirley Jackson (1872-1947) 29, 30

chaplain, chaplaincy 3, 6, 9, 10, 12, 41, 169, 170 -178, 181, 237, 250, 269, 270, 319-320

Charter of Canadian Rights and Freedoms 311

Catholic 63-89, 134, 145, 146, 149, 151, 183n2, 240, 248, 259, 260, 262-267, 270, 273, 276, 278, 283, 293, 304, 305, 307, 308, 310, 315, 318

Chicago, "Chicago School" 30, 34, 36, 151, 154, 156, 310

Colgate, Colgate Rochester Divinity School 25, 30-32, 102

contrapositions 261, 274-275

Council of Trent 65, 71, 73, 75, 81, 88

Cramp, John Mockett (1796-1881) 22n3, 25, 27, 28n22, 30n28, 63-90, 91-96, 98-100, 106, 129, 131, 133 -136, 142

Crawley, Edmund A. (1799-1888) 25-28, 123-127, 130-133

Dalhousie University, 4, 25, 26, 124, 125, 127, 130, 162

Davies, Benjamin (1814-1876) 23, 24, 28

DeBlois, Stephen W. (1827-1884) 29

Dissenting Academies 44

Douglas, Tommy 35, 315

ecumenism, ecumenical 11, 21,39-42, 63, 85, 174, 259, 260, 263, 267, 271, 273

Edwards, Morgan (1722-1795) 57-61

eucharistic 225 -233, 249, 260, 273

European Convention of Human Rights 277

European Court of Human Rights 277, 278, 279, 281, 284, 286, 295

European Commission on Human Rights 291

Evangelical Fellowship of Canada 42

Feller, Henriette Odin 106

Forsman, Rodger E.W. 6, 16

Fosdick, Harry Emerson 22,102

Foster, George B. 22n1, 33, 34

Fuller, Andrew 94

Fundamentalist 34, 102, 153, 154,160, 165

Fyfe, Robert A. (1816-1878) 23n4, 24

Gilmour, George P. (1900-1963) 37, 41

Goodspeed, Calvin (1842-1912) 27, 28, 29

Grande Ligne Association 106, 108

Granville Street Baptist Church 25, 26n12, 124

hermeneutic 207, 215, 216, 219, 220, 230

Horton Academy 26, 29, 30, 109, 128, 131, 150

hymnody, hymn(s) 6, 12, 54, 91, 94, 97, 118, 119, 183, 186, 207, 214-224, 228, 234, 237-238, 243, 248, 257, 324

improvisation 202, 203

institutional religion 10

Inter-Church Council 6

Kant, Immanuel 29, 308, 309

King, Martin Luther, Jr. 22n1

Lewis, C.S. 185

Liberal tradition 22, 23, 33, 36, 38, 41

liturgical 11, 41n54, 59, 85, 183, 193, 225, 226, 228, 237, 238, 241, 243, 262

Lowry, Thomas 189

Luther, Martin 75, 208, 304

Lutheranism 305

Macintosh, Douglas Clyde (1877-1948) 33, 35

McMaster Tradition 23, 37, 41n54

McMaster University 24, 28, 32, 34, 36, 37, 38, 151, 167, 176

Manning Memorial Chapel 4, 9, 10, 237, 255

Maritime Baptists 33, 42n55, 127n13, 132, 136, 137, 141, 162, 169, 176

Methodists 25, 68, 212

multiculturalism 311, 321

narrative 182, 187, 188-192, 195, 204, 210, 222,

Newman, John Henry 65, 76n39

326

INDEX

Nova Scotia Baptist Education Society 125, 126, 128n15, 129n18, 130, 132n29

Oickle, Leanne, 5, 10
Olivet Baptist Church, Montreal 97, 100-104, 109, 119
Oxford Movement 65n10

Passion plays 6, 10, 181, 182, 191, 237, 255
Peace of Augsburg 276, 278, 281, 282, 283, 301, 305n9
Peace of Westphalia 304, 305
Pope Francis 261
post-millennialist 28
prayer(s) 6, 70, 77n44, 83, 87, 88, 91, 93, 94, 96-98,1 00, 102, 105, 107, 108, 112, 115, 119, 121, 141, 146, 183-185, 188, 191,195, 201, 204, 217, 223, 224, 226, 227, 229, 231, 238, 239, 244, 245, 248, 257, 289
Presbyterians 25, 60, 72, 125, 144, 177, 267

Queen's College 124, 125,

Rauschenbusch, Walter 22n1, 31n29, 35
receptive ecumenism 63, 259, 260,267
Reekie, Archibald B. (1862-1942) 38, 39
Regent's Park College 5,8, 33n36, 92, 181, 251
Rhode Island College 46,48
Roman Catholic Church 64, 66, 68,70, 72-90, 134, 145, 146, 152, 240, 248, 259, 260, 273, 276n1, 278, 293, 304, 305, 307-310, 318
Royal Canadian Legion 6

Royal Society of Canada 158, 303

Sabbatarianism 28
sacrament(s), sacramental 9, 75, 184, 198, 199, 225, 227, 229n7, 234
Sawyer, Artemus W. (1869-1896) 131-141
Separatist tradition 33, 63, 307n14
Shields, T.T. 154-157
Shurden, Walter 272
Social Gospel 31,35, 174, 176n31
St. Stephen, New Brunswick 19
Stott, John R.W. 253

temperance 172, 176, 177
theatre 10, 181-205,
Toronto Baptist College 24, 28
Trudeau, Justin 303, 304n5, 311, 314, 320

UN Declaration on Human Rights 276
Universal Declaration of Human Rights 285
University of Chicago 30, 34, 154
United Baptist Association of New Brunswick 175

voluntarism 22, 24

Women's Foreign Mission Circle 106
worship 11, 51, 59, 60, 98, 119, 145, 146, 181-205, 213, 224, 226-229, 234, 241-249, 255, 273
Whidden, Evan M. (1898-1980) 32, 32n33, 158-165.
Whidden, Howard Primrose (1871-1952) 30, 36, 37, 143, 150, 151, 154, 156-158
White, B.R. 5

327

Williams, Roger 22
Wilson, Paul Scott 209, 215n13,
220, 229, 231, 232
Wolfville Baptist Church 27, 62
WWI 156, 168, 177,
WWII 307-309

YMCA 152, 153